WITHDRAWN
NDSU

POLITICS AT MAO'S COURT

Studies on Contemporary China

**THE POLITICAL ECONOMY OF CHINA'S
SPECIAL ECONOMIC ZONES**
George T. Crane

**WORLDS APART
RECENT CHINESE WRITING AND ITS AUDIENCES**
Howard Goldblatt, editor

**CHINESE URBAN REFORM
WHAT MODEL NOW?**
*R. Yin-Wang Kwok, William L. Parish, and Anthony Gar-On Yeh
with Xu Xueqiang, editors*

**REBELLION AND FACTIONALISM IN A CHINESE PROVINCE
ZHEJIANG, 1966–1976**
Keith Forster

**POLITICS AT MAO'S COURT
GAO GANG AND PARTY FACTIONALISM
IN THE EARLY 1950s**
Frederick C. Teiwes

Studies on Contemporary China

POLITICS AT MAO'S COURT
GAO GANG AND PARTY FACTIONALISM IN THE EARLY 1950s

FREDERICK C. TEIWES

An East Gate Book

M. E. Sharpe, Inc.
Armonk, New York
London, England

An East Gate Book

Copyright © 1990 by M. E. Sharpe, Inc.

All rights reserved. No part of this book may be reproduced in any
form without written permission from the publisher, M. E. Sharpe, Inc.,
80 Business Park Drive, Armonk, New York 10504.

Available in the United Kingdom from M. E. Sharpe, Publishers,
3 Henrietta Street, London WC2E 8LU.

Library of Congress Cataloging-in-Publication Data

Teiwes, Frederick C.
    Politics at Mao's court : Gao Gang and party factionalism in the early
1950s / Frederick C. Teiwes.
      p.   cm. — (Studies on contemporary China)
    Includes bibliographical references
    ISBN 0-87332-590-7 — ISBN 0-87332-709-8 (pbk.)
    1. China—Politics and government—1949–1976. 2. Chung-kuo kung
ch'an tang—Purges. 3. Kao, Kang. I. Title. II. Series.
DS777.75.T442   1990
951.05′5—dc20   90-35927
                                                                                                                              CIP

Printed in the United States of America

MV   10 9 8 7 6 5 4 3 2 1

To Inge and Jack

CONTENTS

TABLES AND PHOTOGRAPHS	ix
ABBREVIATIONS	xi
PREFACE	xiii
INTRODUCTION	3
1 THE SETTING	
Beijing Politics, Late 1952–Mid-1953	15
2 THE ATTACK ON LIU AND ZHOU	
The National Conference on Financial and Economic Work, June–August 1953	52
3 FACTIONAL MANEUVERS AND POLICY CHANGE	
The Organization and Agricultural Cooperativization Conferences, September–November 1953	79
4 IN SEARCH OF ALLIES	
Gao Gang's Approaches to Party Leaders in the South and Beijing, Summer–Fall 1953	93
5 THE RESOLUTION OF THE GAO GANG AFFAIR	
December 1953 and After	115
6 CONCLUSION	
Politics at Mao's Court	142
APPENDICES	
I AN OVERVIEW OF THE GAO-RAO AFFAIR	157
II THE TAX ISSUE AND OTHER DEVELOPMENTS	
January–May 1953	177
III THE NATIONAL CONFERENCE ON FINANCIAL AND ECONOMIC WORK	
June–August 1953	183

IV	THE STRUGGLE IN THE CENTRAL ORGANIZATION DEPARTMENT AND THE NATIONAL CONFERENCE ON ORGANIZATION WORK July–October 1953	213
V	GAO GANG'S APPROACHES TO OTHER LEADERS	221
VI	MAO'S REACTION TO GAO GANG'S ACTIVITIES	228
VII	THE FOURTH PLENUM AND SUBSEQUENT MEETINGS, 1954	235
VIII	THE 1955 NATIONAL PARTY CONFERENCE	254
NOTES		277
INDEX		317

TABLES AND PHOTOGRAPHS

Tables

1	Key Regional Leaders, 1949–1953	22
2	Leading Members of the Financial and Economic Committee and State Planning Commission, 1952–1953	28
3	Leaders Selected for Inclusion in *The Great Soviet Encyclopedia*, 1952	100
4	Officials Disciplined as a Result of the Gao-Rao Affair	132
5	The Factional Balance: Key Party and State Positions, 1954–1956	136

Photographs

Deng Xiaoping conversing with Chen Yun, Fall 1952	31
Fourth Plenum of the Seventh Central Committee, February 1954	123

ABBREVIATIONS

Organizations and Policies
CCP	Chinese Communist Party
FEC	Financial and Economic Committee
FFYP	First Five-Year Plan
GAC	Government Administration Council
NPC	National People's Congress
PLA	People's Liberation Army
PRC	People's Republic of China
SPC	State Planning Commission

Publications and Publishing Agencies
AJCA	*Australian Journal of Chinese Affairs*
CB	*Current Background*
CLG	*Chinese Law and Government*
CQ	*The China Quarterly*
DSYJ	*Dangshi Yanjiu* [Research on Party History]
FBIS	Foreign Broadcast Information Service
NCNA	New China News Agency
RMRB	*Renmin Ribao* [People's Daily]
SCMM	*Selections from China Mainland Magazines*
SCMP	*Survey of China Mainland Press*
SW	*Selected Works of Mao Tsetung*
WM	*The Writings of Mao Zedong, 1949–1976*
WS	*Mao Zedong Sixiang Wansui* [Long Live Mao Zedong Thought]
WS 1949–57	*Mao Zedong Sixiang Wansui 1949.9–1957.12* [Long Live Mao Zedong Thought, September 1949–December 1957]
ZDJCZ	*Zhonggong Dangshi Jiaoxue Cankao Ziliao* [CCP History Teaching Reference Materials]
ZDRZ	*Zhonggong Dangshi Renwu Zhuan* [Biographies of Personalities in CCP History]

PREFACE

THIS STUDY began as a relatively narrow reexamination of one of the most elusive cases of Chinese Communist leadership conflict, the 1953–54 Gao Gang–Rao Shushi affair, on the basis of substantial new information from the post-Mao period. While the present account remains very much a detailed analysis of and, indeed, something of a detective story about this obscure conflict, it soon became apparent that the investigation had broader implications concerning the nature of elite politics in the Maoist era. Basic questions of power, policy, ideology, factions, and patterns of leadership interaction generally are all central to the unfolding story. The illumination these issues receive in the context of the Gao-Rao case is relevant not only to the initial post-1949 period of comparative—but flawed—Party unity, but also to the structural fault lines of the political system that were later to contribute so significantly to the Cultural Revolution. The ultimate aim of the book is to home in on these structural features of the Maoist system, which were to have such momentous consequences long after the Gao-Rao affair.

Coming back to the Gao-Rao case after a decade is in some ways a humbling experience. This is not particularly due to the fact that some of the main propositions offered in my 1979 analysis in *Politics and Purges in China* have proven considerably wide of the mark. Indeed, in a fundamental sense the basic theme of Mao's unchallenged position, which underlay the earlier analysis, has been strengthened and clarified by the new data available. Humility is rather engendered by the awareness that my previous interpretation was stated with a degree of certitude not justified by the information then available. It is further created by the realization that even with new, much more revealing post-Mao data, points that seemed clear in both draft form and several brief published accounts of the case have become problematic as further evidence has been unearthed. In fact, the very nature of the matter under investigation means many aspects of the present analysis lie beyond anything approaching definitive proof. The result, then, is an account that may have to be further amended as new evidence appears or particularly perplexing issues are thrashed out with Chinese scholars in the future.

None of the above, however, has prevented me from arguing forcefully a general view of elite politics in the early 1950s as dominated by one man, Mao Zedong. Notwithstanding myriad other factors, in the end high-level politics became court politics, where the name of the game was to divine the preferences of the Chairman and use or adjust to those preferences in ways that furthered individual or group interests. Various conflicts within the elite had diverse sources, but at the top they were all shaped and constrained by the parameters of court politics. This interpretation is supported by a host of specific developments discussed in the following pages; more importantly, in my view at least, it is the only viable interpretation for the overall pattern of events that occurred. It is also a view resoundingly supported in substance, if not precise formulation, by the evidence of a wide range of Chinese scholars specializing in Party history and related disciplines.

But with many aspects of the story uncertain or problematic, how does one deal with the paradox of what seems to me a clear overall picture yet many unclear details? I have attempted to be rigorous in handling each particular event or facet of the story. Where the evidence is ambiguous or contradictory I have sought to bring this to the reader's attention. Where alternative explanations are possible I have attempted to outline the possibilities. I have tried to eschew the temptation to slot particular events into my overall interpretation where such a procedure would be congenial to my argument but lacking adequate independent evidence. I have even repeatedly questioned, in the research if not the writing, the validity of the basic interpretation as against less Mao-dominant interpretations of Chinese politics. As a result, the reader can puzzle with me over the many remaining uncertainties of the story. At the same time, it will also be up to the individual reader to use his or her own judgment to decide whether the general interpretation prevails despite the many problematic specifics.

A number of people have contributed to this study. Bruce Jacobs and Wang Gungwu offered helpful comments on an earlier draft. Gyorgy Markus and Patricia Springborg provided valuable assistance on an obscure but revealing theoretical point. At various times research materials that are difficult to obtain, particularly internal (*neibu*) publications, were generously provided by Keith Forster, Edward Friedman, David Holm, Kenneth Lieberthal, Roderick MacFarquhar, Michel Oksenberg, and Tony Saich. Graeme Gill not only provided relevant Soviet materials but served as an expert source of guidance for those aspects of the study touching on the Soviet Union. I thank them all.

Three people deserve special mention, however. First, David Chambers made available the long *neibu* document that appears as appendix I to this book. David's generous and unsolicited offer of this comprehensive account early in the project provided an essential documentary base that, together with the results of interviews with Chinese sources, encouraged me to embark once again on systematic research into the Gao-Rao affair. Second, Timothy Cheek, in addition to some valuable assistance with sources not available in Australia, provided extensive, insightful comments on the initial draft. Apart from the general encouragement provided, many of his suggestions have been gratefully incorporated into the final version. Indeed, on at least one occasion, Tim will recognize the insertion of his words to emphasize a key point. Finally, but profoundly, this study has benefited from the many contributions of my research assistant, Warren Sun. Although Warren joined the project after the basic interpretation had taken shape, his relentless pursuit of data, judicious weighing of evidence, and careful consideration of the larger issues helped to extend and deepen the analysis. The end result, I believe, has been to enrich greatly the version presented here.

The staff of the University of Sydney's Department of Government has provided major support for this book. I am grateful to Lyn Fisher for her research assistance and the preparation of the index, and to Sandra Donnelly, Pauline Rimmer, Maria Robertson, Sonja Waikawa, and especially John Robinson for their diligent work in preparing the manuscript through a number of stages. I also thank Anita O'Brien of M. E. Sharpe, Inc., for her excellent editorial work, and Doug Merwin for his steadfast backing of the project. Research funding was generously given by the Australia-China Council, the Australia-China Exchange in the Humanities and Social Sciences, the Ian Potter Foundation, the University of Sydney's overseas travel grant awards, and especially by the Australian Research Council. Without this financial support the study could not have been undertaken or executed in anything like its present form.

Special acknowledgment must be made to a substantial number of Chinese scholars and former officials who must necessarily remain nameless. Quite simply, without the assistance of these oral sources this study would not have been possible. Not only did these sources provide the only available information on the key event that set in motion the Gao-Rao affair—Mao's late 1952 or early 1953 talks with Gao Gang—they also introduced and clarified a whole series of other key issues. Over a four-year period from 1985 to 1989, nearly four dozen Chinese scholars were questioned about the Gao Gang affair in the course of broader interviews on Party history; of these, about half provided significant information or insight. While naturally these sources varied in their depth of knowledge, particular perspectives, interpretation of events, and, on some occasions, candor, they by and large made sincere efforts to assist me within the limits of their understanding. I quickly came to respect their seriousness in dealing with the questions raised, and I gratefully acknowledge the invaluable help they so generously offered.

A note on the appendices is also in order. The original translations were largely prepared by Pamela Tan, Warren Sun, and Ai Ping. Several of the appendices are based on previous translations drawn from either official Chinese sources, Western translation services, or the comprehensive collection of Mao's works, *The Writings of Mao Zedong, 1949–1976*, Volume 1: *1949–1955*. I thank M. E. Sharpe, Inc., for permission to use the latter source, and also thank the Corbett Publishing Company for permission to include an excerpt from *History of the Communist Party of the Soviet Union (Bolsheviks): Short Course.*

Finally, no recounting of the support that has sustained this project would be complete without mention of the sacrifices and good cheer of my family. I am deeply indebted to my wife Kath, and to my children Inge and Jack to whom this book is fondly dedicated.

POLITICS AT MAO'S COURT

INTRODUCTION

TODAY'S official view of the initial years of the People's Republic of China (PRC) depicts something of a golden age, a period not only when the Party's policies were usually correct, but also when leadership relations were marked by a high degree of unity and democracy.[1] While there is much to recommend this overview, it at best overstates the case and at worst ignores some key weaknesses of the Maoist system. In these early years considerable unity did exist, but it was a flawed unity involving significant tensions and linked precariously to Chairman Mao Zedong's commitment to Party solidarity. Simply put, the unity and democracy that existed were not structural[2] but rather a result of the Chairman's self-restraint. Moreover, even with Mao's commitment to unity and democracy relatively high in this period, his rather aloof personality and especially the awe surrounding the architect of revolutionary success created an authoritarian distance from other Party leaders and with it uncertainty concerning the Chairman's intentions. Thus the classic conditions for court politics existed at the very start of the PRC—other leaders saw their status, policy priorities, and careers dependent on the favor of the "emperor" and competed for that favor in circumstances where his preferences were often unclear. In the early 1950s the consequences of this were relatively benign if hardly completely harmonious. A decade later the same general conditions set the stage for the Cultural Revolution.

Apart from the basic fact of court politics, various other fault lines potentially threatened Chinese Communist Party (CCP) unity in the early 1950s. First, a number of groupings or "factions" based on the military units and other organizations that won the revolution existed within the Party.[3] While an equitable division of the spoils of victory in 1949 served to underpin unity, each grouping was proud of its particular achievements in revolutionary struggle and jealous of its rewards. Any development that threatened to upset the existing balance naturally endangered the larger unity as well. In addition to the prestige provided by one's revolutionary achievements, status was conveyed by considerations of Party rank and length of service to the revolution. Such status distinctions generally worked for stability, but the possibility of "generational" conflict was another potential threat to unity. Ironically, given that in real terms such conflict seemed relatively low in the immediate post-Liberation period, an effort on Gao Gang's part to stimulate generational divisions apparently did occur as a result of Mao's actual or purported views on the matter. In the 1960s such tensions appeared in much more severe form against the background of the Chairman's far more clearly articulated opinions on the need for generational change within the leadership.

Another source of tension rooted deeply in both the larger culture and the particular traditions of the Communist movement was the moral-ideological approach to politics. The pursuit of philosophically based "correct" positions purportedly linked by an overall "line," the belief that deviations from such a "line" are not uncommon, and the conviction—often validated by personal experience in harsh revolutionary struggle—that even those ostensibly bound to the Party by a lifetime commitment can betray the cause potentially contain the seeds of sharp division. Such phenomena as ahistorical evaluations of past performance from the needs of a current line, the compilation of documentary files to demonstrate a pattern of deviation on the part of targeted enemies, and the use of vague moral terms by political climbers against bureaucratically better positioned opponents, which were such prominent features of the Cultural Revolution, were all present albeit on a much more limited scale in the early 1950s. And while policy differences themselves formed another significant cleavage, more threatening was the possibility that a disgruntled Chairman or an ambitious subordinate would raise policy issues to the ideological level. In a Party environment where correct theory and moral virtue were closely tied, and with a Chairman who showed signs of ideological uncertainty regarding a virulent Stalinist theory at variance with his own policy orientation, the potential for escalating leadership conflict was not insignificant.

These and other features of Chinese elite politics are illuminated by a reexamination of the 1953–54 Gao Gang affair, the one obvious blot on Party unity in the early 1950s. This affair, which culminated in Gao's purge and suicide, has long been one of the least understood and most poorly documented CCP leadership conflicts. While the post-Mao period has produced only a comparatively limited number of new documentary materials dealing specifically with the case, these documents, a wider range of new sources on related developments in 1952–54, and critically important oral sources now provide the basis for a more complete and accurate analysis than was previously possible.[4] These sources allow a deeper understanding of the nature of Party factionalism in this initial post-1949 leadership struggle, an understanding going well beyond the basic outline of the factional activity originally condemned in the 1955 official resolution on Gao's "clique." The new material also provides a much clearer picture of the personalities, policy positions, and bureaucratic interests involved in the case. Finally, the post-Mao sources demonstrate, although not without remaining gray areas, what was always obscured previously—the pivotal role of Mao Zedong in the affair from start to finish. The result is a richer picture of Mao's interaction with other leaders at the apex of the Communist system in these early years.

Previous Studies and New Conclusions

In the decade following the formal purge of Gao Gang and his alleged ally, Rao Shushi, the few Western analyses of the affair advanced speculative interpretations emphasizing such factors as possible policy differences,[5] regionalism,[6] and Gao's possible ties to the Soviet Union.[7] Surprisingly, unlike Hong Kong accounts, these studies paid relatively little attention to the central official charge that Gao and Rao had engaged in factional activities that aimed to split the Party and seize supreme power, nor to the crucial questions of the precise nature of these factional maneuvers or the individual leaders targeted by Gao.[8] Materials provided by the Cultural Revolution changed this situation only to a degree; the small number of new analyses to appear still dwelled on the same issues, although now with greater focus on the factional activities and targets themselves.[9] In addition, a new consideration was raised in the form of Mao's health as a possible factor precipitating the affair.[10]

In 1979 I published the most systematic analysis of the Gao-Rao case to date using early 1950s', Cultural Revolution, and post-Mao sources.[11] The major conclusions of this study were: (1) despite charges that Gao established an "independent kingdom" in the Northeast, regionalism was not a major factor in his purge as his Northeast region had not been beyond the effective control of the central authorities; (2) while Gao had good relations with the Soviet leadership and particularly Stalin, those relations were not a major aspect of his activities or a precipitating factor in his fall; (3) policy issues played a secondary role at best in the efforts of Gao and Rao, who did not put forward a coherent policy program; (4) the main factional appeal used by Gao Gang—an attempt to fan the resentment of army leaders against those with "white area" or underground careers during the revolutionary period, especially Liu Shaoqi and Zhou Enlai—was poorly conceived and had limited impact; (5) the key circumstantial factor in the situation was Mao's poor health, which led Gao to begin maneuvers for a possible succession struggle; and (6) overall, the effort of Gao and Rao was marked by inept politics and was easily beaten back with only minimal damage to Party unity.

The new materials available since 1979 necessitate some important alterations to the above conclusions. While the first two conclusions substantially hold, new information allows a fuller understanding of the regionalism and Soviet aspects of the case. With regard to the Soviet factor, although the Gao-Stalin link still seems peripheral, a greater if somewhat indirect impact resulted from the generational implications of the post-Stalin succession and from Mao's weakness for Stalinist theory. The third conclusion on the comparatively minor role of policy also retains some validity, but Gao and Rao openly raised policy issues as a significant part of their activities. Moreover, the general policy debates of the period were an essential factor shaping the attitudes of key figures in the drama. The fourth and sixth conclusions must be substantially revised; the effort to manipulate tensions between "red" and "white" area cadres was far more potent than originally believed, and Gao made considerably more headway than previously seemed likely—even though the activities of Gao and Rao can in many respects still be considered inept. Finally, Mao's health—although somewhat poor in this period and relevant to the unfolding events—was not a precipitating cause of Gao's activities. Instead, what set Gao in motion was several personal discussions with Mao in which the Chairman indicated dissatisfaction with Liu Shaoqi and Zhou Enlai. Rightly or wrongly, Gao interpreted these conversations as providing an opportunity to displace Liu and himself become Mao's successor.

The broad outlines of the Gao-Rao case can be sketched briefly. As part of a more general shift of regional leaders to the capital, Gao Gang was transferred to Beijing in late 1952 from his position as the leading Party, government, and military figure in China's Northeast to become head of the State Planning Commission (SPC). In early 1953, Rao Shushi, the leading Party and government official in East China, similarly came to Beijing to head the Central Committee's organization department. Sometime after Gao's arrival his fateful discussions with Mao took place, and after Rao appeared on the scene he tacitly aligned himself with Gao. The first major effort to undermine Liu and Zhou took place at the National Conference on Financial and Economic Work, held from mid-June to mid-August 1953. The centerpiece of this effort was an attack on the tax policies of Minister of Finance Bo Yibo, an attack actually aimed at Bo's close colleague, Liu Shaoqi, and also implicating Premier Zhou Enlai. While Mao may have been initially impressed with Gao's criticisms of Bo, by the end of the conference he emphasized unity and mitigated the seriousness of Bo's rather significant errors. Later in the year, at the September–October National Organization Work Conference, Rao continued an attack that had begun at the time of the earlier conference on another long-time Liu associate, deputy organization department head An Ziwen. A key aspect of this attack was criticism of An over a draft list for the new Politburo to be chosen at the next Party Congress, a list that assertedly slighted army leaders in comparison to "white area" figures. By the end of the conference Mao and the "Party Center" intervened to support An Ziwen.

Meanwhile, following the Financial and Economic Conference, Gao headed south on "holiday." During his stay in the south, as well as in Beijing both before and after the trip, he contacted various leaders seeking their support for a reorganization of the Party and government. In these efforts he offered various posts to prospective allies and made use of An's list to gain the support of disgruntled army figures. In the same process Gao targeted several key members of a slightly younger generation of CCP leaders and tried to win support in most of China's large administrative regions. Gao's successes included enlisting the backing of Peng Dehuai, a Politburo member and titular head of the Northwest region who had successfully commanded Chinese forces in Korea. He also curried favor with the great general and head of the Central-South region, Lin Biao. He was less successful, however, with Vice-Premier Deng Xiaoping, concurrently Southwest Party leader, although Deng appears to have given Gao's proposals careful consideration. Chen Yun, the CCP's leading economic official and fifth-ranking leader, may also have pondered the situation for a considerable period of time, but eventually both Chen and Deng rejected Gao's entreaties and reported his activities to Mao.

The affair came to a climax at a series of Politburo meetings in December when Mao indicated his intention to go on holiday and, as was the custom, proposed that Liu Shaoqi take over in his absence. Gao objected, proposed instead that leadership be exercised "by rotation," and indicated his desire to be Party vice-chairman or general secretary and concurrently premier. Finally, at a late December meeting, Mao denounced Gao's "underground activities" and Gao's cause was lost. Mao subsequently left for his holiday and entrusted Liu with conducting a Central Committee plenum to deal with the case. When the plenum met in February 1954 the intention was to allow Gao and Rao a way out in return for appropriate self-criticism, but they would not show the required contrition. Gao's recalcitrance was manifested in an attempt on his own life during February, and a successful suicide in August 1954. The case was finally put to rest at the March 1955 National Party Conference when Gao and Rao were denounced by name and expelled from the Party, and a brief resolution elusively detailing their "crimes" was adopted and openly published.[12]

What is the precise political meaning of the above events? What do they tell us about Chinese leadership politics in the early 1950s? Before these questions are addressed in detail in the body of this study, it is necessary to consider problems of sources and methodology.

Sources and Methodology

All of the various sources used in this analysis raise vexing problems. Each category of documentary evidence, at least as far as the case per se is concerned, is relatively sparse in volume, contains major gaps of substance, reflects a particular bias, and is inconsistent in important respects with information from other sources. Contemporary documents from the 1950s dealing specifically with the Gao-Rao affair are limited to two periods of several months duration each—the period following the February 1954 Fourth Plenum of the Seventh Central Committee, and that after the March 1955 National Party Conference. In 1954 the names of Gao and Rao were not even mentioned, and only general statements concerning deviations threatening Party unity appeared.[13] A year later Gao and Rao were officially denounced, and a few charges especially concerning their alleged "unprincipled" factional activities and Gao's setting up of an "independent kingdom" in the Northeast were laid but hardly elaborated upon.[14] In the period from 1955 to the Cultural Revolution there was a virtual total blackout on the Gao-Rao case in official sources; only a handful of major statements made any reference to the affair.[15]

Pre–Cultural Revolution documents project an image of Party unity. As I shall argue, to an important extent this unity was a reality notwithstanding various strains, but the image was also the result of a conscious decision not to wash dirty linen in public any more than absolutely necessary and to play down any divisions that existed within the elite. Moreover, with regard to Gao and Rao specifically, once it was officially determined that their activities were "unprincipled," that is, involved seeking power and position rather than "principled" differences over policy, there was an obvious inhibition to discussing policy issues, particularly as some of those issues remained subject to debate after the purge. Beyond these considerations, the political sensitivity of a situation where various figures involved in Gao's activities continued to hold key positions, including (as of 1955) two Politburo members, Peng Dehuai and Lin Biao—not to mention the role of Mao himself—argued for silence. Finally, the fact that, relatively speaking, Gao and Rao had clearly violated official norms of leadership behavior, and that Gao's core group of supporters had been relatively weak politically, gave little impetus for any reconsideration of the case. Because of such factors, 1950s' sources only give general clues to the reasons behind the affair; however, particularly when combined with subsequent information, these sources provide considerable insight into the general developments in 1953 against which the activities of Gao and Rao unfolded.

Cultural Revolution sources brought to light some new information concerning the case but never addressed it directly. The polemics of the period in both official and Red Guard publications were limited to comparatively few attacks linking active or recently deposed officials to the Gao-Rao "conspiracy,"[16] or articles criticizing the lingering prestige of Gao and Rao in areas where they had served.[17] Apart from the continuing inhibitions created by the role of Mao and lack of a strong pro-Gao constituency within the leadership, the long absence of Gao and Rao from power made them uninteresting targets of attack, while the fact that Gao's major protagonist had been Liu Shaoqi left little scope for fitting the affair into the demonology of a Mao-Liu "two-line struggle." While the fragments of information released were not necessarily inconsistent with those from earlier and later periods, the overall gloss of fierce leadership conflict stood in sharp relief to the emphasis on unity in both 1950s and post-1978 sources. Moreover, the use of Cultural Revolution sources—both official and Red Guard but especially Red Guard—raises not only the question of their interpretive slant but also the factual validity of events described in the polemics of the period.[18] Nevertheless, these Cultural Revolution polemics have raised a few issues of importance.

The Cultural Revolution period also produced various collections of Mao's hitherto unpublished writings and speeches to internal Party gatherings, particularly the *Wansui* volumes.[19] These collections contain a fair number of references to Gao and Rao, but they are always in the form of elusive passing remarks. Overall there is little doubt that these documents are genuine, although not every comment can be vouched for confidently.[20] In terms of understanding the Gao-Rao case, the most vexing problem is the unsystematic nature of Mao's remarks concerning that affair.

Perhaps the most difficult source to come to grips with is the official volume 5 of Mao's *Selected Works*, published in 1977 during the initial post-Mao phase.[21] This collection covering 1949–1957 is both authoritative and suspect. Much as the Hua Guofeng leadership itself, volume 5 was transitional in nature, reflecting not only the comparatively stable elite politics of the 1950s but also the "two-line struggle" perspective of the Cultural Revolution—particularly as it dealt with Liu Shaoqi and Bo Yibo. This legacy of the Cultural Revolution, which also distorted other sources from 1977–78,[22] resulted from both Hua's need to link himself firmly to Mao and the fact that volume 5 was based on a draft compiled by the so-called Gang of Four.

According to an authoritative oral source, in the haste to get volume 5 out there was not a great deal of revision to the selections already made under the direction of Zhang Chunqiao and Yao Wenyuan. As a result, significant distortions appeared: the editors added pointed titles to the selections; mitigating terms such as "comrade" were dropped; and phrases, sentences, and whole sections of Mao's talks were deleted, resulting in an unbalanced picture of the Chairman's meaning. In the case at hand, volume 5 excerpts from Mao's August 12, 1953, speech to the Financial and Economic Conference harshly criticize Bo Yibo under the title "Combat Bourgeois Ideas in the Party"[23] when, according to sources with access to the complete text, the Chairman's full talk ranged much more widely and was less severe overall. Moreover, the editors specifically excluded the section of the speech where Mao absolved Bo of errors of political line, thus leaving quite the opposite impression. Finally, while some oral sources believe there was no altering—as opposed to the deletion of—Mao's actual words, a comparison of volume 5 to the *Wansui* texts more generally does indicate some differences in wording, seemingly modifying intent.[24] In any case, the deletion of individual phrases or whole passages is more than sufficient to distort Mao's meaning.

Another problem with volume 5, or with any other Mao texts for that matter, has less to do with the intent of the editors than with that of the Chairman himself. Mao, particularly in his rambling comments to internal Party gatherings, often lacked rigorous consistency or clarity.[25] Thus, in an August 1953 speech Mao articulated the ostensibly threatening opinion that "the contradictions between the working class and the bourgeoisie are antagonistic," but in the same passage he spoke of "the alliance of the working class and the national bourgeoisie."[26] The latter statement was clearly compatible with Mao's backing of moderate united front policies toward private businessmen, while the former stands in uneasy tension with those policies. Of course, Mao may have simply meant that there was an underlying antagonism between the two classes but it could be transformed into a nonantagonistic contradiction by proper policies—a position he elaborated in 1957.[27] Nevertheless, such apparent imprecision, particularly when married to politically truncated texts, makes even more difficult the task of getting a fix on Mao's intent.

Following the historic December 1978 Third Plenum of the Eleventh Central Committee, the discipline of Party history began once again to attract serious attention and a new, more objective interest in the CCP's past emerged.[28] A rich vein of new materials appeared, including official histories, memoirs, scholarly articles on specific events and problems, collections of speeches and writings by leading Party figures and other official documents, detailed chronologies, and internal discussions of historical developments. In nearly all of these sources the Gao-Rao affair has received remarkably short shrift. Official histories, while adding some enticing details, steer clear of the key issues and present only brief discussions of the case in much the same stilted language as the formal 1955 verdict.[29] The 1981 resolution on Party history makes only a passing reference to Gao and Rao, while the extensive compendium of notes on the resolution offers no summary of the affair.[30] Scholarly articles rarely deal directly with the case, although studies of other developments in the early 1950s are sometimes extremely useful for the light they shed on it. Similarly, general and specialist chronologies produce information of great value concerning the context but often ignore the Gao-Rao case itself.[31]

Memoir material, despite some extremely revealing brief accounts,[32] also largely avoids mention of the affair, while collections of leaders' speeches and writings—even including remarks by Liu Shaoqi, Zhou Enlai, and Chen Yun to the Fourth Plenum in 1954[33]—are remarkably vague concerning the actual factional activities of Gao and Rao. Only the post-Mao speeches of Deng Xiaoping directly raise the events of 1953, revealing publicly for the first time such crucial developments as Gao's approaches to Deng and Chen Yun.[34] Significantly, Deng's raising of the issue seemingly reflected less of an interest in the Gao-Rao affair itself than an effort to debunk the hated "two-line struggle" interpretation of Party history pushed during the Cultural Revolution.[35]

Finally, *neibu* sources also generally ignore the case, with two major exceptions of which I am aware.[36] One exception, a 1980 article by Chen Shihui published by the Anhui Party School,[37] provides a major source for this analysis. This extensive 15,000-character account, which is translated nearly in full in appendix I, provides rich insight and detail into the activities of Gao and Rao, including such key aspects as An Ziwen's list and the attack on Bo Yibo. This account, in turn, is to a significant extent based on internal "teaching reference materials," which include seven directly relevant documents from 1953–55 that to my knowledge are unavailable in any other source, among them Zhou Enlai's summing up speech to the Financial and Economic Conference and Deng Xiaoping's report on the Gao-Rao affair to the March 1955 National Party Conference.[38] Yet both Chen Shihui's account and the documents from the teaching materials avoid direct discussion of Mao's role in the launching of Gao's activities and remain elusive on other issues.

The reasons for this continued comparative lack of attention to the Gao Gang affair involve some familiar considerations that have taken on new force in the post–Third Plenum period. First, there is only a limited constituency with a possible interest in a thorough reexamination of the Gao-Rao case, although the seriousness of their sins has been somewhat played down. Since Gao and Rao fell well before the hated Cultural Revolution, their cases were largely irrelevant to the large numbers of officials demanding a review of the 1966–1976 period. While several of those denounced as members of Gao's clique in 1955—notably Ma Hong and Guo Feng—assumed responsible positions after the Third Plenum,[39] generally speaking no one in a truly high place has had a vital interest in airing the case.[40] The two dominant leaders of the post-Mao era, Deng Xiaoping and Chen Yun, can have no interest in exploring the story beyond Deng's account of their rejection of Gao's approaches. The legion of followers of Liu Shaoqi and Zhou Enlai still active in high-level CCP politics also have no particular interest in reopening the case since their patrons emerged unscathed from the affair. But perhaps the most important political factor is the taboo on discussing Mao's role.[41] Not only does the departed Chairman remain a key to legitimacy in the elite's own eyes,[42] but the need for compromise in the official 1981 assessment of Mao's merits and faults provided a strong impetus for ignoring difficult questions concerning the period up until 1957 when, by consensus, Mao assertedly "gave full play to democracy."[43] With so much contention over the evaluation of the later Mao, it was best to leave such questions alone.

Apart from the sensitivity of Party historians to political currents in the post-Mao era, other factors have also conspired to inhibit scholarly investigation of the Gao-Rao affair. Quite simply, the data available to scholars have limited the possibilities of thorough analysis. As one academic source put it, once Gao had been purged it was felt there was no need to gather materials on his career; thus whole topics of historical investigation, such as the Shaan-Gan-Ning Border Region where Gao had been a leading figure, suffered as a result.[44] As for the events of 1953 themselves, scholars are frustrated by the fact that the records are semi-open at best. Even academic historians who have seen the minutes of the Financial and Economic Conference or the discussion meetings on Gao and Rao convened after the Fourth Plenum have had only partial access, and the record of the crucial December 24 Politburo meeting reportedly is totally closed. Such historians recognize the importance of memoir material, but many sensibly regard recollections to be of variable quality and often unreliable. Thus it is unsurprising that one scholar declared that documentation was inadequate for drawing a correct conclusion on the case. Nevertheless, when one considers the full range of post-1978 documentary sources dealing with both the affair and the background events, the basis is laid for a quantum leap in our understanding of the Gao-Rao case.

In terms of interpretation, none of the limitations of reform era sources means that the basically reaffirmed 1955 verdict on Gao—or the overall characterization of Mao in the early 1950s—is necessarily wrong, although they do suggest that a bias toward unity not unlike that in contemporary 1950s' material affects these sources. Nevertheless, in Party history circles in China today, a subtle reconsideration of the Gao-Rao affair has occurred. Concisely put, while there is no fundamental controversy concerning the historical verdict that Gao and Rao had carried out Party-splitting activities aimed at toppling Liu Shaoqi—at least within the main-line scholarly and political circles consulted—there is considerable feeling that the traditional characterization of Gao and Rao was too harsh. In particular, the 1955 conclusion that Gao and Rao formed an anti-Party "clique" or "alliance" is no longer used in Party history accounts,[45] and scholars are deeply skeptical that the two men engaged in any explicit coordination of activities. Yet the larger verdict and accompanying biases remain in the published sources of the reform era.

If the documentary record of the present period has, for all its shortcomings, provided the basis for a significant advance in the analysis of the Gao Gang affair, oral discussions with informed Chinese scholars and political figures (usually retired) have been absolutely crucial to this study. Not only have these discussions produced the only PRC sources providing explicit information on Mao's late 1952 or early 1953 talks with Gao Gang,[46] they have also yielded additional unique information as well as a richer, more finely detailed account of matters raised in Chen Shihui's *neibu* article and the wider array of post-1978 sources.

Those consulted, numbering nearly four dozen in total, varied considerably in their knowledge of the case or, in at least some cases, their willingness to discuss it. They also varied considerably in type, including scholars whose main source of information was the (restricted) documentary record, other academics with wide leadership contacts who heard or read about aspects of the case in an unsystematic fashion, political figures on the periphery of the events (including those who subsequently heard accounts from the principals), and even one political figure who had been intimately involved himself. In some cases, particularly with academics, it was possible to have repeated, detailed discussions allowing a homing in on perplexing issues. Two approaches were adopted in the discussions. One was to focus on events and allow broader interpretations to emerge naturally; in this manner care was taken to avoid leading respondents to any particular point of view. This was, however, supplemented by a more exploratory approach where I put certain interpretations to Chinese scholars to facilitate discussion of difficult questions. Together these methods yielded an impressive amount and range of information.

A number of general points can be made concerning oral sources and the problems involved in using them. First, information remains tightly held within the Chinese system, and even individuals of similar high rank and function will have access to vastly different amounts and quality of information. Rank itself is naturally one key determinant of access,[47] but personal connections and specific work responsibilities are often crucial. Moreover, communication among scholars working in Party history and personally familiar with one another is seemingly flawed to a significant extent. I was struck by the number of times a most authoritative source excitedly interjected with "this is new, this is fresh" when a colleague discussed some Party history question; seemingly it took a foreign presence to facilitate the exchange of information. Another key point is that debate that exists within scholarly circles and differences in interpretation will be expressed to a foreign interlocutor. That said, however, certain restrictions seem to operate. Thus the taboo on dealing with Mao's talks with Gao Gang prevailed in most discussions.[48] More generally, while there did not appear to be a "line" on the Gao-Rao affair, there clearly was a conventional wisdom; thus, diverse sources reaffirmed that Mao's discontent with Liu Shaoqi in 1953 was strictly limited. While I am inclined to agree on the basis of a review of the total evidence, I am nevertheless left with the uneasy sense that the Chinese scholars concerned have in at least some cases simply accepted at face value a plausible interpretation.

How, then, can the interviewer know whether to have confidence in the testimony of his respondents? Such confidence must be based on a number of factors: an intuitive sense of reliability built up in the course of extensive discussions, thorough questioning to the extent feasible as to how the sources in question came by their information, by checking the compatibility of information provided with the contemporary 1950s' record and other documentary sources, and ultimately through one's own feel for the politics of the matters under examination. Similarly, the reader will have to evaluate the information gathered from such sources and the accompanying interpretations on the basis of the total pattern of evidence presented and his or her own confidence in the scholarship of the analyst.

The above discussion of sources still leaves some basic methodological questions. When sources conflict, how does one choose? Are the main questions at issue in understanding the Gao-Rao affair subject to rigorous standards of evidence? Can one avoid imposing one's own bias on elusive and sometimes contradictory evidence? Concerning conflicting sources, some rules of thumb apply. First, contemporary evidence must obviously take precedence when issues of fact arise. Thus, the actual December 1952 tax regulations drafted by Bo Yibo's Ministry of Finance must be regarded a better guide to their real nature than either Mao's criticism as reported in volume 5 or Chen Yun's September 1953 speech as presented in his 1984 *Selected Works*. Unfortunately, as is so often the case, the key issues are not the nature of the regulations but the attitudes and political actions of figures such as Mao and Chen toward them, and here no truly contemporary sources are available. Another rule of thumb is that when Cultural Revolution and post-Mao sources conflict, preference is normally given to post-Mao sources, which, although hardly completely objective, are far less polemical and considerably more reliable than those from 1966–68.[49] On the key issue of the relative merits of Mao's volume 5 and other 1977–78 materials versus post-1978 sources, cautious preference is given to the latter concerning overall interpretation while a close examination of each point at issue is undertaken. Finally, I rely heavily on those oral sources in which I have the most confidence, but each detail provided must be evaluated carefully against documentary material to the extent possible. Where the views of even the most trusted oral sources are incompatible with the documentary record, they must be rejected.

Even the most meticulous weighing of source materials cannot settle some of the basic questions at issue in this study. The analysis concerns the political motives and intent of Mao in particular and the degree of trust and reservation in the relations of leading figures, factors unclear not only to observers but perhaps even to the individuals themselves at the time. It also concerns the degree of unity or conflict within the elite as a whole and between specific segments, something that could only be grasped imperfectly even with much more systematic evidence. Conclusive proof cannot be offered on such matters, but what can be done is to present alternative possibilities and reasoned argument for one's own preferred explanation. Finally, analysts must confront the inescapable fact that their general overview of Chinese politics shapes specific interpretations of cases such as the Gao-Rao affair. This is unavoidable since an overall sense of Chinese politics must inform the effort to sort out ambiguous evidence. The task is to avoid imposing preconceptions on evidence that will not sustain them, to modify past views when required by new information, and to make sure that the evidence takes precedence in any irreconcilable conflict.

1
THE SETTING
Beijing Politics, Late 1952–Mid-1953

WHEN Gao Gang and Rao Shushi moved to Beijing in late 1952 and early 1953, they entered a national political environment that was in many ways stable but at the same time undergoing important changes. With economic recovery completed and the Korean War stalemated, a new era of planned economic development and socialist transformation beckoned. This, of course, meant new policies, and with them came a changed ideological overview. It also meant the elaboration of new institutions, which required extensive personnel reassignments to staff them. At the very top it meant that personalities previously serving in the large administrative regions, such as Gao and Rao but also including others like Deng Xiaoping, would now interact on the most important issues of state.

This chapter, in addition to analyzing the key developments in the story before the Financial and Economic Conference was convened in June 1953, examines those broader policy, bureaucratic, ideological, and personality factors that set the stage upon which the events of the Gao-Rao affair enfolded. But before turning to the specifics of late 1952 to mid-1953, a more general review of leadership cohesion and conflict in the early 1950s is in order.

**Mao, Party Unity, and Conflict in the Early 1950s:
An Overview**

How adequate is the official view of a golden age of inner-Party unity and democracy?[1] Much evidence indeed suggests significant unity in the initial post-Liberation years. With the exception of the Gao-Rao affair, there were no major leadership purges in the early 1950s. Perhaps even more telling, there was remarkable leadership stability over the full period from the Seventh Party Congress in 1945 to the Eighth Congress in 1956: only a handful of Central Committee members apart from Gao and Rao were not reelected in 1956, and, moreover, the overall pecking order among top officials changed comparatively little.

A number of factors contributed to this relative stability and unity. The victory of 1949 against considerable odds was a crucial factor that greatly enhanced the authority of Mao and other top leaders who had developed the successful revolutionary strategy. Revolutionary success also provided the spoils of power, which were widely shared within the elite. Different groups within the Party—"factions" if one prefers—all benefited from the parceling out of positions, a process that not only satisfied their sense of revolutionary merit but also fulfilled deep feudal notions of getting one's own share. While a common ideological commitment to Marxism in the abstract need not be a force for unity, as the fissiparous history of the Communist movement demonstrates, a decade of indoctrination in a specific CCP version of Marxist-Leninist orthodoxy did contribute to cohesion. Moreover, a broad consensus formed quickly on ambitious industrialization and social transformation along the lines of the Soviet model. While this did not obviate spirited debate on how the model should be adjusted to Chinese conditions or how rapidly it should be implemented, the existence of a broadly accepted model avoided the type of fundamental divisions that rocked the Soviet Communist Party in the 1920s. Finally, solidarity was a result of the reinforcing interplay of Party unity and policy success. Unity contributed to effective solutions in terms of both constructive debate and disciplined implementation, while success in solving problems further deepened the commitment to leadership cohesion.

Overall unity, however, did not mean an absence of leadership cleavages. One potential source of division was the diversity of revolutionary careers within the Party elite. Different career patterns produced the various groups or "factions" within the larger elite; moreover, each group was jealous of its position, and any change upsetting the existing balance among them was potentially disruptive. Indeed, the effort to manipulate tensions among such groups was a key feature of the activities of Gao Gang. But as in the latter revolutionary period, the overall pattern in the early 1950s was to mitigate factional tensions by the broad sharing of power and positions recognizing the claims of each group. As Mao reportedly rejoined to the complaints of Gao and Rao in summer 1953 that certain leaders belonged to a faction, "China's revolution was made by many mountaintops [i.e., factions]."[2]

Another source of tension carried over from revolutionary days was the inevitable personal friction affecting various personalities at the apex of the CCP, friction derived from conflicts over power, different policy preferences, or sheer personal incompatibility. Examples of relevance to the Gao-Rao affair, as will be seen, were strained relations between Rao Shushi and Chen Yi, and between Gao Gang and Peng Zhen. In both cases, as in others, Mao had sought to dampen tensions in the name of Party unity. A further source of limited, nonpolarized conflict was the growing identification of individual leaders with the institutions and departments they headed as the new system took shape and became increasingly bureaucratized in the early 1950s. Finally, related to the above, cleavages inevitably arose from the large agenda of policy issues facing the CCP in power. Different policy inclinations and institutional interests led to recurring conflict on such questions as how quickly to press ahead with economic development and social transformation. In the 1949–1953 period in particular, an inevitable tension existed between an emphasis on securing economic revival and broad political acceptance through general reassurance and tangible concessions to key social groups, on the one hand, and the desire to establish firm organizational control and quicken the steps to planned development and transformation, on the other.[3] Such differences generated spirited debate, but the range of contending views by and large remained relatively narrow.

Party unity, then, did not mean a lack of tensions but a willingness on the part of CCP leaders to minimize those tensions that did exist. It meant falling in behind official decisions once made, and a broad acceptance of the existing configuration of power at the top. Crucial to this type of unity was the role of Mao. Mao's unchallenged leadership provided the foundation upon which broader stability could be built, but by its very nature it could undermine that stability at any moment of the Chairman's choice. Mao's position was that of the charismatic leader whose strategic insights had solved the mysteries of the Chinese revolution; it was further bolstered by the traditional aura of an awesome founder of a new dynasty. In legal terms, Mao's authority rested on not only a 1943 Central Committee decision giving him formal powers to act unilaterally in certain instances,[4] but also the fact that after 1949 he was, in the words of one oral source, "Chairman of everything"—the individual placed "in charge" (*zhuchi*) of Party, government, and army affairs. By 1953, moreover, Mao's reputation for political wisdom had been furthered by the perceived successful outcome of Chinese intervention in the Korean war—a policy imposed on the Party by Mao despite widespread reservations within the leadership concerning the costs and dangers of such a venture.[5]

Mao's authority thus created the basis for broader elite solidarity but it did not guarantee it. The unity that existed to a large extent reflected Mao's conscious strategy of leadership and rule. In the early 1950s the Chairman normally observed the official norms of collective leadership and democratic discussion, although in a manner that retained enormous discretion in his own hands. While reserving the right to insist on his own way in matters of prime concern such as the Korean decision, Mao's general approach was to encourage broad discussion in order to reach a consensus position. He by and large avoided harsh rebukes to those who took positions contrary to his, and—especially in areas such as industrial policy where he acknowledged his own inadequacies[6]—he would concede to a strong majority view despite his own reservations.

If this approach to dealing with policy debates enhanced Party unity, so did Mao's orthodox and mainstream intellectual position in the early period of the PRC. Throughout these years Mao emphasized the need to steer a course between "leftist" excesses and "rightist" timidity. Although the Chairman's policy preferences may have on occasion been somewhat to the "left" of other key leaders, these were still relatively centrist in terms of the overall range of elite opinion, at least in the period up to mid-1955. Thus, when debate did intensify, generally Mao's centrist position served to ameliorate conflict and build consensus rather than polarize differences within the leadership. However, Mao's intense concern with ideological probity, especially when taken in conjunction with the political/moral tradition of "correctness" within the Communist movement, had the contrary effect of potentially exacerbating what in fact were relatively narrow policy differences.

Crucial to Party unity was Mao's approach to the politics of leadership. Basically his approach was akin to that used in revolutionary struggle: to isolate the handful of diehard opponents (i.e., Wang Ming and his followers up to the early 1940s) by attracting the support of as broad a coalition of "factions" within the Party as possible. This meant shaping a leadership at the Seventh Congress in 1945—and again in 1956—that contained men of talent and independent prestige. In 1945 this further meant a Politburo consisting of leaders at least half of whom had stood on opposite sides of crucial issues from Mao in the CCP's past. To unify the "factions," there was also a recognition of existing status in the leadership as reflected in a marked continuity of Politburo membership; virtually all members apart from Wang Ming's group were retained. In addition, Mao drew in new figures reflecting the diverse constituencies of the Party, including Gao Gang representing the pre-1935 North Shaanxi base area and Peng Zhen of the "white areas," while studiously avoiding raising any member of his own "faction," such as Lin Biao, to the Politburo.[7] Equally important is that once this leadership structure was established, Mao did not alter its makeup dramatically. Of special importance is that Liu Shaoqi was confirmed as number two in the Party and Mao's successor in 1945, and from 1945 to 1953 the order of rank on the highest Party body of the period, the five-man Secretariat, was clearly Mao, Liu, Zhou Enlai, Zhu De, and, by 1950, Chen Yun.[8] Such stability at the top was the basis for stable expectations lower down in the hierarchy; conversely, any threat to that stability could potentially pose a severe threat to Party unity.

The relations between Mao and other high-ranking Party leaders—particularly members of the Secretariat and Politburo—were obviously crucial to Party unity. While these relations involved a generally consensual style, at root they can hardly be said to embrace democracy, other than the democracy of the Chairman's self-restraint. In fact, the essence of Mao's relations with his leading associates might be termed "authoritarian distance." Factors of personality,[9] Mao's often noncommittal approach to policy discussions,[10] the elevation conferred on the holder of any ultimate office, the revolutionary prestige of a successful maximum leader, and the cultural awe surrounding the founder of a new Chinese regime all contributed to an aloof remoteness on the Chairman's part. While not the most unbiased observer, in 1953 Mao's old foe Zhang Guotao offered from afar perhaps the best summary of the Chairman's interpersonal style based on experience well before Mao was crowned with revolutionary success: "[Mao] is usually courteous in his relations with others, but he is very dictatorial and firm in his views. . . . Although he knows how to use power in the top leadership, he has little talent for building up a large personal following except as a remote symbol."[11] Although underestimating the degree to which Mao balanced his forceful ("dictatorial and firm") bent with the pursuit of consensus, this assessment captures an essential aspect of Mao's rule immediately after 1949.

The fundamental basis of this authoritarian distance undoubtedly was Mao's status as the successful revolutionary leader, a status amplified by the Chinese cultural tradition. While access to Mao became more difficult for leading colleagues used to dropping casually by the Chairman's cave in Yan'an, even with Mao ensconced in Zhongnanhai and shielded by the accoutrements of power, other top leaders of Secretariat or Politburo status either had fairly constant contact, as in the case of Zhou Enlai, or apparently could arrange for a meeting on short notice, as happened with Rao Shushi.[12] The distance was not a function of access per se but rather due to the dangers perceived in getting too close to the awesome power in Mao's grasp. As I shall demonstrate, throughout the events of 1953 various actors remained hesitant to approach Mao on sensitive matters for fear of misreading the Chairman's intent. While this tendency was much less pronounced than during the Cultural Revolution,[13] the same basic phenomenon played a vital role in leadership politics during the "democratic" early 1950s.

Although remote in the above sense, the Mao of the early 1950s was deeply immersed in ongoing policy. Ironically, given his relatively consensual style, Mao paid greater attention to detail than he did in the more absolutist final decade and a half of his life. This, of course, served to keep close colleagues and more distant officials on their toes and sensitive to the Chairman's wishes. His interventions were decisive; thus there was no question of his authority to rewrite important sections of Liu Shaoqi's 1950 report on land reform.[14] Yet in the period up to 1953 such interventions seem to have been largely courteous. When Mao corrected someone's "erroneous" views, generally no names were mentioned, although usually his displeasure with other leaders was widely known within the top circles.[15] Moreover, without prejudging the Gao-Rao case, up to that time there is little evidence of Mao using divide-and-rule tactics to undercut specific leaders or play off different groups in any systematic sense.[16]

Yet the ability to single out any view or individual for criticism was a profoundly effective tool for reinforcing the Chairman's authority. However much Mao may have believed that criticism and self-criticism enhances Party unity, he surely was aware of the political benefits of a situation where anyone bar himself was subject to criticism, where he could provide the impetus for decisive criticism, and where he could sit in judgment in all cases. The uneasiness this must has engendered even in the context of a broadly consensual style was useful to Mao, but his "unify the factions" approach required that it be used with restraint. Party leaders could accept their vulnerability to such rebuke if they were likely to be spared once the ritual of criticism and self-criticism was over, and if the substance of the criticism would more often than not prove correct. Mao's track record and prestige was such in the early 1950s that both assumptions were widely held. But the vast amount of discretion in the Chairman's hands meant uncertain times if Mao deviated from his standard practice. Unity did prevail to a significant degree in the early 1950s, but it was unity with an Achilles' heel.

Gao and Rao Come to Beijing, Late 1952–Early 1953: The Political Context

Gao Gang and Rao Shushi moved to Beijing from their respective regional bases in late 1952 and early 1953. The exact dates cannot be pinned down; post-Mao sources only say that Gao arrived at the end of 1952 (*1952 niandi*) and Rao at the start of 1953 (*1953 nianchu*).[17] Gao had formally been named head of the newly formed SPC in November 1952 and was last reported in the Northeast at the end of that month.[18] Rao's official posting to replace Chen Yun as head of the Central Committee's organization department came in February 1953,[19] and he did not attend a major regional government meeting in East China in middle of that month.[20] The move of these two high officials to the national capital was part of the process of centralization, which saw many other key regional leaders such as Deng Xiaoping also take up central posts.

The Implications of Centralization

The process of centralization had numerous political and administrative implications. Basically it furthered the long-anticipated transition to a new period and new tasks. The regional form of government established in 1949 whereby great de facto power was vested in six large administrative regions had always been regarded as a temporary measure required by the diverse conditions initially facing China's Communist rulers.[21] Centralization had been carried out incrementally and on the whole quite smoothly from 1950, and the process would continue until the dissolution of the six regional Party, government, and military structures in 1954–1955. It was, moreover, linked to the successful completion of economic recovery in 1949–1952 and the beginnings of planned economic construction in 1952. Thus, with a new stage of development emerging, preparations under way for China's First Five-Year Plan (FFYP) based on Soviet-style centralized planning, and new economic ministries being established in Beijing, the transfer of leaders of the rank of Gao and Rao to assume part of the increasingly heavy administrative work load was a natural outcome. The setting up of institutions and the assumption of duties, however, also created new bases of power for key CCP leaders and new patterns of interaction within the top echelons of the Party and state.

Gao Gang and Rao Shushi were not the first major regional leaders to be transferred to Beijing. That honor apparently went to Deng Xiaoping, who arrived at the Center from the Southwest in July 1952 and the next month was named a vice-premier of the Government Administration Council (GAC), the predecessor of the State Council.[22] About the same time Xi Zhongxun came from the Northwest and assumed a vice-chairmanship of the GAC's Culture and Education Committee.[23] In January 1953, shortly after Gao and about the same time as Rao, Deng Zihui was transferred from the Central-South to Beijing, where he took up the post of head of the Central Committee's rural work department and thus direction of the agricultural cooperativization movement;[24] even before his arrival he had been named vice-chairman of both the GAC's Financial and Economic Committee (FEC) and Gao's SPC. While all these leaders now had heavy central duties, they still retained their regional posts—perhaps as a result of Gao Gang's lobbying.[25] Their influence continued to be great in the regions, but they appear to have been physically absent on the whole and relied on subordinates to exercise control.[26] Table 1 summarizes the positions of these and other key regional leaders.

Several implications of this situation bear comment. First, all of the regions—apart from North China, whose leading figures had started to move into key central posts from 1949 by virtue of already being stationed in Beijing—were involved in the new postings. Thus the same careful balancing of the underlying military units and other Party constituencies in evidence since 1949 and earlier continued. Moreover, the ongoing importance of the various military "mountaintops" is clear with regard to power within the various regions themselves. The loyalties forged during the revolutionary period within these organizations were apparent in the continued exertion of authority by the former key regional figures after they had been sent to the capital. Even more dramatic is the fact that two key military figures unable to assume much of an administrative role in their regions throughout the early 1950s—Lin Biao in the Central-South for reasons of health[27] and Peng Dehuai in the Northwest by virtue of his role as commander of Chinese forces in Korea—not only retained their formal posts when new regional governments were elected in January 1953 but remained the key political leaders of their regions. This was clearly demonstrated when Gao made Lin and Peng, as well as Deng Xiaoping, his key targets in his efforts to secure regional support later in the year.

Here the emphasis is on the broader point—the importance of status in the key revolutionary-military organizations of the pre-1949 period for regional and national political influence as the quite different tasks of economic construction came to the fore. Ironically, given his later appeals to army leaders, Gao was perhaps least suited of the top regional leaders in terms of military experience and achievements to draw on such factors for personal support. Not only were Lin and Peng great generals, but Deng Xiaoping, although a political commissar by position, was one of the outstanding military figures of the Chinese revolution.[28] Even Rao Shushi, with his substantial period as political commissar of the New Fourth and

Table 1

Key Regional Leaders, 1949–1953

(1) Main regional positions	(2) Important historical ties to key leaders[a]	(3) Main central posts[b]
NORTHEAST		
Gao Gang*		
Party secretary	Chen Yun#	Chm SPC 11/52
Chm government	Lin Biao	
Commander and political commissar MR	Li Fuchun	
Lin Feng		
Deputy Party secy	Liu Shaoqi#?	—
Vice-chm government	Peng Zhen*?	
	Bo Yibo?	
NORTH CHINA		
Bo Yibo		
Party secy (1948–49)	*Liu Shaoqi* #	Vice-chm FEC 10/49
Vice-chm government	*Peng Zhen**	Finance minister 10/49–9/53
	Deng Xiaoping	
	An Ziwen	
Nie Rongzhen		
2nd Party secy	Mao Zedong#	Deputy (later acting) PLA chief of staff 10/49
Commander and political commissar MR	Zhou Enlai#	
	Peng Dehuai*	
	Peng Zhen*	
	Lin Biao	
	Deng Xiaoping	
	Bo Yibo	
	Liu Lantao	
Liu Lantao[c]		
Party deputy secy and secy	*Liu Shaoqi* #	—
	Gao Gang*	
Chm government[d]	*Peng Zhen**	
Deputy political commissar MR	*Bo Yibo*	
	Nie Rongzhen	
	An Ziwen	
EAST CHINA		
Rao Shushi		
1st Party secy	Liu Shaoqi#	Head CC organization dept 2/53
Chm government		
Political commissar MR		
Chen Yi		
2nd Party secy	Mao Zedong#	—
Commander MR	Liu Shaoqi#	
Party secy and mayor Shanghai	Lin Biao	
	Deng Xiaoping	
	Tan Zhenlin	

Tan Zhenlin
   3rd Party secy
   Vice-chm government
   Deputy political
     commissar MR
   Party secretary and
     governor Zhejiang

Mao Zedong#
Liu Shaoqi#
Deng Xiaoping
Rao Shushi?
Chen Yi

—

CENTRAL-SOUTH
Lin Biao
   1st Party secy
   Chm government
   Commander MR

Mao Zedong#
Zhou Enlai#
Chen Yun#
Gao Gang*
Peng Dehuai*
Deng Xiaoping

—e

Deng Zihui^f
   2nd Party secy
   Vice-chm government
   Deputy commander and
     deputy political
     commissar MR

Mao Zedong#
Liu Shaoqi#
Lin Biao
Deng Xiaoping
Rao Shushi

Head CC rural work dept
  1/53
Vice-chm SPC 11/52
Vice-chm FEC 11/52

Ye Jianying
   Party 3rd secy and acting
     secy^g
   Vice-chm government
   Party secy South China
     Subbureau
   Party secy and governor
     Guangdong
   Party secy and mayor
     Guangzhou

Mao Zedong#
Zhou Enlai #
Peng Dehuai*

—

NORTHWEST
Peng Dehuai
   1st Party secy
   Chm government
   Commander MR

Mao Zedong#?
Zhou Enlai#
Lin Biao
Deng Xiaoping

—h

Xi Zhongxunⁱ
   2nd Party secy
   Vice-chm government
   Political commissar MR

Gao Gang*
Peng Dehuai*

Vice-chm GAC Culture
  and Education Com-
  mittee 8/52
Head CC propaganda
  dept 6/53

SOUTHWEST
Deng Xiaoping
   1st Party secy
   Vice-chm government
   Political commissar MR

Mao Zedong#
Zhou Enlai#
Peng Dehuai*

Vice-premier 8/52
Vice-chm FEC 9/53
Finance minister 9/53

Liu Bocheng
   2nd Party secy
   Chm government
   Commander 2nd Field
     Army

Mao Zedong#
Zhou Enlai#
Peng Dehuai*
Deng Xiaoping
Bo Yibo
He Long

—j

He Long		
3rd Party secy	Zhou Enlai#	Chm Physical Culture and
Vice-chm government	Peng Dehuai*	Sports Committee
Commander MR	Liu Bocheng	11/52

Sources: Donald W. Klein and Anne B. Clark. *Biographic Dictionary of Chinese Communism*, 2 vols. (Cambridge: Harvard University Press, 1971); Wang Jianying, ed., *Zhongguo Gongchandang Zuzhishi Ziliao Huibian* [Collection of Materials on the Organizational History of the CCP] (Beijing: Hongqi chubanshe, 1983); oral sources; and sources cited in this chapter, notes 22–25, 27, 41–42.

Notes: * = Politburo member; # = Secretariat member; italics = no. 1 regional leader (column 1), particularly close personal or political ties (column 2); FEC = GAC Financial and Economic Committee; MR = Military Region; ? = circumstantial evidence (Lin Feng), Taiwan report of hostile relations (Tan Zhenlin), or history of close but testy relations (Peng Dehuai).

a. The most significant criteria for historical ties with Mao are: (1) support for Mao early in his career when his position was under threat; and (2) close working relations over a substantial period. Thus, the cordial Mao-Gao relationship is not included as it does not meet either criterion. The criteria for important ties among leaders other than Mao are looser; those with significant common work experience or documented personal links are listed. With regard to such ties, however, where relations of coworkers have been particularly conflictual (e.g., Rao Shushi and Chen Yi, Gao Gang and Peng Zhen), they have not been included. Those included in column 2 have been limited to Secretariat members excluding the nonpolitical Zhu De, important regional leaders, and several figures (Li Fuchun, An Ziwen) who played important roles in the Gao-Rao affair. Leaders are listed in order of status as follows: (1) Mao; (2) other Secretariat and Politburo members; (3) the number 1 leader in each region; and (4) other important regional leaders. For the number 1 regional leaders, only ties with people from categories 1–3 are normally listed; for other regional leaders, people from categories 1–3 and category 4 officials from the same region are included. For listing purposes, An Ziwen is treated as the equivalent of a category 4 leader and Li Fuchun as a category 3 figure.

b. Operational posts only with dates of appointment.

c. De facto regional leader given other duties of Bo and Nie.

d. Minister of North China Affairs under GAC 1950–52; chairman of North China Administrative Committee 1/53.

e. Unavailable for major central post as ill and on sick leave for much of this period.

f. De facto regional leader given Lin's illness.

g. Appointed acting secretary and acting commander MR 5/53.

h. Unavailable for major post due to serving as commander of Chinese forces in Korea.

i. De facto regional leader given Peng's absence in Korea.

j. President of PLA Military Academy in Nanjing from 1951.

---

subsequently Third Field armies,[29] arguably had superior military credentials than Gao, whose post-1935 role apparently was more civilian than military.[30] In any case, it appears that in comparison to Lin, Peng, and Deng, the regional clout of both Gao and Rao was based far more on their organizational positions per se than on military accomplishments.

Further inferences about Gao Gang's regional authority and the nature of regional power generally can be drawn from reports of Gao's suspicious response to the summons to the Center. According to Chen Shihui's *neibu* article, 1954–55 documents collected in post-1978 teaching materials, and oral sources, Gao saw his move to Beijing as a mixed blessing.[31] While caution must be exercised since these accounts portraying an arrogant, power-hungry individual may simply reflect the Chinese tendency to denigrate those who have fallen, there nevertheless appears to be substance in them. These sources assert that Gao regarded his transfer as "luring the tiger out of the mountains"—an effort to take him away from his power base in the Northeast. Gao reportedly initially refused to go unless he could keep his position as secretary of the Northeast Party Bureau. He argued he was needed in the Northeast and allegedly only put his anxieties to rest when Mao eventually agreed to the holding of concurrent posts; similar arrangements were then made for other regional leaders who came to Beijing in order to maintain parity.

Another aspect of Gao's reluctance, according to an oral source, was dissatisfaction with the SPC job, which he assertedly regarded as a "promotion in name but demotion in fact." This latter claim seems somewhat questionable in view of the key role the SPC would play in national construction and other accusations concerning Gao's efforts to use the SPC to promote his aims (see below). Nevertheless, even granting the significance of his new role, which together with his 1949 appointment as vice-chairman of the central government conveyed very high rank, Gao's actual status was still less than that of Liu Shaoqi and Zhou Enlai and, somewhat more ambiguously, that of Secretariat member Chen Yun.[32]

The above account raises several important issues. How reasonable was Gao's attitude? What does it tell us about regionalism in the pre-1953 period? Gao's posture suggests a degree of suspicion that sits uneasily with the Party unity said to exist in the early 1950s. While an authoritative oral source insists that his attitude reflected his power-thirsty nature, and that others such as Deng Xiaoping did not feel the same way about moving to the capital, a degree of skepticism is necessary. But such an evaluation cannot be dismissed out of hand. Individual character does vary and is crucial to political behavior at the top; moreover, Gao's overall performance throughout 1953 suggests a lust for power that got the better of his judgment.

Yet surely there were systemic factors influencing Gao's attitude, especially the large degree of power placed in the hands of regional leaders. Here new sources allow a fuller understanding of the charge that Gao had established an "independent kingdom" in the Northeast, or, as Deng Xiaoping put it in 1955, the region had become "Gao Gang's kingdom."[33] Notwithstanding the repetition in post-Mao sources of 1955 allegations that Gao's Northeast opposed the leadership of the Party Center,[34] the key to this phenomenon was not any lack of responsiveness to central directives[35] but the monopoly of power within the region by Gao Gang and his close followers. Gao reportedly placed authority in the hands of a small number of subordinates—particularly the so-called five tiger generals.[36] He denied real power to other officials with whom he did not have close personal ties, most notably Lin Feng (an old "white area" cadre), who was second secretary of the regional bureau. Gao reportedly continued to squeeze Lin out after moving to Beijing and, at some indeterminate time, was criticized by Mao for this behavior.[37] Here, too, Gao's actions may have been abnormal, but the capacity for regional leaders to be local monarchs with far-reaching power over everything undoubtedly generated some ambivalence more widely about moving to the necessarily more constrained national stage, or at least concerning giving up one's regional base.[38] Still, in the context of the times, the move to Beijing was natural and an opportunity for ambitious officials to enhance their status; thus, Gao's attitude as depicted does appear somewhat extreme.[39]

New Relationships at the Center

Another consequence of the centralization process revolves around the relations of the newly transferred leaders to Mao.[40] While there is no doubt that by 1952 Gao Gang had established cordial relations with the Chairman (see below), as table 1 demonstrates he was by no means unique in that regard. Deng Zihui had been one of Mao's closest supporters since the dark days of the early 1930s when Mao had been under attack by the Returned Student leadership;[41] now Mao personally sought Deng out to offer him the rural work post.[42] Deng Xiaoping was a similar and perhaps even more striking case. He had also stood with Mao against the attacks of others during the Jiangxi Soviet. Moreover, the Chairman had subsequently been most impressed with Deng's abilities; in 1951 he declared, "whether politics or military affairs, Deng Xiaoping is good at everything."[43] But the Mao–Deng Xiaoping relationship was significant for more than old loyalties and the Chairman's regard for his younger colleague; vitally important for both the events of 1953 and subsequent CCP history was Deng's subtle understanding of Mao. This understanding, combined with a toughness Mao admired and an ability to work smoothly with others, made Deng a key actor in Beijing well above his formal status even before Gao Gang arrived.[44]

In general terms, the old ties to Deng Zihui and Deng Xiaoping, as well as to others who also assumed important central posts, meant that an even greater role was played by Mao's historical allies in the affairs of the Center. While the natural administrative consequences of the new period remains the most persuasive overall explanation for the new appointments, the political side-effects are of some import. In a real sense, the emerging core leadership just below the Secretariat was more Mao-oriented than the balanced Politburo elected in 1945. This should not be overstated; the overall balance of the "factions" had not been upset, and Mao's power rested on factors far more fundamental than the gains derived from the new postings. But in theory at least—practice would prove somewhat different by late 1953 given Deng Zihui's differing views from those of Mao on cooperativization, not to mention the confusion caused by the Gao Gang affair—Mao's hand was strengthened for pushing his policy preferences, or even for shaking up the leadership if that were his intent. For Gao Gang, however, the implications were more mixed. Not only was his military clout less than that of other key players like Deng Xiaoping, but his claims to Mao's affections were less solidly based historically than those of at least two of the newly transferred leaders. Beyond this, his revolutionary links to movers and shakers more generally suffered in comparison not only to those of several of the other new boys in town, but also to those of additional key figures who remained in the regions. In this regard, one of the few leaders Gao seemed better placed than was Rao Shushi.

Further implications of the centralization process concerned the bureaucratic and working relationships among leaders now being forged at the Center. Of particular significance, both intrinsically given the new national priorities and in terms of the Gao Gang affair, were the new organizations and relationships in the sphere of economic management. The crucial relationship, of course, was between Gao Gang's State Planning Commission and the body that had been in charge of the overall direction of the economy since 1949, Chen Yun's Financial and Economic Committee, and its parent body, the Government Administration Council (see table 2). Perhaps the most striking thing about this relationship in retrospect is the confusion surrounding it: quasi-official contemporary 1950s sources,[45] outside observers at the time,[46] post-Mao documentary sources,[47] and oral sources[48] all give conflicting stories on whether the SPC was of equal status to the GAC (and thus of higher rank than the FEC), or under the GAC and of equal or even lower status than the FEC. This was in part due to the ambiguous wording of the original announcement on the setting up of the SPC,[49] but it is nevertheless clear that in formal terms the SPC was of equivalent status to the GAC under the Central People's Government Council.[50] In political and administrative terms, however, the situation remains somewhat uncertain; it is no accident that scholars today are confused concerning precisely what the relationship was.

I would argue that, on balance, the precise relationship was not fully clear to the actors themselves. Clearly, the SPC was a body of great significance given not only the status of those making up its membership but also the centrality of its main function—the drawing up of the FFYP—to current policy. This task had been under Chen Yun's control since 1951, and he had formulated three drafts before Gao took over; in 1954, control would again revert to Chen.[51] Moreover, the SPC clearly had some operational authority in the management of the economy, but its nature and scope remain unclear and were in any case shared with the GAC and FEC.[52] A clear case in point concerns the State Statistical Bureau, which was formally set up in January 1953 by the GAC and reported to the GAC, but still was charged with close working relations with the SPC and seemingly received instructions from Gao personally.[53] Another source of confusion was the overlapping membership of the two bodies; Chen Yun himself served as a member of the SPC, as did many of his FEC vice-chairmen. Moreover, these leaders had other concurrent posts in the economic sphere, which resulted in close working relations with Chen Yun. Finally, while the size of the SPC apparatus was apparently substantial,[54] it would still pale beside the total economic apparatus under the FEC.

Quite apart from the specific institutional role of the SPC, it is clear that Gao

Table 2

Leading Members of the Financial and Economic Committee and State Planning Commission, 1952–1953

GAC Financial and Economic Committee	Other positions	State Planning Commission
Chairman		**Chairman**
Chen Yun**	(Vice-premier)	
	(Vice-chm central govt, leader NE)	Gao Gang*
Vice-chairmen		**Vice-chairmen**
Deng Zihui	(Head CC rural work, de facto leader CS)	Deng Zihui
Li Fuchun	(Ex-Heavy Industry min)	Li Fuchun 9/53
Jia Tuofu	(Ex-official NW)	Jia Tuofu 9/53
Bo Yibo	(Finance min, leader NC)	
Ma Yinchu#	(Pres Beijing University)	
Zeng Shan	(Commerce min)	
Ye Jizhuang	(Foreign Trade min)	
Deng Xiaoping 9/53	(Vice-premier, leader SW)	
Li Weihan 9/53	(GAC secy-gen, head CC united front)	
Members		**Members**
47 members as of 7/53		Chen Yun**
	(Commander Korea, leader NW)	Peng Dehuai*
	(Leader CS)	Lin Biao
		Deng Xiaoping
	(Head CC org, leader EC)	Rao Shushi
		Bo Yibo
	(Vice-chm GAC Political and Legal Com, Party secy and mayor Beijing)	Peng Zhen*
		Li Fuchun
	(Vice-chm GAC Culture and Education Com, head CC propaganda, de facto leader NW)	Xi Zhongxun
	(Deputy chief of staff PLA)	Huang Kecheng
	(De facto leader NC)	Liu Lantao
	(Ex-Party secy Henan)	Zhang Xi
	(Ex-official NE)	An Zhiwen
	(Ex-official NE)	Ma Hong
	(Head State Statistical Bureau)	Xue Muqiao

Sources: Wang Jianying, *Zuzhishi Huibian*, pp. 612–13; *Renmin Shouce 1953* [People's Handbook 1953] (Tianjin: Dagongbao, 1953), pp. 176–80; *Ta Kung Pao* (Hong Kong), December 8, 1952, in *SCMP*, no. 468, pp. 18–19; and NCNA, Beijing, September 18, 1953, in *SCMP*, no. 654, pp. 5–7.

Notes: * = Politburo; ** = Secretariat; # = non-Party; italics = on both FEC and SPC. FEC and SPC positions as of 11/52 unless otherwise indicated.

Gang's importance in the economic realm was on the rise. The most dramatic evidence of this was a May 1953 GAC notice on the leadership of financial and economic departments. This notice divided these departments into five work organs formally designed as FEC offices and placed under the personal authority of individual top leaders. Seemingly the most important of these, designated Office Number 1, dealt with heavy industry, light industry, the construction and fuel industries, geology, and the First and Second Ministries of Machine Building; this potent industrial complex was given to Gao Gang. Chen Yun was given Office Number 2, responsible for finance, food, commerce, foreign trade, and the People's Bank, while transport and communications went to Deng Xiaoping, agriculture and related matters to Deng Zihui, and labor to Rao Shushi. Responsibility for coordinating the work of these offices was given to Premier Zhou Enlai.[55] These arrangements certainly would have confirmed Gao's sense of great economic clout.

What, then, are the political implications of this generally, and particularly for the relationships of Gao Gang and Chen Yun and Gao and Zhou Enlai respectively? It has been argued that the setting up of the SPC was a political setback for Chen that marked a decline in his fortunes lasting to at least mid-1953.[56] While this cannot be ruled out, and while Gao was obviously on the rise, the actual picture seems more complex. Although the situation clearly was prone to tension over bureaucratic turf, and one piece of evidence suggesting this will be discussed later, overall there is little explicit information to indicate major conflict or a decline in Chen's status.

Chen's whereabouts are difficult to trace throughout the first half of 1953, but he was positioned by his seat on the SPC to continue to exert influence, and his earlier drafts served as the basis for the SPC's revised FFYP, which was finally presented to the Financial and Economic Conference.[57] Oral sources, moreover, say that while there were of course contradictions between Chen and Gao in concrete work, they have seen no materials indicating personal conflict or maneuvers by either Chen or Gao against the other. To the extent that Chen was in "decline" in the first part of 1953, it was most likely due to health problems. The May 1953 notice on economic responsibilities stipulated that when Chen was on sick leave, Bo Yibo would assume his duties,[58] and oral sources report not only that Chen's health at this time was poor but that his practice was to work for a period and then take a complete rest. Thus, while Chen's influence may have waned somewhat at the very time Gao's increased, the circumstances were not necessarily those of personal conflict.

Generally speaking, the strongest evidence for conflict in the economic sphere are the post-Mao accusations that Gao thought he had organized an "economic cabinet" (*jingji neige*) with a great deal of power which allowed him to grasp much of the economic authority of Zhou's GAC.[59] These, however, are vague and perhaps biased charges. In a situation where new bodies were set up, uncertain relationships and a degree of conflict were inevitable, but hard evidence of major bureaucratic conflict in the period leading up to the Financial and Economic Conference is lacking. The GAC–SPC tensions that did exist were undoubtedly subtle. Thus, in addition to his coordinating role under the May 1953 decision, Zhou Enlai had already in fall 1952 "spent a good deal of time with the responsible comrades of the SPC" and offered oversight and corrections to the commission's work.[60] Notwithstanding the ambiguities of formal governmental rank, Zhou's position was still bureaucratically superior to that of Gao Gang. Yet the problem was Gao's rising political fortunes, and particularly the esteem in which he was held by Mao (see below). While Zhou had the authority to oversee at least some of Gao's work, probably more important was the fact that, according to oral sources, Gao had direct access to Mao. In such circumstances, formal chains of command were an imperfect guide to actual power. The most that can be said with any confidence is that the relative positions of Zhou, Chen Yun, and Gao Gang were delicately balanced in early 1953.

In broader personal terms, the implications of the situation were also significant. Overall, the transfer of key figures to Beijing saw the creation of either new working relations cross-cutting previous ties based on revolutionary "factions" or the revival of old relationships from an earlier period. Perhaps crucial here are the relationships among Zhou Enlai, Chen Yun, and Deng Xiaoping. Upon arriving in the capital Deng not only renewed a warm personal relationship with Zhou, dating from the 1920s,[61] but served under Zhou as vice-premier. Although not formally a vice-chairman of the FEC until September 1953, Deng was before too long involved in economic work with special responsibilities in the transport and communications sphere.[62] While one must be wary of post-1978 accounts in this regard, these sources depict a close and supportive relationship between Chen and Deng on economic policy.[63] Similarly, the relationship between Zhou and Chen in guiding the economy in the early 1950s was reportedly extremely close.[64] More broadly, all three, but particularly Zhou and Chen, developed intimate working ties to other key economic actors, such as Bo Yibo and Li Fuchun.[65] Thus, when Gao Gang stepped into his key economic post, he was met by a closely cooperating group of economic decision makers.

Like Deng Xiaoping, Chen Yun is clearly one of the decisive actors in the Gao-Rao affair—perhaps even more so than Deng. Crucial to note is Chen's relationship to both Gao Gang and Mao. Of all the figures shaping China's economic program in 1952–53, Gao had the most developed pre-1949 work ties to Chen and Li Fuchun based on their experiences together in the Northeast from 1945 to 1949 (1950 in Li's case). At least in Li's case, however, this contact may not have been entirely smooth. According to an oral source, when Zhou Enlai denounced Gao's dictatorial tendencies in 1954 he claimed that Gao had ignored Li's suggestions in the Northeast. On the other hand, Chen and Gao had stood

Deng Xiaoping (right) conversing with Chen Yun, Fall 1952

together in an important conflict with Peng Zhen over revolutionary strategy in 1946 (see below), and both appear to have been deeply immersed in the region's political and economic affairs. Thus, it was not surprising that Chen became one of the key people Gao tried to win over to his cause in the latter part of 1953, a fact that makes any pronounced tensions between them earlier seem unlikely.[66]

But the most important factor bearing on Chen's role in the crucial events of 1953 was his relationship with Mao. Although Chen, unlike Deng Xiaoping, was not an early follower of the Chairman, from 1937 on he developed close and immensely significant ties to Mao.[67] While some differences over economic policy cannot be ruled out,[68] the picture presented in post-1978 sources is of enormous trust in Chen's economic leadership on the Chairman's part throughout the early 1950s.[69] But perhaps most crucial is that Chen, like Deng, had a subtle understanding of Mao. Chen seems to have been able to read Mao extremely well; in later years this would mean a discreet fading into the background whenever the Chairman was on a different wavelength, only to reemerge when Mao was more willing to listen.[70] It does not appear that matters reached this state in 1953 but rather, as I shall argue, that Chen's understanding of Mao allowed him to play a critical policy and political role throughout.[71]

Apart from the changes to economic bureaucracies already under way, the latter part of 1952 and 1953 saw the consideration of important changes in political institutions and leadership personnel now that the recovery period had been completed. On the agenda were a new state structure, the convening of the Eighth Party Congress, the filling of top leadership posts in both the Party and state, and Mao's idea of dividing the leadership into "two fronts"—a "first front," which would be responsible for ongoing routine work, and a "second front," where the Chairman would ponder larger problems. Conflicting dating in the source material causes some confusion,[72] but it seems clear that these and related issues were under discussion within the leadership from summer 1952 and, in terms of the Gao-Rao case, reached a particularly decisive stage in late 1953. According to well-informed oral sources, the whole question of the "two fronts" was first raised during Politburo discussions of about August to October 1952 on when to hold the Eighth Party Congress.[73] A source close to Liu Shaoqi further claimed that in 1952 Mao talked the matter over privately with Liu and suggested that Liu be on the "first front." Thus these matters were on the agenda when Gao arrived in Beijing.

In January 1953 a constitutional drafting committee under Mao and a committee to organize national elections under Zhou Enlai were established with the aim of convening a National People's Congress (NPC) before the end of the year.[74] A new constitutional structure would mean new state officers; this, together with staffing the economic ministries recently set up to guide planned construction, meant important personnel decisions would have to be made. Similarly, with plans afoot to hold the Eighth Party Congress and thus elect a new central leadership, some of the key offices of the Party as well as state would potentially be up for grabs. In this context, the possibility of creating the positions of Party vice-chairman and general secretary was apparently raised.

All these issues, which came to a head at the end of the year, were related to Mao's health. While not facing serious physical disability, Mao did suffer from circulatory problems and dizzy spells and desired a lightening of his load. Again, precise dating is impossible, but it would appear that this would have been known within the higher circles in early 1953.[75] Thus, possibly significant changes in structures, positions, and Mao's role were under discussion as Gao Gang established himself in Beijing. Yet it is important to note that such changes did not necessarily foreshadow instability; both the process of centralization to that date and the future revamping of the Party at the Eighth Congress when it was finally convened in 1956 were carried out without disturbing the inner-Party balance. But the situation did create temptations, and in conjunction with other developments Gao assertedly believed a fundamental redistribution of power was at hand.[76]

Overall Policy Orientation

Apart from these developments on the personnel and organizational fronts, in early 1953 basic policy was also up for reassessment. With economic recovery complete and the tasks of planned construction and social transformation looming ahead, the time was ripe for laying down a new overall guideline for the CCP's work. On various occasions beginning in September 1952, Mao spoke in relatively unsystematic form about a "general line for the transition period."[77] True to the Communist tradition, various areas where policy makers confronted particular bureaucratic interests and immediate problems were required to fit into the overall "line." By early 1953 a number of issues that would be central to the general line were under discussion. These included the policy toward the national bourgeoisie, agricultural mutual aid and cooperativization, and the pace of economic growth. The former two would be the subject of some controversy in 1953, whereas the latter appears to have remained noncontroversial for the remainder of the year. By the spring of 1953, the "errors" involving departing from the general line were under criticism in a number of areas, most notably concerning Bo Yibo's new tax system introduced in January. These controversial issues, as well as the difficult question of the policy orientation of different leaders, will be looked at in greater detail subsequently. Here I shall limit myself to a general assessment of the overall thrust of policy in late 1952 and the first half of 1953.

Somewhat paradoxically, while the broad strategic thrust of this period was to press ahead toward planned development and socialist transformation, what might be termed the tactical approach was decidedly cautious. This caution can be summed up under the rubric of "oppose rash advance" *(fan maojin)*.[78] After various excesses in 1952, the time had come to move in a more deliberate manner. Thus, in mid-February 1953 the Central Committee issued a directive that characteristically attacked both right and left deviations but also emphasized problems of precipitate haste in setting up agricultural cooperatives; in March it followed up with a spring planting directive warning against "rash advance" in cooperativization, which reportedly undermined peasant enthusiasm for production.[79] Meanwhile, in January and February, Bo Yibo complained of blind initiative smashing the state budget and blindness in state construction planning producing great waste.[80] This was a theme that had developed in the latter part of 1952 and would continue with regard to various economic sectors throughout 1953. The prescribed antidote reflected the asserted virtues of planned construction—economic cadres were exhorted to link work with actual conditions, avoid unrealistic targets, appreciate the complicated nature of construction, and plan minutely. While "conservatism" in economic work was also criticized, the emphasis was on careful preparations rather than on enthusiastic but unrealistic surges forward.[81] In this there was apparent leadership unanimity, with Gao Gang's SPC standing with other economic organs in the forefront of the attack on rashness.[82]

While, to my knowledge, neither blind development nor rash advance was criticized with regard to treatment of the national bourgeoisie, the basic spirit of policy toward that group from mid-1952 was similar to that concerning cooperativization and the economy generally. After the harsh attack on this class during the Five-Anti Campaign, the leadership adopted a conciliatory posture toward China's private capitalists. With the independent power of the bourgeoisie broken, Party leaders sought to overcome the economic disruption and stagnation that had resulted from the movement by once again affirming the legitimate role of capitalists in national life and through various concrete concessions. In March and April 1953, a group under the Central Committee's united front department head Li Weihan carried out investigations among capitalists in various cities. While this investigation group was to design policies to facilitate the transition to socialism, its work continued the solicitous posture of the previous eight months or so. The report of this group became one of the first items on the agenda when the Financial and Economic Conference convened in June.[83]

All these policies would be up for reconsideration as the general line took shape. The inevitable debate on policy details, particularly in view of the latent contradiction between pressing forward and cautious tactics, would naturally be a potential source of strain, especially since rejected policy views could be pictured as deviant from the general line. Thus, much as the pending organizational and personnel changes offered an opportunity, the debate impinging on the general line also assertedly stimulated Gao Gang to launch his bid for power.[84] But undoubtedly, key to Gao's perception of opportunity were his conversations with Chairman Mao.

The Key Personalities: Mao, Liu, Gao, and Rao

Mao and Gao Gang

According to the understanding of an authoritative oral source, Mao and Gao Gang had three private conversations sometime after Gao's arrival in the capital. These talks must be seen against the background of the Mao-Gao relationship over the previous seventeen years. Although they had no contact before 1935, Mao and Gao quickly developed political and personal ties after the Long Marchers reached the North Shaanxi base area of Liu Zhidan and Gao Gang. When the Long Marchers arrived, Liu and Gao had been arrested by representatives of the same old pre-1935 Central Committee leadership that had tormented Mao, and Mao soon ordered their release.[85] Liu and Gao were now reestablished as leaders of the local base area, and Gao became the preeminent local leader following Liu's death in 1936. An oral source spoke of Mao's respect for Gao Gang as a founder of the Shaanxi revolutionary base and as a local cadre who knew the area very well. During the 1942 rectification campaign Mao articulated his admiration: "I came to northern [Shaanxi] five or six years ago, yet I cannot compare with comrades like [Gao Gang] in my knowledge of conditions here or in my relations with people of this region."[86] According to my source, this professional respect was linked to a personal closeness; during their decade together in Yan'an, Gao often visited Mao's cave and Mao attended dances organized by Gao. By the time Gao was dispatched to the Northeast after the Anti-Japanese war, a personal friendship had been established.

Gao's accomplishments as a leader during the struggle against the Guomindang in the Northeast and later as the supreme leader of the region after Liberation further earned Mao's favor. The Northeast played an unusually large role as a model for the rest of the country in the early 1950s. This was clearly due to the early consolidation of regional power, comparatively advanced economic conditions, and access to Soviet aid and advice as Chinese leaders projected Soviet-style development for their nation. The role of the Northeast as a pathbreaker in both economic construction and political movements created high prestige for the region and its leader[87]—even if Gao's claims that the region was "ever correct" would later leave him open to derision.[88] In fact, "correctness" did not involve any public political posture distinct from that in Beijing. Gao's public statements were generally in tune with central policy, and his position usually shifted as did circumstances and the Party line.[89] Yet the achievements in reconstruction were manifest, and by 1952 Gao was recognized not only by Mao but by the Secretariat as a whole as one of the most capable of the younger Politburo members with rich experience in construction who should play a key role in the emerging period of centralization and planned economic growth. Moreover, the fact that the Northeast had already established its own local planning commissions made Gao a logical candidate for the SPC post.[90]

Despite the absence of a distinct public posture, the question remains whether Gao Gang brought any particular policy orientation with him to Beijing. As implied above, standard Pekinological methods are not of much help. Particular speeches by Gao can be read as evidence of a "rightist" leaning, as in his October 1952 warning that agricultural cooperativization should not push ahead rapidly in the absence of mechanization;[91] or as indicating a "leftist" inclination, as reflected by his attack on "bourgeois thought" and "rightist thought within the Party" in January of the same year.[92] Ironically, in view of future events, perhaps one of the strongest public statements of a "leftist" view was offered by Bo Yibo in August 1952 when he chastised those who underestimated the speed of development, complained of leaving too much planning and designing in the hands of unreformed old technicians, and praised the creativeness of the masses.[93] In short, under rapidly changing circumstances it is risky to read too much into the open declarations of CCP leaders.

Nevertheless, convincing evidence comes from oral sources that in the context of late 1952 and early 1953 Gao Gang's policy orientation was on the "left" of the spectrum occupied by CCP leaders. These sources picture Gao as favoring a comparatively rapid elimination of the national bourgeoisie as a class and a quick transition to socialism, and a close adherence to the Soviet model.[94] Most interestingly, a source close to Liu Shaoqi reported the perception that Gao's work and economic ideas were "leftist" in 1952 but attached no great political moment to this for the period *before* late 1953. Apparently such differences were all accepted features of leadership politics.

Of particular significance was the relationship of Gao's "leftist" tendencies to Mao's policy preferences. While oral sources see Mao and Gao sharing similar views on at least some issues, as one scholar put it, Gao's "leftism" had something in common with Mao's, but there were also differences. Indeed, the general pattern of evidence from 1953 suggests a more complicated situation where Mao's position is better characterized in the "centrist" tenor previously argued, and also by not insignificant tension between his broad ideological leanings and his concrete policy advocacy. As will be seen, whatever policy affinities were shared by Mao and Gao, the Chairman's policy preferences sometimes diverged from those of his younger colleague on issues of great significance.

In any case, when Gao arrived in Beijing the Chairman had good reason to be well disposed toward him based on past contact, recent achievements, and most probably a degree of policy affinity. While Mao's relations with Gao were warm and marked by respect and trust,[95] however, they were clearly the relations of leader and subordinate. Apart from differences in Party rank, not to mention the distance created by Mao's position as the supreme revolutionary leader, the superior-subordinate relationship was further accentuated by the contrast in a significant Chinese index of prestige—cultural level. According to oral sources, Gao was of relatively unsophisticated peasant background, comparatively low in educational level, stubborn and forthright in character, with an explosive temperament.[96] One authoritative source claimed that Gao looked up to the more learned Mao, while the Chairman regarded Gao as a rather rough type who wasn't very literate. Unlike his attitude toward Liu Shaoqi, Mao had no profound respect for Gao's theoretical abilities. But Mao was pleased whenever he perceived signs of Gao's intellectual development—not only in the sense of a Marxist theoretician but also as a learned man. A case in point was Gao's 1949 article (reportedly written by Gao's talented subordinate Ma Hong), "To Whom Is the Glory."[97] The Chairman is said to have felt this showed that his rough comrade was making progress. The same factor would again play a role in the critical events of summer 1953.

This, then, was the nature of the relationship when Mao and Gao discussed issues facing the CCP in late 1952 and/or the early months of 1953. While the exact content of these talks may be forever lost,[98] it is the understanding of an authoritative oral source that Mao expressed dissatisfaction with certain aspects of the work of Liu Shaoqi and Zhou Enlai during the three exchanges. According to his understanding, Mao complained of rightist conservatism (*youqing baoshou*) in their work. While some of this criticism was directed at past errors (see below), it still had relevance for current policy. Reportedly of particular concern to Mao was that he believed Liu and Zhou were too cautious concerning the pace of socialist transformation. This, or course, was inevitably linked to policy toward the national bourgeoisie, and, in the context of early 1953, Mao was particularly upset by Bo Yibo's tax concessions to the bourgeoisie. The Chairman apparently also criticized the views of Liu and Zhou concerning the pace of agricultural cooperativization, although it is not clear whether he was complaining about past or present attitudes. In any case, the overall posture of "opposing rash advance" in economic construction seemingly was not raised.[99] But whatever the precise catalogue of Mao's discontent, it appears certain that significant unhappiness with Liu and Zhou was conveyed to Gao Gang.

What was Mao's intent in raising his discontent in the conversations with Gao? A range of explanations is possible. The most innocent interpretation would be that Mao was simply letting his hair down with an old friend to vent some frustrations with his highest collaborators; yet surely Mao knew that any exchanges with a Politburo member would have political implications. Or, as one oral source suggested, Mao's object may have been to warn Gao that he should not develop a "rightist" tendency similar to that of Liu and Zhou, but this too seems unlikely given Gao's comparatively "leftist" posture. Related to this, Mao may have been encouraging Gao to take a forceful position in favor of a faster pace of transformation within Party councils. Given the overall consensual approach to decision making in these years, it may be that Mao was hesitant to impose his views too baldly but wished to enhance their likelihood of prevailing in open debate.

Less benign is the possibility that Mao wished to bring pressure on Liu and Zhou to force them into greater conformity with his own preferences. Conceivably, his displeasure was such that he was willing to entertain a significantly increased degree of contention within the Politburo or even to impose his will through divide-and-rule tactics. An even less benign interpretation is that Mao was indeed considering or seeking to get rid of Liu and/or Zhou. One variant of this interpretation would be that Mao was pondering such a move but had not made up his mind; another is that he had determined that one or the other should go but was unwilling to expend his own political capital on this task and hoped a few hints would encourage Gao to do the dirty work while leaving himself a line of retreat. Indeed, this apparently was Gao's interpretation of the Chairman's intent since he seemingly acted independently of Mao throughout 1953 although attempting to draw on the Chairman's prestige. The more extreme version would be that Mao was explicitly endorsing a full-blooded attempt to unseat Liu and Zhou, but the attempt somehow went wrong. Finally, a theoretically possible but most unlikely motive is that all along Mao was trying to set up Gao Gang for a fall.[100]

Oral sources, sources which are quite willing to see questionable motives in Mao's actions in other contexts, do not believe that Mao was trying to remove Liu and Zhou. They conclude that Gao, driven by ambition, misinterpreted the Chairman's intent as a green light to replace Liu as the successor when in fact Mao's trust in Liu—various irritants notwithstanding—remained high. While retaining reservations concerning the conventional wisdom reflected in this consensus, my own view also doubts any intention to remove Liu or seriously disrupt leadership cohesion for a number of reasons.

First, Mao would have been reluctant to depart from his "unifying the factions" approach, which had contributed to the startling successes of the previous decade. Related to this, these successes left Mao in a stronger political position than ever, one where he need fear no threats or take radically new measures to secure his dominance. Moreover, as shall be argued in more detail below, the overall pattern of his relations with Liu Shaoqi in the preceding years indicates a high degree of confidence and relatively limited differences; there were no tensions of such magnitude as to require drastic action. Another consideration is that to encourage Gao to take on both Liu and Zhou would have been unnecessary as well as clumsy. While the comparative strength of Liu's character conceivably could have made Mao wary, Mao saw Zhou as a pliable subordinate albeit one with rightist inclinations.[101] Zhou, who in any case prided himself on being Mao's assistant, was moreover widely loved within the higher echelons of the CCP, and any effort to remove or demote him would have produced considerable discontent for non-essential gains. Finally, the course of events in 1953 demonstrates an awesome authority on Mao's part which surely could have been used more effectively to limit or remove Liu and/or Zhou had that been the Chairman's purpose.

In any case, Gao Gang apparently took Mao's meaning to be that he should try for the number two position in the CCP. Chen Shihui's *neibu* account, while avoiding all mention of the Mao-Gao talks, flatly asserts that Gao felt he could "count on Chairman Mao's 'trust' in him"[102] as he undertook his factional maneuvers. Gao's sense of the Chairman's backing in the effort to unseat Liu, who was clearly the primary target of his activities, would have been reinforced by Mao's May 1953 circular criticizing the issue of Central Committee documents without his approval, a circular at least partially if unfairly aimed at Liu Shaoqi and more than likely related to issues raised in the talks with Gao.[103]

Moreover, Gao's perception of the Chairman's intent dovetailed with his own discontent with Liu Shaoqi. According to a well-informed oral source, relations between Gao and Liu had been good in Yan'an, and when Gao was sent to the Northeast Liu took him aside and asked him to help Peng Zhen, who, as the new ranking secretary of the region, might not be able to handle everything himself. But Gao-Liu relations began to sour as a result of Gao's dispute with Peng over military strategy in the Northeast in 1946. At that time Peng Zhen advocated a more frontal strategy in opposing Guomindang armies than Gao, Lin Biao, and Chen Yun, who favored building up Communist forces in the countryside.[104] Even at this stage a favorable disposition on Gao's part toward Liu was apparent in an appeal from Lin and Gao to Liu that he himself come to the Northeast to take over from Peng.

In the event, the matter was settled by Mao's support of Lin, Chen, and Gao, with the result that Lin replaced Peng in the top role; Peng, however, continued to work in the region for over a year, and his relations with Gao assertedly were very bad. In fall 1947 Lin and Gao sent an emissary to the Party Center to discuss the continuing problems of the Northeast Bureau, but Liu apparently equivocated and, rather than come down against his close associate Peng, called on the bureau's leaders to concentrate on unity.[105] This reportedly led Gao to begin to develop a grudge against Liu; this was seemingly intensified in 1948 when there was a ten-day delay in Gao's appointment as regional secretary after Lin Biao moved south, a delay for which Gao held Liu responsible. Accordingly, it was from this time that Gao began to spread his theory of "red" and "white areas" and his claims that "white area" cadres like Liu Shaoqi and Peng Zhen had no experience in leading revolutionary war or building revolutionary bases. This account makes intelligible what would otherwise seem dubious, that is, the charge that Gao was fomenting discontent with leading comrades at the Center—especially Liu Shaoqi—for the entire period since 1949.[106] Yet it is important to emphasize that any such stirring up of dissatisfaction appears to have been relatively low-level grumbling before 1953.

In the early post-Liberation period another conflict arose between Gao Gang and Liu Shaoqi, although in this case the issue resulted in Liu being severely embarrassed.[107] The matter began in July 1950 when Deng Zihui gave a report to a trade union meeting in the Central-South region. This report argued that in state enterprises there were contradictions between the concrete interests of the workers and management, and that the trade unions should represent worker interests. Deng sent his report to Mao and the Party Center while Liu commented on behalf of the Center that the report was very good. Liu's comment had been circulated to and approved by all members of the Secretariat, including Mao. Quite independently, however, Gao Gang had already formed a different view that in state enterprises the interests of workers and management were identical since there was no exploitation in such enterprises. He then organized the writing of an essay expressing his viewpoint and submitted it to Mao, seeking approval to publish the piece as a *Northeast Daily* editorial. The article and accompanying letter were distributed to both Mao and Liu, but in the event it appears that Mao did not read them. Instead, Liu responded, suggesting that the essay temporarily not be published, but that the issue be discussed directly with Deng Zihui at the Party's Fourth Plenum, scheduled to be held shortly with the trade union issue at the top of the agenda. Following this, Liu began drafting an article of his own that was critical of both Deng and Gao but fundamentally sided with Deng. At the same time, this draft article developed the idea that different types of contradictions existed within state enterprises, a notion that Mao would by 1957 expand into his concept of antagonistic and nonantagonistic contradictions.

As with most high-level differences, the key to settling this dispute was apparently Mao himself. According to an oral source specializing in trade union affairs, Mao read Liu's reply to Gao but did not express an opinion. Yet sometime between Liu's May 1951 reply and the end of the year, when an enlarged trade union meeting was held that severely criticized union head Li Lisan for, inter alia, supporting Deng Zihui's view, a dramatic shift in policy occurred. My source explained that "evidently Mao changed his mind, but no one knows why," and only Li Lisan was directly criticized, although again "nobody knows why." Although Liu may not have been openly rebuked, since he had made his position clear and was the Secretariat member with overall responsibility for trade union affairs, he was hugely embarrassed by the affair. Not only was he unable to publish his article on contradictions within state enterprises—an article that would eventually be published posthumously in Liu's *Selected Works*—but the Fourth Plenum had to be postponed given the leadership's disarray on the issue, and Liu chose to leave Beijing rather than attend the trade union meeting, which attacked Li Lisan when it was convened in December.[108] For Gao Gang, the lesson of this affair must have been that with Mao's backing Liu could be defeated on a policy issue and embarrassed politically.

Thus it would seem that preexisting discontent with Liu and past experience that Liu could be bested with Mao's help, when taken in conjunction with his late 1952–early 1953 conversations with the Chairman, provided ample motivation for Gao Gang's factional activities during the remainder of 1953. But before examining these activities in detail, a closer look at Mao's relationship with Liu Shaoqi is in order.

Mao and Liu Shaoqi

By the Seventh Congress in 1945 Liu Shaoqi clearly ranked second in the CCP hierarchy.[109] When Mao departed on the physically dangerous mission to Chongqing for negotiations with Chiang Kai-shek, he not only left Liu in charge of the daily operations of the Party but made it clear that if anything happened to him Liu should take over as primary leader. Two years later, when Yan'an was under Guomindang attack, the leadership was split, with Liu placed in charge of a "Central Committee working committee" sent to Hebei, which would take over if the worst befell Mao, who remained in the Northwest. Oral sources are absolutely clear that Liu was considered the successor within the elite even though the term itself was not used.

Whether Mao individually chose Liu as his successor or whether Liu's elevation was more due to a leadership consensus is uncertain, but the Chairman clearly accepted and valued Liu's new role. In his eyes, Liu's suitability was due to his status as a long-time Party leader, his important "white area" constituency within the CCP, his great practical abilities in work, but above all his political and ideological firmness in the struggle against Wang Ming. Liu's political insight was demonstrated in 1937 when he became the first CCP leader to offer a systematic critique of Wang Ming's "erroneous line" of the early 1930s. Unlike his attitude toward Zhou Enlai and others, Mao regarded Liu as someone of sufficient ideological capability and political strength to take over if the situation ever arose. This, of course, did not mean that Mao and Liu did not have their share of disagreements in the period before 1953, although these obviously have been exaggerated in Cultural Revolution sources.[110] Exaggerations notwithstanding, there were a number of instances after 1945 where Mao criticized Liu's "errors," cases that were well known within the CCP and brought up by Gao Gang in summer 1953, and again in the Cultural Revolution. The most significant of these were Liu's "leftist" mistake in land reform in 1947-48, the spring 1949 Tianjin talks where he declared "exploitation is beneficial" in an effort to reassure local capitalists, and his 1951 criticism of agricultural cooperatives in Shanxi.

The circumstances varied from case to case, but none of them involved a profound confrontation between Mao and Liu. On the 1947-48 case, Liu was indeed responsible for framing the "leftist" land reform regulations, although Mao accepted these at the time. When Mao subsequently began to speak out against the excesses that had resulted, Party cadres clearly understood this as a criticism of Liu, but no names were mentioned.[111] Moreover, in a 1950 letter to Liu and a 1951 Politburo resolution Mao brought up the erroneous practices of 1947-48, although again without directly criticizing Liu. While such references were clearly relevant to rural policy at the time, these mild rebukes also had the effect of reminding Liu of his past errors and who set the standards of ideological correctness.[112]

Of greater significance given their bearing on policy toward the national bourgeoisie were the Tianjin talks. These talks resulted from Mao dispatching Liu to curb the chaos caused by overly radical Party cadres who had recently entered the cities, and to revive the economy with the cooperation of China's capitalists. Not only were Liu's actions fully in accord with Mao's policy directive, but the Chairman affirmed the basic spirit of Liu's talks and expressed delight when Liu's wife, Wang Guangmei, reported on Tianjin developments in May 1949.[113] Subsequently, at the June 1950 Third Plenum, Zhou Enlai praised Liu's explanations as still an important guideline for united front work with the bourgeoisie and indicated Mao's approval.[114]

According to oral sources, it was only in the latter part of 1952, during early discussions on the general line, that Mao began criticizing the Tianjin talks, that is, well after the event and in a new context. This ahistorical approach, which falsely claimed that the talks violated the line of the March 1949 Second Plenum, seemingly reflected Mao's overriding theoretical concern with transforming the bourgeoisie in late 1952 and early 1953 rather than his practical concern with the necessity of using that class for economic recovery in 1949. Related to this was the fact that the Chairman's ire was drawn not by the actual policies of 1949 but by the ideologically careless statements made by Liu, such as asserting that exploitation involved no evil and lauding private businessmen as "red capitalists."[115] What was political rhetoric in 1949 designed to assuage the fears of an insecure but vital group was now judged in terms of theoretical niceties of the transition period. It is important to note, however, that there is no evidence that this was a serious source of conflict between Mao and Liu; oral sources assert once again that the Chairman did not use Liu's name. But Mao's displeasure was definitely known by high leaders about the time Gao Gang arrived in Beijing.

The 1951 Shanxi case probably marked a sharper and, in a sense, more justified instance of Mao's displeasure with Liu, but there were notable similarities with the Tianjin talks issue. In July 1951 Liu wrote and distributed in his own name a critical comment on a report on mutual aid and cooperativization by the Shanxi provincial Party authorities. This report proposed supporting and developing into a campaign a move on the part of some peasants to convert mutual aid teams into advanced cooperatives of the Soviet type. Given the chaotic rural conditions created in Shanxi by this program, Liu sharply attacked it as "agrarian socialist thought." Mao had used the same term in 1948 to attack leftist excesses as reactionary and backward; according to an authoritative oral source, in offering his brief comments Liu proceeded without consultation and had no idea that Mao now had different views.

Mao, however, seems to have been annoyed, indeed very angry according to another well-placed source. On the one hand, Mao was seemingly upset by Liu's acting without consultation—the kind of concern that was to find voice later in the Chairman's May 1953 circular declaring that he must approve all Central Committee documents. In policy terms, in 1951 Mao was interested in pushing cooperativization forward, and in September 1951 he began drafting a resolution on developing mutual aid and cooperativization. When this resolution was issued in December it implicitly criticized Liu, although yet again no names were mentioned. Significantly, in this directive Mao was not completely out of sympathy with Liu's concerns; a direct leap from mutual aid teams to full-scale collective farms was not on. But Mao outlined an intermediate step, the semisocialist lower-stage cooperative to smooth the transition, which Liu had not considered. Whereas Liu seemingly saw higher collective forms as something that would come only after mechanization—a view widely shared after the failure of the Second Plenum to deal with the issue clearly, Mao devised a method for a smoother and quicker transition to socialist agriculture. Finally, in theoretical terms, Mao apparently was particularly upset with Liu's use of the term "agrarian socialist thought," his own prior usage notwithstanding. Such a term conflicted with Mao's desire to push cooperativization along, and as a result the term generally fell into disuse after September 1951.[116]

If Mao again raised this earlier dissatisfaction at the beginning of 1953—and there are strong indications that this was the case by the middle of the year[117]—the question remains as to how it related to issues then facing the leadership. As already indicated, in the first half of 1953 policy toward cooperativization was in the mainstream of the *fan maojin* approach. The stress was on correcting leftist adventurism, stopping blind attacks on private ownership, avoiding overemphasis on cooperatives at the expense of mutual aid teams in old liberated areas, and insisting on the voluntary principle for guiding the movement.[118] What is crucial for our purposes is that the available evidence points to Mao's approval of this policy orientation. In a major statement in March 1953 he was in perfect harmony with the previous month's Central Committee directive on cooperativization: "Our . . . agricultural economy remains basically a scattered, small peasant economy . . . ; this is vastly different from the mechanized collective farming of the Soviet Union. Therefore, in the present transition period we cannot introduce unified and planned production in agriculture, . . . and interfere too much with the peasants."[119] The next month, moreover, Mao provided a notice affirming that the spring Central Committee directives on agriculture provided theoretical knowledge and important policy principles for current work.[120] Thus, while Mao may have reflected unfavorably on the general thrust of Liu Shaoqi's 1951 position on cooperatives, and while his own position would drift in a somewhat more radical direction later in 1953, in the spring his concrete position was apparently in line with the counsels of caution.

Whatever Mao may have felt about these and other "errors" on Liu's part,[121] what is politically crucial, oral sources assert, is that Liu always accepted the Chairman's criticisms.[122] For Mao's part, he does not appear to have attacked Liu by name at any stage, and oral sources are convinced that as of early 1953 Mao retained a substantial degree of trust in Liu. Moreover, Mao's grousing to Gao Gang notwithstanding, it is difficult to find evidence of fundamental Mao-Liu differences at this point. It is striking that Cultural Revolution sources raise no substantial Mao-Liu issues for the 1952–early 1953 period itself;[123] and on the key 1953 issues Mao's position was hardly polarized from that of other leaders. Thus, as of spring 1953, while Mao undoubtedly had cause for dissatisfaction with Liu Shaoqi, neither past incidents nor current policy seemed sufficient cause for a major breach that might lead to an effort to displace Liu. Nevertheless, the Chairman's expressions of discontent, both in general terms over such matters as the Tianjin talks and in his talks with Gao Gang, were sufficient to introduce an element of uncertainty, which potentially put at risk the leadership approach that had served him so well over the preceding decade.

Rao Shushi Decides to Support Gao Gang

Rao Shushi arrived in Beijing sometime after Gao Gang as one of the top twenty or so leaders of the CCP.[124] Although not a Politburo member, Rao's importance is indicated by both his old positions as top Party and government leader in East China and his new posting as head of the organization department, which controlled key personnel assignments. As with Gao Gang, recently available sources tell several stories about Rao that reflect poorly on his character. Again, one must be wary of such accounts concerning disgraced officials. In Rao's case one must be doubly wary since a certain parallelism exists between the picture drawn of him and that of Gao Gang. Both are seen as uncontrollably ambitious, excessively suspicious, and seeking total control of their local kingdoms.[125] These reservations notwithstanding, the stories are worth recounting.

One case concerns Rao being summoned from Shanghai to Beijing in February 1952 for treatment of an eye disease. A leading military figure stationed in East China, Su Yu, had recommended that Rao take sick leave and accompanied him on the luxury train for high-level cadres. Rao reportedly was so suspicious he regarded Su's presence as an effort to keep him under surveillance and additionally worried that his errors in East China would be discovered. Once in Beijing, Rao assertedly was further upset when he heard that the Center wanted to dispatch a leading cadre to Shanghai to help with Three- and Five-Anti work. These considerations, so the story goes, left Rao so agitated he couldn't sleep, and he got up in the middle of one night to request a meeting with the nocturnal Mao. When the Chairman received him at 3 A.M., Rao asked whether or not he had been courageous in the struggle with the enemy, whether he had made mistakes of line in his East China work, and why Su Yu had accompanied him to the capital. Even when Mao reassured him that he had been brought to Beijing because of the Center's trust in him, Rao was reportedly still ill at ease and only relaxed when the Chairman proposed that Rao himself decide when to terminate his sick leave and resume his duties.[126] As with Gao Gang, this instance may, as oral sources believe, reflect Rao's abnormally suspicious nature, but the question must remain open as to what it implies about the general level of trust within the leadership.

Another case that bore heavily on subsequent events concerned Rao's uneasy relations with Chen Yi. In 1943, when Rao was political commissar of the New Fourth Army in East China and Chen commanded the same force, Rao assertedly launched a struggle against Chen, whose frank manner frequently resulted in unorthodox statements. This was essentially a "surprise attack" initiated without prior discussion with Chen or a request to the Central Committee for instructions. A struggle meeting was held where Rao charged Chen with opposing Mao and the political commissar system, and with wanting to drive him [Rao] away. Having won support within the New Fourth Army, Rao then telegraphed the Central Committee attacking Chen and asking for him to be replaced. The Center obliged in 1944 and Chen was sent to Yan'an. Chen made a self-criticism of his "liberalism" assertedly for the sake of unity, and Mao declared that Chen had made contributions to the revolution, that the conflict between Chen and Rao concerned a working relationship, and that the argument should come to an end.[127]

Later, in 1949, the tensions between Rao and Chen again surfaced when the time came to hand out posts in the six large regions then being established. The practice was to appoint the leading regional military figures to head the new governmental structure, which in East China would have meant Chen Yi, who had earlier returned to take up again military command. While Chen reportedly adopted a modest or prudent stance, Mao still pushed the idea. Rao, however, objected on the (allegedly false) grounds that most local commanders opposed Chen's appointment. Mao reportedly accepted Rao's request because Party secretaries were responsible for personnel and to reject his opinion would have caused a serious loss of face.[128] Nevertheless, Chen gained important local posts as East China Party Bureau second secretary and Shanghai Party secretary and mayor, while other leaders with close ties to Chen also held key regional posts (see table 1). Thus, whatever his desires, at the time of his transfer to the Center Rao had not achieved the same degree of regional dominance as Gao Gang in the Northeast.[129]

At some point in spring 1953, after his arrival in the capital, Rao apparently decided to back Gao Gang. Undoubtedly influenced by both Gao's increasing prominence and signs of Mao's dissatisfaction with Liu Shaoqi, Rao reportedly concluded that Gao would be successful in his efforts to "seize power" and that his increasing importance meant Gao "had already replaced Liu Shaoqi as Chairman Mao's successor," and very quickly joined forces with him.[130] Yet, in some ways, Rao was an odd person to throw his lot in with Gao. His revolutionary career involved not only important underground ("white area") assignments, but also working relations with Liu.[131] There is some uncertainty concerning the closeness of Rao's links to Liu. Chen Shihui describes the relationship as "comparatively close" in work,[132] but an authoritative oral source considers the links of no great significance. However intimate or otherwise, the political importance of the links were indicated by Liu's 1965 comment that it was he who promoted Rao and placed him in a major position.[133] In policy terms, moreover, Rao apparently was out of step with Gao Gang; in contrast to Gao's leftist posture, Rao assertedly had consistently made rightist errors in his East China work after 1949, errors which Chen Yi had reportedly opposed.[134] Finally, Gao and Rao were very different types of people. In contrast to the rough, open personality of Gao who, as accusations after his fall revealed, was a notorious ladies' man, Rao was well-educated, spoke very good English, adopted a strict moral code, and gave very little away.[135] The incongruence of both personal and policy factors in Rao's "alliance" with Gao has seemingly not only caused the particularly sharp criticisms of him as a typical hypocrite who was especially good at feigning,[136] but has also given rise to doubts both at the time and subsequently that anything so formal as an alliance actually existed.

While the accusation of an alliance was leveled against Gao and Rao as early as spring 1954,[137] there are many reasons to believe that little more than parallel action by the two men existed. Doubts concerning an alliance surfaced as soon as the case was exposed in 1954, and such disbelief was again present when the formal verdict was handed down in 1955. According to a well-informed oral source, doubts were widespread enough that Liu Shaoqi brought them to Mao's attention, whereupon Mao directly addressed the matter at the 1955 National Party Conference. While Mao did raise some specific matters to justify the notion, which will be discussed later in this study, overall official charges on this point speak vaguely of Gao and Rao mutually coordinating their activities, of the two being identical in nature, and their evil deeds manifesting the same form. Very few specifics are given, and Chinese scholars today report having seen no material demonstrating that Gao and Rao ever held talks concerning their "anti-Party" activities. This picture of at best tacit support on Rao's part was the defense of Rao himself, who at the February 1954 discussion meeting on his case declared that he and Gao "agreed without prior consultation and happened to have the same view" (*bu mou er he*). That there was little evidence to shake Rao's position is indicated by the fact that the conveners of the meeting weakly concluded that they had insufficient time to probe the matter further. Finally, oral sources report that Gao Gang's former secretaries claim there was little connection between Gao and Rao.[138]

For the remainder of the analysis I shall therefore treat the Gao-Rao "alliance" as essentially a case of parallel actions by the two leaders pursuing linked goals but not acting in close concert, although evidence suggesting the contrary will also be noted. But this brings us back to the question of why Rao decided to back Gao Gang. Paradoxically, it may be that Rao's significant but not overly close connections with Liu help explain his attitude to Gao. Apart from simply positioning himself to be on the anticipated winning side, if Rao did not support Gao he might lose out in the coming shake-up given his past links to Liu. According to Chen Shihui, Rao "feared that if he again followed Liu Shaoqi he would suffer a loss in status."[139] By this logic, if Liu's associates would suffer as a result of the bloodletting, then it was best to abandon ship. In addition, by early 1953 Rao had his own grievances with Liu. As shall be examined in detail in chapter 3, Rao evidently believed that the much closer relationship between Liu and An Ziwen was denying him real control over the organization department. Thus ambition, fear, and resentment all argued for Rao distancing himself from Liu and aligning with Gao Gang, while prudence suggested avoiding direct plotting, which clearly violated Party rules.

From Gao's point of view, as Rao's actions from the Financial and Economic Conference on demonstrated support, there probably was no need to engage in the type of lobbying efforts that he later applied to Lin Biao, Peng Dehuai, Deng Xiaoping, and Chen Yun. But whether tacitly or involving still hidden personal contacts, Rao was a valued ally. Not only was he the leader of East China, but Gao reportedly saw great advantage in Rao's control of personnel.[140] He also apparently saw Rao as a younger cadre who would be part of a new generation displacing the somewhat older Liu Shaoqi and Zhou Enlai. This issue of Party generations, strangely, is involved in the difficult question of a possible Soviet connection in the Gao-Rao affair.

The Soviet Connection, Party Generations, and Ideological Orientation

From the very first, outside observers speculated about Soviet involvement in the demise of Gao Gang given the major role of the Soviet Union in the Northeast in the early 1950s.[141] Although contemporary sources kept silent about any Soviet connection, the Sino-Soviet dispute produced Russian sources claiming that Gao's only error was his friendship for the Soviet Union,[142] while Cultural Revolution and post-Mao materials have indicated Chinese suspicion of Gao's "illicit relations" with Moscow.[143] There is little doubt that Gao had established both warm personal relations with Stalin—even if the political implications of these relations have been exaggerated[144]—and smooth working relations with Soviet officials in the Northeast, adjacent Soviet territory, and Korea.[145] What was dubious were private discussions Gao held with the Soviet ambassador and other Russian officials.[146] Interestingly, in these talks, at least some of which took place about the time Mao was expressing his discontent with Liu Shaoqi and Zhou Enlai to Gao Gang,[147] Gao reportedly spoke critically of Liu and Zhou, depicting them as hostile to the Soviet Union and claiming they had said uncomplimentary things about Stalin. These conversations, as both Khrushchev's memoirs and Chinese oral sources attest,[148] were revealed to Mao by Stalin at some indeterminate time, perhaps as early as 1950.[149] But according to a well-placed oral source, there was no particular reaction on Mao's part. Whether this was due to the lack of clear guidelines for dealing with China's Soviet allies,[150] to the fact that Stalin already knew what Gao conveyed in any case, or to the fact that the Soviet Union made it risky to make any move made against a "friend" of Moscow (notwithstanding Stalin's double game), it was only *after* Gao's fall that both the issue of his links to Moscow and the more general question of appropriate relations with the Soviet "big brother" became sensitive.[151]

But what could Gao's calculations have been in cultivating the Soviets? Did these calculations play a role in his activities in 1953? The contacts in question probably began before Gao was emboldened to strike at Liu Shaoqi and, quite apart from any bold power plays, a top CCP politician could potentially benefit from a favorable Soviet attitude. At the time Sino-Soviet relations were close and the PRC was economically and militarily dependent on the Soviet Union. There was also the fact of Soviet leadership of the international Communist movement of which the CCP considered itself a firm member, not to mention the considerable respect in which Stalin personally was held. In this context, Soviet backing was a significant political asset. Several well-informed oral sources believe Gao was seeking Soviet support and, as one put it, such support combined with Mao's blessing would have made Gao extra strong—"a tiger with wings."

A potential problem, however, was Mao's burning nationalism and resentment of Soviet slights[152]—an attitude shared by a substantial segment of the elite. While this should not be exaggerated in the context of the early 1950s, a blatant use of Soviet support would have been potentially counterproductive. Thus, combining the two sources of support was hardly a sure thing. Moreover, the nature of any Soviet support for Gao was problematic. Not only was doubt cast by Stalin's turning over information to Mao, but there was no reason for the Soviets to rely excessively on Gao given their extensive dealings with other Chinese leaders.[153] In any case, I have encountered no oral or documentary sources that suggest that Gao actively used the "Soviet card" in his unfolding efforts to win support throughout 1953.

The Generational Issue

If Gao's links to the Stalin leadership played only a submerged role, the post-Stalin succession in the Soviet Union apparently had a direct impact on his calculations. According to an authoritative oral source, Gao took heart from the emergence of Malenkov as the initial successor to Stalin. Gao, already aware of Mao's discontent with Liu, noted that Malenkov was of a younger generation than such leaders as Molotov and Kaganovich. More to the point, this source reports having seen documents claiming that Gao had told others that Mao said it was better to let younger people be successors. Whatever Mao may have meant by this,[154] Gao seemingly reasoned that people of his generation could replace the older Liu and Zhou, that is, people such as Chen Yun, Deng Xiaoping, Rao Shushi, and Lin Biao as well as himself. While there is a degree of absurdity in Gao's generational analysis since Liu and Zhou were vigorous men in their mid-fifties, it does provide a clue to his actions. Although Cultural Revolution sources picture Gao's claims that he was "young and capable" as an effort to push the older and somewhat unhealthy Mao aside,[155] the Malenkov analogy suggests a different aim. The contrast to the "young and fit" Gao was not Mao but Liu and Zhou; the issue was who was best endowed for the role of successor. In this light, it is not surprising that most of the key figures Gao approached—Rao, Chen, Deng, and Lin—were roughly the same age as Gao and five to nine years younger than Liu and Zhou.[156]

In any case, the appeal to younger leaders was an odd strategy given the relative youth of Liu and Zhou, Chinese attitudes toward age, and the fact that other ties would undoubtedly be more significant than generational bonds for those concerned. As with so much else about this case, it seems that only Mao's attitudes, or perceived attitudes, were sufficient to make the generational question a significant factor.

Ideological Orientation

One final aspect of Sino-Soviet relations influenced the Chinese political scene generally in early 1953 and was to impinge, somewhat indirectly, on the Gao-Rao affair. This concerned broad ideological orientation, a factor of obviously critical importance as a new general line took shape. Notwithstanding Mao's suppressed resentment toward aspects of past and present Soviet behavior, or various assertions of Chinese ideological independence in the early 1950s,[157] Chinese ideology was profoundly affected by Stalinist orthodoxy. This was reflected not only in the heavy exposure of cadres and population to Soviet theories, but also in Mao's request to Stalin to send a theoretician to China to assist with the revision of the Chairman's *Selected Works*. Stalin obliged, and Mao subsequently held nocturnal working sessions with theoretician Yudin during the early post-Liberation period.[158] Moreover, in the second half of 1952, at Mao's behest, Liu Shaoqi and seemingly Zhou Enlai as well consulted Stalin on the emerging general line.[159] For all his political boldness and, less dramatically, theoretical inventiveness, Mao was still uncertain in the ideological sphere and wary of straying too far from Soviet canon.

Soviet ideological influence was explicitly manifested in April 1953 in the form of a new study program for senior and intermediate cadre study groups.[160] This theoretical study was specifically designed to accompany the Soviet-style economic construction China was then embarking upon and to provide a Marxist-Leninist ideological groundwork for socialist transformation. The basic text for study was the 1938 Stalinist *History of the Communist Party of the Soviet Union (Bolsheviks): Short Course*. Specifically, cadres were to read chapters of the *Short Course* dealing, respectively, with the period of economic reconstruction (1921–25), the struggle for socialist industrialization (1926–29), the collectivization of agriculture (1930–34), and the completion of the building of socialist society (1935–37). In conjunction with these chapters cadres were also to study twenty-five articles by Lenin, Stalin, and other Soviet leaders dealing with economic construction. This study program continued until the end of the year and into 1954, and by fall 1953 it was explicitly linked to study of the general line, with particular emphasis on the chapter covering 1921–25.[161]

What explains this new theoretical study program? What messages might it have conveyed to those officials who did indeed dutifully read the prescribed texts? The simplest explanation for launching this course of study is, given the expressly ideological nature of Marxist-Leninist regimes, the felt need for theoretical guidance and the fact that Soviet theory was the only orthodox source of doctrine then existing. Yet while the use of Soviet theory was perhaps at root a reflex action, i involved theories and attitudes strangely out of tune with the emerging general line of the CCP. As will be seen in greater detail later, the Chinese general line would emphasize gradualism and peaceful methods of transition. To be sure, scattered throughout the assigned study materials—particularly in the *Short Course* chapter on 1921–25, the selections from Lenin, and the remarkably skillful Stalin selections from the 1920s—were sentiments compatible with contemporary CCP policy: emphasis on maintaining the alliance with the middle peasantry, the need to fight a two-front battle against deviations of the left and right, the desirability of regrouping one's forces rather than engaging in headlong advance, the necessity of learning from experts and setting practical goals, and the importance of persuasion rather than pressure in achieving the Party's objectives.[162] Moreover, an underlying theme of the Soviet literature was precisely the core idea of the general line—that society was in a process of transition from capitalism and socialism and policy must be oriented to making that transition a success.[163]

The above features of the Soviet texts notwithstanding, any cadre bothering to read them carefully would undoubtedly have been confused concerning the lessons to draw. Apart from the lack of overall coherence of the texts themselves, particularly significant was the tension between the predominant message of the study program as a whole, on the one hand, and the aims of CCP policy and existing norms of inner-Party life, on the other. Despite warnings concerning both the left and right and the moderate themes noted above, perhaps the sharpest rebukes were reserved for rightist policies associated with Bukharin. In contrast to contemporary Chinese policy discussions, where class struggle was rarely mentioned, Bukharin was denounced for his theory of subsiding class struggle when assertedly such struggle became more intense and vicious as capitalist elements attempted to resist the transition. Moreover, the Soviet materials denied that the dispute between Stalin and Bukharin involved shades of difference; instead it was characterized as a conflict of two opposing lines,[164] a notion that had not been a feature of post-1949 CCP policy debates hitherto but would have an ominous echo in summer 1953.

Above all, it was the characterization of inner-Party life as involving organized anti-Party factions, a leadership infested by agents of class enemies, and a politics of violent sabotage and murderous plots that more than anything stood at variance with the practice of Chinese communism in the early 1950s. In contrast to the Chinese situation, the Soviet texts depicted an environment where even debate on the modalities of policy implementation was a reflection of bitter class struggle within the Party—e.g., the advocacy of a slower rate of industrial growth was treated as tantamount to speaking for the enemies of socialism.[165] While the Soviet view of factional conflict had elements of historical accuracy as well as distortion, it was a jarring message in the context of 1953 China.

While this ambiguous Soviet ideological legacy was probably a vague background factor introduced more for reasons of pointing out a general policy direction and keeping up theoretical appearances than for any specific political purpose, it nevertheless operated in a Party where theoretical disputation and related political conflict had a firm tradition, albeit a comparatively more restrained one than in the Soviet Party. Arguably, the type of impulses it conveyed fit into both Gao Gang's general orientation and his specific efforts to change the shape of the CCP's leadership configuration. While the literal implications of the Soviet texts were undoubtedly far removed from the consciousness of most leaders in spring 1953, this factor would play an elusive but not insignificant role as the rest of 1953 unfolded.

Conclusion

In sum, as summer 1953 approached, Gao Gang, with or without good reason, believed he had Mao's backing—or at least acquiescence—for an attempt to replace Liu Shaoqi as the Chairman's successor. He apparently thought he could emulate Malenkov and sweep aside such older figures as Liu and Zhou Enlai. Zhou was not the same formidable obstacle as Liu, but as an older official of conservative tendencies whose faults had been noted by Mao and who stood above Gao in the hierarchy, Zhou would have to go too. To do this Gao would recruit figures of his own generation and reward them with the new positions that would result from the reorganization of the state and the holding of the Eighth Party Congress. Although the country was undergoing a process of centralization, Gao reportedly thought in terms of winning over the leaders of the great administrative regions as one key to achieving his aims; in any case, most of these figures now occupied critical central posts in addition to their regional offices. Somewhere in the background stood Gao's assiduously cultivated Soviet ties, presumably to be invoked at the appropriate moment to demonstrate that he could secure China's international objectives. Finally, with a full-fledged discussion on the general line about to unfold, Gao's leftist inclinations were apparently in tune with some of Mao's preferences as well as in resonance with officially promoted Soviet theory. In this context the opportunity for attacking Liu and Zhou on the policy front arrived with the convening of the Financial and Economic Conference in mid-June.

2
THE ATTACK ON LIU AND ZHOU
The National Conference on Financial
and Economic Work, June–August 1953

HOWEVER ADVANCED Gao Gang's plans concerning a bid for enhanced power may have been in early summer 1953, the National Conference on Financial and Economic Work would inevitably be of great significance quite apart from his activities. With planned economic construction starting, a review of economic policies across the board was essential. With the whole notion of socialism bound up in patterns of economic ownership, programs affecting structural economic change would be high on the agenda. Moreover, as already emphasized, the fact that policies were to be placed in the context of a general line had important political implications; they would be examined not only in terms of technical and bureaucratic considerations but above all with regard to ideological correctness.

In terms of leadership politics, the Financial and Economic Conference would also have inevitable consequences for top officials. In the case at hand, despite claims that Gao Gang's "conspiratorial activities" can be traced to 1949,[1] it is clear that the major maneuvers of the Gao-Rao affair began at the summer conference. Even apart from this, the very review of economic policies was bound to affect individual leaders in this sphere, as it did so dramatically in the criticism of Bo Yibo. Given Mao's apparent displeasure, Zhou Enlai was vulnerable; as premier, he bore the ultimate responsibility for the administrative decisions affecting the economy. The case of Liu Shaoqi was somewhat different, however, since he was not in charge of concrete economic work, although in his role of assisting Mao with all Central Committee work he gave considerable attention to economic construction.[2] Moreover, the fact that general ideological issues were paramount in Mao's eyes—plus the significance of Liu's personal ties to Bo Yibo—left Liu in a particularly difficult position in view of Mao's discontent with his past "errors." In examining developments at the Financial and Economic Conference, the focus will be not only on Gao's specific activities, but on the key issues affecting the overall leadership equation—the general line, policy toward the national bourgeoisie, and Bo Yibo's new tax system.

The Financial and Economic Conference met on and off between about June 14 and August 12;[3] it is not always clear precisely which events during this period took place at the conference per se and which transpired in other forums, such as Politburo meetings. For reasons of simplicity, all events relating to the work of the conference will be considered together here regardless of whether they actually occurred at the conference itself. Sources differ as to who was responsible for the conference; a variety of post-Mao sources state that Zhou Enlai was in charge of the meeting[4] while several Party histories assert that Gao Gang "used the opportunity of being in charge of this conference" to carry out his activities.[5] On balance, Zhou would seem the better bet given the weight of evidence and the overall responsibility of the GAC for economic construction. In either case, both Gao and Zhou played major roles at the conference—Gao made a major report on economic construction plans, while Zhou conveyed Mao's views on the general line to the participants and gave the summing-up report at the end of the meeting. Apart from the vital role played by Mao himself, others assigned key functions were Li Fuchun, who also reported on economic construction; Party united front head Li Weihan, who reported on transforming the bourgeoisie; and Chen Yun, who, as the Party and state official in charge of financial and economic work, subsequently assumed overall responsibility for shortcomings.[6] Of the vital actors in the unfolding Gao-Rao affair, only the sick Lin Biao and Peng Dehuai as commander of Chinese forces in Korea were missing from the conference.

The conference agenda was wide-ranging. It included the Five-Year Plan; the January–April 1953 budgetary performance and problems; revising the tax system; the food question and the problem of providing food for disaster relief; problems of adjusting commerce (especially procurement and price policy); problems concerning capitalist industry and commerce; and basic construction. These issues were linked together by the "main responsibility" of the conference to discuss how to implement the general line, to unify the understanding of officials too prone to the narrow perspectives of their own departments, and to criticize and correct ideas departing from the general line and mistakes committed in work during the preceding half year. It was this process of summarizing experience and correcting mistakes that Gao and Rao assertedly seized upon to launch their attacks on Liu, Zhou, and others. Particular areas receiving criticism were Bo Yibo's industrial and commercial tax system, public finance, banking, and agricultural taxes, and in several talks Mao also raised rural transformation. Errors in these areas allegedly— albeit usually unconvincingly—involved violations of principles laid down by the March 1949 Second Plenum of the Seventh Central Committee. Clearly, the question of how each of these concrete policies fit into the overall Party line provided considerable potential for manipulation and attack.[7]

Events during the Financial and Economic Conference proceeded on two levels—open policy discussions at the conference sessions, and behind-the-scenes efforts by Gao Gang to win support while at the same time denigrating Liu and

Zhou. Although the official 1955 verdict depicts the Gao-Rao affair as largely conducted "behind the back of the Party" in which "they never openly put forward any program against the Central Committee,"[8] and Deng Xiaoping twenty-seven years later declared that "so far as Gao Gang's real line is concerned . . . I can't see that he had one,"[9] Gao and Rao used the open sessions of the conference to develop a critique of others that reflected Gao's general orientation and had a certain policy coherence. It may be the case that they "had no policies of their own concerning practical work"[10] in the sense of offering concrete alternative measures, but their criticism of Bo Yibo in particular clearly contained the basis for a program of stepped up socialist transformation with fewer concessions to the bourgeoisie. The apparent lack of specifics suggests the asserted opportunist motives of the challenge, but it also most likely reflected uncertainty about Mao's precise policy position. In any case, in a manner that would reappear in much more virulent form during the Cultural Revolution, relatively vague ideological criteria were applied to specific policy questions in the pursuit of political gain.

The three crucial areas of discussion at the summer 1953 conference for the purposes of the present study—over the content of the general line itself, on policy toward transforming the national bourgeoisie, and concerning Bo Yibo's tax system—are related in substance, but on available evidence there is no way of knowing precisely how the course of debate on one affected the others. Each will be dealt with separately below, although likely points of contact will be noted. Finally, the behind-the-scenes activities of Gao and Rao will be examined independently, although these maneuvers were intertwined with developments at the open sessions of the conference.

The General Line

Once the conference opened, the "general line for the transition to socialism" was quickly the center of attention. On June 15, in a comment on Li Weihan's report on the national bourgeoisie,[11] Mao went beyond earlier unsystematic discussions and for the first time laid down the general line in comparatively complete form:

> The general line and the overall task of the Party during the period of transition is basically to complete national industrialization and the socialist transformation of agriculture, handicraft industries, and capitalist industry and commerce within a period of ten to fifteen years or a bit longer. This general line is a beacon illuminating every task we undertake. One must not deviate from this general line. If one is divorced from this general line, errors either of "left" deviation or of right deviation will occur.[12]

Notwithstanding at least nine months' consideration, this formulation apparently was not the subject of any extensive debate at the conference, and Mao fine tuned the formulation, as was his habit, both during the meetings by revising documents and reports—particularly Zhou Enlai's conference summary in August—and subsequently.[13]

The general line was formally issued to the nation in September, followed by a six-month propaganda campaign. In the course of the campaign the "basic principles" of the line were elaborated, largely emphasizing such concrete tasks as the Five-Year Plan, concentrating on heavy industry, modernizing national defense, developing transport and communications, and ensuring the gradual rise of living standards.[14]

The lack of contention at the Financial and Economic Conference over the formulation of the general line undoubtedly was a result of Mao clearly declaring himself at the outset, and also because a consensus had already been reached. The real turning point in the leadership's attitude toward the transition occurred during the less systematic discussions in fall 1952. In that period, under the influence of the success of the Five-Anti Campaign in bringing the bourgeoisie to heel, the previous view that the transition to socialism could *start* after ten, fifteen, or twenty years shifted to one foreseeing the basic *completion* of the process in a similar period. Mao took the lead in this change, but during fall 1952 Liu, Zhou, and other Party leaders climbed on board.[15]

The new understanding had important political implications both from a general theoretical perspective and, as will be seen, less clearly for specific policies. From an overall point of view, the general line provided a new emphasis in the ongoing debate over precisely how much attention to give to reassuring key social groups and how much to controlling and transforming them. With economic recovery achieved, the FFYP scheduled to begin, and the Korean war rapidly moving toward a settlement, the emphasis on transformation intensified. Yet it is important to note that in some critical respects there was continuity with the preceding period. First, the hallmark of the general line was gradualism; both industrialization and transformation would take place over a fairly long period in a step-by-step manner. Moreover, as shall be discussed in greater detail below, the framework of the united front remained, and the bourgeoisie would continue to play a vital role. In terms of speed, Mao still charted a middle course: in his June 15 statement he warned against both the left error of "going too fast" and the right error of "standing still."[16]

In strict policy terms, then, while the new general line marked a somewhat more radical approach, it remained a moderate program around which a consensus could easily be formed. Moreover, as will be seen with regard to the national bourgeoisie, it offered cautious elements within the leadership a basis for arguing their point of view during the Financial and Economic Conference. As for Mao, his basic position seems little changed during the course of the conference, although there is some evidence suggesting a slightly more leftist view at its close. This is perhaps seen in Mao's reversing the order of the deviations to be avoided in August so that now rightist errors took pride of place. Moreover, the August version of the general line explicitly dated the transition as starting from the founding of the PRC rather than with the FFYP, although this change may have been prompted by a hardly radical source, Zhou Enlai. Finally, but more ambiguously, on the question of speed the Chairman altered June's "ten to fifteen years or a bit longer" to the vague formulation of "a considerably long period of time," which might arguably be used by those advocating a shorter period of time but could also be used by proponents of a longer transition.[17] Thus, overall the results of the formulation of the general line were somewhat equivocal, with various elements within the leadership able to find solace in its centrist orientation.

The discussions on the general line, however, shed further light on the leadership equation in early summer 1953. Interestingly, one person who came out well despite apparently being at variance with Mao on a significant matter was Gao Gang. This is demonstrated by a June 28, 1953, letter from Zhou Enlai to Mao for the Chairman to read and pass on to Gao. In this letter Zhou politely argues that a formulation in Gao's draft report for the Financial and Economic Conference that spoke of the socialist transition solely in terms of realizing socialist industrialization was incomplete as it failed to take agricultural collectivization and transforming capitalist industry into account, and that an earlier draft mentioning agricultural collectivization was to be preferred. This letter was significant in several senses. First, it shows Zhou's willingness to engage in discussion concerning the general line despite the political difficulties he was facing as a result of Bo Yibo's tax policy, something reflecting a relatively noncontentious debate. Zhou was even game to be critical of Gao Gang, although a leading Chinese scholar working on Zhou insists this was by no means an attack on Gao. Also interesting is that Gao was out of step with Mao, who had cited agriculture, handicrafts, and capitalist industry and commerce as part of the process of transition on June 15;[18] this undoubtedly was the key reason for Zhou to feel confident in raising the matter. But most interesting is the tremendous care with which Zhou posed the issue, asking that both Mao and Gao inform him if his opinion was suitable. My very well-placed source agrees with the analysis that Zhou's letter was a clear sign of Gao's high standing at the time, which Zhou fully respected, notwithstanding Gao's theoretical carelessness.[19]

While the precise formulation of the general line provided little scope for attacking Liu or Zhou, in another sense Mao provided grounds for both general pressure on those skeptical of stepping up the pace of change and pressure on Liu Shaoqi personally. The effect of laying down a "comparatively complete" general line at the outset of the conference was to settle the overall debate in favor of the need for a stepped up process of change. The emphasis was clearly on moving toward socialism, albeit in gradual fashion, and those hesitant to do so ran the risk of being out of step with the Party line. Moreover, as indicated above, past performance was to be judged in terms of deviation from the line. This was something of a fraudulent exercise since the new line was retrospectively seen as embodied to a significant extent in the line of the 1949 Second Plenum, something explicitly added in Mao's August formulation.[20] In fact, Mao's speech to the Second Plenum and subsequent major statements of 1949, while acknowledging the socialist future, placed major emphasis on recovery and reconciliation in the short term.[21] In addition, there was no theoretical clarity about the relationship between New Democracy—the official designation of the PRC's stage of development before Mao's mid-1953 formulation—and socialism, or about the process of transition from one to the other.[22] Thus, the criteria for "deviating from the general line" was uncertain and dubious at best, and the very fact that the issue had been raised to the ideological level made concerned officials vulnerable—thus opening up opportunities for Gao and Rao. Furthermore, the manner in which Mao chose to illustrate the danger of "standing still" had potentially adverse implications for Liu Shaoqi. In his June 15 statement the Chairman warned that those who pushed New Democracy instead of socialist transformation risked rightist errors.

According to the volume 5 text, Mao further argued:

> "Firmly establish the New Democratic social order." This proposition is harmful. In the period of transition things are changing every day; every day socialist elements come into being. How could this so-called "New Democratic social order" be "firmly established"? . . . Our present revolutionary struggle . . . will thoroughly bury the capitalist system and all other exploitative systems. The idea of "firmly establishing the New Democratic social order" . . . impedes the development of the socialist cause.
>
> "Go from New Democracy toward socialism." This proposition is too vague. . . . If we go in a direction year after year, in fifteen years can we still say [that we are simply] going in that direction? Going in a direction means that [the goal] has not yet been reached. At first glance this proposition looks acceptable but after detailed analysis [one can see] it is not a sound one.[23]

Since Liu had been associated with a slogan similar to "firmly establish the New Democratic social order," such remarks inevitably affected him. Indeed, Cultural Revolution sources declare that in articulating the general line Mao smashed Liu's "New Democratic order," a view echoed by the editors of volume 5.[24] Several things should be said about this turn of events. First, in an important sense it was unfair to Liu. Although he had apparently emphasized the slogan or a variant[25] several years before, the evidence is unclear as to whether or how strongly Mao objected at the time.[26] Moreover, Liu was on record in May 1953 that China was entering the new epoch of the transition to socialism.[27] Earlier, while endorsing the slogan, Liu apparently linked it with movement toward socialism which, notwithstanding Mao's strictures of June, was the central energizing concept of the general line. Certainly no recorded statement by Mao before mid-1953 provides more precision than "movement," and the time envisioned for the transition was similar in the public views of the two men.[28] These considerations notwithstanding, Mao appears to have been expressing discontent with a slogan that may have had utility earlier but now clashed with the impetus he wished to give to socialist transformation. Considerations of historical fairness aside, the vital question remains as to how significant Mao viewed the issue. Obviously, in raising it the Chairman gave it considerable weight, yet in a *Wansui* version of the same June 15 text Mao plays down the issue's seriousness by observing with regard to "going from New Democracy toward socialism" that it was not a big mistake.[29] Moreover, oral sources know of no evidence that Mao raised this question before June 15.[30] While it is certainly plausible that he mentioned it in his private talks with Gao Gang, this too is far from certain, and a few days before the Financial and Economic Conference opened Rao Shushi spoke somewhat vaguely of "the gradual transition from New Democracy to socialism."[31] Thus, although the matter was undoubtedly important to Mao, it fell short of the major issue portrayed by Cultural Revolution sources and the editors of volume 5. Still, given the Chairman's apparent dissatisfaction with the cautious views of both Liu and Zhou Enlai on the pace of socialist transformation, i.e., the length of the New Democratic period, the issue had contemporary policy implications even as it revolved around past slogans.[32]

In any case, by attacking the New Democracy slogan (and perhaps through other criticisms raised simultaneously[33]), Mao inevitably created problems for Liu. As with Mao's talks with Gao Gang, one can speculate over the Chairman's motives in raising the question. These might vary from an attempt simply to discredit the slogan, which had considerable currency within the Party,[34] to slapping Liu across the wrists for perceived ideological shortcomings, to contributing to an effort to remove him. Criticism and self-criticism, except of course for Mao himself, was normal, and Liu among others admitted mistakes at the conference.[35] Whether Liu's mistakes would ultimately be treated as isolated errors or as more serious faults was not immediately apparent, but in a system emphasizing moral-ideological correctness the potential for harsh conclusions was present. For Gao Gang, aroused by his talks with the Chairman and moreover stimulated by Mao's May circular on the improper issuing of documents, Mao's comments on the slogan during his formulation of the general line could only be a source of further encouragement.

Using, Limiting, and Transforming the National Bourgeoisie

The importance of policy toward the national bourgeoisie at the Financial and Economic Conference has already been indicated by the fact that Mao's definition of the general line came in the form of comments on Li Weihan's report on capitalist industry. The ownership of industry and commerce would obviously be a fundamental aspect of any transition to socialism, and Mao had personally asked his long-standing acquaintance Li to carry out the spring investigations into the actual condition of China's national capitalists, who had recently suffered the trauma of the Five-Antis.[36] Mao's statements in the year preceding the conference, with the possible exception of one brief, ambiguous comment allegedly critical of Li

Weihan reported in volume 5,[37] suggest a conciliatory approach toward the national bourgeoisie. In a September 1952 letter to Huang Yanpei, a leading minor party figure and a government minister, Mao criticized Huang's draft speech to a capitalist group as "a bit too radical," and he went on to observe that it was impossible and improper to "disallow such things as the bourgeoisie's making money by exploitative means."[38] In March 1953, in another letter to Huang and the democratic personage Chen Shutong, the Chairman endorsed conveying to industrial and commercial circles his observation "that things should be fair, that people should do as much business as they have capital for."[39]

Nevertheless, policy toward the national bourgeoisie was not entirely moderate, particularly as it applied to commercial capitalists. Reflecting the Marxist bias against commercial activity as opposed to industrial production, in 1952 and early 1953 Party leaders favored "eliminating" (*paichu*) a part of capitalist commerce each year. In March 1952 Mao noted the greater importance of industry than commerce and called for converting commercial capital into industry. This, moreover, was not simply Mao's personal view; it expressed a commonly held opinion within the leadership at the time.[40] Thus, there were several aspects of policy and leadership attitudes toward the national capitalists as the Financial and Economic Conference approached, but the overall thrust was decidedly pragmatic. By the time Li gathered his data and prepared his recommendations, Mao had indicated a wariness about pressing capitalists too hard and a desire to utilize their energies even as he prepared to increase the pressure for socialist transformation.

Li Weihan's investigations and the reaction to them are revealing in terms of both the Gao Gang affair and leadership interaction generally. Much of the information on these developments comes from Xu Dixin, a participant who took up posts in both the Central Committee's united front department and the GAC's industry and commerce administration bureau in fall 1952 and who was sometimes present at the summer 1953 Politburo discussions on the question. Li's investigations involved visits to major centers of the private economy—Wuhan, Shanghai, Nanjing, Wuxi, Zhangzhou, and Jinan—from March to May, and his investigation group included not only personnel from the united front department and industry and commerce administration bureau but also from Gao Gang's SPC. When Li wrote two reports upon his return to Beijing in May, they initially went to Liu Shaoqi as the official responsible for all routine work at the Center. In the event, Liu, perhaps chastened by the Chairman's criticism of his handling of documents in mid-May, reportedly concluded that the issues raised were very serious and must be considered by the Politburo, which was duly convened. For his part, Mao was reportedly delighted with Li's work and personally phoned him to say it would be discussed by the Politburo.[41]

It was presumably at the earliest of quite a few Politburo sessions dealing with the issue that Mao laid down the first comprehensive statement of the general line on June 15. According to Xu Dixin, while everyone supported Mao's formulation of the general line, discussion ensued on how long transformation would take. As suggested earlier, in this regard Mao's relatively moderate formulation of the transformation period—"ten to fifteen years or a bit longer"—provided a convenient opening for cautious leaders on the crucial issue of how long it would take to transform capitalist industry. Zhou Enlai, reported Xu, argued that transformation could not proceed too quickly for excess speed would not be beneficial to the national economy. In his opinion, even fifteen years might not be enough, and a bit longer would possibly be required. Zhou also emphasized that the process must be smooth and based on a policy of unity and education toward the private capitalists, while Liu Shaoqi took a similar position in criticizing leftist thought. Thus, as with Zhou's letter on the general line, in these discussions Zhou and Liu did not appear to be inhibited from advancing their moderate views. Mao's indications of dissatisfaction notwithstanding, their policy advocacy was within the broad parameters laid down by the Chairman. Presumably Gao Gang favored a faster pace of transition (see below), but the available sources do not indicate whether he argued the case or held his peace on this question. In any case, as with agriculture and handicrafts, a ten-to-fifteen-year guideline was laid down for the transformation of capitalist industry.[42] Thus, while the guideline may not have been quite as cautious as Zhou desired, it was still well within the bounds of moderation.

Another issue raised in these Politburo meetings concerned bureaucratic turf. According to Xu, both Mao and Zhou felt that an organ with overall responsibility was needed to take charge of the transformation of private capital. In this context Chen Yun made his influence felt by saying that the SPC already had too much to do, and if it were assigned this task the work might be done poorly. Whether this was in response to a suggestion by Gao or someone else was not indicated, but it is the strongest available evidence of possible bureaucratic tension between Chen and Gao. The result was not simply that the united front department and Li Weihan would take primary responsibility, but that Li was simultaneously appointed to Chen's FEC as a vice-chairman. Moreover, the FEC set up a sixth office under Xu Dixin to deal directly with transformation. To the extent this was a bureaucratic tussle between Chen and Gao, Chen Yun emerged as the clear winner.[43]

Chen's considerable influence was also reflected in the reconsideration of policy as it affected *commercial* capitalists. The unsympathetic official attitude toward private commerce had not changed by the start of the Financial and Economic Conference, and Li Weihan's proposals dealt basically with industrial capitalists. Some officials, apparently headed by Chen, however, felt that existing policy caused problems and began to consider the other side of the issue. In a major speech to the conference on August 6, Chen attacked "blindly eliminating private commerce" and warned against the attitude that "the left is better than the right"— a warning that probably had other issues in mind as well. Chen argued that as long as state commerce didn't contract, there could be a gradual process of squeezing out the private commercial sector. The matter was not finally settled at the conference, but shortly thereafter, in early September, Mao came down firmly on Chen's side in a talk to representatives of democratic parties and industrial and commercial circles when he declared that commercial capitalists could carry out state capitalism and the "elimination" method could not possibly be used in dealing with private commerce.[44]

While the position of Gao Gang can be inferred on the above issues, only on the question of the methods of transformation is explicit information available. At the June 15 meeting where Mao formulated the general line, Li Weihan proposed a number of concrete measures designed to transform the ownership of capitalist industry by peaceful methods summarized under the rubric of *shumai*—the method of peacefully buying out the capitalists step by step. Li proposed three specific methods: (1) nonmonopoly purchase of the production of capitalist enterprises (*shougou*); (2) processing and ordering goods to monopolize the purchase and marketing of private enterprise products by the state; and (3) joint state-private ownership as the state took over a substantial share of formerly private ownership.

In the discussions that followed, the dominant opinion was that *shougou* was a primitive form of transformation that no longer was in much use, and emphasis should be placed on the latter two methods. Zhou and Chen Yun further pointed to the need to advance gradually to joint ownership. Apparently in this context Liu declared his support for the peaceful *shumai* method and criticized the leftist thought of those who equated peaceful transformation with "class conciliation"— an attitude officials could easily have picked up from the study of Soviet texts then under way. By the end of June the issue was settled. Mao had approved Li's *shumai* approach, Liu, Zhou, Zhu De, Chen Yun, Deng Xiaoping, and Li Fuchun had all agreed, and Li Weihan was instructed to revise his report for the conference.[45] After the conference, in September, Mao gave a ringing endorsement of peaceful transition in his address to democratic party leaders and national capitalists when he emphasized that transformation must be voluntary, warned against impatient rash advance (*jizao maojin*), and noted that private industry and commerce "in the main serve the nation's economy and the people's livelihood."[46]

In all this Gao Gang was the odd man out. When the others expressed their support of *shumai* he remained silent. While he said nothing, his silence was correctly perceived as disagreement. Mao, according to an authoritative oral source, felt Gao was a bit overly left on this issue but chose not to confront him. Instead Mao dispatched Li Weihan, who had worked with Gao in the mid-1930s,[47] to speak privately to Gao in an effort to persuade him of the policy's virtues. Gao, however, was in no mood to listen and, ironically revealing his theoretical ignorance, said to Li, "Have you ever read *On the Opposition*[48] by Stalin? . . . Didn't Bukharin also advocate a peaceful entry into socialism?"[49] Here, unlike the "New Democratic social order" issue, Gao could gain no encouragement from Mao's position. On the other hand, he had not been directly rebuked by the Chairman for his left leanings, and he continued to express those leanings forcefully at the conference. As an oral source noted with some awe, while prudently maintaining his silence in Mao's presence he continued to hold to his view on *shumai* after Mao's decision and even disrupted Li Weihan's discussion of the issue at the conference proper, where Mao presumably was not present—proof positive in my source's eyes that Gao was indeed fierce and daring in his ambition.[50]

The Criticism of Bo Yibo's New Tax System

In sharp contrast to the transformation issue, Gao Gang took a much more forthright position on another major question raised at the Financial and Economic Conference—Bo Yibo's new tax system. Here, moreover, in at least some respects Gao was able to secure considerable backing from Mao. Indeed, Gao seems to have been following Mao since it is likely that the Chairman raised the tax question in their private talks. In the course of the conference, however, Gao seemingly pushed the issue harder than Mao intended, and in any case by the end of the meetings the Chairman rejected the full implications of Gao's attack on Bo. Yet for much of the conference Mao and Gao took a similar stance on a question that engendered considerable tension among the assembled officials.

The new tax system was promulgated on December 31, 1952, by the FEC on behalf of Bo's Ministry of Finance. Ironically, this system was a response to the new conditions emerging as China moved down the road toward state planning and socialism. The concerns behind the changes, however, were fiscal and technical rather than ideological. The former regulations, adopted in 1950, suited the conditions of economic restoration when economic reforms had not yet been undertaken. This original system was complex and could not be adequately simplified. It was also out of step with changing ownership and economic patterns; with the growth of the public sector the source of state revenues shifted to that sector, and the economic functions performed by both state and private sectors also changed. In these circumstances the new tax system was designed to simplify tax collection procedures and guarantee state revenues which were being lost due to the out-of-date nature of the old regulations. Related to these concerns was the decline in business activity that resulted from the shock the private sector received during the Five-Anti Campaign in the first half of 1952—a decline that also meant reduced tax collections and the need to find supplementary revenues.[51]

In striving for these goals, the new system introduced two innovations that were later considered serious mistakes: the principle of "equality between public and private enterprises," and altering the tax payment link from a wholesale enterprise tax to a factory turnover tax. The new payment link resulted in effectively eliminating the business tax paid by private wholesale enterprises, while the drafters of the system itself recognized that equal treatment of public and private sectors would result in increased tax burdens on the state and cooperative sectors. The equal-treatment approach reflected a broader trend in policy that had been in evidence since the peaking of the Five-Antis in June 1952—namely, an effort to reassure businessmen after their recent ordeal through such measures as lowering interest rates, expanding credit, increasing orders, and readjusting processing fees. Another aim was to force better performance from the public sector. By putting state and cooperative enterprises on the same footing as private ones it was hoped that they would be stimulated to improve their business methods, introduce business accounting systems, lower production costs and trading charges, and accelerate capital turnover. In fact, however, the new system resulted not only in an enhanced competitive advantage for the private sector and increased taxes for the state and cooperative sectors, but also in decreasing state enterprise profits. This produced considerable conflict with local leaders since the great regions relied on state enterprises for their revenue. Thus, apart from any ideological considerations, this situation gave Gao Gang direct practical cause for discontent since the advanced Northeast suffered a particularly heavy decline in profits.[52]

A second, related issue emerged in early 1953 that also would soon place Bo Yibo in the firing line. This concerned the excessive stockpiling of goods in state commercial warehouses, which resulted in part from the overambitious plan for 1953 reflected in Bo's large budget deficit. In January 1953 a National Commercial Conference under Bo's leadership met to consider the problem and decided to deal with it by having the state warehouses disgorge their stocks. Together with the policy of "loosening one's bowels," the commercial departments also ceased to purchase the output of state light industry and refused to allow those enterprises to sell on the market. A number of problems resulted. First, the affected state factories found themselves overstocked with various goods; interestingly, the problem was apparently especially severe in the Northeast, thus giving Gao Gang another practical reason for unhappiness with Bo. Naturally, this problem caused a decline in production and business turnover. Moreover, since market demand had been underestimated, shortages appeared and the variety of goods on the market suffered, which further affected the flow of materials and supplies. Finally, another problem—one with ideological overtones—was that private commerce was able to buy up products disgorged from state warehouses and thus strengthen their influence over the market. Another "error" was to increase purchasing from private factories while cutting back on purchases from the state sector, which was obliged to continue producing in order to support its workers. All of this, together with the new tax system, was summed up as causing "the public to retreat and the private to advance." Mao reportedly was critical of these developments, and they came under attack at the Financial and Economic Conference, where, like the tax system, they were regarded as a "mistake in principle" and corrected.[53]

Apart from the practical problems resulting from the new tax system and the disgorging policy, the ideological issues involved were especially sensitive. A program placing the bourgeoisie and the state on equal footing at a time of transition carried potential political risks. As was pointed out at the conference, it was the duty of financial authorities not just to secure funds for the state but to regulate the income of different classes and develop the socialist economy.[54] Vulnerability was further created by the absence of any clear Central Committee policy on the issues involved. Despite Mao's subsequent claim that Bo had violated the resolution of the March 1949 Second Plenum,[55] that plenum had manifested a desire to see some development of private enterprise, albeit not unlimited development, an objective that had not been effectively changed since. Whatever injustice this may have involved, in these circumstances it is clear that at least the tax issue, and most likely the disgorging policy as well, came under critical scrutiny before the Financial and Economic Conference.

What is less clear is whether this resulted in formal criticism at this early stage, and exactly who was under attack. While Mao later claimed that mistakes in financial and economic work had been "seriously criticized" since Bo put forward his tax system in December 1952, there is little other evidence to suggest that criticism began immediately following the issuing of the tax regulations.[56] Mao's own attitude in the earlier mentioned March 1953 letter to non-Party figures Huang Yanpei and Chen Shutong was relaxed and solicitous; he merely noted that concrete methods to resolve the problems of businessmen should be studied by Bo's Ministry of Finance, the taxation office, and other offices.[57] Further evidence suggesting restraint on the Chairman's part is provided by a 1981 recollection by Bo Yibo of an "unforgettable impression" concerning a spring 1953 encounter with Mao. According to Bo, the Chairman summoned him for a talk and advised him to learn some dialectics. Mao reportedly noted "sternly and sincerely" that Bo liked to blame his mistakes on being busy, but that this was wrong. The fault rather lay in Bo's inability to penetrate to the essence of the matter.[58] While this advice was more than likely prompted by the tax issue, it—and Bo's willingness to recall it twenty-eight years later—does not suggest unrelenting criticism. Nevertheless, a well-placed oral source describes Mao as "furious" over the "equality of public and private" slogan, and apparently a consensus on the need to criticize Bo had been reached before the conference, but without full agreement on the nature of the criticism.[59]

Uncertainty over the seriousness of the preconference mood is mirrored in the lack of clarity concerning the targets of any criticism. In addition to Bo Yibo himself, it seems reasonably clear that Zhou Enlai and Liu Shaoqi were at least somewhat at risk although the circumstances varied in their cases, while the possible implication of Chen Yun is much less certain. Zhou's vulnerability came not simply from the fact that the GAC was the organ ultimately responsible, but also from direct involvement on his part. Zhou not only supported Bo but together with him was responsible for the December 31, 1952, *People's Daily* editorial that explained and promoted the new tax system.[60] According to a well-placed oral source, Mao criticized Zhou sharply before the conference began.

Liu, in contrast, was less directly involved in economic decision making but, like Zhou, offered his support. This perhaps was one of instances Mao had in mind in his May 1953 criticism of Liu's handling of documents. Oral sources report that the Politburo did not discuss the tax system, and Mao claimed at the conference that the revisions had been introduced without reference to the "Central Committee." This is perhaps true if the "Central Committee" equals Mao, who reportedly knew of the tax changes in a general sense but had not seen the regulations and the offensive "equality between public and private" slogan before publication. While oral sources believe it was unnecessary for Mao to review the regulations beforehand since the matter concerned concrete government work, Liu, in his capacity as the responsible person for routine Central Committee work, apparently did receive and approve the relevant documents. In this regard it is noteworthy that when raising the issuing of documents question, Mao directed that all relevant materials from August 1952 to May 1953 be checked, that is, for the period covering the tax issue.[61] Thus, Liu's culpability in Mao's eyes may have involved organizational procedures as well as policy issues. As will be seen, by virtue of Liu's close personal and political relationship to Bo, it bore on the issue of "factional" ties as well.

On the face of things, an obvious additional target for any recriminations would be Chen Yun. Not only was Chen the official in charge of overall economic policy, he also signed a notice on the tax regulations, assumed responsibility for these errors after the conference, and during the Cultural Revolution was accused of being the main culprit.[62] But putting aside the questionable assertions of Cultural Revolution sources, no direct evidence of Chen's *primary* responsibility exists. The most one well-placed oral source could say is that he thought the tax system "had some relationship to Chen Yun"; I have encountered no oral or written source explicitly citing Chen's active involvement, Mao's dissatisfaction with him over the issue, or any attack on Chen in this regard before, during, or after the conference.

Given Chen's key role in the economic sphere and his close working relations with Zhou and Bo, not to mention his signature on the notice, it is inconceivable that he bore no responsibility. Yet while the desire of post-Mao sources to minimize differences between the Chairman and other leaders in the early 1950s may explain the absence of information concerning Mao-Chen conflict,[63] it hardly explains the failure to acknowledge an attack by Gao Gang on Chen if one had occurred. The conclusion, while necessarily speculative, is that Chen's involvement was minimal. Perhaps Chen had simply ceded primary responsibility to Bo while he focused on other issues, or he may have deliberately stood aloof from an issue where other sections of the economic bureaucracy—notably the Ministry of Commerce and Ministry of Light Industry[64]—had expressed opposition or reservations, or perhaps he limited his activity in view of his health problems. Whatever the reason, Chen Yun seems to have escaped significant blame for Bo's alleged sins.

Whatever the precise situation before the conference, once it was under way an intense attack on Bo Yibo began. According to oral sources, one of the sharpest attacks came in a comprehensive and theoretically sophisticated speech by Gao

Gang that had been drafted on his instructions by his Northeast and SPC subordinate Ma Hong.[65] Gao took up the question of equal treatment of the state and private sectors and pictured it as a rightist tendency of surrendering to the bourgeoisie. This speech, as well as additional ones drafted by Gao's subordinates, was full of references to Marx, Lenin, and Stalin. Moreover, although apparently outside the conference rather than in the formal sessions, Gao used Stalin's attack on Bukharin's peaceful transition, which he referred to in his private conversation with Li Weihan concerning the transformation of the bourgeoisie, to criticize Bo.[66] Finally, in one of his talks at the conference, Gao declared that Bo's mistake was an error in line.

Gao's attacks on Bo were supported by the fierce criticism of Rao Shushi who, in Mao's view at least, was "working hand in glove" with Gao at the conference, and of officials assertedly organized by Gao or Rao.[67] Among the less theoretical attacks coming from these officials and others were charges that Bo was a domineering finance lord, knew only about finance and had no politics, had turned the Ministry of Finance into an independent kingdom, and had surrendered to the rich peasants as well as the bourgeoisie. In addition, people like Li Fuchun and various local leaders who were not involved in Gao's activities also criticized Bo harshly but with a difference. Whereas Gao emphasized mistakes in line implying that Bo should be dismissed, Li and others did not adopt this formulation. Many objected to Gao's position and a big argument ensued. As the pressure against Bo increased, one of Bo's old comrades who had survived prison with him in the 1930s, An Ziwen, used the tactic of silence rather than join in the criticism.[68]

But, both oral and documentary sources assert, Bo was only Gao's ostensible target—under the guise of criticizing Bo he was inciting dissatisfaction with Liu Shaoqi. Here it is significant to note that, at least in the minds of Gao and Rao, the important connection was "factional" rather than functional. It was Liu, much more than the functionally responsible and more directly involved Zhou, who was the main target, while Bo's immediate superior, Chen Yun, seemingly escaped criticism. Although Liu was culpable for having approved the tax system, it apparently was Bo's historical links to Liu Shaoqi in "white area" work that were crucial.[69]

While Rao and others joined Gao's attack, and those like Li Fuchun took a different but still severe tack, the most important reaction to Gao's speeches was that of Mao himself. Initially, an authoritative oral source reports, Mao was impressed with Gao's arguments and particularly their theoretical erudition, although it would seem the Chairman was unaware of Gao's conclusion that Bo had committed line mistakes.[70] After his downfall Gao would be attacked as someone with little understanding of Marxism-Leninism who fooled others by plagiarizing the work of his subordinates,[71] but in summer 1953 the arguments put together by those subordinates stood Gao in good stead with the Chairman. Having always considered Gao crude intellectually if successful as a Party leader, Mao seemingly saw signs of substantial progress on Gao's part in the realm of theory. It was not clear just when or how Mao's favorable attitude was conveyed to the conference, as he seemed normally not to have been in attendance,[72] but his views apparently became known to the participants and contributed to the growing tension. In the heat of midsummer Beijing, with Bo fanning himself with a large tropical leaf, the finance minister came under great pressure and made two self-criticisms acknowledging that he had not taken the overall situation into account.

The identity of those joining in the criticism of Bo is unknown with a few exceptions.[73] Moreover, their precise motives, which undoubtedly varied from individual to individual, must remain a matter of speculation. Were those adding their voices to the anti-Bo chorus seeking to oust him from office? Who apart from the "conspirators" themselves realized that the attack on Bo was aimed at Liu and Zhou? While Deng Xiaoping claimed in 1955 that Gao never openly or formally expressed opinions against Liu or Zhou, Chen Shihui's *neibu* account states that the link to Liu was obvious to the more alert since in their criticism of Bo they "cleverly used comments from Comrade Liu Shaoqi's previous speeches."[74] An authoritative oral source, however, tends to believe that apart from those organized by Gao and Rao, many cadres did not fully realize what was going on and joined in out of the belief that Bo was guilty of errors, and in any case criticism and self-criticism over such matters as tax policy was seen as a normal part of Party life.[75] Yet surely crucial was the fact that an apparent signal from Mao made Bo an inviting, even obligatory target. As a result, the tension became intense, with not only Bo but Zhou Enlai described by oral sources as very nervous. Zhou, as was his practice, accepted some responsibility for the tax system and admitted rightist errors.

As with other issues during the summer of 1953—i.e., policy toward private commerce and bureaucratic control of the transformation of the bourgeoisie—Chen Yun now played a key role in resolving the tax question. A speech by Chen late in the conference was the turning point. On August 6 Chen attempted to redress the balance at the conference by stating that although financial and economic work had suffered from a bit of a rightist tendency, it was necessary to emphasize that what was not wanted was the view that "the left is better than the right."[76] It was apparently in a section of that speech not recorded in Chen's *Selected Works* that he addressed squarely Bo Yibo's errors. According to an authoritative oral source, Chen argued that Bo's tax policy was a secondary matter: "I controlled the main road of financial and economic work but did not give enough attention to the smaller lanes. Bo Yibo's problem is a small lane problem, it is not a line." Thus Chen both assumed overall responsibility for work in this sphere[77] and lessened the significance of the tax policy issue. At this stage, however, perhaps with a view to Mao's sensibilities, he formally concluded that the tax system was a mistake of principle that violated the line of the Second Plenum.[78] But the thrust of his argument was to downplay the importance of the errors made, and the immediate effect of Chen's intervention was to lower the temperature at the conference.

On this evidence alone Chen's intervention is surprising since nothing in his career before or since indicates a willingness to stand up to Mao. Chen had been close to Mao since Yan'an, and throughout his career he followed a guiding principle of not offending the Chairman, of not speaking out in opposition once Mao had nailed his colors to the mast.[79] In the case at hand, this suggests that Chen had reason to suspect—or know—that Mao was not committed to an all-out attack on Bo Yibo. In the event, once the reportedly relaxed Chen had stated his main road/small lanes analysis, both Mao and Zhou expressed agreement. Just as Mao's initial favorable attitude toward Gao had apparently resulted in the buildup of pressure against Bo, the Chairman now contributed to its easing both by this support of Chen and through active lobbying of conference participants. With Mao having modified his position, Zhou's nervousness apparently abated, and he too joined in the process of reducing tension.[80]

The circumstances of Mao learning of the full extent of Gao's attack on Bo and reacting negatively to it are obscure. Moreover, not only is the degree to which he rebuked Gao's views—although not Gao personally—unclear, but there is a tension between the analyses of post-Mao sources and a crucial document from the Financial and Economic Conference, Zhou Enlai's summary report. Nevertheless, it seems clear that toward the end of the conference Mao became more aware of Gao's onslaught. This, as some oral sources suggest, may have been the result of briefings Mao received on the progress of the conference; one such source claimed that when Liu Shaoqi reported on developments the Chairman was upset and disapproving. Alternatively, Mao may have understood Gao's anti-Bo activities through his reported attendance at one of Gao's talks late in the conference.[81] In either case the Chairman felt the matter had to be dealt with, and Zhou reportedly proposed that Mao speak to the conference. The Chairman agreed but said that Zhou should address the meeting as well. As a result, on the penultimate day of the conference, August 11, Zhou gave his summary report, which had been corrected and approved by Mao.[82] Finally, on August 12, Mao gave his closing speech.

In his summing up speech Zhou explicitly absolved Bo Yibo of line mistakes and agreed with Li Fuchun's opinion that financial and economic work had basically been in accord with the decisions of the 1949 Second Plenum. Nevertheless, the full text of Zhou's speech has a much sterner tone than either oral sources or Chen Shihui's *neibu* analysis suggest. While Zhou acknowledged some responsibility for himself and Chen Yun, a whole range of serious errors was slated home to Bo as the principal responsible comrade. Although assertedly unsystematic, these errors were characterized as "right opportunist mistakes in principle," said to reflect "bourgeois thought in the Party," and at least some of them violated the Second Plenum's line. Furthermore, while Zhou acknowledged Bo's past bravery in revolutionary struggle, his achievements in work, and his correct carrying out of the Party line "at various times," he nevertheless claimed that despite some progress Bo's two self-examinations still had not uncovered the root of his problem. Tellingly, Zhou expressed agreement with Gao Gang not only on the economic issue of the need to concentrate on heavy industry but also on Gao's characterization of Bo as dishonest, as someone who put himself before the Party. Finally, while clearly indicating a way out for Bo, Zhou suggested that it was only Mao's criticisms and those of local Party committees (i.e., Party organs such as Gao's Northeast Bureau) that saved Bo from completely departing from the general line.[83]

Even more than Zhou's report, Mao's August 12 concluding speech to the Financial and Economic Conference was a profoundly contradictory statement that both damned Bo Yibo ideologically and absolved him politically. This contradiction may be partially explained by conflicting sources; volume 5 of Mao's *Selected Works* provides an extended harsh critique of Bo while Chen Shihui's internal document focuses on the Chairman's absolution of Bo. As indicated in the section on sources and methodology,[84] oral sources report that volume 5 distorts Mao's talk by presenting only his negative comments. Nevertheless, these same sources attest that Mao's comments recorded in the *Selected Works* are genuine.

Politically, the crucial aspect of Mao's talk was that he followed the analysis of Chen Yun and Zhou Enlai that Bo had not violated the general line. Somewhat illogically given his other comments, Mao observed with direct relevance to Bo's tax policies that "two points join a line, but the problem of the 'new taxation system' is only one point and one point doesn't make a line. The mistakes in previous financial and economic work were serious, but they were not mistakes in line."[85] Thus Mao had taken a tack that was more like that of Li Fuchun than Gao Gang—harsh criticism short of branding Bo guilty of a wrong line. This, together with the Chairman's statements and lobbying concerning unity (see below), settled the matter. In the view of both oral sources and Chen Shihui, Gao Gang was again rebuffed.[86]

Nevertheless, the waters were muddied by the very strength of Mao's biting critique of Bo. Bo's type of error, according to Mao, was not an ordinary mistake but one of principle, a tendency toward capitalism. To those inclined to attribute his shortcomings to "petty bourgeois individualism," Mao rejoined that "he ought to be criticized [mainly for] his bourgeois thought, which is beneficial to capitalism and harmful to socialism."[87] Bo was also a person who both "politically and ideologically [is] somewhat corrupted."[88] Concerning Bo's tax system, Mao argued, "if [it] develops further it will inevitably become *divorced* from Marxism-Leninism and from *the Party's general line for the period of transition* and will develop toward capitalism."[89] Moreover, in this context Mao raised the organizational issue that apparently touched Liu Shaoqi: in framing the tax system, Bo allegedly "sought the opinion of the bourgeoisie . . . and made a gentlemen's agreement with the bourgeoisie, but he did not report to the Central Committee."[90] Apart from thoroughly discrediting Bo's tax policy, Mao added allegations that Bo had belittled socialist agriculture in an article critical of "agrarian socialist thought"—allegations that were not only patently unfair but also again pointed to Liu Shaoqi.[91] In sum, this criticism amounted to a damning ideological indictment of Bo Yibo that also indirectly implicated Bo's chief political supporter despite Mao's final judgment on the question of line.

The texts of both Zhou's complete speech and the truncated version of Mao's talk suggest a more serious attitude toward Bo Yibo than post-Mao accounts of their efforts to emphasize unity, which assertedly rebuked Gao Gang. Clearly, Mao's other concern, ideological correctness, still weighed heavily in the verdict on Bo. Significantly, Zhou found it necessary to affirm his agreement with Gao on several points, including at least some of Gao's strictures against Bo. In their emphasis on the unity theme, what oral sources seem to be saying is that at the end of the day Mao gave Bo a reprieve from political oblivion. Various such sources extended this theme to Liu and Zhou. One very well-placed former official held that Zhou was "saved" when Mao began to turn his attention to unity, while several scholars expressed the view that if Mao had not intervened, Liu's position would have been precarious. But none of this amounts to the major rebuff to Gao suggested by Chen Shihui and other documentary materials.

In any case, the seriousness of Bo's ideological "errors" could not but have immediate political ramifications. For one thing, Mao indicated his continuing discontent by mentioning Bo's mistakes on several occasions in fall 1953.[92] Again, different sources suggest different shades of seriousness on Mao's part; thus a *Wansui* collection renders a November 1953 comment as merely saying Bo's mistakes "concerned the general line problem" while the *Selected Works* version notes a more weighty "error in deviating from the general line."[93] In any case, by the end of the conference, although relieved by the intervention of Chen, Zhou, and Mao, Bo Yibo still suffered from the strain and relinquished his key post, to be replaced in September as minister of finance by Deng Xiaoping. While this may have been, as an authoritative oral source claims, a voluntary sick leave on Bo's part,[94] it clearly reflected the political reality that Bo was down though not out. However, it was not long before Bo was put in charge of industry, communications, and transportation on the proposal of Mao, Zhou, and Deng,[95] and when the State Council was established a year later, he assumed the major post of chairman of the State Construction Commission. The rectification principle of using those who admitted their mistakes was apparently still in force in this case.

The picture was also mixed on the policy front. While Mao's insistence that the tax system was a mistake in principle was readily accepted, how this was to be translated into policy was not straightforward. It was one thing to reject the "equality between public and private" slogan; it was quite another to design a policy that both took into account this ideological rejection and dealt effectively with the practical problems the new tax system had been designed to overcome in the first place. Again, it was left to Chen Yun to address the conundrum. In a September 14 speech to the Central People's Government Council a month after the conclusion of the conference, Chen argued that with [private] business activity declining and tax collections down, it was necessary for Bo and others to think of ways to supplement revenue. Under these conditions it was reasonable to propose changing the tax system, but the method should have been better considered. While criticizing equal treatment as a wrong formulation and a mistake of principle, Chen's analysis of its shortcomings emphasized the economic functions performed by the state sector in supporting the state treasury, maintaining production, promoting balanced regional growth, and stabilizing the market rather than large ideological themes. Finally, he stated that suddenly reversing the changes introduced by the new tax system would produce chaos, any change would have to be carefully studied, and it was necessary to proceed with caution.[96]

Chen's counsel seemingly carried the day, although much remains uncertain about precisely what was done. While one set of taxes on wholesalers who had been exempted under Bo's system had already been restored on August 1,[97] it does not appear that a systematic revamping of the system was undertaken. A reform period source speaks of a "comparatively big adjustment" in tax work, but it subsequently describes the tax policy toward the bourgeoisie during socialist transformation with the ambivalent formula, "[although] differently to some extent, treat equally without discrimination" (*yousuo butong, yi shi tong ren*).[98] Compendia of tax regulations from both the late 1950s and 1980s include Bo Yibo's system, but no further changes or additions before 1955.[99] And a 1978 source claiming, exaggeratedly, a turnaround in policy toward the bourgeoisie following the Financial and Economic Conference largely listed nontax measures such as curbs on speculation and stepped up planned placing of orders with private enterprises by the state.[100] On balance, in the tax sphere adjustments appear minimal given Chen's concern about disrupting the economy.[101] Mao's ideological concerns were listened to, but in a manner combining statements of principle with pragmatic adjustments, and this approach seemingly satisfied the Chairman.

Factional Activities Inside and Outside the Conference

Despite post-Mao reassertions of the 1955 verdict that Gao and Rao were basically involved in clandestine activities without programmatic content, the foregoing discussion clearly indicates that Gao was openly expressing a distinct policy orientation. Through criticism of Bo Yibo's tax policy, Gao and others advocated a tougher posture toward the national bourgeoisie. Nevertheless, references to activities "inside and outside the conference"[102] point to factional maneuvers beyond the statement of a policy preference both at the open conference sessions and privately behind the scenes. These maneuvers centered on a concerted effort to create dissatisfaction with the performances of Liu Shaoqi and Zhou Enlai.

From all accounts, Liu was by far the main target,[103] although Zhou was also under strong attack particularly on the tax issue. According to an authoritative oral source, Gao did not regard the unambitious Zhou as a major threat; but undoubtedly responding to Mao's dissatisfaction with Zhou's "rightist" tendencies and the fact that he was an older official above Gao in the hierarchy, he too was targeted. This, of course, reflects the official interpretation of an unprincipled bid for power.

But before proceeding, it is appropriate to weigh further the policy versus power aspects of the Gao-Rao affair. Might it not be argued that, at least in this early stage, Gao Gang was largely motivated by the policy/ideological concerns he voiced at the conference?[104] Indeed, as I shall emphasize, many of Gao's actions, particularly at the open conference sessions, mirrored those of Mao and in that sense were both politically sound and "legitimate" according to the norms of inner-Party life. Outside the conference, however, he clearly went beyond policy considerations and agitated for a leadership shake-up. And in a system so sensitive to status, the very fact of criticizing two leading members of the Secretariat, a level of the hierarchy above Gao, leaders who moreover were singled out for the highest accolade of "Chairman Mao's close comrades-in-arms," was profoundly threatening to the established way of doing things. While Mao, from a still higher status, might criticize Liu and Zhou—and always up to this point by indirection rather than by the direct attack he endorsed on the lower-ranking Bo Yibo—for Gao to do the same thing from his lesser position points squarely to the power motive.

The general nature of the attack on Liu and Zhou is described as spreading rumors, sowing discord, and using certain gaps in their work to incite dissatisfaction with them.[105] As Mao complained later, Gao and Rao caused instability by exaggerating small defects into a larger pattern.[106] This tactic of "attacking a single fault without considering the other good aspects" and presenting isolated and ordinary mistakes as opposition to the Party line had been clearly in evidence concerning Bo Yibo; it was vigorously extended to Zhou and especially Liu during Gao's behind-the-scenes activities when he argued that Bo's mistakes in line should be traced to the two senior leaders. At the open conference meetings, while Gao assertedly made unprincipled speeches and created a tense atmosphere, the attack was conducted by indirection. As indicated above, in criticizing Bo, Gao used various quotations from Liu's previous speeches, which made it immediately apparent that Liu was also being criticized.[107] Presumably, however, what remained unclear to many of the assembled officials was just how much of this was normal criticism—even if unusual given the levels of those involved—and how much was something more.

In this process Gao used "isolated inappropriate expressions" from various past statements by Liu to portray "questions that had already been corrected or self-examined" as serious current problems. Thus quotations from Liu's Tianjin talks and his "Opinion on the Problem of Handling Rich Peasant Party Members" were presented in a manner to suggest surrendering to the bourgeoisie and rich peasants.[108] The latter rich-peasant Party member issue, like the Tianjin talks question, was another clear case of dwelling on something that had been superseded by present policy.¹⁰⁹ What is striking, however, is the degree to which Gao's approach in this regard followed Mao's. With the Tianjin talks in particular, it is clear that Mao ripped "isolated inappropriate expressions" out of historical context and applied them to the contemporary situation. Moreover, as in the cases of criticizing Bo for not reporting to the "Central Committee" and for his article that attacked "agrarian socialist thought,"¹¹⁰ the Chairman's allusions to Liu were unmistakable. But again, what was acceptable from Mao would not necessarily be acceptable from Gao Gang, especially when taken in conjunction with his activities outside the conference.

Whatever the possibility that Gao's actions at the plenary meetings of the conference stayed within the bounds set by Mao himself, there is little doubt that he overstepped the mark outside the conference unless we assume that the Chairman was closely guiding his activities. Privately, Gao and Rao assertedly raised both a number of issues relating to the open sessions and additional themes that they were to develop for the remainder of 1953. Apart from tracing Bo Yibo's "line errors" to Liu and Zhou, whom they cited by name, this included likening Bo's mistakes to those of Bukharin, and further elaborating on Liu Shaoqi's past indiscretions. In the latter endeavor, in a manner that would be repeated a thousandfold during the Cultural Revolution, Gao Gang's "clique" prepared a documentary file collecting seven of Liu's earlier speeches and memoranda as ammunition to be used against him. These seven "fatal materials," which were reportedly distributed to some conference participants, included not only those bearing on such well-known sources of Mao's discontent as the 1947–48 leftist deviation during land reform, the 1949 Tianjin talks, and the 1951 comment on Shanxi cooperatives, but also Liu's January 1946 report calling for peaceful struggle and coalition rule with the Guomindang. Mao had made no known criticism of this last document, although his own position at the time had a somewhat different emphasis from Liu's,¹¹¹ but this did not prevent an effort to play on the differences that had existed. In this manner Gao attempted to provide documentary "proof" of Liu's consistent departure from the true path.¹¹²

In addition to these efforts to discredit Liu, Gao and Rao stirred the pot with a number of themes that would be aired more extensively as the year wore on—themes that will receive more thorough analysis in subsequent chapters. These all revolved around the factional issue. It was apparently at this time that the question of An Ziwen's list for a future Politburo, which assertedly shortchanged leading military figures, was initially raised.¹¹³ Linked to An's list was Gao's theory of the two parties of the army and base areas (the "red areas") and of the "white areas"; this theory was presented with the argument that a thorough reorganization was needed since "white area" cadres had grasped an undue portion of Party power. Significantly, in contrast to the 1955 claim that Gao had asserted *he* was the representative of the army and revolutionary bases, recent sources indicate that the argument was that Mao was the representative of the "red areas" and Liu of the "white areas."[114] It was also in this context that Gao apparently made his earliest approach to the great absent general, Lin Biao, by flattering him as, strangely, Mao's true successor, and also by visiting him outside the conference.[115]

Gao laid the charge of factionalism at the doors of Liu and Zhou. Liu was charged with forming his own clique, evidence for which was supposedly An's list, while Zhou was also said to have his own faction; it was these accusations that allegedly drew Mao's rejoinder that the revolution consisted of many mountaintops.[116] But perhaps the most potent "rumor" spread by Gao related directly to Mao. According to an authoritative oral source, it was apparently at this time that Gao claimed Mao's backing and "reorganized and spread Mao's words" critical of Liu and Zhou, which the Chairman had expressed in their private conversations.[117] Those who might have been susceptible to Gao's other appeals now had a strong additional cause to at least consider opposition to Liu and Zhou, while even those out of sympathy with Gao had reason to temporize given the claims being made about Mao's views.

All of these activities "outside the conference" took place through intense private lobbying, including dinner parties and dancing parties organized by Gao as he sought to establish alliances and incite dissatisfaction with Liu and Zhou. Among those participating in these activities were not only former Northeast officials like Ma Hong but also Rao Shushi's East China subordinate, Xiang Ming, thus raising some doubts as to how coincidental the parallel activities of Gao and Rao were. In one of the many ironies that abound in this case, many of these parties were held in Gao Gang's residence at the former French Embassy, which happened to be located near the home of Liu Shaoqi's closest Politburo supporter and Gao's old sparring partner in the Northeast during the civil war, Peng Zhen, and next door to the home of one of Peng's closest subordinates, Liu Ren. People from Peng's circle could see the parties from Liu Ren's residence, and Peng would report on Gao's parties in 1954 once Mao had determined Gao's fate.[118]

As with the specific criticism of Bo Yibo, it is difficult to know exactly who was involved in attacks on Liu and Zhou during the Financial and Economic Conference or how much various participants knew of Gao's aims. Undoubtedly there were those who had thrown in their lot with Gao Gang, and others who knew something was up because of approaches they received from the Gao camp, those who suspected a larger design given what was said at the conference, and others who blissfully assumed that what was going on was just part of normal inner-Party criticism. At the 1955 Party conference that put the seal on the case, in speaking of those involved in the affair Mao distinguished between those who "have been influenced generally and have merely been brushed by [Gao's and Rao's] wings" and those "few comrades [who] have been more deeply influenced, . . . talked with [Gao and Rao] about many questions, and carried on clandestine activities, doing propaganda work for them."[119] Mao further noted that some people "knew some bad things in general about [Gao and Rao] but did not recognize [the existence of] the conspiracy" and conceded that "This is understandable because [it] was difficult to see."[120] Of course, some of these officials undoubtedly did discern something but chose to lie low in an uncertain political situation.[121] Finally, Mao warned those who were not involved against being conceited and argued that Gao and Rao did not approach them because they were regarded as enemies, looked down upon as being of no consequence, considered not the sort of people wanted for the conspiracy, or simply that there had been insufficient time to attend to them.[122] Thus, while it is impossible to draw precise distinctions, it seems clear that in the lobbying behind the scenes at the conference and afterward there were many levels of involvement and understanding.[123] As to the individuals actually involved in attacking Liu or Zhou apart from various close subordinates of Gao and Rao, only South China Subbureau head Tao Zhu, who by his wife's later account "opened fire" on Liu and was used by Gao during the conference, can be identified with any confidence.[124]

If it is unclear precisely how much various participants at the conference knew or understood about the actions of Gao and Rao, it is also uncertain what the targets—Liu and Zhou—and above all Mao himself were aware of. According to Mao's 1955 version, "one could see that they were [behaving] abnormal[ly]. At the time of the [conference] their abnormal activities were discovered, and each time they were rebuffed,"[125] but this awareness assertedly still fell short of full knowledge of the aims of Gao and Rao. As for Zhou, oral sources state that he had no knowledge of Gao's ultimate objectives,[126] while Liu reportedly was unaware of rumors spread by Gao. In the view of several such sources, the most the Secretariat sensed at this point was that Gao wanted to oust Bo Yibo—an analysis consistent with the efforts of Chen Yun, Zhou, and Mao to absolve Bo of line mistakes.[127]

In the event, the action taken was less than decisive, but it still altered the political climate. Apart from the reprieve for Bo, this involved an effort to emphasize Party unity. Post-1978 sources claim the "Party Center" criticized the mistaken methods of Gao and Rao and corrected the erroneous ideas spread by them. Both Mao and Zhou clearly opposed the exaggeration of work mistakes. Having rejected in his summing-up speech the notion that mistakes in financial and economic work systematically opposed the Party line, Zhou reportedly stressed the significance of unity during the final days of the conference. Most important, Mao placed great weight on discipline and unity in his closing speech: "If there are any opinions, please raise them openly. To damage Party unity is the most shameful thing." He also reportedly sought out people from all aspects of the Party for talks, and "all [he] talked about was the need for unity, destroying cliques, and leveling mountaintops."[128] As previously indicated, post-Mao sources uniformly treat this as a clear rebuff to Gao, but there are reasons for doubt. Gao himself had attacked cliques and factions, so it is by no means impossible that Mao's remarks on unity could be taken as at least partially backing Gao.[129] Moreover, as has been seen, Gao received Zhou's praise at the end of the conference while, according to oral sources, Gao's offering to the self-criticism ritual merely dealt with an overemphasis on conditions in the Northeast, which resulted in proposals not suitable for the nation as a whole. Most significantly, for all his heightened awareness of the unity issue, Mao apparently never confronted Gao Gang; according to an authoritative oral source, he remained very polite (*keqi*) to Gao and still took him seriously. Mao's only approach during the conference had been the indirect one of sending Li Weihan to argue the virtues of the peaceful transformation of the bourgeoisie. The larger issue of behavior damaging Party unity was never directly taken up with Gao Gang.

There is, of course, no way of being confident about the meaning of this situation. Was Mao, as he claimed, only dimly aware of Gao's actions and motives? Had he been told in any detail of what had transpired outside the conference? Was he inhibited by embarrassment over his own role in stimulating Gao's actions? Did he limit his intervention because he saw error on all sides and in any case wished to mediate among Liu, Zhou, Gao, and Rao rather than come down decisively against any individual? Had an effort to stir the pot to a limited degree proven more difficult to manage than anticipated? Or did Mao continue to harbor some still unfulfilled plan to use Gao to topple Liu Shaoqi that had somehow gone awry? Whatever the case, general appeals for unity by Mao and Zhou were insufficient as Gao Gang assertedly turned a deaf ear to their warnings.[130]

Conclusion

While ultimate meanings necessarily remain elusive, it is nevertheless possible to offer a reasonable interpretation of the outcome of the Financial and Economic Conference—an outcome involving policy, ideology, and Party unity. If one sets aside possible Machiavellian motives on Mao's part, it appears that the Chairman put great weight on all three considerations but in ways that were somewhat contradictory. Throughout the conference Mao exhibited great concern for ideological correctness, in general terms of focusing all work on socialist transformation, in criticism of suspect policies such as the "equal treatment of public and private" tax system, and through a somewhat unreasonable ahistorical preoccupation with past "errors" in theory and expression, such as Liu Shaoqi's Tianjin talks and his criticism of "agrarian socialist thought." Mao's concern with theoretical deviance was most dramatically expressed in his blistering critique of Bo Yibo's alleged surrender to bourgeois ideology. Yet Mao claimed his criticism of Bo was designed to help those with errors[131] and seemingly believed that there was no incompatibility of his onslaught with Party unity. When signs appeared that ideological struggle was getting out of hand, he shifted the emphasis toward unity but still maintained his basic theoretical position. The Chairman's political message was that Bo (as well as Zhou) was wrong and the issue important, but let's not overdo it and damage Party unity. How effective this message was vis-à-vis Gao Gang without more direct intervention on Mao's part is another matter.

There was also a tension between Mao's ideological concerns and concrete policy. In broad terms he was interested in hastening the transition to socialism and realizing the final victory of the proletariat over the bourgeoisie. In practical terms, however, he was not only committed to gradualism but willing to endorse such measures as concessions to the commercial bourgeoisie, which on the face of it sat uncomfortably with his theoretical orientation. Sometimes Mao would seem to settle for a statement of principle, as in the condemnation of Bo Yibo's tax system, while allowing pragmatic considerations to limit substantially actual policy adjustments. This, in turn, reflected a willingness to listen to the advice of specialist colleagues, a willingness seen in several instances of the Chairman following the lead of Chen Yun in the economic sphere.

In overall policy terms, although a new impetus had been given to socialist transformation, nothing like the harsh stance implicit in many of Gao Gang's statements emerged. Li Weihan's peaceful transition had been approved, while Bo Yibo's tax system remained largely in place. Moreover, the overall conclusions reached by the conference were consistent with the perspective of "opposing rash advance," which had been necessitated by the overambitious 1953 yearly plan, although in this respect there was no apparent conflict with Gao's SPC. These conclusions called for emphasizing planning and preventing blindness in financial and economic work, focusing on keypoint projects and step-by-step advance while reducing impetuosity in construction, and generally enhancing unified leadership over the economy.[132] In his concluding speech, Mao criticized both "impetuous rash advance [and] conservatism [as] subjectivism."[133] Similarly, within a month of the conference Zhou Enlai warned in early September against "blind rash advance sentiments" while also criticizing the conservative tendency of not making full use of advantages.[134] And for the remainder of the year, *People's Daily* editorials called for meticulous investigation, planning, and coordination in construction work while stressing the need to overcome impetuosity.[135] By the end of the conference and for the subsequent period, Mao accepted the preferences of the Party's economic specialists and endorsed a cautious, pragmatic economic policy notwithstanding his ambitious ideological goals.

While policy had been set on a moderate course and Party unity was reemphasized by the end of the conference, the overall political result was still ambiguous. Various leaders, including not only Liu Shaoqi and Zhou Enlai but also the influential Chen Yun and the rising Deng Xiaoping, were required or felt it prudent to admit mistakes. Zhou, at least, was reportedly much relieved by the conclusion of the conference, but his confidence arguably had been damaged by the sharp attacks on the tax policy. While Mao had opted for reaffirming Party unity, his biting rebuke to Bo Yibo on the last day of the meetings must have left considerable uncertainty in the minds of those supporting moderation. As subsequent events would suggest, even those like Chen and Deng who had great skill in reading Mao's moods and were apparently not directly in the firing line had reason to pause. For Gao Gang and Rao Shushi, in terms of both policy decisions and Mao's intervention to save Bo Yibo, the outcome should have been a warning against reckless action. But the ambiguities provided by Mao's overall ideological posture, his apparent continuing anger over Bo's errors, his various indirect criticisms of Liu, and his failure to take Gao directly to task for the disruptive activities at the conference all provided hope. While more prudent actors undoubtedly would have hesitated, in the months following the Financial and Economic Conference Gao and Rao plunged ahead.

3
FACTIONAL MANEUVERS AND POLICY CHANGE
The Organization and Agricultural Cooperativization Conferences, September–November 1953

AFTER the closing of the Financial and Economic Conference in mid-August, whether or not they actually coordinated their activities, Gao Gang and Rao Shushi sought their objectives in several interrelated ways. One crucial aspect, to be examined in the following chapter, was Gao Gang's personal lobbying of high-ranking leaders, including Lin Biao, Peng Dehuai, Deng Xiaoping, and Chen Yun, in an effort to win them over to his cause. Another aspect, to be analyzed in the present chapter, was to use another of the various conferences then being held for the purpose of unifying policy according to the general line[1] to carry on the attack on Liu Shaoqi—in this case the National Organization Work Conference in September–October. Here another of Liu's loyal comrades, An Ziwen, replaced Bo Yibo as the surrogate for Liu. It has been asserted that this conference was the second main forum for factional activity in 1953, one that added to the awareness of the "Central Committee" that Gao and Rao were engaged in abnormal behavior.[2] This chapter will also examine another conference apparently not entangled in the activities of Gao and Rao, the October–early November National Conference on Agricultural Mutual Aid and Cooperativization, which is nevertheless an important part of the overall course of CCP politics at this time. This conference, convened by Deng Zihui's rural work department, involved a shift in policy direction on Mao's part in line with his general emphasis on socialist transformation and produced a somewhat different interaction of ideology and policy than had occurred at the Financial and Economic Conference.

The Struggle in the Organization Department
Before the National Organization Conference

The attack on An Ziwen, which became the key issue of the September–October conference, had its origins in events earlier in 1953. As indicated in chapter 1, tensions emerged between Rao and An as Rao assumed his position as head of the Central Committee's organization department in February 1953 and worried that he was unable to exercise real control over his new assignment. This fear was apparently based on two considerations, both of which centered on An's close ties to Liu Shaoqi.

The first consideration was a specific conflict, a late 1952 or early 1953 clash between subordinates of An sent to Shandong in Rao's East China region to carry out investigations of the "New Three-Anti" Party rectification, on the one hand, and the local Shandong establishment, on the other. While hardly reflected in the sketchy contemporary record,[3] problems arose when An's men, led by Wang Fu, head of the Party members administration section, and Zhao Han, head of the general office,[4] were given responsibility for observing the new campaign and rectification in the Shandong countryside, and for assisting the Shandong discipline inspection committee in collecting materials on the newly defined evils of bureaucratism, commandism, and violation of law and discipline. The materials collected were reportedly sent to Mao by An in January 1953, and the Chairman then personally issued a directive on the movement. In Shandong, however, the investigation team met with resistance from the local Party apparatus, which could easily dominate the provincial discipline inspection committee under the administrative arrangements then in force.[5]

The leading Shandong Party secretary, Xiang Ming, who later participated in the activities of Gao and Rao at both the Financial and Economic and Organization conferences and was subsequently denounced as a member of the "alliance" in 1955, assertedly restricted the activities of the provincial disciplinary body and "drove out of Shandong" the central investigation group. After their return to Beijing, An reported the matter to Liu Shaoqi and Zhou Enlai but apparently not to the leader of East China, Rao Shushi. When criticism of An began within the organization department in mid-July, Rao raised this matter, sharply rebuking An for reporting directly to Liu and Zhou and claiming that he was supporting "the branches against the areas," that is, an overly vertical form of administration that curbed regional authority. The administrative issue notwithstanding, what really seems to have upset Rao was that the incident demonstrated An's links to Liu.[6]

But more fundamental than this incident was the established pattern of running the organization department, which placed overall control firmly in the hands of Liu Shaoqi. An had been in charge of the daily work of the department for much of the period since 1945, but the department had always been accountable to a member of the Secretariat. This had either been Ren Bishi or Liu Shaoqi, with Liu exercising clear dominance in the organizational sphere following Ren's death in October 1950. Usually another top leader was designated department head and stood between the Secretariat member responsible and An; at various times in the 1940s it was Peng Zhen and, apparently from the time of Ren's death, Chen Yun. While Chen had played a key role in organization work as department head from 1939 to 1945, in the early years of the PRC his role was nominal as he devoted his energies to economic issues. Chen's position in this period was most likely related to the always important questions of status; as the leader who replaced Ren Bishi on the Secretariat, he seems to have inherited his formal responsibilities. But given the weight of Chen's economic duties and his questionable health, the authoritative role in organization work shifted to Liu, who had exercised it during Ren's illness. Subsequently, it was Liu who played the key role at the First National Organization Work Conference in 1951, and who would again play that role at the second conference in 1953 after Rao's appointment as department head.[7]

Thus Rao Shushi found himself in a situation where he had to contend with a close working relationship between Liu, on the Secretariat above him, and An, with a long-term career and extensive connections in the department below. The fact that this working tie was reinforced by "factional" links of the strongest kind, sealed by Liu's role in securing the release of An and others from Guomindang custody in the 1930s, could only have added to Rao's being ill at ease. Moreover, An's responsibilities led to well-developed work links with other key figures. He served under Zhou Enlai in 1951–52 in the general Party committee for Party, government, and army organs directly under the Center, and in this period his main job was to assist Zhou during the Three-Anti Campaign. In this task An also served under his old comrade from Guomindang confinement, Bo Yibo, both in the Three-Antis general office and on the Central Austerity Inspection Committee, which played an important guiding role for the Three- and Five-Anti drive. While Rao may have been unusually suspicious as claimed by an authoritative oral source, there were solid reasons for him to wonder how much authority he could exercise when thrust into the middle of such a well-established network.[8]

With this background, and with the Financial and Economic Conference under way, Rao assertedly launched an "unreasonable struggle" without the approval of the "Party Center" in a meeting of department heads within the organization department in mid-July and in subsequent meetings. Here Rao raised the "branches against areas" issue and the question of An's Politburo list, which had recently earned An a disciplinary warning. He also sharply attacked An's unwillingness to participate in the criticism of Bo Yibo. At the Financial and Economic Conference itself, Rao tried to pressure An into speaking by saying, "in a big inner-Party struggle like this you should make your position clear." In the organization department meetings he claimed An's reticence demonstrated a lack of a "good [political] sense of smell" and proved that An and Bo belonged to a "small circle"; moreover, through such attacks Rao attempted to reflect on the attitudes of Liu Shaoqi at the Financial and Economic Conference.[9]

Within the department this was conducted with unusual harshness: Rao reportedly shouted at An, jumped up and down, and rudely pointed at him. Such actions allegedly presaged an attempt to reshuffle the department's leadership, and this produced great resentment and severely disrupted departmental work. As for the normally cheerful An, he reportedly could neither sleep nor eat. At some point

Mao's attention was called to the situation and, in an effort to stop the conflict, the Chairman reportedly criticized Rao. Mao supposedly said that Rao shouldn't think he knew everything because he had been a big region secretary when in fact he was inexperienced at the Center, and questioned his launching of a struggle against An without notifying the Center.[10] Whether Mao's rebuke was less sharp than this account implies is unclear,[11] but Rao seemingly was more impressed with the current setbacks suffered by both An and Bo Yibo and with Gao Gang's high standing. In any case, Mao's criticism was insufficient to prevent Rao from renewing the attack on An at the Organization Work Conference in the fall.

The National Organization Work Conference, September–October 1953

The National Organization Work Conference began sometime in September 1953 and ended on October 27. This conference, like the Financial and Economic Conference before it, was linked to the general line; its objectives were to lay down the tasks of organization work in mobilizing the Party to fulfill the general line and FFYP and also to discuss cadre policy.[12] As with the earlier conference, this meant a review of shortcomings that could be used by Gao and Rao, including those already raised at the summer meeting. Once again the target was Liu Shaoqi, but the broader cast of characters was somewhat different than that during the summer. Rao Shushi led the attack on An Ziwen, but there is no evidence that Gao played a personal role at the conference. In fact, according to oral sources, Gao was outside of Beijing for most of the Organization Conference carrying out his lobbying activities,[13] and in any case this situation reflected the functional duties of both Gao and Rao.

Functional considerations apparently determined the other main actors. While Zhou Enlai gave a political report on the current situation and the general line on September 29,[14] he does not appear to have played a prominent role overall. As befitted the Secretariat member with overall responsibility in the organizational realm, Liu Shaoqi chaired both the conference as a whole and the conference's leadership small group. In addition to Rao and An and the six regional organization heads, this small group included Zhu De, who had relevant functional responsibilities as head of the Central Discipline Inspection Committee;[15] Qian Ying, vice-chairman of the government's Supervision Committee; and key figures from the propaganda/ideological sphere—propaganda head Xi Zhongxun and theorist Hu Qiaomu. Also included was Yang Shangkun, who as head of the CCP's general office had an important coordinating role, and Li Fuchun, who despite past work in the organization department had the weakest functional reason for involvement given his economic duties.[16] Interestingly, Chen Yun, the main economic policy maker, who had stronger reason to participate as immediate past organization department head, apparently did not take part. Finally, and even more interesting,

Deng Xiaoping, who would play a crucial role within the small group at the end of the conference as Mao's apparent troubleshooter and subsequently take over the organization department, was not listed among the leadership group members.[17]

As the conference approached, An came under new pressure. Rao made An's life difficult by telling him at the last minute that he should deliver an organization department work report to the meeting. The need for such a report had not been decided upon during the conference preparations, but now Rao suddenly cited An's long experience in the department as an apparent excuse to "put [him] in a difficult position." An, however, endured by working day and night to prepare a report that confirmed achievements but at the same time criticized faults and errors in the department's work. Once the conference began, plenary sessions divided into regional groups were held to discuss general organizational work. Familiar themes that had already been raised during the summer were aired in these sessions, and, as with the Financial and Economic Conference, references to activities "inside and *outside* the conference" suggest the same type of extracurricular maneuvers as on the previous occasion.[18]

The old issues again raised in one context or another included An's Politburo list, which reportedly was widely distributed at the conference and presented as proof of Liu's alleged attitude of despising military cadres. Also on the factional theme was the accusation that the pre-1953 organization department had become a small clique. More general organizational issues were also raised: An and the old organization department were charged with "blurring the distinction between enemies and friends," "lacking sufficient vigilance concerning bad people," and having "right-leaning thought." This critique of laxness in the personnel sphere had already been aired in the summer concerning economic cadres. At the Financial and Economic Conference Gao and Rao had condemned the organization department concerning the appointment of cadres, and particularly certain individuals with "complicated" past histories, whom they named. An ordered a review of the files of these officials and discovered that their complications came from their participation in "many different kinds of complex struggle . . . against the enemy under the instructions of the Party," i.e., from working under "white area" conditions much as Bo Yibo and An himself had done. It is unclear what defense An was able to offer for such cadres, but the issue and its revival at the Organization Conference indicates how the necessarily ambiguous nature of underground work in enemy organizations created both a general issue of "vigilance" against traitors and a special vulnerability for those individuals involved in such work.[19]

Similarities also existed between the two conferences in terms of political tactics. As was the case with Bo Yibo at the Financial and Economic Conference, the Organization Conference assertedly involved "condemning An to knock down Liu." While building a case for An's dismissal, Rao's attacks on various aspects of organization work "pointed the spearhead" at Liu.[20] Here the link was functional, as it had been with regard to Zhou Enlai during the summer conference given

Liu's overall responsibility for organizational matters, as well as "factional" in respect to Liu's close ties to An. As with the earlier conference, it is unclear precisely who was involved. There were, however, some apparent differences in what transpired. Existing accounts imply that fewer people not "in the know" joined the criticism than was the case in the summer, and that the bulk of it was carried out by close associates of Gao and Rao operating in an even more coordinated fashion.

In this case there were specific developments suggesting coordination. Thus the attack on An's alleged lack of vigilance and rightist tendencies was made by the organization chief in Gao Gang's Northeast, Zhang Xiushan, while Rao declared another of Gao's subordinates, Guo Feng, should become the "core of [the organization department]." Meanwhile, Rao organized his East China subordinates, Shandong secretary Xiang Ming and organization department head Lai Keke, who had clashed with An's investigation team at the start of the year, to join in the criticism of An. Lai's attack, which centered on the Party rectification movement then under way,[21] reportedly mirrored that of Zhang Xiushan. Although some oral sources suggest that these developments only reflected Rao using his organization department powers to direct regional organization leaders such as Zhang Xiushan, Deng Xiaoping's 1955 report attributed preparation of Zhang's Organization Conference speech to the "Gao Gang clique." Mao would also seize on these developments in 1955 as proof of a genuine "alliance" between Gao and Rao. Nevertheless, none of this rules out a tacit relationship between the principals, even if some of Gao's subordinates actively cooperated with Rao within his functional sphere.[22]

Developments at the Organization Conference differed in two other crucial respects from those at the Financial and Economic meetings. First, related to the seemingly more coordinated attacks at the fall conference, they were more blatant. However clear the inferences, at least at the open sessions during the summer the attacks on Liu Shaoqi remained indirect and uncertain in their ultimate intent. Now, according to one Party history, *direct* attacks were launched against Liu,[23] while oral sources report that Rao traced An's mistakes to Liu and openly used Liu's name. In contrast to Gao, who assertedly never spoke publicly against Liu, Rao's activities, as one oral source put it, were too obvious, and it became increasingly clear that Liu was the real target. This situation, which violated existing hierarchical status, resulted in sharp criticism of Rao and probably led Gao to approach Mao in an effort to protect his supporter.[24]

A second vital difference, one undoubtedly explaining why the criticism at the conference was undertaken by a more narrow group, concerned the role of Mao. Whereas Mao's well-known anger over Bo Yibo's tax system goes a long way toward explaining events from June to August, there was no such clear pattern of discontent with either An Ziwen or the work of the organization department. Although An apparently had been censured over his list even before the Financial and Economic Conference (see chapter 4), Mao's role in such a censure is unclear although likely. As for the performance of the organization department, apart from a few minor past issues that arguably displeased the Chairman,[25] his only known comments *in 1953* indicated approval of the conduct of the New Three-Anti Campaign.[26] Thus, when Rao Shushi orchestrated activity at the Organization Conference, he was on much shakier grounds than Gao Gang had been a few months earlier.

Rao's vulnerability became apparent after Liu Shaoqi, who was aware of at least some of what was going on in his role as conference chairman, reported to Mao. Mao's reaction was reportedly sharp, but its full implications were again clouded, this time, ironically, due to the intervention of Zhou Enlai. According to well-informed oral sources, Mao was greatly angered by Rao's activities and wanted to expose Rao before the full conference membership. Mao made three points: first, suspend the conference; second, Rao's problem should be made public; and third, when the conference representatives go back to their units, emphasis should be placed on Party unity. Zhou, however, argued that making the matter public to all conference participants was not appropriate as they included provincial-level cadres who were not even Central Committee members. Once again, status considerations came to the fore. In Zhou's mind it would not do to wash the dirty linen of the highest levels before mere provincial officials, and Mao accepted his advice.

As a result, the "Party Center" called a halt to the conference proceedings, and Mao entrusted Liu with presiding personally over a leadership small group meeting to expose and criticize the "problem of the contradiction between Rao and An." Quite a few leadership small group meetings were held, during which Liu not only exposed Rao Shushi but invoked Mao's authority: "Chairman Mao instructed me to bring the struggle within the organization department out into the open and solve it, and he pointed out clearly, 'in the past the central organization department has made achievements and [it] has carried out the correct line in its work.' " Liu, however, was quick to add that there had been mistakes and he took responsibility for them. In addition to Liu, others, including Zhu De and particularly Deng Xiaoping, who now appeared at the group meetings, weighed in with strong appeals to strengthen Party unity in order to realize the general line. Deng, apparently on October 27, the last day of the conference, also spoke to the conference as a whole and openly affirmed that the organization department had been carrying out the Party's correct line. He also added an explicit endorsement of both Liu and An Ziwen: "[The department's achievements are] indivisible from the leadership of Chairman Mao and especially of Comrade Shaoqi. However, Comrade Ziwen also has achievements, one cannot consider that only the leadership is good, that it could produce achievements if the work was badly carried out."[27] Rao's own concluding speech to the full conference endorsed this view by acknowledging that the organization department had carried out the Party line for many years, An's contributions had been essential, and strengthening Party unity was a vital task.

The conflict with An lay buried in the leadership small group, and Rao had at least for the time being been forced to concede defeat on the issues at hand.[28]

While Mao had played a decisive role in determining the course of the Organization Conference, by accepting Zhou's advice and keeping the issue largely in the leadership group, the rebuff to Rao had been somewhat diluted. Moreover, Mao seems to have personally kept at arm's length from the conference. Several sources assert that the Chairman reaffirmed Party discipline and unity at the Organization Conference,[29] but this is stated in a formalistic manner and not supported by detail, whereas detailed accounts make no mention of Mao's presence. The one known message Mao sent to the conference was a letter sent to Yang Shangkun on October 22 requesting the distribution to participants of an extract from the Stalinist *Short Course*, and that "Comrades Liu, Rao, and Hu Qiaomu" be notified of this.[30]

The content of this extract sat uncomfortably with both the theme of unity then being preached at the conference and the moderate policy course affirmed at the Financial and Economic Conference. This concluding section of the *Short Course* attacked "compromises and capitulations" (i.e., the color Gao Gang had attempted to paint Bo Yibo and thus Liu Shaoqi) and called for smashing "petty bourgeois parties" (i.e., the small democratic parties representing the national bourgeoisie, whose continuing role had just been affirmed). In typical Stalinist fashion, Party unity was made dependent on "uncompromising struggle against opportunists within [the Party's] own ranks." Perhaps the hidden message was in the warning against "conceit"—a main theme in the campaign against Gao after his fall—and the call for serious criticism and self-criticism, but overall the *Short Course* extract presented a different vision of Party unity than that which had been advanced since the latter stages of the Financial and Economic Conference.[31] Whether the surfacing of this peculiar piece of study material simply reflected a disjunction between Mao's political aims and his theoretical interests, was a by-product of the ideological routine that was normal at such conferences, or conceivably was a deliberate measure on the Chairman's part to keep people guessing, must, of course, remain a matter for speculation.

Finally, it is likely that one of two occasions on which Gao Gang asked Mao to protect Rao Shushi took place at the end of or just after the conference when Gao returned to Beijing.[32] Mao, recounting the event in 1955 as yet more proof of an "alliance," said that Gao informed him that Rao was in big trouble and asked the Chairman's help. Mao claimed to have brushed aside Gao's entreaties with the observation that as they were both in Beijing "[W]hy should he want you to represent him and not come directly to me [himself]?"[33] Assuming this exchange did take place following the Organization Conference and Mao's account is substantially accurate, it indicates some uncertainty concerning Mao's intentions. That Gao Gang would seek redress for Rao from the Chairman while, under this scenario, some of Mao's closest colleagues had just called Rao to account in his name suggests that at least in Gao's mind the rebuff the anti-Liu cause received at the Organization Conference was not an accurate guide to Mao's wishes. Moreover, Mao apparently did not use this opportunity to chastise Gao Gang. According to well-informed oral sources, at this stage there was still no sign that the Chairman had made up his mind to take decisive action against Gao or Rao, or a clear indication that Liu Shaoqi was completely trusted.

Yet by the time the Organization Conference closed on October 27, Gao and Rao had suffered a greater setback than had occurred in the summer. The affirmation of An Ziwen and the organization department had been much stronger than the tepid conclusion that Bo Yibo's major ideological mistakes did not amount to errors of line. Liu Shaoqi's special role in guiding a fundamentally correct organizational policy had been affirmed, in contrast to Mao's various innuendoes against Liu, which had marked the Financial and Economic Conference. Rao had been directly rebuked in the leadership group meetings as the Center's understanding of Gao and Rao assertedly deepened, and Party unity was emphasized anew. Indeed, it appears that Rao's efforts had badly backfired.

But once again uncertainties were present. Mao sent a peculiar message to the conference which, if read carefully, seemed to endorse the Stalinist approach to handling policy disagreements. Moreover, notwithstanding the defense of An's achievements, his actual position in the organization department remained vulnerable. While the precise causes are unclear, in early 1954 An lost control of the daily affairs of the department.[34] Interestingly, Deng Xiaoping ultimately took authority as department head in April 1954 after Rao's demise; as a result, during and after the Gao-Rao affair Deng became the key figure in both Bo Yibo's Ministry of Finance and An Ziwen's organization department. Most importantly, Mao had again failed to confront Gao. Thus, while the warning signs were arguably clearer than they had been at the end of the Financial and Economic Conference, a degree of ambiguity still surrounded Mao's position. As before, Gao Gang ignored the warning signs and pressed ahead.

The National Conference on Agricultural Mutual Aid and Cooperativization, October–November 1953

As the Organization Conference reached its conclusion, events were under way that produced a shift in policy toward agricultural mutual aid and cooperativization—one of the key areas of Mao's general concern with the process of socialist transformation. In fact, moves toward realizing Mao's concern with advancing the cause of socialized agriculture had been apparent since July. The Central Committee held the Third National Conference on Agricultural Mutual Aid and Cooperativization from October 26, the day before the closing of the organization meeting, until November 5.[35] Out of this meeting came a new directive formally promulgated on December 16.[36] Thus, at the very time the Gao-Rao affair was coming to a head, one of Mao's key policy concerns was resolved, at least for the time being.

Again, the cast of characters was apparently somewhat different from the earlier meetings, although considerably less is known in this case. Although the conference appears to have been held under the auspices of the rural work department, its head, Mao's old close comrade and the key official for agriculture, Deng Zihui, was out of Beijing carrying out investigation and research during this period.[37] Deng's deputy, Liao Luyan, seemingly was the key official on hand, and other participants undoubtedly included personnel from the central agricultural bureaucracies as well as local Party leaders whose duties involved major responsibility for the rural sector. As for top leaders other than Deng Zihui, apparently neither Zhou Enlai nor Zhu De attended.[38] There is also no information to indicate Gao Gang's presence, although the socialist transformation of agriculture would obviously have an important bearing on the FFYP; certainly no charges were laid against either Gao or Rao relating to this conference. Likely candidates for attendance given their key roles in shaping policy toward the planned purchase and supply of grain and edible oils in fall 1953 were Chen Yun and Deng Xiaoping, but again I have found no information confirming this.[39] The key actor was Mao himself, who claimed the day before the conference ended that "the Central Committee" was devoting 70 to 80 percent of its efforts to the transformation of agriculture.[40] Although it seems that Mao's activities as usual were largely in the background rather than at the conference proper,[41] his views and actions were decisive.

While Mao reportedly expressed concern to Gao Gang over rightist tendencies in mutual aid and cooperativization sometime in the first half of the year, his known statements as late as March–April were consistent with the cautious policy laid down by the February directive on mutual aid and cooperatives, which he explicitly endorsed.[42] Even at the end of June, in a brief remark on the mutual aid and cooperative movement, Mao emphasized such cautious sentiments as the principle of voluntary peasant participation, careful preparation, and step-by-step progress while warning against both right and left deviations.[43] In this remark and others during the summer, however, the Chairman raised the danger of reversion from the socialist to the capitalist road if the movement was not promoted.[44]

A clear indication that Mao's views were beginning to be reflected in policy was a late July speech by Deng Zihui to the New Democratic Youth League, and subsequent comments by Deng in the following months. Deng articulated several themes that became increasingly prominent as the year wore on. He argued that the small-peasant economy would develop on either the socialist or capitalist path, and it was the Party's task to see to it that the socialist solution was adopted. The rural economy could not be allowed to remain forever at its present state, nor could it be allowed to grow on a free basis. Another theme was the need to place limitations on rich peasants, a more restrictive interpretation than in the past of the policy allowing the development of the rich-peasant economy. There were still cautious elements in Deng's formulation, particularly a warning against hasty and adventurous attitudes and a call to respect the ownership rights of small peasant producers even while enforcing changes in the private ownership system, but these were not out of step with the emerging policy.[45]

The apparent causes of this shift in policy lay in the dynamics of rural policy in 1952 and early 1953. As indicated earlier, such excesses as blindly setting high targets for the number of mutual aid teams and cooperatives, impatiently seeking higher forms of organization with more socialist content, and overaccumulating common property produced widespread peasant discontent and panic. This, in turn, led to the February directive and the drive against "rash advance," but, as Deng Zihui acknowledged in 1954, a lack of control in carrying out this policy in some areas turned "rash advance" into "rash retreat" and a failure to push the movement forward.[46] Another consideration coming to bear in 1953 was the realization that the small-peasant economy was not producing sufficient agricultural products to keep pace with the demands of socialist industry.[47] But probably the greatest concern for Mao himself, and one that had conceivably surfaced during his private talks with Gao Gang, was one particular manifestation of "hasty retreat"—the dissolution of large numbers of cooperatives.[48] This would be raised in the context of the Chairman's growing discontent over rural policy during the October–November conference.

Mao's discontent had some familiar elements. It involved a critical judgment concerning a key leadership colleague, Deng Zihui, and most likely concerning Liu Shaoqi as well. Much of this judgment, as on other matters, was patently unfair and ahistorical. In this case, however, there apparently did emerge a significant policy difference between Mao and Deng, and Deng Zihui, who was perhaps unique among Chinese leaders,[49] remained convinced of his views. Again Mao seized on out-of-date slogans. In laying down the general line on June 15, Mao criticized "firmly protect private property," while during the conference he attacked both this slogan and advocacy of the "four big freedoms" of no restriction on the hiring of labor, trading, money-lending, and renting out land by rich peasants.[50] Both these slogans were clearly associated with Deng Zihui, and less certainly with Liu Shaoqi, but both referred to policies in vogue during the immediate post-1949 period of economic recovery. In fact, in spring 1953 Deng Zihui explicitly criticized both slogans, and his pronouncements during the summer and fall indicated a willingness to push ahead with the process of the socialist transformation of agriculture.[51]

These typically exasperating ideological preoccupations notwithstanding, Mao had some major differences with Deng concerning actual developments in 1953. Even here there was a substantial element of unfairness. By fall 1953 the Chairman was unhappy about developments in the spring, particularly with the dissolution of cooperatives and more generally with the "anti–rash advance" approach, which he considered mistaken *as it applied to mutual aid and cooperativization.* He expressed his feelings in a talk with Liao Luyan as the conference drew to a close:

> It is not right to force the dissolution of cooperatives which meet the [necessary standards], this is wrong no matter what the circumstances. The campaign to

"check impetuosity and rash advance" was a gust of wind, wasn't it? As it flew from above, it brought down a number of agricultural producers' cooperatives that should have survived. An investigation should be made about such cooperatives, the findings made known and the mistake admitted.[52]

In case there were any doubt, Mao went on to note that "Rash advance is wrong, failure to set up cooperatives when they can be set up is also wrong, and forcible dissolution of cooperatives is even worse."[53] But in making these strictures Mao was, of course, overlooking his own endorsement of the *fan maojin* approach. Moreover, there is no clear evidence that he opposed the dissolution of cooperatives at the time; indeed, Deng Zihui's biographer claims that prior to fall 1953 the "Center" was satisfied with Deng and the rural work department and as late as October 4 issued a notice affirming that eliminating impetuosity and rash advance was important and timely. Deng Zihui, for his part, remained unconvinced that the *fan maojin* approach of spring 1953 had been wrong even after Mao spoke, and he explicitly stated this view a year after the fact in April 1954.[54]

This latter attitude of Deng's appears to have been at the crux of differences between himself and Mao as they applied to *ongoing* policy in fall 1953. Mao and Deng agreed that both rightist and leftist errors had occurred in mutual aid and cooperativization. Deng warned against the rightist tendency of "letting things flow," which spontaneously appeared during the process of correcting rash advance since the summer,[55] while Mao criticized "excessive meddling" in the "scattered small-peasant economy" even as he ranted against *fan maojin*.[56] The issue was one of emphasis, and Deng believed that opposing rash advance not only had been essential in the spring but remained relevant for rural work; significantly, his investigations and research, which kept him away from the conference, were especially concerned with correcting leftist tendencies. But with Mao becoming impatient with the rate of progress in cooperativization, different opinions on *fan maojin* emerged at the time of the conference, and both Deng and the rural work department received criticism and blame. Moreover, an authoritative oral source states that Mao's dissatisfaction over "opposing rash advance" extended to Liu Shaoqi and Zhou Enlai, who had supported the policy, and the December resolution on mutual aid and cooperatives was an implicit criticism of Liu and Zhou. In the event, the political result was that Deng Zihui carried out a self-examination, but he assertedly did not believe he had committed serious mistakes or had been anything other than steadfast in his commitment to the socialist path, nor did he change his previous understanding of the rural situation.[57] Whether because his self-examination obscured these attitudes or Mao chose to overlook the recalcitrance of such a long-time close supporter is unclear, but in any case Deng Zihui continued in his position as China's key agricultural official.

In policy terms, the outcome of the conference was to push policy in the direction outlined by Mao. The December directive on mutual aid and cooperativization affirmed points emphasized in Mao's talks just before and during the conference: there was a struggle of the socialist and capitalist roads, it was impossible to adopt a laissez faire attitude toward the small-peasant economy, and rich-peasant exploitation must be restricted. The key innovation to emerge from Mao's speech and take pride of place as the "core" of the December resolution was the increased emphasis on cooperatives. While the importance of going through the mutual aid stage was strongly reaffirmed, cooperatives were now defined as an "essential link" that would impel the entire movement forward, and the pace of building cooperatives increased.[58] Thus, Mao achieved a significant advance in agricultural cooperativization.

Nevertheless, both the Chairman's talks in October–November and the December decision remained within the consensus mold of steering a course between right and left deviations, although more to the "left" than Deng Zihui would have liked. If the rightist tendency had been firmly put in its place, there were still significant warnings directed at the left. Voluntary participation remained a cardinal principle and special provisions were laid down against commandism; "rash advance" and excessive targets were still wrong; the interests of private producers were to be looked after; and "advancing by steady steps," which carefully avoided exceeding the consciousness of the masses, was a basic guide for the movement along with "active leadership."[59] A significant shift of emphasis had occurred, but the movement remained on a relatively cautious footing.

As a result of these developments, Mao had obtained a major policy goal and achieved it without grossly violating the consensual mode typical of the period. This accomplishment paralleled his earlier successes in laying down the general line and shaping a policy for the transformation of the national bourgeoisie—areas where gradualism and "steady steps" were also the hallmarks of consensus. Yet the situation was somewhat different, and Mao was more intent on getting his way in policy as well as ideology. Here Mao was not content to settle for the discrediting of offensive slogans, such as the "equality of public and private," while his specialist colleagues kept concrete policy change limited. If the new emphasis on cooperatives was still a comparatively centrist program, it nevertheless shifted policy more toward transformation than in other areas, including some where, as in the case of the treatment of the commercial bourgeoisie, there had actually been elements of retreat. And while Mao came to regard "opposing rash advance" in agricultural cooperativization as a mistake, he had explicitly endorsed that approach to the national bourgeoisie[60] and at the very least accepted it from his economic policy makers regarding the economy as a whole. In agriculture, as elsewhere, the Chairman demonstrated an ability to set broad policy directions, lay down ideological orthodoxies, and shake major political actors, but here he went further in shaping the details of policy.

Conclusion

The major conferences of fall 1953 produced diverse results both in terms of the designs of Gao and Rao and in general terms. Ironically, the Agricultural

Cooperativization Conference in which Gao and Rao played no apparent role seemingly provided more support for Gao Gang's broad policy orientation than the Organization Conference where Rao Shushi was so active. While the policy shift at the Cooperativization Conference was relatively moderate it still meant a move to the left; no similar movement could be detected at the organization meetings. Moreover, the Chairman's ideological signals, particularly his attacks on the "four big freedoms," seemingly pointed to Liu Shaoqi as well as Deng Zihui, and the subsequent December resolution on cooperatives apparently was indirectly critical of both Liu and Zhou Enlai. On the other hand, notwithstanding ambiguities and an obscure reference to Stalinist texts, the net result of the Organization Conference was a clear if somewhat muffled rebuke to Rao over the issue of Party unity.

From Mao's perspective the Cooperativization Conference undoubtedly had achieved his policy objectives—without any help from Gao Gang. In contrast, the organization meetings had presented scenes of disunity he professed to find distasteful. At this point the Chairman might have wondered whether the policy and ideological support he probably expected from Gao was worth the disruption to higher Party ranks, but he apparently had come to no firm conclusions. It would not be long, however, before Gao Gang's simultaneous efforts to build political support within the highest circles produced a decisive change in Mao's attitude.

4
IN SEARCH OF ALLIES
Gao Gang's Approaches to Party Leaders
in the South and Beijing, Summer–Fall 1953

DURING AND FOLLOWING the Financial and Economic Conference in the summer, and while the various conferences of the fall conducted their business, another critical aspect of the Gao Gang's "anti-Party activities" took place in the form of approaches by Gao to senior Party leaders. Through these approaches Gao sought to secure the leaders' backing for a reorganization of the top leadership and the deposing of Liu Shaoqi as Mao's successor. At least some of Gao's lobbying efforts were initiated while the economic meeting was still in session, and after the conference, under the pretense of taking a holiday, Gao assertedly traveled to East China and the Central-South region where he conducted "roving talks" in his bid to build support.[1] It is unclear precisely when Gao's travels began or how long they lasted, but the best evidence suggests that Gao's trip took place from the latter part of September to the end of October.[2] There was, moreover, continuity between his activities in the South and those he undertook upon his return to Beijing; indeed, his maneuvers reportedly intensified once he was back in the capital.[3] When these maneuvers were finally reported to Mao by Chen Yun and Deng Xiaoping, the Chairman then set out to act against Gao and Rao.

While the appeals used by Gao in these approaches are clear, other aspects remain uncertain. Where specific approaches were made is often unclear, and the full range of leaders involved remains unknown. The numbers were clearly not insignificant, but of the highest echelons only Lin Biao, Peng Dehuai, Luo Ronghuan, Deng Xiaoping, and Chen Yun can be identified with assurance, while of lower-ranking figures People's Liberation Army (PLA) Deputy Chief-of-Staff Huang Kecheng, South China leader Tao Zhu, and Anhui Party Secretary Niu Shucai are also known to have been approached. Lin and Tao were definitely contacted in the South,[4] although Lin was initially approached in Beijing, while Luo Ronghuan most likely and the others probably were contacted in Beijing either before or after Gao's southern trip. It is the question of timing that is most significant. While the conflicting evidence will be examined on a case-by-case basis below, it is necessary to address the issue and its significance at the outset.

The political significance of the timing of Gao's approaches relates to those made to Chen Yun and Deng Xiaoping, *and* precisely when Chen and Deng reported these events to Mao. Deng Xiaoping's version, which is faithfully echoed in Party histories, claims Chen and Deng went to Mao *immediately (liji)* after being approached.[5] This account is dubious. While the evidence is ultimately inconclusive, on balance it appears there was a considerable gap between Gao's approaches and the apparently separate reports of Chen and Deng to the Chairman, a gap on the order of one to two months or even more.[6] I am reasonably confident (see below) that Mao was informed sometime in November, or perhaps the very end of October at the earliest, while it is likely that Chen and Deng were approached in September, if not as early as July or August. Of course, the situation might have been different for the two leaders, with one or the other approached by Gao considerably before his colleague. But in contrast to the official version, which implied a high degree of commitment to Party unity, any significant delay in reporting to the Chairman points more to uncertainty concerning Mao's attitudes and the all importance of those attitudes for his leadership colleagues.

Gao used a variety of appeals in his effort to build support. The various alleged shortcomings of Liu and Zhou were, as at the Financial and Economic and Organization conferences, used against them. A major ploy was the lure of high office in a period when, with the general line laid down, the issue of electing personnel for the new state structure and Central Committee members for the projected Party Congress was increasingly large. In this context, it has been reported that Gao proposed holding supplementary elections for Central Committee and alternate Central Committee membership and pushed a reorganization (*gaizu*) of the Central Committee and government in his talks with high-ranking Party figures.[7] Specific offers were made as well; a Red Guard source asserts Gao dangled the promise of a vice-premiership in a Gao-led administration before Tao Zhu during a visit to Guangzhou,[8] while in one of the best-known instances he suggested that a Party vice-chairmanship would be appropriate for Chen Yun.

But clearly an important, if not the crucial, aspect of Gao's approaches—an aspect that gained support or caused pause—was his claim to have Mao's backing. That this was credible indicates that Mao's speech and private talks about unity at the end of the Financial and Economic Conference were not decisive. Faced with Gao's claims of the Chairman's support, Mao's failure to rebuke Gao forcefully, and the fact that Liu Shaoqi indirectly and his close associate Bo Yibo had been criticized during the summer, major leaders apparently saw reason to back Gao or at least to temporize in their responses. As will be seen, the reemphasis on unity and especially Mao's anger with Rao Shushi during the Organization Conference would have a more significant effect, but even then various leaders continued to hedge their bets.

Manipulating Factional Tensions

Apart from the claim of Mao's support, undoubtedly one of the most potent weapons in Gao's arsenal was the exploitation of "factional" tensions between army cadres and those whose revolutionary careers centered in the army and rural base areas, on the one hand, and "white area" cadres, on the other. The official 1955 verdict on the case focused on this aspect as the central element in Gao Gang's activities:

> He even tried to instigate Party members in the army to support his conspiracy against the Central Committee of the Party. For this purpose he raised the utterly absurd "theory" that our Party consisted of two parties—one, the so-called "party of the revolutionary bases and the army," the other, the so-called "party of the white areas"—that the Party was created by the army. He claimed himself as the representative of the so-called "party of the revolutionary bases and the army" and [that he] should hold the major authority, that the Central Committee of the Party and the government should therefore be reorganized in accordance with his plan.[9]

Post-1978 sources, moreover, affirm the importance of this factor; on his travels Gao assertedly incited leading army cadres with the argument that Party and state power was in the hands of "white area" Party members.[10] The focus on military leaders during Gao's southern trip is also suggested by the logic of the situation. As most of the key figures Gao sought to win over attended the Financial and Economic Conference and held bureaucratic posts in Beijing in any case, there was no need to head south to consult them, but most army leaders would not have been at the conference. In the event, an authoritative oral source judges Gao's effort to split the Party along "base area" and "white area" lines as having produced substantial successes.

In my earlier analysis,[11] I concluded that although a central ploy in Gao's bid for power, the "base area"/"white area" appeal was ultimately a weak one with little impact. There were three basic reasons for this conclusion. First, in the Central Committee as a whole, army and "base area" cadres dominated, and PLA military and political officers had moved into leading Party and government positions at all levels after 1949. Thus, there was little basis for widespread grievances within this group. Second, as noted in chapter 1, to the extent that army and base area grievances did exist, Gao Gang lacked the contacts to represent those forces. Indeed, despite the official verdict that Gao pictured himself as the representative of these areas and the undoubted fact that Gao hoped to identify with them, as noted earlier, newly available sources indicate that he portrayed *Mao* as the representative of the "red area party" in contrast to Liu representing the "white area party."[12] As a northerner whose pre-1935 experiences were isolated from the mainstream of armed revolution in the South, and as someone who was not a major military figure in his own right, Gao was poorly positioned to tap any resentment.

Finally, while Gao attempted to paint Liu and Zhou as "white area" representatives who grasped power at the Center, the careers of both men were too complex for such simple labeling. Zhou Enlai in particular had deep ties with army leaders going back to the Whampoa Academy in the 1920s, and oral sources argue strongly that he was deeply admired by all major groups within the military. As for Liu, his career included work in the Jiangxi Soviet, participation in the hallowed Long March, a period as political commissar of the New Fourth Army in 1941-42, and a leading role in Yan'an. There was, however, a basis for Gao's characterization of Liu in the CCP's major historical resolution of 1945, which praised Liu as "the exponent of the correct line for work in the [w]hite areas" while Mao was assigned the same role in the more important base areas.[13] In any case, according to oral sources, military leaders not only knew Liu well, they accepted him as the successor given his contributions to revolutionary victory. Before 1953, these sources say, there is no evidence of military dissatisfaction with Liu.

An Ziwen's Politburo List

While nothing in post-1978 sources indicates that the above reasons for downgrading the impact of Gao's "base area"/"white area" appeal were incorrect, clearly the conclusion was. Why? The answer seemingly was An Ziwen's list of prospective Politburo members as portrayed by Gao Gang. While the existing pre-1953 division of power and positions did not disadvantage army leaders, except perhaps in terms of a narrow reading of Politburo membership,[14] An's proposal, which after being attacked at the Financial and Economic Conference apparently became an even more widely used device on Gao's southern tour and at the Organization Conference,[15] ostensibly promised to upset the existing balance in favor of "white area" representatives. Oral sources and Chen Shihui's *neibu* account are the only sources to provide any detail concerning An's list, and they present basically compatible accounts. With a Party Congress on the agenda, An Ziwen prepared a name list for election to the new Party Politburo. Gao Gang reportedly seized upon the list and presented it as including some important "white area" figures while slighting army leaders. Gao's key claims were that the list allegedly included An's old close associate Bo Yibo but not the great general, Lin Biao, and that it originated with Liu Shaoqi. In this context, Gao pictured the new Politburo An Ziwen was assertedly proposing as an example of the "white area faction" further aggrandizing its already too great power, with Liu, An, and Bo all belonging to a small circle favoring its own while despising military cadres.[16]

The story of An's list is obscure. Not only is it rarely mentioned in written sources, but most oral sources consulted professed little knowledge of the matter. The best-informed source on the question presents a version of events that has the initiative coming not from Liu Shaoqi,[17] but from Gao Gang. According to this source, Mao apparently raised the matter of arrangements for leaders of the great regions with Gao and asked him to consider the matter. Gao then went to An sometime in spring 1953 and, using Mao's name, instructed him to prepare a Politburo list including the existing members and the key figures of the regions. It was not, in this version, An's job to do this and he hesitated, correctly understanding this was something within Mao's responsibilities. But in the face of Gao's representation he finally produced the list. People aware of the list were befuddled as to how someone of An's rank could produce it, and thus they were susceptible to Gao's claim that Liu Shaoqi was behind it. From this perspective, the list was a trap to ensnare the uninvolved Liu. In producing the list, An reportedly accepted Gao's guidelines and dutifully added those great region leaders not already on the Politburo—Bo Yibo, Deng Xiaoping, Rao Shushi, and Lin Biao.[18] Gao Gang, however, assertedly spread the rumor that Lin was not on the list.

Clearly, An Ziwen was in hot water over the list even before the Financial and Economic Conference and received a formal disciplinary warning (*jinggao chufen*) as well as criticism.[19] In addition to ongoing criticism by Gao and Rao over the matter at the Financial and Economic Conference, the summer organization meetings, and the Organization Conference, An's reduced position in the department *after* the fall of the "conspirators" indicates that all was not forgiven. Finally, in commenting on the Gao-Rao affair in 1955, Mao referred to "a slate of candidates for the [Politburo] illicitly (*sini de*) put together by An Ziwen."[20] The precise meaning of these rebukes to An is unclear, but the most likely explanation is that An was carpeted for an action that fell within Mao's sphere—a situation not unlike Mao's criticism of Liu Shaoqi and Yang Shangkun for issuing documents that he had not checked. Whether the matter of the *composition* of the list had a bearing on Mao's attitude is not clear. Nor is there any evidence that An tried to defend himself by citing Gao's instructions or Lin Biao's actual presence on the list. While it is totally speculation on my part, An's apparent silence on the matter may have been similar to his tight-lipped posture at the Financial and Economic Conference concerning Bo Yibo. In the face of uncertain attitudes at the highest levels—including most importantly those of Mao—simply enduring criticism may have seemed the safest course.[21]

Whatever the true story of An's list, the resentment it generated sheds light on the larger issue of Party factionalism in the initial postrevolutionary period. As Mao often pointed out, various groupings—what he liked to call "mountaintops"—had formed within the CCP during the revolutionary period. These included, apart from the "white area" cadres, such groups as the Jiangxi Soviet mountaintop, the Second Front Army and Fourth Front Army mountaintops, and the various field army mountaintops. Even inside these groupings there were small mountaintops based on shared revolutionary experiences. Of course, nothing was absolutely binding about such experiences. Rao Shushi and Chen Yi clashed as the leaders of the New Fourth Army, while Rao's career ties to Liu Shaoqi did not prevent his defection to Gao Gang despite few if any ties to Gao. Yet as a general rule, an authoritative oral source maintains, those who knew each through shared experience drew together.

Of all the mountaintops, none was apparently tighter than the "white area" group led by Liu Shaoqi in North China in the mid- to late 1930s. Of particular importance was what came to be known in the Cultural Revolution as the case of the "sixty-one traitors." Jailed by the Guomindang, these Party cadres, including Bo Yibo and An Ziwen,[22] were released in 1936 as a result of Liu's proposal that they make false statements renouncing communism, a proposal approved by Mao and Zhang Wentian, who was then formally the ranking Party secretary. Thus, these figures were grateful to Liu and to Peng Zhen, who played a key role in implementing the policy for their release, and they had a high degree of solidarity from sharing the deprivations and uncertainty of captivity together. These links were maintained as they assumed important posts after 1949; therefore, Gao's aim of getting at Liu Shaoqi through Bo Yibo and An Ziwen had an inherent logic.

Mao's approach, while seeking to overcome excessively narrow factional perspectives, was to unify the mountaintops by recognizing their separate claims. As has been argued, part of this effort was to distribute positions widely among various groupings and to balance carefully representation on the most powerful bodies. The initial arrangements made in 1949 were apparently satisfactory to all the major constituencies, but there clearly was potential for tension as new arrangements became necessary by 1953 and a new share out of power and status loomed. An Ziwen's list stimulated this tension on at least two counts. First, by allegedly increasing the relative position of "white area" cadres versus "base area" and army cadres, An's list upset the delicate balance and opened up the old question of who deserved credit for the victorious revolution.[23] While military leaders were apparently willing to accept Liu Shaoqi's status, an authoritative oral source reports resentment over the prominence in the proposed leadership structure of Bo and Peng Zhen, both of whom had careers comparatively more restricted to the "white areas" than Liu. As a sitting Politburo member it is unlikely there would have been much objection to Peng Zhen's reelection, but to add Bo to Peng on the Politburo must have seemed unbalanced, even outrageous, to army leaders in the absence of the great majority of top military figures on that body.[24]

A second source of friction among the mountaintops occurred when an individual from one group was promoted rapidly; this was likely to fuel objections among members of other groupings. Sometimes such a promotion might be accepted with relative equanimity, as in the case of Deng Xiaoping, whose military achievements were widely recognized,[25] but in the view of an authoritative oral source it would normally produce discontent over perceived favoritism. By placing Bo Yibo on the Politburo list, An Ziwen was seen to be proposing such a disproportionately fast promotion. The best indication of relative status in the early 1950s—status reflecting not only the positions allocated at the Seventh Congress in 1945 but also subsequent changes during the civil war and initial post-1949 period—was a list of leaders personally selected by Mao in 1952 in response to a Soviet request for twenty-one biographies to be published in *The Great Soviet Encyclopedia*.[26] Bo was not among the twenty-one leaders selected (see table 3); moreover, Mao's choices included ten figures—Lin Biao and Deng Xiaoping among them—who had played major military roles during the revolutionary struggle. If the new Politburo was to be of roughly the same size as the seventeen-man body subsequently elected in 1956, An's alleged proposal would have involved a striking rise indeed for Bo, who ranked a lowly forty-fourth on the 1945 Central Committee.[27] The rapidity of this promotion—together with the fact that it was to be at the expense of top army figures among the twenty-one—meant that An's list as portrayed by Gao Gang was doubly dangerous in Gao's hands.

Factions and Regions

Factional considerations were also closely involved in Gao's goal of winning the support of five of the six administrative regions.[28] Gao's own Northeast was of course secure, and he presumably felt that Rao Shushi would take care of East China—although this must have been a somewhat optimistic view given the strength of Chen Yi's influence in the area. Only North China could not be won over—there Peng Zhen as Party secretary and mayor of Beijing and Bo Yibo were the key figures. Thus, the Central-South, where Lin Biao was the ranking figure despite illness; the Northwest, where Peng Dehuai was the key even though he was physically in Korea; and the Southwest, where Deng Xiaoping was crucial, were to be courted. Clearly, Gao calculated on using the army versus "white area" issue that An Ziwen's list had created to win over Lin, Peng, and Deng. Yet more was involved. Gao was not simply appealing to an "army and base area" faction, he was seeking support of the various field army mountaintops which had been deposited in each of these regions by the battles of the civil war.

To elaborate on the analysis in chapter 1, what was crucial was not amassing regional support qua regional support in some central/regional equation, but gathering the significant strands of the predominant "base area" wing of the CCP and turning them against the "white area" cadres. As has been seen, nearly all the key figures with the exception of Lin Biao had moved out of their regions by 1953 even though they retained concurrent local responsibilities. The key to mobilizing these networks was through the dominant individual in each—regardless of whether that individual was a professional commander like Peng Dehuai or a political commissar like Deng Xiaoping. The importance of these leading figures is suggested by Gao's—probably correct—calculation that Peng Dehuai could "deliver" the Northwest even though he had not been there or concerned with its problems for three years. The same conclusion is suggested by an oral source commenting on Gao's approach to Tao Zhu: Tao (the Party chief of the South China Subbureau and former Fourth Field Army cadre) would be no problem as long as

Table 3

Leaders Selected for Inclusion in *The Great Soviet Encyclopedia*, 1952

	CC/Politburo rank 1945	CC/Politburo rank 1956	Main positions 1952–53[a]	Main "factional"[b] association
Mao Zedong	1/1	1/1	Party and state chm	—
Liu Shaoqi	3/3	2/2	Party Secretariat	North China white areas
Zhou Enlai	23/4	6/3	Premier	—
Zhu De[c]	2/2	5/4	Commander PLA	—
Chen Yun	8/6	8/5	Vice-premier Chm FEC	—
Gao Gang	12/8	—	Chm SPC	North Shaanxi base area
Peng Dehuai[c]	33/13	22/14	Commander Chinese forces in Korea	1st Field Army
Dong Biwu	7/10	7/9	Vice-premier Chm GAC Political and Legal Com	—
Lin Boqu	5/11	3/8	Secy-general Central People's Govt	—
Peng Zhen	18/9	29/10	Party secy and mayor Beijing Vice-chm GAC Political and Legal Com	North China white areas
Deng Xiaoping	28/-	4/6	Vice-premier	2nd Field Army
Liu Bocheng[c]	24/-	20/15	2nd Party secy SW Pres PLA military acad	2nd Field Army
Rao Shushi	14/-	—	Head CC organization dept	3rd Field Army
Chen Yi[c]	22/-	21/12	2nd Party secy East China	3rd Field Army
Lin Biao[c]	6/-	9/7	Party secy and chm C-S (inactive)	4th Field Army
He Long[c]	21/-	37/16	2nd Party secy SW Chm Physical Culture and Sports Com	1st Field Army

Xu Xiangqian[c]	9/-	18/-	PLA chief of staff (inactive)	4th Front Army
Deng Zihui	34/-	40/-	Head CC rural work dept	New 4th Army
Ye Jianying[c]	31/-	43/-	3rd Party secy C-S	—
Li Fuchun	13/-	13/13	Vice-chm FEC	—
Luo Ronghuan[c]	16/-	14/11	Chief procurator	4th Field Army

Sources: Oral source; Wang Jianying, Zuzhishi Huibian, pp. 480–81, 640–42; Klein and Clark, Biographic Dictionary; and William W. Whitson with Chen-hsia Huang, The Chinese High Command: A History of Communist Military Politics, 1927–71 (New York: Praeger Publishers, 1973).

Note: Order of listing, while reflecting status broadly, is based on completion of the biographies.

a. Main operational posts only; concurrent regional positions (see table 1) not included.

b. Not exhaustive; based on estimate of strongest ties during revolutionary period. None given where strongest links to post-1935 Party/military center or individual is a Party elder (Dong Biwu, Lin Boqu).

c. Named PLA marshal in 1955.

Lin Biao (Tao's superior as head of the Central-South region and the supreme leader of the Fourth Field Army) came on board. In sum, such considerations suggest strong and cohesive ties among the officials staffing most of China's great regions.

This perspective also supports my understanding of regionalism in this period. As with Gao's "independent kingdom" in the Northeast, regional power was highly concentrated in a few hands in each great region. Lower-level officials looked to leading individuals and those around them for direction, but this did not mean that regional policy was unreceptive to central directives. What it did mean was that such individuals were the vehicles for maintaining policy responsiveness to the Center while at the same time monopolizing political power vis-à-vis subordinate levels. These individuals were indeed local kings through the maintenance of revolutionary career networks only incidentally linked to specific regions, but rulers whose kingdoms were hardly independent of the overall policy direction provided from Beijing despite inevitable tensions between central departments and local bureaucratic units. As long as unity prevailed in Beijing, local authority was enhanced by carrying out central policy; only central retaliation provoked by local disobedience could undermine the rule of regional leaders.[29] But with factional tensions on the rise within the top leadership such regional figures were faced with more difficult choices.

Gao's Approaches to Key Party Leaders

Gao Gang apparently believed that if he could present Mao with the support of the five regions plus additional key figures such as Chen Yun and Luo Ronghuan at the Center, he would provide the Chairman with sufficient grounds for changing the succession in his own favor, a change that Gao presumably believed was Mao's desire. If such leaders, who all ranked among the top twenty-one PRC officials at the time, could be won over, then presumably strong influence could be brought to bear on Mao if he were inclined to a general leadership shake-up in any case. Lesser figures like Huang Kecheng, Tao Zhu, Anhui Party Secretary Niu Shucai, or the various officials such as Ma Hong from the Northeast and Xiang Ming from East China who would be denounced as members of the alliance in 1955,[30] could play supporting roles, but success would depend on those at the highest levels and a receptive Mao.

Lin Biao

Post-1978 written sources place great weight on the support allegedly lent to Gao Gang by Lin Biao. According to Deng Xiaoping, Gao "first gained the support of Lin Biao, which was what emboldened him to go ahead full steam."[31] Given Lin's fall from grace in 1971, such assertions are suspect, but it nevertheless does appear that Lin was an early target for Gao's blandishments. As has been noted above, Gao allegedly spread rumors at the Financial and Economic Conference flattering Lin. According to an oral source specializing on Lin Biao, although not attending the conference Lin was staying at the Summer Palace at the time, and Gao visited him there. Moreover, on his southern trip Gao met with Lin Biao in Hangzhou in October for consultations,[32] while Lin, who was still on sick leave, reportedly sent a letter to Gao as late as the end of November.[33]

In these dealings Gao, undoubtedly using the various appeals discussed above, raised plans for a reorganization of the Party and state leadership. Gao and Lin reportedly discussed at great length a name list for an "election of the Center" (*zhongyang renxuan*). Apart from the undoubted impact of An Ziwen's list on Lin, Gao could have reasonably hoped that certain past events would have made Lin sympathetic to him and antipathetic to Liu Shaoqi's group. Gao and Lin had apparently developed close ties during their service together in the Northeast. In particular, the dispute in the early stages of the civil war between Peng Zhen, then the leading Party secretary, on the one hand, and Lin, Gao, and Chen Yun, on the other, both deepened Gao-Lin relations and left a residue of bitterness between Lin and a leading member of Liu's group. As noted in chapter 1, Peng argued for a policy of protecting Communist-held cities and railways, while Lin, Gao, and Chen called for abandoning these holdings and retreating to the countryside to establish rural base areas. Mao decided the issue in favor of retreating to the countryside, Peng was demoted, and leadership tension in the Northeast continued to fester over the following year until Peng was transferred to North China, where he took up duties under Liu Shaoqi and was also reunited with Bo Yibo. While Mao reportedly minimized the incident as only a difference of opinion in work when Gao raised it in 1953 as a mistake in line, this particular conflict left its mark on Lin-Peng relations, and it dovetailed perfectly with the situation created by Gao's use of An's list.[34]

Beyond fanning past resentments, Gao appealed to Lin on the basis of future position. Here the issue is clouded by uncertainty over both the specific role outlined for Lin and Gao's intent in putting such a role forward. According to a well-informed oral source, at the Financial and Economic Conference Gao flattered the absent Lin by saying that neither Liu nor Zhou would be Mao's successor, that the true successor was Lin Biao. Presumably similar sentiments were expressed in the face-to-face exchanges between Gao and Lin. While such advocacy is odd given both Lin's ongoing health problems, which had kept him away from most major Party meetings in the post-1949 period,[35] and Gao's alleged objective of himself becoming the successor, that Gao might have expressed it has a certain plausibility for several reasons.

First, if Mao were to discard Liu Shaoqi as his successor, Lin had at least some credentials making him a succession candidate, despite the obvious problem created by his health. Lin still possessed great prestige based on his outstanding revolutionary achievements; he ranked sixth of all Party leaders in the voting for the Central Committee in 1945 even before the remarkable military successes of the civil war in 1945–49. Later, after more years of ill health, he still had considerable credibility—if far from universal approval—as the successor when Mao tapped him for that role in 1966.[36] This, in turn, was linked to another asset of Lin's—his very close ties to Mao. A close follower of Mao's since the late 1920s who had developed something of a student-teacher relationship with the Chairman, Lin was clearly highly trusted by Mao.[37] Lin was not above disputing military matters with Mao in strong terms during the revolution, but as the Chairman put it later, "in the end he still did what I wanted."[38] Thus, Lin Biao would be a key figure to have on one's side, not only in terms of military support but all importantly as someone Mao trusted.

But perhaps the key for Gao in advocating Lin as the successor lies in his ill health.[39] Gao may have been content to flatter Lin with the idea that he, Lin, could be the successor while all the time calculating that this could not be a reality given Lin's physical condition.[40] This same motive may have been involved in the specific position Gao apparently had in mind for Lin Biao. While the sources at hand only refer to Gao raising the matter with others rather than Lin himself, Gao reportedly proposed in the context of whether a Soviet-style Council of Ministers system should be adopted in the new Chinese constitution that Lin Biao be chairman of the Council of Ministers (*buzhang huiyi zhuxi*).[41] These revelations, too, are puzzling since such a position was the equivalent of premier and thus unlikely for Lin, given both his inability to carry a heavy administrative load and Gao's alleged desire that he himself become premier. While once again forced to rely on speculation, it may be that Gao's knowledge of Soviet administration was as hazy as his knowledge of Stalin's writings (cf. his confusion in thinking *On the Opposition* was an anti-Bukharin text). In speaking of the Council of Ministers system (*buzhang huiyizhi*), Gao may have actually been addressing less the administrative apparatus (the Council of Ministers in the USSR and the GAC, later the State Council, in China), which was fundamentally similar in both countries, than the formal legal organs above this apparatus. Thus he may have been advocating a Supreme Soviet type of arrangement whereby the chairman of that body became the titular head of state—an honorific position but one without power.[42] Such an arrangement was being considered, and, according to one oral source, there was some sentiment that the top state post should be filled by a military man. If the chairmanship of a Chinese version of the Supreme Soviet was the position Gao had in mind for Lin, it would have fitted both Lin's reduced capacities and Gao's designs. Ironically, according to another well-informed oral source, a bit earlier in this period Gao had said he would let Liu Shaoqi be a Shvernik, the titular head of state in the Soviet Union until Stalin's death. In any case, if Gao put any specific proposals directly to Lin, they were possibly along these lines.

While Gao's apparent suggestion of a prestigious status or post may have appealed to Lin Biao, undoubtedly as important, if not more so, was Gao's assertion that he had Mao's support. Indeed, an authoritative oral source reports that when the crunch came Lin—and Peng Dehuai and Tao Zhu as well—was able to escape serious repercussions by claiming that Gao cheated him into believing Mao had sanctioned Gao's proposals. In this regard it is perhaps significant that Lin had not attended the Financial and Economic Conference; the same applied to Peng Dehuai. Thus, the two key leaders who came over to Gao's side at least to some degree had not been present when Mao sought to limit the criticism of Bo Yibo and restore Party unity. Two leaders who were present—Deng Xiaoping and Chen Yun—and who presumably were in a better position to evaluate Mao's intentions as a result, did not go along with Gao. Clearly, as has been repeatedly emphasized, there was ambiguity in Mao's position, and on the evidence of mid-1953 Gao's story could not be dismissed, but absence from the scene of conflict may have contributed to erroneous perceptions of Mao's attitudes. In any case, as Deng Xiaoping would assert nearly three decades later, Lin's support does appear to have strengthened Gao's intention to press ahead. But in contrast to the insinuations of the present official version, Lin's support appears to have been largely passive. According to my authoritative oral source, while he expressed agreement with Gao's views, Lin did nothing concrete to support the plans of Gao Gang.

Peng Dehuai

Even less information is available concerning Gao's approach to Peng Dehuai sometime following Peng's return to China from Korea on August 11. In the heated atmosphere of the 1959 Lushan plenum Peng was identified as a principal member of the Gao-Rao conspiracy. The decision of the plenum also claimed that Peng's "co-conspirators" on that occasion, Huang Kecheng and (unconvincingly) Zhang Wentian, had been part of Gao's factional activities.[43] Little detail was provided during the 1959-1978 period, however, and it is clear that whatever Peng's involvement with Gao Gang, the issue was only raised as a result of his clash with Mao over the Great Leap Forward at Lushan. Once Peng was rehabilitated at the landmark Third Plenum in December 1978, moreover, his new status as a victim of Mao's excesses and a model upright man resulted in a reluctance to examine the more questionable parts of his past.[44] As a result, the rich memoir literature of the post-1978 years has passed over in silence the relationship of Gao Gang and Peng Dehuai in 1953.

Peng's case is similar in several respects to that of Lin Biao. Like Lin, Peng had developed good relations with Gao, although in his case this seemingly came largely after the revolutionary period. During the revolution their careers took different paths. Peng had been a mainstay of the southern revolution while Gao was a leader of the North Shaanxi base area before 1935. In the Anti-Japanese period Peng was a key military figure second only to Zhu De in the overall command structure; Gao dealt largely with Party and government affairs in the Shaan-Gan-Ning Border Region surrounding Yan'an. Ironically, Peng became the leading figure in the Northwest and developed close ties with some of Gao's old associates, most notably Xi Zhongxun, after Gao departed for the Northeast in 1945. The personal ties between Peng and Gao became significant during the Korean war. At that time Gao's Northeast provided important support services for Peng's armies in Korea, and oral sources stress Peng's appreciation of such support. Indeed, Red Guard sources claim that Peng was so impressed with Gao's abilities that he wanted him made PLA chief-of-staff during the Korean war,[45] although military informants doubt this on the grounds that as officials of equal [Politburo] status it would have been "impossible" for Gao to serve in the subordinate chief-of-staff position.[46]

Another similarity to Lin Biao was that Peng Dehuai had developed a long-standing antipathy to Liu Shaoqi, in this case of even deeper dimensions. The difficulties in the Peng-Liu relationship went back to the early 1940s. At that time Peng had succeeded Liu and Yang Shangkun as head of the Party's Northern Bureau, and in May 1942 a Japanese attack on the Taihang region had resulted in big CCP losses. Part of this, it was believed, was due to Peng's neglecting to organize the peasants thoroughly or carry out rent reduction. At this time Liu arrived in North China on his way from Central China to Yan'an and gave a report to the Northern Bureau. According to an oral source who attended the meeting, Liu compared the recent failures to his own earlier correct leadership of the area and declared the then current situation a great mess. Subsequently, in winter 1942–spring 1943, the Taihang Subbureau of the Northern Bureau held a high-ranking cadres conference where Liu's close associates Bo Yibo and An Ziwen took the lead in criticizing Peng on the same issues Liu had raised earlier. Liu also paid a visit to the area during these meetings and expressed his views to Bo and An. The volatile Peng, however, was unwilling to accept this criticism.

Peng's resentment apparently deepened further when, since he wouldn't admit fault, he and Bo were summoned to Yan'an and Deng Xiaoping took over his duties in the Northern Bureau. In Yan'an Peng was seriously criticized for not paying sufficient attention to the peasant movement, not simplifying administration, nor improving the army, all of which were said to have led to the defeat at the hands of the Japanese in May 1942. Finally, Peng's grievances with Liu were again exacerbated at the famous 1944 criticism of Peng's conduct of the 1940 Hundred Regiments campaign, criticism which led to well-documented bitterness on Peng's part toward Mao, who sanctioned the attack.[47] But what is not generally known is that Liu presided at the criticism sessions, thus providing another reason for Peng's ill feelings toward the CCP's number two leader, which seemingly still lingered in 1953.

With this background, when Gao approached Peng, apparently in Beijing "about September,"[48] it seemingly was in much the same vein as his approach to Lin Biao. Given Gao's representation of An Ziwen's list, Peng apparently was displeased with the ostensible discrimination against army leaders, and he also apparently believed that Mao had objections to Liu and Zhou, especially Liu. While no information is available concerning any position Gao may have suggested for Peng, if a proposal was forthcoming nothing would have been more appropriate than the defense portfolio, which Peng received in the event when the new government was set up in 1954. In any case, as with Lin Biao, the decisive consideration for Peng Dehuai undoubtedly was his belief that Gao did indeed have Mao's support. But also like Lin, Peng reportedly limited himself to agreeing with Gao rather than undertaking any specific actions.[49]

In terms of winning over the Northwest, logic suggests that Xi Zhongxun, who was the most powerful figure in the region after Peng departed for Korea, would have been a major figure for Gao's blandishments. Not only did Xi play a crucial role in the Northwest, by the latter part of 1952 he had assumed key duties in the culture and educational sphere at the Center. Moreover, Gao's links to Xi go back to the pre-1935 North Shaanxi base area. Indeed, according to one oral source, at some indeterminate time Gao expressed to Xi resentment over the relative underrepresentation of North Shaanxi cadres on top Party bodies with the observation that "North Shaanxi saved the Center." This phrase pointing to the vital support given by northern Communists to the gravely weakened remnants of the Long March in 1935 reportedly sat poorly with Mao. But to the extent that resentment existed on Gao's part, it reportedly was relieved first by his elevation to the Politburo in 1945 and then by his appointment as one of the vice-chairmen of the Central People's Government Council in 1949—an appointment specifically made by Mao to recognize the contributions of the North Shaanxi base.[50]

In any case, whatever Gao may have said to Xi earlier or even in 1953, and notwithstanding an intriguing Hong Kong source claiming a tussle over Xi's loyalties in 1953,[51] my most authoritative oral source reports no knowledge of Xi's involvement in the Gao-Rao affair and believes his rise in 1952–53, which included taking over leadership of the Center's propaganda department in 1953, was largely the product of the shift of regional personnel to Beijing and extraneous factors.[52] Regardless of the actual situation with Xi Zhongxun, who almost a decade later would be arbitrarily dragged into the affair (see chapter 5), it nevertheless appears that the primary effort to win over the Northwest and its associated field army mountaintop was through Peng Dehuai.

Luo Ronghuan

Even less is known about Gao's approach to another major military figure, Luo Ronghuan. Indeed, the only available information is provided in a brief account in a 1978 journal article.[53] This approach, said only to have occurred "in 1953," most likely took place sometime in the second half of the year, perhaps even as late as December.[54] Luo was an inviting target for several reasons. Not only was he one of the great military leaders of the revolution, as would be recognized by his 1955 selection as a PLA marshal, but Luo had also been a key officer in Lin Biao's Fourth Field Army and its predecessors since 1930 and had developed good working relations with Gao in the Northeast during the late 1940s.[55] Thus, in addition to having an established relationship with Gao, Luo was both a military cadre presumably sensitive to any real or imagined slights to the PLA and a Fourth Field Army stalwart who should have been responsive to any plan to recognize Lin Biao's status. Yet, according to the version of events on hand, things did not quite work out that way.

The 1978 account has Gao unexpectedly turning up at Luo's house, presumably in Beijing, one evening in 1953. Gao referred to the possibility of setting up the Council of Ministers system, which was then under discussion within the leadership, and proposed Lin Biao as its chairman. Luo, in this version, was astonished by Gao's suggestion and quickly hastened to ask, "Has this question been discussed by the Center? Is this Chairman Mao's intention?" Luo's reaction fits perfectly into the pattern of leadership responses throughout 1953: the key question was what was Mao's position. In this case, at least, Gao reportedly backed off in embarrassment, admitting the Center had not discussed the issue and Mao did not know of it, and suggesting that they discuss the issue first. Having apparently determined to his satisfaction that Mao was not behind the suggestion, Luo rejected any discussions on the grounds that it would be inappropriate for them to discuss such a large matter.

Interestingly, Luo assertedly went on to say that it was unsuitable for Lin to hold such a post as Gao suggested since he was the leader of only one of several major military groupings, and it was up to Mao and the Center to make the arrangements concerning which leaders of these groups should assume what new posts. In these remarks Luo seemingly demonstrated a sensitivity to the balancing of the various army "factions," and to the danger of singling out any particular group. Yet even given this, as portrayed, relatively forthright rebuff to Gao, Luo may have been sensitive to his seemingly inadvertent involvement as he stayed away on grounds of illness from meetings held after Gao's exposure, presumably the Fourth Plenum and the discussion meeting concerning Gao in February 1954 (see chapter 5), and limited himself to sending a written speech. It would seem that while Luo may not have responded positively to Gao's approach, the very fact of contact was enough to produce unease on his part.

Deng Xiaoping

All the evidence suggests that Deng Xiaoping was, along with Lin Biao, a crucial objective of Gao Gang's search for allies. As with Lin and Peng Dehuai, Deng was both a military hero and a regional leader; as with Lin, he was one of Mao's closest personal followers throughout a long period of Party history. But unlike Lin and Peng, and also unlike Chen Yun, there is little to indicate that Deng had developed any significant career links to Gao before 1953.

There is no unambiguous evidence of either precisely when Gao Gang approached Deng or when Deng went to see Mao and report on Gao's activities. The evidence (see below) is reasonably strong that Deng, about the same time as but separately from Chen Yun, went to Mao in November, if not late October or possibly early December.[56] If Deng's story about "immediately" reporting to Mao is true, then Gao's approach also came sometime between the end of October and the start of December. Moreover, Deng himself strongly implied that the approach came at "the end of 1953" (*1953 niandi*), a term indicating November or December, but in a manner less than totally credible.[57]

Various oral sources, however, speaking independently of one another, believe that Gao's approach came considerably earlier. One source expressed a fairly typical view in claiming that Lin, Peng, Deng, and Chen were all approached following the Financial and Economics Conference "about September," with the last three leaders contacted in Beijing, although on balance it seems Gao's meetings with Lin Biao came both earlier and later (see above). This fits the sequence given in Party histories where Gao allegedly first secured the support of Lin and then turned his attention to Deng Xiaoping, although here again the precise timing is left vague.[58] Thus, the weight of the evidence suggests a September approach to Deng if not an earlier one at the Financial and Economic Conference, which both Gao and Deng attended, but there is still enough uncertainty that the official view of a November or early December approach followed by an immediate report to Mao cannot be categorically rejected.

Other evidence, from Deng's own lips, also suggests that reporting to Mao, when it did come, was a considered rather than a reflex act. According to Deng's remarkable 1980 account:

> So far as Southwest China was concerned, [Gao] tried to win me over and had formal negotiations (*zhengshi tanpan*)[59] with me in which he said that Comrade Liu Shaoqi was immature. He was trying to persuade me to join in his effort to topple Comrade Liu Shaoqi. I made my attitude clear, saying that Comrade Liu Shaoqi's position in the Party was the outcome of historical development, that he was a good comrade on the whole, and that it was inappropriate to try to oust him from such a position.[60]

This, of course, is the version of an interested participant, and the degree to which Deng "made his attitude clear" must remain uncertain. In any case, the fact that Deng felt it necessary to undertake "formal negotiations" with Gao speaks volumes. Deng, as suggested above, may have felt in his own mind on the basis of events at the Financial and Economic Conference that Mao was not out to get rid of Liu, but he could not be sure. As an authoritative oral source put it, Deng had to be extremely careful in dealing with Gao since he might indeed represent Mao. To the extent Deng did "make his attitude clear," it is plausible that Deng, as he implied, was motivated in part by a desire to avoid the damage to Party unity that would follow from "highly irregular . . . behind-the-scenes deals."[61] Related to this was a sensitivity to status that has been repeatedly noted in this study. What Deng was saying was that Liu's status had been affirmed by a long process in Party history, and any attempt to tamper with such historically validated status might result in a major leadership upheaval that could only threaten the CCP's major objectives.

Yet undoubtedly Deng's key calculation was his estimation of Mao's actual desires. As desirable as unity might be, political success was dependent on staying on the right side of Mao. In this he would have been guided not only by what he saw at the summer conference, but by his long-term association with the Chairman as one of Mao's oldest and closest supporters. While Deng probably temporized even more than he implied in 1980 and delayed for perhaps two months in reporting to Mao, it is reasonable to conclude that at the very least he had reason to doubt Gao's claim of Mao's support and held aloof from throwing his lot in with Gao Gang.

Chen Yun

Chen Yun played a role similar to that of Deng Xiaoping in several respects. This, of course, was not simply by virtue of their being both major objectives in Gao's effort to win allies, but in their shared subtle understanding of Mao and the fact that the decision of each to report to Mao became a critical turning point in the unfolding of the Gao Gang affair. From Gao's perspective there were similarities between Chen, on the one hand, and Lin Biao, Peng Dehuai, and Deng, on the other. As with Lin Biao and Peng Dehuai, Gao had some reason based on past history to hope for Chen's support. They had stood together against Peng Zhen in the dispute over military strategy in the Northeast and had worked together in that region for a number of years before 1949. Chen also fit into Gao's concept of a younger generation, which also included Deng and Lin, to take over from Liu and Zhou. Also, as an able and younger leader already on the powerful Party Secretariat, it behooved Gao to win Chen's support.[62]

But there were also some important differences between Chen and the others. Chen Yun was not a military man, and while his revolutionary career had been predominantly in the base areas, first in the South and later in Yan'an, it was not devoid of "white area" work either. Nor was Chen a long-time follower of Mao like Lin and Deng, although a close working relationship since the late 1930s had apparently led to a very high appraisal of Chen on the Chairman's part. And, as seen in chapters 1 and 2, unlike Lin and Peng, who apparently had no detailed economic views, and setting aside Deng, where lack of evidence prevents any firm conclusion concerning compatibility or incompatibility of policy orientation,[63] differences between Chen and Gao can be safely assumed. While there is insufficient evidence to indicate any fundamental differences, Gao's somewhat leftist general posture and his seemingly harsh attitude toward the national bourgeoisie were at variance with Chen's cautious approach on both scores. Also, oral sources note Gao's strong commitment to the Soviet model while Chen, although also committed to the model in general terms, had already by 1953 indicated reservations about uncritically adopting Soviet practice.[64] Finally, the overlapping responsibilities of the SPC and FEC undoubtedly generated some tension between Gao and Chen. Yet, for all these potential obstacles to cooperation, Gao pursued Chen's support, a pursuit suggesting either that the policy differences between them were not as great as might be imagined or that at least in Gao's mind the political logic of the situation would easily override any such differences, or a combination of the two.

In any case, the apparent thrust of Gao's approach to Chen, also termed "formal negotiations" by Deng Xiaoping, was an offer for an enhanced position within the hierarchy, a proposal whereby Gao and Chen would hold key responsible positions under Mao. According to Deng Xiaoping, "Gao Gang also approached Comrade Chen Yun . . . and told him that a few [Party] vice-chairmanships should be instituted, with himself and Chen each holding one of them."[65] Chen, however, was assertedly unmoved by this "one for you, one for me" proposal. Again, the time and place of the offer is unclear, with "about September" in Beijing the best bet. There is evidence, however, pointing to the incident taking place both earlier and later. One oral source, who learned of the event years later from Zhou Enlai, recounted how after a Politburo meeting Gao reportedly drew Chen to his car to make the "one for you, one for me" offer and said it *probably* happened during the Financial and Economic Conference in July or August. Whether in July–August or September, both versions are consistent with the view of oral sources questioned on the matter that there was a delay in Chen reporting to Mao. On the other hand, several post-Mao written sources treat the sequence of events in such a way as to suggest that the "one for you, one for me" ploy occurred after the initial round of early December Politburo meetings.[66]

Of course, various alternatives are possible. Gao could have approached Chen on a number of occasions spanning the entire July–December period. Or Deng and the others might have been approached "about September," but given Chen's somewhat different situation, Gao may have delayed pursuing him until late in the piece. Obviously other possible variations exist as well. Whatever the circumstances, Chen Yun's response was possibly more decisive than Deng's.[67] While it is unclear what he told Gao, an authoritative oral source states that Chen was the first to bring the story of Gao's activities to the Chairman and in so doing brought about a fundamental turning point in the entire Gao-Rao affair.

Chen and Deng Report to Mao

While Deng Xiaoping stated in 1980 that after being approached by Gao, "Comrade Chen Yun and I realized the gravity of the matter and immediately brought it to Comrade Mao Zedong's attention,"[68] oral sources indicate that their actions were separate and uncoordinated—and also that they were the only leaders of those lobbied by Gao Gang who went to Mao, although the lesser-ranking Huang Kecheng reportedly submitted a written report to the Secretariat at some comparatively early stage.[69] According to these oral sources, Chen informed Zhou Enlai first and then told Mao of Gao's proposals. Somewhat later, Deng went directly to the Chairman and told his story of Gao Gang's approach. Chen apparently shared Deng's concern with Gao's surreptitious wheeling and dealing and the damage to Party unity that would be caused by a leadership split. Ties of work and sentiment to Zhou Enlai may also have contributed to their unreceptiveness to Gao's entreaties. Deng's links to Zhou, as noted earlier, went back to their days together in France in the early 1920s, and Deng would later claim to "have always looked upon him as my elder brother."[70] Chen, for his part, worked closely with Zhou as a member of the Party Secretariat and especially as the leading government economic official under the premier. Also significant were the implications of Chen reporting *first* to Zhou before seeing Mao, perhaps both to warn his comrade and to check with another close observer of the Chairman. By contrast, reportedly no one told Liu Shaoqi, something explained by a well-informed source as reflecting Chen's belief that it would be inappropriate to tell Liu since the matter was primarily directed against him. The different treatment of Liu and Zhou might also be explained by more intimate Chen-Zhou and Deng-Zhou ties.

Yet, as suggested above, skepticism concerning Gao's claims of speaking for

Mao must have played a crucial role. As emphasized earlier, both Chen and Deng had been close to Mao in a political or work sense during key portions of the revolutionary period and had developed a subtle understanding of his thinking and motives. In the period in question, they both observed Mao's attitude toward Bo Yibo and his efforts to promote the theme of Party unity at the Financial and Economic Conference, with Chen in particular playing a key role linked to that of Mao. But perhaps the critical development in their understanding of Mao's current intentions was the Organization Conference. All sources addressing the issue indicate that Chen and Deng reported to Mao after the Organization Conference closed on October 27. Oral sources generally nominate November as the time Mao was informed, although those written sources implying that Gao's "one for you, one for me" proposal came in early December would seemingly put Mao's awareness in December also. Moreover, whatever the exact date, Chen and Deng going to Mao after the Organization Conference makes sense for it was during that conference that Mao's anger concerning Rao Shushi's activities became clear—so clear that Zhou Enlai had to restrain the Chairman from going "public" in an inner-Party sense. Deng Xiaoping, as Mao's apparent troubleshooter at the conference, would have been in a particularly good position to observe the Chairman's intensified expressions of concern with Party unity. With Mao's position now comparatively clear, it may have appeared safe and perhaps essential to speak out against Gao Gang.

Mao reportedly expressed dismay and disgust at Gao Gang's activities. Of course, this could have been a feigned disgust covering up chagrin that his efforts to either unsettle or remove Liu and/or Zhou had come unstuck,[71] but Chen Shihui and oral sources claim it was an honest reaction to the discovery of prohibited factional activities by a trusted colleague, and they believe that Gao had completely miscalculated Mao's intentions in the first instance. Mao himself claimed to be greatly upset not only with Gao's activities but also with the fact that he had not been informed earlier. Mao reportedly expressed his dissatisfaction in a November or December conversation with Minister of Public Security Luo Ruiqing.[72]

According to the recollections of Luo's daughter, the Chairman asked Luo who would take over on the "first front" if he retired to the "second front." In the charged political atmosphere of the time, Luo dared not respond directly but indicated that while Liu was the obvious choice there were now doubts. Mao cut Luo off and criticized his lack of a political sense of smell:

> some [people] sleep on beds and some . . . in a drum [i.e., in the dark]. I can see you're in the dark. Do you know there are people carrying out conspiracies, organizing an underground headquarters in Beijing. You say you support my flag, why is it when you hear certain things, you don't question if they're true or false? . . . The one who is conspiring, organizing an underground headquarters, is Gao Gang. When I retreat to the second front, he wants to be the Party vice-chairman. He told [Chen Yun] you will be a Party vice-chairman and so will

I. You think he supports Lin Biao? This time there's no Lin Biao here . . . .[73] [Gao Gang] will not only strike down Liu Shaoqi, he will strike me down, and he will strike down Lin Biao.[74]

Luo Ruiqing was apparently convinced by Mao's rebuke. But whatever the Chairman's innermost feelings, perhaps the greatest significance of the exchange is that it is yet another piece of evidence of a high official being unwilling to stand up and be counted while he was unsure of Mao's intentions.

In the event, once Chen and Deng reported to Mao action soon followed. The initial steps were to order an investigation conducted by the Secretariat, and to hold talks with key figures who had been lobbied by Gao Gang. Chen Shihui reports that "when the Secretariat discovered the splitting activities of Gao and Rao, comrades Mao Zedong, Zhou Enlai, Deng Xiaoping, and Chen Yun personally sought out people for talks."[75] Apart from Mao's chat with the man in charge of the security apparatus, the key discussions were those of Deng with Peng Dehuai and Chen with Lin Biao.[76] Peng, for his part, reportedly had become aware that something was amiss following what must have been an early or mid-December Politburo meeting (see chapter 5) and planned to raise Gao's activities with Zhou Enlai, but he was approached by Deng before having a chance to follow through on his intention.[77] In addition, Deng visited Luo Ronghuan about this time although it is not known whether the subject of Gao Gang was raised.[78] According to an authoritative oral source, both Peng and Lin claimed to have been deceived by Gao into believing he had Mao's backing and this, together with their willingness to disown Gao Gang, was accepted as sufficient reason for absolving them of serious errors. Mao's believed preferences were all-important. They not only seemingly led Peng and Lin to go along with Gao but were seen as an understandable, if not wholly legitimate, cause for doing so. But once credible emissaries from Mao in the form of Deng and Chen appeared, Peng and Lin, notwithstanding any lingering resentment over An Ziwen's list or past differences with Liu Shaoqi, immediately disassociated themselves from Gao Gang. As a result, the major support Gao had gathered during his southern trip and into Beijing was withdrawn by the time the decisive events of December 1953 unfolded.

Conclusion

By early December 1953 Gao Gang had completed over three months of heavy behind-the-scenes politicking in an effort to win high-level support for his bid to supplant Liu Shaoqi as Mao's successor. As with his efforts at the Financial and Economic Conference and Rao Shushi's at the Organization Conference, the results were mixed. Gao's effort to use the new leadership lineup allegedly projected by An Ziwen's list to prove discrimination against the PLA at the hands of Liu Shaoqi and his "white area" followers seemingly fanned considerable resentment within military circles and, according to oral sources, produced a great deal of support.

The specific approaches to Lin Biao and Peng Dehuai produced positive if cautious responses, while those to Luo Ronghuan, Deng Xiaoping, and Chen Yun had less positive but still ambiguous results. At the very least, nothing so strong as to stop Gao in his tracks was said. Thus, as the last month of the year arrived, it was still conceivable for Gao to overestimate his position in terms similar to those attributed by post-1978 sources: he could assume support in at least four of China's six great regions, he had a powerful bureaucratic base in the SPC, and in Lin Biao and Peng Dehuai he had the backing of two of the PRC's most important military figures.[79]

But unbeknownst to Gao Gang, the key factor he had been counting on—Mao's political support—had now undergone a fundamental change. Whatever Mao's precise plans for Liu Shaoqi, Zhou Enlai, and Gao Gang earlier in the year, it had seemed clear for a considerable period of time that Mao intended Gao to play an important role and looked to Gao for support in some of his more impatient endeavors. With the Organization Conference, however, Mao was being increasingly pushed into a position where he might have to choose between sympathy for Gao's ideological orientation and the great weight he attached to Party unity. The revelations of Chen Yun and Deng Xiaoping apparently forced that choice.[80] It is by no means clear what reprimand Mao had in mind for Gao at this stage, but some sanction seemed inevitable. As events unfolded throughout December, the stage was set for Gao's exposure while Gao himself continued his activities unabated. The collision was unavoidable, and by the end of 1953 Gao Gang's political endeavor had collapsed, although it would take more than a year before the case was finally put to rest.

5
THE RESOLUTION OF THE GAO GANG AFFAIR
December 1953 and After

WITH MAO apparently having made up his mind to rebuff Gao Gang by late November or early December, events in December saw Gao continuing his "conspiratorial" efforts to denigrate Liu Shaoqi and build support for himself. Significantly, in view of the issue of whether there actually was an "alliance," there is little sign of Rao Shushi in accounts of the December developments, just as he did not appear to be involved in the previous months' lobbying of top leaders. Meanwhile, Mao secretly carried out investigations and made preparations both to inform key Party leaders of his intentions and to set the stage for Gao's exposure. The context was a series of Politburo meetings starting in early or mid-December that focused on the issues of Party and government reorganization and the attendant questions of power already raised in the latter part of 1952 and subject to discussion throughout 1953: the nature of the state system under the projected new constitution, whether the Party should have vice-chairmen and/or a general secretary, the personnel arrangements required by the state constitution and by convening the Eighth Party Congress, and the implications of Mao's proposal to divide the leadership into "two fronts." Linked to this was the more immediate issue of Mao's proposed holiday and who should take over as acting chairman in his absence.

Such questions of power rather than policy were at the heart of leadership politics in December 1953. Unfortunately, the details of this period are even less accessible than those concerning earlier developments in this elusive case. If we leave aside events such as Gao's approach to Luo Ronghuan, which I have treated as happening earlier but which may have taken place in December, memoir and related literature bearing on the December events is almost nonexistent apart from the recollections of Luo Ruiqing's daughter. We are reliant to a greater than usual extent on the pat accounts of formal Party histories. Oral sources are still of considerable help but somewhat less than usual; their knowledge of the events is restricted in some key respects.

Nevertheless, what is almost certain is that an enlarged Politburo meeting[1] on December 24 was the moment when Mao, for the first time, directly confronted Gao Gang and Gao's plans came completely unstuck. Here too, little is known of the content of this crucial meeting apart from a brief account offered by Mao when he discussed the case in March 1955 and the somewhat confused memoir of Luo Ruiqing's daughter, and the record of the meeting remains closed to high-ranking scholars in the PRC. But, while little information is available on exactly what happened on December 24, it is reasonably clear that important issues concerning the ultimate fate of Gao Gang and Rao Shushi, the extent of the involvement of others, and precisely how the affair would be handled within the Party were left unsettled. These matters would only gradually be dealt with, first at the February 1954 Fourth Plenum and the subsequent special discussion meetings separately investigating Gao and Rao, then at various local meetings over the following months, and finally at the March 1955 National Party Conference. Even then there were further ramifications of the Gao-Rao affair over the subsequent years.

The December Events

As during the Financial and Economic and Organization conferences, Gao Gang assertedly furthered his aims both openly at the Politburo sessions and secretly "behind the back of the Center."[2] Precisely what happened openly and what took place behind Mao's back is not always clear, nor is it completely clear what transpired at the December 24 meeting as opposed to the Politburo sessions earlier in the month. Despite this uncertainty, it is clear that unlike the earlier conferences when Mao's ambiguous posture most likely reflected an incomplete awareness of Gao's activities, an as yet undetermined judgment concerning the pluses and minuses of his ideologically sympathetic but overly ambitious friend, and, in the case of the Organization Conference, the restraint urged on the Chairman by Zhou Enlai, now Mao was acting in a deliberate manner to mask his intention of turning on Gao Gang. According to his daughter, Luo Ruiqing gained a deeper understanding of Mao from those developments, of how the Chairman "devised strategies" and "by remaining calm and collected forced his opponent into an obvious disadvantage."[3] This disadvantage would come in the form of Gao overreaching himself at and outside Politburo meetings then under way.

Gao had reportedly been advancing his claims for the positions of Party vice-chairman or general secretary and premier of a reorganized state apparatus at least since his trip south and return to Beijing,[4] and he now assertedly became particularly active in lobbying for that outcome. But the issue that drew Gao into a vulnerable position within the Party, and one on which he was arguably set up by Mao,[5] concerned not the basic issues of institutional structure and personnel assignments being considered throughout 1953, but the specific question of Mao's holiday. This, however, was related to the more fundamental structural issue of the "two fronts." As indicated in chapter 1, Mao had raised the "two fronts" idea in the second half of 1952, but he had made no concrete proposal before December

1953. Mao had, however, spoken privately to Liu Shaoqi on several occasions about the possibility of organizing "two fronts" and asked him to head the "first front." With the broader institutional questions under renewed discussion, Mao seemingly again placed the "two fronts" near the top of the agenda.[6] Gao Gang allegedly saw this as an opportunity to seize power on the "first front" in charge of everyday affairs while leaving Mao empty handed on the "second front,"[7] but of course Gao's key aim was that he and not Liu Shaoqi would be preeminent on the "first front."

Several factors apparently influenced Mao in suggesting this new leadership structure. First, there was the question of his poor but not threatening health, something well known within the top leadership even though Cultural Revolution claims of a letter by Gao-Rao supporters asking the Chairman to "take a rest" are questionable.[8] Mao had been in bad health periodically since 1946, and now in 1953 had suffered from dizzy spells related to overwork and circulatory problems.[9] In this situation Liu presided over routine work for much of 1953 even though Mao remained at his post, circumstances that perhaps contributed to Mao's displeasure over Liu's handling of documents.[10] Mao, in any case, wanted relief from his taxing schedule. Apart from health issues, he reportedly particularly hated the routine task of receiving diplomatic credentials and suggested that the head of a Supreme Soviet type body, that is, what turned out to be the NPC Standing Committee in the institutional setup introduced in 1954, take over those duties.[11] Mao saw the "two fronts" arrangement as an opportunity to devote his energies to what really interested him, especially theoretical issues. Unlike later developments with the "two fronts" where Mao was notionally attempting to prepare for an orderly succession, no question of ceding real power was involved.[12] According to an authoritative oral source, it was simply a question of easing Mao's administrative burdens.

Mao again raised the matter with Liu in December 1953 and suggested that he take charge of the "first front," a clear indication of confidence in Liu notwithstanding the various oblique criticisms of the Chairman's statements throughout 1953. Liu, an authoritative oral source reports, argued against the type of arrangement Mao proposed on the grounds that the Chairman's leadership was required as the new China had just recently been established. But to ease Mao's burden concerning Party work, Liu suggested appointing Deng Xiaoping as secretary-general (*mishuzhang*) to assist with CCP affairs, and this proposal was accepted.[13] Whether this was a grateful Liu who knew of Deng's refusal to back Gao Gang at this point, whether his nomination of Deng was simply a shrewd recognition of the close personal ties of Mao and Deng, or even whether Deng's rejection of Gao possibly reflected an awareness of Liu's proposal remains unclear.[14] In the event, these arrangements behind Gao Gang's back further set the stage for Gao's comeuppance.

Related to the "two fronts" question were Mao's plans for a holiday. Those plans, according to an oral source, were under way before the Gao Gang affair came to a head. As with the "two fronts," Mao's health and the need to ease his burdens were at issue. Also involved, according to oral sources, was Mao's desire to ponder issues concerning the new constitution and state structure away from the pressures of the capital, and to carry out investigation and research on various policy issues.[15] But in the context of Mao's changed attitude toward Gao Gang by November–December, the arrangements for Party leadership in Mao's absence took on a pointed political meaning since these plans called for Liu Shaoqi to take over control of the Central Committee as acting chairman. Like the "two fronts" scheme, they not only suggested Mao's confidence in Liu but represented a distinct threat to Gao's plans. In the view of informed oral sources, Gao would have been encouraged to oppose this arrangement both by the results of his lobbying efforts and by the fear that his opportunity might pass if he did not act against Liu in the immediate circumstances.

The sequence of fateful events was set off when Mao proposed to one of the December Politburo sessions that while he was on holiday Liu should, "according to convention," take over the work of the Party Center in his absence. By this proposal Mao referred to the established practice dating back to the Chongqing negotiations in 1945 that when Mao was absent on work assignment, ill, or on holidays, Liu as number two in the Party would be responsible for overall CCP affairs. It is my assumption that Mao raised this matter in a routine manner, perhaps even in question form.[16] For, according to Party histories, Gao Gang, who had earlier apparently suffered in silence when Mao approved Chen Yun's suggestion concerning limiting the tasks of the SPC, and who had kept his peace when Mao sanctioned a peaceful approach to the transformation of the bourgeoisie which he opposed, now immediately objected to the Chairman's "proposal."[17] In the ensuing discussion Gao reportedly made a counterproposal that leadership should be exercised by rotation. The details of this plan—how long the rotating periods of leadership would be and who would be eligible to fill the role—are unclear. If, as one oral source speculated, leadership was to rotate among members of the Secretariat, Gao himself would be excluded from the rotation and Zhou Enlai would be included, but such an arrangement would at least have the advantage of reducing Liu's status.

In any case, according to oral sources, support for Gao's proposal came from a surprising source—Zhu De.[18] Zhu's support is surprising as he had not been one of those approached by Gao and was regarded as a generous and open-minded man who never tried to grasp for power; one source who worked closely with Zhu at another time attributed it to Zhu being a political innocent who did not have a clear idea of Mao's thinking.[19] If, as this view suggests, Zhu was unaware of Mao's new disposition toward Gao Gang, it would be yet another case of a key leader being uncertain of Mao's aims. Although Zhu had been involved along with Liu and Deng in the effort to hose down Rao Shushi's activities at the Organization Conference, he was now apparently willing to countenance a move by Gao Gang in the face of what assertedly was Mao's formal position. While the charitable interpretation is that Zhu naively thought the rotation proposal a legitimate one for consideration, and a less charitable explanation would be that he bore some hidden grudge against Liu, the one conclusion that does seem reasonable is that he was unconvinced of the seriousness of Mao's support for Liu taking over in his absence on this occasion.

Whatever was said in the Politburo following Mao's proposal, Gao was apparently stimulated into frantic action behind the scenes. Now he assertedly demanded that he be appointed a Party vice-chairman or general secretary (*zong shuji*—a much weightier post than *mishuzhang*), and that a new election for premier be held so that he could take over that post as well.[20] Gao's lobbying reportedly also brought up the idea of a leading post for Lin Biao in a Council of Ministers system. According to the fascinating if apparently confused account of Luo Ruiqing's daughter, it seems that on the evening of this meeting Gao phoned Luo, saying he wanted to drop by for a visit. Luo responded that he would go to Gao's house instead, phoned Mao for instructions, and then went to see Gao to learn what he had to say, as instructed by the Chairman. When Luo arrived, Gao proposed that Lin Biao be head of a Council of Ministers if there were to be one and urged Luo to take good care of the Chairman's health. Luo extracted himself from the situation by saying he would look after Mao but could not agree on the Council of Ministers as Lin Biao was not in the best of health.[21] Undoubtedly other such inconclusive approaches took place at this time, including perhaps the similar meeting with Luo Ronghuan discussed in the previous chapter.

As before, Mao seemingly did not criticize Gao for his actions during the first three weeks of December. This time, however, Mao had presumably made up his mind but let Gao go on and incriminate himself. According to oral sources, before the December 24 meeting Mao had already called for the organization of the Fourth Plenum to deal with Gao and Rao, and the Secretariat had informally decided that Liu would indeed take over in Mao's absence. These developments, however, were kept from Gao Gang. In public he retained his high rank of sixth in the leadership, just outside the Secretariat.[22] And according to Mao's own account, on December 23 Gao tried for a second time to secure Mao's protection for Rao Shushi,[23] apparently unaware of the Chairman's intentions. The fact of seeking protection for Rao indicated that Rao was still in bad odor from the Organization Conference, but that Gao would still go to Mao also suggests at least some confidence at this late date in the Chairman's support, notwithstanding Mao's proposal that Liu serve as acting chairman.

The December 24 Politburo Meeting

It was only at the enlarged Politburo meeting on December 24 that Mao finally confronted Gao Gang. This meeting reportedly was the first step in exposing and putting a stop to the activities of Gao and Rao, but it also had the declared function of trying to save them.[24] Mao now criticized the rotation proposal, formally decided on Liu's acting role, and revealed Gao and Rao's various sins. As recalled by the Chairman fifteen months later, the essence of Mao's attack, and the core of his own defense, was that Gao and Rao had behaved in a planned conspiratorial manner unknown to him: "I said there were two headquarters in Beijing. One was . . . led by me; we blew a positive wind and lit a positive fire. The other was a headquarters commanded by someone else; it blew a sinister wind and lit a sinister fire and was operating underground."[25] Charging that their aim of "knocking down a group of people" was a threat to Party unity, Mao both issued a "serious warning" (*yanzhong jinggao*) to Gao and Rao and proposed a draft resolution on strengthening Party unity. When the Chairman demanded to know whether those present agreed with his views, Gao reportedly turned red in the face and unnaturally muttered his assent. Thus, the key consequence of Mao's denunciation was that the challenge of Gao and Rao was finished. The draft resolution was "unanimously" endorsed by the Politburo, all Central Committee members in Beijing lent their support to the anti-Gao cause, no one else was "dragged in," and those key leaders like Lin Biao and Peng Dehuai who had earlier dallied now openly disassociated themselves from Gao and Rao.[26] Mao had spoken and the "conspiracy" collapsed; all that was left was mopping up.

From the Fourth Plenum to the National Party Conference: Handling the Gao-Rao Affair

While the main political issue was settled on December 24—Gao and Rao would not succeed in their aims and they would have to suffer some as yet undefined setbacks to their careers—the mopping up of the affair involved a number of complex issues. All of these issues would relate to the principle of Party unity which Mao had reaffirmed, for the third time at a major Party meeting in 1953, on the 24th. Now the overriding political problem was how to restore as much inner-Party harmony as possible after all the maneuvering and factional tensions of 1953. This involved, first, the disposal of Gao and Rao themselves. Would they still have a leadership role to play? What degree of self-criticism would they be required to undertake to salvage something from their careers? How would they respond to this challenge?

A second major issue concerned who else was involved and how they would be treated. This would require the investigation of facts and involve difficult political choices concerning how much to own up to for those who had been involved in the affair to one degree or another.[27] It would necessitate such decisions as: Who would be basically absolved from culpability, as was the case with Lin Biao and Peng Dehuai? Who would be denounced as core members of the "conspiratorial clique" and on what criteria? Finally, it was necessary to address Party unity in broader terms, to deal with the larger "factional" issues stirred up by Gao Gang throughout 1953. This again drew attention to the personnel questions raised by a new state structure and the Eighth Party Congress. How could the discontent of the military stimulated by Gao's representation of An Ziwen's list be calmed? Could a satisfactory balance of groupings be sustained? Who would receive the key positions of power in the new Party-state structure?

These issues were dealt with over a number of stages between early 1954 and the Eighth Party Congress, which was finally convened in September 1956. First, the Fourth Plenum itself in February 1954 attempted to deal with Gao and Rao. This was not totally successful, and following the plenum two special discussion meetings were convened, one to deal with "the Gao Gang problem," the other to handle "the Rao Shushi problem." These meetings involved not only attacking and exposing Gao and Rao—apparently an experience of sufficient intensity to contribute to Gao Gang's first, unsuccessful suicide attempt—but also the investigation of the involvement of others. Over the following months, lasting until summer 1954, various regional meetings were held to blacken the reputations of Gao and Rao, who had by now shown themselves unwilling to make the required admissions of guilt, and to check further on the participation of others in their activities. In September–October 1954 the NPC was convened and a new state structure introduced, and the first post–Gao Gang "factional" balancing took place in the assignment of government posts. Then, in March 1955, after more than a year of investigations, Gao and Rao were expelled from the Party and a small group of comparatively low-ranking officials were labeled as members of their "clique" as the case was formally wound up. Finally, the Eighth Party Congress in September–October 1956 saw the "factional" balancing act applied to the new Party leadership.

The Fourth Plenum, February 6–10, 1954

As indicated above, Mao had begun to make preparations for the Fourth Plenum even before December 24. According to the biography of An Ziwen, Mao left Beijing for Hangzhou after "deploying [forces]" for the plenum and carried out the work of publicizing the Gao-Rao affair and strengthening Party unity while outside the capital, thus adding a critical new purpose for his "holiday."[28] The key preparation was to entrust Liu Shaoqi with management of the plenum. By this step, an authoritative oral source confirms, Mao not only carried out his previously made plans for a holiday but deliberately underlined Liu's position as the second-ranking leader in the CCP.

If the intent behind Mao's actions in 1953 had been to knock Liu down a peg, the result of the Gao Gang affair had quite the opposite effect. Even if he had never intended to raise doubts about Liu's status, events had forced a significant reaffirmation of Liu's position as the Chairman's successor, which may or may not have been in the cards otherwise.[29] Nevertheless, this reaffirmation was not at the expense of Mao's authority as the ultimate leader. In case anyone had any doubts, Gao Gang's defeat on the issue of Party unity did not absolve Liu or other leaders on questions of ideological propriety. Liu not only admitted to mistakes in work including some bourgeois thought on behalf of the Politburo in his formal report to the plenum, he also engaged in self-criticism on at least two of the issues that most upset Mao at the time of his private talks with Gao Gang, and which Gao used against Liu in 1953—the 1949 Tianjin talks and the 1951 Shanxi cooperatives question. In addition, Liu made a self-criticism concerning the 1951 trade union issue on which he had directly clashed with Gao. Liu's political status had been secured for the time being, but the Chairman still had the power to define his subordinate's theoretical errors.[30]

If there was little ambiguity concerning Liu's position as of early 1954, the precise fate of Gao Gang and Rao Shushi was still in the balance. All available evidence indicates that while it was unclear exactly what they had to do, a way was provided for Gao and Rao to retain some position in the leadership and thus help bind their particular followings to the cause of Party unity. Clearly, they would have to make a clean breast of their activities, and Mao apparently had set something of a test for them in this regard. According to an authoritative oral source, in his December 24 broadside Mao did not reveal all that he knew. Thus, both the formal requirements of rectification principles for owning up to one's mistakes and the crucial political need to satisfy Mao that they were willing to turn over a new leaf were at issue.

This account of a reform emphasis is not simply derived from the assertions of post-Mao sources. It is also based on what we know of actual developments before and during the plenum. First, Mao's draft resolution on Party unity gave pride of place to carrying out rectification principles for those comrades who "are willing to mend their ways and actually make amends"; only secondly did it deal with the need for struggle against unrepentant factionalists.[31] Second, Gao and Rao were not disgraced in public, nor did they immediately disappear. On the day after the December 24 meeting Gao went to Anshan to preside at the launching ceremonies for three Soviet-assisted projects at the Anshan Iron and Steel Company,[32] and he continued to make public appearances until January 20, when, ironically, he was listed in his normal position just after Chen Yun at a rally addressed by Liu Shaoqi.[33] During the plenum itself, moreover, Gao and Rao still retained their status on the evidence of a group photograph of the participants.[34]

As a third indication of potential leniency, there apparently was a studied avoidance of naming names in the speeches delivered at the plenum attacking behavior threatening Party unity. Indeed, the available partial texts of the report by Liu at the start of the plenum and the speeches by Zhou Enlai and Chen Yun delivered on the last day not only avoid names but, in the cases of Liu and Zhou, address the questions at issue through stilted formulas. Only Chen Yun rose

Fourth Plenum of the Seventh Central Committee, February 1954
From left, first row: Xu Teli, Gao Gang, Dong Biwu, Zhou Enlai, Liu Shaoqi, Zhu De, Chen Yun, Zhang Wentian, Peng Dehuai, Wu Yuzhang, and Peng Zhen.
Second row, fourth from left is almost certainly Rao Shushi; eleventh from left is Deng Xiaoping.

above the banal with an apparent reference to Gao's stubbornness ("it is never easy for a water buffalo to make a turn"), an acknowledgment of Mao's crucial role which made it possible to deal with the problem "more easily and sooner," and an argument that as Mao was mortal, special measures were necessary to guard against such cases in the future.[35] While Gao and Rao clearly were confronted at the plenum, even as it ended there was apparent reluctance to take the significant step of naming Gao Gang and Rao Shushi in formal addresses to the Central Committee.

But the most persuasive evidence that a way out existed for Gao and Rao comes from oral sources. In part this is opinion. Thus, one very well-placed source assumes that if Gao had admitted errors and had taken back the theory of the two parties of the base areas and "white areas" it would have been possible for him to continue to work. Even more significant is a report of Mao's own attitudes, at least as claimed by the Chairman ex post facto. According to an authoritative source, when Mikoyan visited Mao in Qingdao in 1957 to seek support for Khrushchev's move against the so-called anti-Party group in the Soviet Union,[36] Mao offered China's support but suggested mild measures in dealing with the oppositionists. By way of example, the Chairman told Mikoyan that he would have kept Gao Gang on the Central Committee and sent him to work in his old bailiwick in the Northwest, and expressed remorse that he had not spoken about this to Gao after the December Politburo meeting to stabilize Gao's mood and thus prevent his suicide attempts, which ultimately succeeded in August 1954.

All of the above suggests claims that Gao and Rao were offered "many opportunities for a fresh start"[37] during and after the Fourth Plenum have considerable validity. Further evidence of a rectification approach is provided by oral sources, who claim that at the plenum Party leaders focused on self-criticism rather than attacking others. In addition to Liu Shaoqi, a case in point was Peng Zhen, who related to these sources that because of Mao's call for self-criticism he did not air his old grudge against Gao Gang but instead admonished himself for quarreling with Lin Biao in the post-1945 Northeast.[38] But such evidence notwithstanding, the claims of post-Mao sources, both written and oral, that the plenum's emphasis was on unity and its conduct low key are not fully persuasive, for several reasons.

First, two groups of people were under considerable pressure at the Central Committee meeting—those who had been approached by Gao Gang, and Gao, Rao, and their close followers. All of those who had been lobbied by Gao, oral sources report, were required to make a self-examination on this point. Since only Chen Yun, Deng Xiaoping, and Huang Kecheng had reported before Gao's disgrace, this left some uncomfortable questions for the substantial number of others approached by Gao.[39] Some stayed away on the excuse of ill health, including Luo Ronghuan, who sent a written report, and seemingly Lin Biao, who remained in Guangzhou;[40] Peng Dehuai attended and undoubtedly was one of the forty-four leaders making "important speeches." Presumably this was the occasion when, according to the resolution on Peng's case at Lushan five years later, Peng and Huang Kecheng made an "ostensible" self-criticism that allegedly concealed important facts about their participation in the activities of Gao and Rao.[41] But whatever pressure these figures were under, the situation was clearly worse for Gao and Rao. They undoubtedly were held to stricter standards in their self-examinations, and assertedly neither responded adequately. Gao reportedly only made a superficial self-criticism and Rao a vague self-examination, and they both were judged to have failed to express genuine repentance.[42]

Another cause for a degree of skepticism concerning the benign picture of the Fourth Plenum is the tough rhetoric it produced. Although both Liu's report and the resolution on strengthening Party unity gave prior mention to the rectification of errors over merciless struggle against those intentionally damaging unity,[43] only Zhou Enlai's speech had an overall conciliatory gloss as befit his moderate image.[44] Liu's report and the resolution included a harsh Stalinist outlook ironically not incompatible with Gao Gang's apparent views: in a period of socialist transformation and imperialist encirclement, domestic and foreign enemies seek to sabotage the revolutionary cause first and foremost by undermining Party unity through agents within the Party itself. In addition, these documents cited a sinister rogue's gallery of Trotsky, Bukharin, Chen Duxiu, Zhang Guotao, and Beria as the type of people who threatened Party unity.[45] Chen Yun, moreover, began by speaking of past splits in the Party and emphasized the need to be vigilant against future splits, came close to naming Gao by referring to that comrade carrying the burden of [the self-label of always being] "correct," and repeatedly compared the unnamed Gao to one of the greatest renegades in CCP history, Zhang Guotao.[46] Finally, a *People's Daily* editorial declared that the plenum adopted rules for inner-Party struggle based on the same concluding section of the Stalinist *Short Course* that Mao had singled out during the previous fall's Organization Conference.[47]

Thus, the contrast between Mao's apparent objectives—Party unity, self-criticism, keeping the temperature of proceedings under control—and Stalinist rhetoric again surfaced. As earlier, one suspects that a certain reflex action in searching for appropriate ideological formulations at a moment of considerable intraelite tension and the Chairman's own uncertainty vis-à-vis Soviet orthodoxy came into play. Nevertheless, the use of such rhetoric at a time when Mao had *clearly* targeted the political losers of the previous year's conflict could only add to the tension and the discomfort of Gao, Rao, and their followers. While it may be, as oral sources assert, that a fierce struggle was avoided at the Fourth Plenum, the position of Gao and Rao was precarious as the meeting came to a close. This general situation, and particularly the unsatisfactory nature of their responses to the self-criticism ritual, apparently contributed to the decision to hold separate discussion meetings to probe more deeply into the cases of both leaders.

The Discussion Meetings on Gao and Rao, February 15-25, 1954

With Gao Gang and Rao Shushi refusing to admit serious fault and the roles of others still unclear, discussion meetings (*zuotanhui*) were convened in mid-February in Beijing to verify facts, check what had been claimed in statements made at the plenum, and listen to the explanations of Gao and Rao, on the one hand, and to continue to expose them, on the other. While Gao and Rao themselves and various top leaders attended, the participants were mainly lower-ranking officials who had worked with the two principals at the Center and in their respective regions. Fact finding was clearly in order, but a negative finding to at least some degree was undoubtedly preordained. The meeting on Gao Gang was chaired by Zhou Enlai, who gave a summing up speech on February 24 or 25, while Gao reportedly made a self-criticism on the 24th, which only admitted that he was against "certain leading Central Committee comrades" and had engaged in illicit factional activities but assertedly touched lightly on the fact that his mistakes might split the Party if they were further developed. The choice of Zhou to chair this meeting might be explained by several factors: as a member of the Secretariat he had been deeply involved in the investigations conducted since Chen Yun and Deng Xiaoping reported to Mao; he was one of Gao's main targets of attack; and he had most likely been in charge of the Financial and Economic Conference where Gao's activities first surfaced.[48]

Over the same period the separate meeting dealing with Rao Shushi was held under the joint leadership of Deng Xiaoping, Chen Yi, and Tan Zhenlin. Deng was clearly a logical choice for such a responsibility given both his involvement in breaking the case and the subsequent investigations, and his major troubleshooting role during the Organization Conference where Rao's activities so badly backfired. Chen and Tan were undoubtedly assigned their tasks as leading East China officials who should have been in a position to uncover Rao's activities in his regional base. Moreover, given Chen Yi's history of bad relations with Rao, he could presumably be relied on to take a sufficiently critical stance, while there are suggestions that Tan may also have had poor past relations with Rao. In Tan's case, however, the situation is muddied by Cultural Revolution allegations that he had been deeply involved in Gao-Rao activities at the time of the Financial and Economic Conference.[49] Whatever the truth of those specific charges, and on balance they are unpersuasive, Tan's career ties were strongly to both Deng and Chen Yi rather than to Rao.[50]

In any case, the outcome of the discussion meeting on Rao was similar to that of the Gao meeting. Rao's efforts at self-examination were again judged inadequate; his preliminary self-criticism at the meeting reportedly touched on light points but dodged serious problems, while a written self-examination after the meeting admitted some facts but assertedly avoided many crucial problems. Although acknowledging various past shortcomings, Rao refused to accept fully errors starting with the Financial and Economic Conference and particularly concerning his involvement in Gao Gang's activities, a position that was credible to many of the participants. It was not, however, acceptable to those in charge. On March 1, 1954, Deng, Chen, and Tan submitted a report to the Center on the results of meeting that emphasized Rao's long-term character defects as an inveterate factionalist and a typical hypocrite, and also alleged his role as Gao's "accomplice."[51]

The key accusations to come out of the discussion meetings, however, were those outlined in Zhou Enlai's February 24 or 25 indictment of Gao Gang's errors. Many of these charges became the standard pieces of both the press campaign against unnamed factionalists in the months after the plenum and the propaganda against Gao and Rao after the 1955 Party conference, while a few that were not aired publicly touched on particularly sensitive issues. Zhou's list of "conspiratorial" activities included such prominent features of future public denunciation and important aspects of Gao's actual 1953 maneuvers as the effort to split military and "white area" cadres; carrying out sectarian activities and spreading the mistakes of central leaders in order to build an alliance against Liu Shaoqi; spreading rumors especially concerning An Ziwen's list to create discord within the Party; his demand to be made Party vice-chairman and premier; the conduct of a factional cadre policy using lavish promises to broaden his influence; and plagiarizing the work of others to laud himself.[52]

But two other charges Zhou laid against Gao—that he had built an "independent kingdom" in the Northeast and had "mixed up right and wrong in foreign relations"—were not central features of his 1953 activities. Rather, oral sources believe, they were matters that, like Gao's reputed dictatorial work practices, his decadent life style centering on a notorious attraction to the opposite sex, or Rao's old clashes with Chen Yi, came to prominence only once Gao and Rao were placed under the spotlight. Such issues served a useful function in denigrating Gao and activating anger against him. With regard to "independent kingdoms," leaders such as Lin Feng in the Northeast, who had effectively been cut off from real power, could now savor the new situation.[53] But "independent kingdoms" were a broader phenomenon of the Chinese political system in the early 1950s than simply a failing of Gao Gang. Mao's criticism of decentralism and "independent kingdoms" at the summer 1953 Financial and Economic Conference had been aimed at least as much at Bo Yibo as Gao Gang,[54] and in the months after February 1954 press attacks were launched against "independent kingdoms" and related bureaucratic deviations affecting the entire Party and state structure.[55] Thus the situation and the issue were used both to address endemic structural problems and to discredit Gao. Nevertheless, there is also evidence that at least *after* his fall from grace, Gao's activities generated concern about the regional administrative setups. Thus the regional Party organs were abolished in April 1954 on the same day that Deng Xiaoping became CCP secretary-general, and the government and military organs at the great region level followed suit over the next year.[56] Subsequently, Mao also linked this development to Gao Gang,[57] but given the long process of centralization that began well before the Gao-Rao affair, it is most likely that affair's only impact on the fading away of the regions concerned its timing.

Similarly, Zhou Enlai's accusation that Gao had "mixed up right and wrong" in foreign relations in a way disadvantageous to Sino-Soviet unity pointed to an issue that could stir indignation against Gao but did not deal with a major aspect of his "conspiracy." Unlike the "independent kingdoms" question, since this dealt with the crucial foreign policy issue of Sino-Soviet relations it remained unmentioned in public discussion. In chapter 1 a number of reasons were given as to why the Soviet connection was not vital; developments at the discussion meetings further support this conclusion. The charge itself suggests a fairly limited concern, namely, by his conversations with Soviet officials concerning the CCP's internal affairs, Gao complicated the conduct of Chinese foreign policy. Very well-placed oral sources report that no evidence of Soviet interference in CCP affairs was uncovered, nor were Gao's Soviet ties regarded as traitorous or illicit.[58] Furthermore, these sources are not aware of Mao making a big issue out of the relationship.

Indeed, it was only in the process of dealing with the Gao-Rao affair that rules were drawn up to govern the exchange of information with Soviet officials. Earlier, going back to 1945 when, with Mao's knowledge, the Soviet Communist Party established direct links with the CCP's Northeast Party Bureau, there were no guidelines for Sino-Soviet contacts. Now the Central Committee informed Party members that if any information had been given to Soviet representatives in the past it was not a matter of great concern, but if information had been passed on recently it must be reported, and in the future anything to do with the Soviet Union must go through the Central Committee. As one oral source put it, Mao and others *now* became very sensitive to this matter. Thus, Gao Gang's Soviet ties brought about a tightening up of procedures for dealing with the Soviet ally, but those ties themselves were not a significant factor in Gao's fall. But what the raising of this question did produce, according to an authoritative source, was a general sense within leadership circles that denigrating Liu and Zhou to the Soviets was improper, if not illegal, and thus contributed to the further blackening of Gao Gang's reputation.

Finally, Zhou Enlai touched upon the most sensitive issue of all, one that would not be mentioned publicly at the time and only most obliquely to this day, the question of the Mao-Gao relationship. By charging Gao with "fabricating Comrade Mao Zedong's words" and "falsely using the name of the Center" to spread slanderous rumors and lower the prestige of the Center,[59] Zhou undoubtedly was referring to Gao using and allegedly distorting Mao's private critical comments concerning Liu and Zhou to suggest that his efforts to displace these leaders had the Chairman's blessing. The fact that such "rumors" had a degree of credibility in the context of 1953 given both Gao's perceived closeness to Mao and Mao's known displeasure with Zhou over Bo Yibo's tax system and with Liu on a number of issues, had surely been the key factor in some leaders lending support to Gao and in causing others to temporize. Now Gao stood damned for assertedly having misrepresented the Chairman.

Facing such charges, even before Zhou's summary, Gao attempted suicide during the discussion meetings.[60] The degree to which this act reflected pressure that was perhaps greater than at the plenum,[61] a hot-headed, unsophisticated personality, a sense of profound betrayal by Mao, or some combination of these and other factors cannot, of course, be known. Oral sources, however, place great weight on Gao's distraught state of mind due to his dismay that, contrary to all his expectations, he did not have Mao's backing. According to one of his secretaries at the time, as relayed by an oral source, Gao was extremely upset and would not discuss "things which could not be revealed"—presumably his fateful 1952–53 conversations with the Chairman. Throughout this period Gao reportedly made many attempts to talk to Mao but was always rebuffed, thus perhaps giving rise to the remorse Mao expressed to Mikoyan three years later.[62] But whatever the reason, by the attempted suicide Gao placed himself further outside the path of possible redemption, and when he finally succeeded in poisoning himself in August 1954 it was regarded as "an expression of his ultimate betrayal of the Party."[63]

Local Party Conferences and the National Party Conference, March 1954–March 1955

With Gao and Rao having failed to redeem themselves at the Fourth Plenum and subsequent discussion meetings, it was necessary to spread further word of their predicament and undercut their reputations at lower levels of the Party, particularly in their regional power bases of the Northeast and East China. Mao had already laid some of the groundwork for this during his "holiday," and now in the last days of February Zhou Enlai was dispatched to Shenyang, where he gave a marathon fifteen-hour speech detailing the perfidious deeds of Gao Gang.[64] Starting in late March and lasting into the summer, a series of regional, provincial, and municipal conferences were held, initially in the Northeast, again under the guidance of Zhou Enlai, and then throughout the country. These meetings continued to undermine the prestige of Gao and Rao, but they also had the further function of investigating the involvement of others and defining the scope of disciplinary action to be taken.[65]

Despite the thorough attack on Gao and Rao, the rectification policy of "cure the sickness to save the patient" was consistently advocated and practiced during the investigations and in determining sanctions at both the local meetings and the National Party Conference in March 1955, which formally wound up the case. As Deng Xiaoping put it in 1980: "the Gao-Rao case was handled rather leniently. Hardly anyone was hurt. In fact, care was taken to protect a number of cadres."[66] The scope of the struggle was limited, and few disciplinary sanctions were handed out; according to an oral source, only about twenty officials received some form of punishment. Apart from Rao himself, and Gao posthumously, even those publicly identified as members of the "Gao-Rao clique" in 1955 (see table 4) retained their Party membership and were assigned new, if reduced responsibilities.[67]

During the local meetings various leaders were apparently let off on grounds similar to Lin Biao and Peng Dehuai, who had successfully claimed they had been cheated by Gao Gang into believing he had Mao's backing. This was certainly the case with Tao Zhu, who made a self-examination to the Guangdong provincial Party committee.[68] It may also have been the case, although by no means certainly, with Shanghai leaders Chen Peixian, Pan Hannian, and Gu Mu, who made "strict self-criticisms" during the East China meetings held under the auspices of Chen Yi and Tan Zhenlin,[69] but Pan was not out of the woods, as will be seen. Even in the Northeast where the regional meeting was apparently particularly tense, the extent of those actually punished was quite limited. This and other aspects of the process are illustrated in table 4, which lists those punished at the March 1955 conference as members of the "Gao-Rao anti-Party alliance," together with several others who definitely suffered although they were not formally named.[70]

What is striking about the officials listed in table 4 is not only their concentration in the Northeast and East China, but their relatively low status. This is particularly apparent if one considers the leading Northeast cadres involved who, although having a virtual stranglehold on the key positions within the Northeast Party Bureau, were still of comparative low rank in the Party as a whole. In contrast to Bureau Second Secretary Lin Feng, who had assertedly been frozen out of real power by Gao, and to leading regional figures in all other regions, none of these men held Central Committee or even alternate Central Committee rank. This undoubtedly reflected the historical pattern of the Chinese revolution whereby the high-ranking leaders who had come to the Northeast in 1945 almost all went south with the victorious army of Lin Biao in 1948–49 or moved on to key posts in Beijing shortly after 1949. But it seemingly also reflected Gao's "factional cadre policy," his desire for a dominant position secured through patronage. The effect was to place in key regional posts lesser figures of limited prestige, figures who were even more beholden to the top regional figure—Gao Gang—than was normally the case.[71]

A key example of the above is Ma Hong, the talented theorist who wrote many of Gao's key articles and reports, apparently including statements attacking Bo Yibo at the Financial and Economic Conference. According to an oral source, Ma Hong had been demoted during the Yan'an period for unacceptable personal behavior. Ma was then picked up by Gao as a personal secretary, and Gao subsequently took the extremely unusual step of raising Ma's cadre ranking by three grades over a two-to-three-year period.[72] Thus Ma was tied to Gao by exceptionally strong patronage bonds; conversely, he was in no position to resist

Gao's demands for participation in the "conspiracy." A similar if less dramatic situation, perhaps reinforced by old revolutionary ties,[73] probably also existed for the other officials intimately entangled in the activities of Gao and Rao. When Rao asked people of the rank of Xiang Ming or Lai Keke to participate in the attacks on An Ziwen, they did not have much scope to refuse.[74] They did not have sufficient status to allow them to temporize when approached, or to escape serious repercussions when their involvement was finally revealed. It was undoubtedly a recognition of their plight that helps explain the still lenient treatment most of the concerned officials received in March 1955.

Rao Shushi and the Case of Pan Hannian and Yang Fan

If recognition of the dynamics of leadership interaction and the general priority given to leadership unity explain the overall leniency apparent in handling the Gao-Rao case, other features of Chinese politics were involved in the cases of those who were not leniently dealt with—Rao himself, Pan Hannian, and Yang Fan. While Rao's political disgrace is most likely explained by his apparent refusal to confess his alleged misdeeds, he was also arrested in April 1955, languished in jail until August 1965 when he was sentenced to fourteen years imprisonment but paroled the following month, again placed "under examination" during the Cultural Revolution, and finally expired in 1975.[75] Meanwhile, Shanghai First Deputy Secretary Pan and Public Security Chief Yang had also been arrested in the same month, and they would be incarcerated until after the "Cultural Revolution decade" when their names would be finally cleared, in the case of Pan posthumously. But in spring 1955, Rao, Pan, and Yang found themselves enmeshed in criminal as well as political matters.

The story of this case is too complicated and tangential to be dealt with in full here. Briefly put, Pan's arrest and imprisonment grew out of a number of issues having to do with underground work before 1949 and security work after the founding of the PRC. Pan was accused of having been a double agent for both the Guomindang and the Japanese during the revolutionary period and, as head of Shanghai's social affairs bureau, which oversaw police work after 1949, of having infiltrated the security apparatus with Guomindang agents and having assisted in the 1950 bombing of Shanghai by Taiwan military forces. Yang was implicated by his functional role directly under Pan as well as close personal ties to Pan, and he was further vulnerable due to the enmity of Jiang Qing relating to events in Shanghai literary circles during the 1930s. The various charges against Pan and Yang became particularly salient in the context of the *sufan* campaign against hidden counterrevolutionaries, which got under way in spring 1955. There was really no convincing proof of their guilt at the time, but by the same token there was no unambiguous evidence of their innocence. According to an authoritative oral source, in the context of the *sufan* campaign and the Gao-Rao affair, Mao made

Table 4

Officials Disciplined as a Result of the Gao-Rao Affair

Official	Main early 1950s' positions	Main postdisciplining positions
(a) Members of the "Gao-Rao Anti-Party Alliance" named 3/55		
Xiang Ming	2nd Party secy Shandong Subbureau Vice-governor Shandong	Transferred to Hebei 1955 (Died 1969)
Zhang Xiushan[a]	Deputy Party secy NE Bureau Head NE organization dept	Military attaché Vietnam 1971 Military attaché Albania 1975 Deputy head State Council office of educated youth affairs 1979 Vice-chm State Agricultural Commission 1980–82
Zhang Mingyuan	3rd Deputy Party secy and secy-general NE Bureau Vice-chm NE govt	Responsible person 5th Machine Building Ministry 1970 Deputy head PLA rear services dept 1970
Zhao Dezun	Party secy and governor Heilongjiang Head NE rural work dept	Party secy Heilongjiang 1979
Ma Hong[b]	Deputy secy-general NE Bureau Member and secy-general SPC	Economic work with Bo Yibo 1961 Vice-pres and pres Chinese Academy of Social Sciences 1979–85
Guo Feng[a]	Party secy Liaoxi Deputy head NE organization dept	1st Party secy Liaoning 1980–85
Chen Bocun	2nd Party secy Port Arthur-Dairen Deputy head NE organization dept	Vice-min of Finance 1981–82
(b) Others disciplined		
Pan Hannian[c]	Deputy Party secy and vice-mayor Shanghai	(Died in prison 1977, rehabilitated 1982)
Yang Fan[c]	Head public security Shanghai	(Rehabilitated 1983)
Niu Shucai	Party secy Anhui	Vice-mayor Shanghai 1957–58 Vice-gov Hebei 1960–62 Vice-chm Hebei People's Congress 1980

Lai Keke	Head organization dept Shandong Subbureau	Head Shandong CCP industry bureau 1958 Party secy, vice-chm Revolutionary Com, deputy Party secy, and secy Zhejiang 1966–76
Han Tianshi[d]	Party secy Anshan	Party secy Yunnan 1979 Party secy Beijing University 1980

Sources: CB, no. 324, p. 5; Teiwes, Politics and Purges, pp. 179, 654; ZDRZ, 25:49–50; Xinhua Wenzhai, no. 1 (1987): 170–71; SCMP (Supplement), no. 162, p. 14; Hangzhou Ribao, August 17, 1977; Malcolm Lamb, Directory of Officials and Organisations in China, 1968–1983, Contemporary China Papers no. 17 (Canberra, 1983); Gendai Chugoku Jimmei Jiten [Modern China Biographic Dictionary] (Tokyo: Kasumiyamakai, 1982); Gongdang Wenti Yanjiu [Research on Communist Party Questions] (Taibei, June 1988), pp. 80, 83; Documents of the Thirteenth National Congress of the Communist Party of China (1987) (Beijing: Foreign Languages Press, 1987), pp. 178–80; and oral sources.

Note: Dates given incomplete regarding holding of posts; various posts too low ranking to trace.

a. Central Advisory Committee member 1982– .

b. Central Committee Alternate 1982–87.

c. Wrongly accused.

d. Central Advisory Committee member 1987– and Central Disciplinary Inspection Committee member 1982–87.

---

the final decision to keep Pan and Yang under arrest, although present-day sources insist they were in fact blameless.[76]

Ironies abound in this case. First, the history of relations between Rao, on the one hand, and Pan and Yang, on the other, was reportedly marked by sharp conflict going back to the early 1940s,[77] but in the immediate post-1949 period they shared responsibility for security matters, with Rao having direct leadership over Pan's anti–special agent work.[78] This work relationship worked against all of those concerned. When investigations were carried out in 1954 into Rao's affairs in Shanghai, the matter of Pan's deliberate use of Guomindang agents in the security organs, today explained as a device to uncover the Guomindang special agent network, was discovered and, given Rao's political disgrace, treated seriously. This issue was reportedly played upon very hard by Ke Qingshi, who became the leading Party secretary in Shanghai by 1955.[79] Apart from reflecting asserted strong leftist tendencies and ties to Jiang Qing, arguably Ke used the situation to clean out Rao's associates and solidify his own dominance over the local apparatus.[80]

Whatever the motives, the political attack on Rao had opened the security issue involving Pan and Yang as well as Rao. In turn, the security issue seemingly further influenced Mao's negative view of Rao. Thus, in an exchange of letters with Chen Yi during the March 1955 conference, Mao responded to Chen's suitably humble presentation of his draft speech attacking Rao with the observation that Rao's crime might even be worse than Gao's.[81] While Rao would, like Pan and Yang, ultimately be absolved of any criminal wrongdoing,[82] unlike his East China associates Rao's political verdict would remain unchanged. In 1955, the strong tendency in Chinese politics to paint with the same brush the associates of a fallen leader, resisted to a considerable extent in the handling of the Gao-Rao case, ironically was extended to two associates of Rao with whom he was not on particularly good terms because of the security issues involved.

This leads to another irony worth comment. Pan, and by association Yang and Rao, were vulnerable precisely because of the nether world of underground work that was Pan's revolutionary assignment—and also Rao's for part of *his* career. Such a world involved daily dealings with the enemy at great personal risk; it also involved a risk to the Party that those so assigned might themselves be double agents. In the event it was Rao who led the accusations against An Ziwen and the old organization department for lack of vigilance concerning enemy agents who had wormed their way into responsible positions through participation in such complicated work. How exquisite that the same shadowy, unprovable sins came to contribute to Rao's woes.

If the push for Party unity could not extend to Rao—who probably would have been expelled from the Party in any case because of his asserted role as "co-conspirator" with Gao and his reluctance to make an appropriate admission of guilt—and to those who were willy-nilly entrapped by the security issue, a move toward greater unity occurred at the April 1955 Fifth Plenum convened at the close of the National Party Conference. This plenum elected Lin Biao and Deng Xiaoping to the Politburo;[83] in this it continued an effort begun at the 1954 NPC to placate those upset by the developments of 1953, an effort that would reach fruition at the Eighth Party Congress.

Maintaining the Factional Balance: The 1954 NPC and the 1956 Eighth Party Congress

The election of Lin and Deng to the Politburo in April 1955 addressed one of the lingering tensions aroused by the Gao Gang affair, the question of adequate representation of military leaders on high Party bodies. While it is not totally clear why this still should have been an issue if Gao Gang had misrepresented An Ziwen's list as claimed,[84] an authoritative oral source states that Mao and other leaders realized that there was still considerable discontent within the military over the list episode. This not only meant that no action would be taken against Lin or Peng Dehuai for their involvement, but what better way to ease this tension than name two of the PLA's greatest heroes to the Politburo.

Other factors were also at play in moves at the very top. In the case of Deng Xiaoping, unlike that of Lin Biao who did not take up an active political career for health and perhaps other reasons,[85] the Politburo appointment merely punctuated an ongoing rise, which had already seen him take a leading role in economic, Party organization, and general Party affairs. Such a rise was undoubtedly linked to his key role in bringing the Gao-Rao affair to its end, and more fundamentally to his long-standing close ties to Mao. The other key figure in terminating the Gao Gang case, Chen Yun, also gained in status when by mid-1954 he joined Liu Shaoqi, Zhou Enlai, and Zhu De as one of Mao's "close comrades-in-arms."[86]

But if "army and base area" figures, particularly those who exposed Gao Gang, were on the rise, key "white area" figures benefited as well. This was seen most clearly in the strong reaffirmation of Liu Shaoqi as the successor, and of course also in the ongoing crucial role of Zhou Enlai. Most ironic in terms of Gao Gang's objectives, another "white area" beneficiary was Peng Zhen. According to a source who worked closely with Peng Zhen throughout this period, his role in the immediate post-1949 period was fairly limited to his official responsibilities in Beijing municipality despite his Politburo status. This situation was probably a result of his mistakes in the Northeast during the civil war, which Gao Gang had so forcefully opposed. But with Gao's demise Peng Zhen's actual status rose, and by 1955 he was a de facto participant in all meetings of the Secretariat. While restoring Party unity meant sensitivity to the claims of the military, this was not at the expense of "white area" leaders. In this key instance the outcome of the Gao Gang affair had enhanced the position of one of the most significant "white area" figures.

Thus, there was more involved than simply soothing ruffled military feathers in the personnel arrangements of 1954–56 although, as table 5 demonstrates, that aspect was a major one. When the new state structure was established at the NPC in September 1954, Peng Dehuai was duly installed as minister of defense as well as the third-ranked vice-premier, while Lin Biao, physical problems notwithstanding, was named the second vice-premier behind Chen Yun, although apparently without concrete duties. Moreover, half of the ten vice-premiers were major military figures during the revolutionary period. Then, at the Eighth Party Congress in 1956, the military received ample recognition on the new enlarged Politburo, with over 40 percent of the full members consisting of PLA marshals and all of the new full members having "army and base area" careers. While this was undoubtedly in part a continuing effort to dampen the tensions stirred up in 1953, it was also significant as a larger statement of the requirements of factional balance and harmony. The new Politburo, as the immediate post-Gao arrangements, did not represent so much a victory of the "army and base areas" over the "white areas" as continuity in the existing shareout of positions. Liu Shaoqi and Zhou Enlai—Gao Gang's "white area" targets—were reaffirmed as the second- and third-ranking figures in the hierarchy, and Liu's position as the successor was further solidified.[87] At the same time, the cause of so much trouble in 1953, Bo Yibo, was named the last-ranking alternate member of the Politburo. Overall, the top leadership that Mao had designated for celebration in *The Great Soviet Encyclopedia* prior to the Gao-Rao affair was maintained apart from Gao and Rao themselves, as was longer-range continuity with the 1945 Politburo.[88] Factional problems had arisen in 1953 in large part because An Ziwen's list, as presented by Gao Gang, would

Table 5

The Factional Balance: Key Party and State Positions, 1954–1956

Politburo rank 1956 (1945)	Primary institutional identification	1949–1954 region	Party posts at 8th Congress 1956	State posts at 1954 NPC	Main "factional" association[a]
1 (1) Mao Zedong*	P	—	Chairman Chairman MAC	Chairman PRC	—
2 (3) Liu Shaoqi*	P	—	Vice-chairman	Chairman NPC	N. China white areas
3 (4) Zhou Enlai*	G	—	Vice-chairman	Premier Minister of Foreign Affairs	—
4 (2) Zhu De*	M	—	Vice-chairman MAC member	Vice-chairman PRC	—
5 (6) Chen Yun*	G	—	Vice-chairman	1st vice-premier	—
6 (–) Deng Xiaoping*	P	SW	General-secy	4th vice-premier	2nd Field Army
7 (–) Lin Biao*+	M	CS	MAC member	2nd vice-premier	4th Field Army
8 (11) Lin Boqu*	G	—	—	Vice-chairman NPC	—
9 (10) Dong Biwu*	P/G	—	Secretary Central Control Committee	President Supreme People's Court	—
10 (9) Peng Zhen*	P	NC	CC secretary 1st secretary Beijing	Mayor Beijing Vice-chairman and secy-gen NPC	N. China white areas
11 (–) Luo Ronghuan*	M	CS	MAC member	Vice-chairman NPC 7th vice-premier	4th Field Army
12 (–) Chen Yi*	G/M	EC	MAC member	Mayor Shanghai 9th vice-premier Chairman SPC	3rd Field Army
13 (–) Li Fuchun*	G	NE	—	—	—
14 (13) Peng Dehuai*	M	NW	Vice-chairman MAC member	3rd vice-premier Minister of Defense	1st Field Army
15 (–) Liu Bocheng*	M	SW	MAC member Party secy PLA military academy	NPC Standing Committee	2nd Field Army

Name		Region	CC position	Gov position	Background
16 (–) He Long*	M	SW	MAC member	6th vice-premier Chm Physical Culture and Sports Committee	1st Field Army
17 (–) Li Xiannian	G	CS	—	10th vice-premier Head finance and trade staff office Minister of Finance	4th Front Army
alt 1 (–) Ulanfu	P/G	NC	1st secretary Inner Mongolia	8th vice-premier Chm Nationalities Affairs Com Chm Inner Mongolia	Mongol progressive circles
alt 2 (12) Zhang Wentian	G	NE	—	Vice-minister Foreign Affairs NPC Standing Committee	—
alt 3 (–) Lu Dingyi	P	—	Head CC propaganda dept	NPC Standing Committee	—
alt 4 (–) Chen Boda	P	—	Deputy head CC propaganda dept Dep head CC rural work dept	—	—
alt 5 (7) Kang Sheng#	P	EC	—	—	—
alt 6 (–) Bo Yibo	G	NC	—	Vice-premier (1956) Head heavy industry and construction staff office Chairman State Construction Com	N. China white areas
Wang Jiaxiang	P	—	CC secretary Head CC international liaison dept	Vice-minister Foreign Affairs	—

Table 5 (continued)

Politburo rank 1956 (1945)	Primary institutional identification	1949–1954 region	Party posts at 8th Congress 1956	State posts at 1954 NPC	Main "factional" association[a]
Tan Zhenlin	P	EC	CC secretary	—	3rd Field Army
Tan Zheng	M	CS	CC secretary	Vice-min Defense NPC Standing Committee	4th Field Army
Huang Kecheng	M	CS	CC secretary	Vice-min Defense NPC Standing Committee	New 4th Army
Li Xuefeng	P	CS	CC secretary Head CC industry and communications dept	NPC Standing Committee	2nd Field Army
Liu Lantao	P	NC	CC alt secretary Dep secy Central Control Com	NPC Standing Committee	N. China white areas
Yang Shangkun	P	—	CC alt secretary Head CC gen office	—	—
Hu Qiaomu	P	—	CC alt secretary	NPC Standing Committee	—
Deng Zihui*	P/G	CS	Head CC rural work dept	5th vice-premier Head agriculture staff office	New 4th Army
Li Weihan	P/G	—	Head CC united front dept	Head united front staff office Vice-chairman NPC	—

Name	Category	Region	MAC	Position	Link
Xi Zhongxun	G	NW	—	Secretary-general State Council	North Shaanxi base
Luo Ruiqing	PS	NC	—	Head internal affairs staff office; Min of Public Security	N. China Field Army
Lin Feng	G	NE	—	Head culture and education staff office; NPC Standing Committee	N. China white areas?
Jia Tuofu	G	NW	—	Head light industry staff office; Min of Light Industry	North Shaanxi base
Wang Shoudao	G	CS	—	Head transport and communications staff office	?
Ye Jianying*	M	CS	MAC member	NPC Standing Committee	—
Xu Xiangqian*+	M	—	MAC member	NPC Standing Committee	4th Front Army
Nie Rongzhen	M	NC	MAC member	NPC Standing Committee; Vice-premier (1956)	N. China Field Army

Sources: Klein and Clark, *Biographic Dictionary*; Whitson with Huang, *The Chinese High Command*; table 3 above; and oral source.

Notes: * = Included in Mao's selection for *The Great Soviet Encyclopedia* (see table 3 above); + = inactive due to illness; # = Inactive due to claimed illness to 1955; P = Party; G = government; M = military; PS = public security; MAC = Party Military Affairs Committee.

a. Not exhaustive; based on estimate of strongest ties during revolutionary period. None given where strongest links to post-1935 Party/military center or individual is a Party elder (Dong Biwu, Lin Boqu).

have upset the existing balance. The new 1956 Politburo sought to bury these problems by reaffirming the established pattern. The emphasis was on giving each "mountaintop" its fair share, an approach apparently deemed necessary if Party unity was to be fully restored.

Strains on Party Unity: The Gao Gang Case and Subsequent Leadership Turmoil

The various efforts of the 1954–56 period could not completely bury intraleadership tensions, however. For lower-ranking figures in particular, the legacy of the 1953 conflict left some officials fearful of airing their thoughts. As late as April 1956, Mao noted that a side effect of the Financial and Economic Conference and Fourth Plenum was a cat-and-mouse situation where the lower-level mice would not say much to the higher-level cats.[89] Within the top leadership a different sort of tension lingered as Liu Shaoqi in particular harbored resentment over the support given Gao Gang by Peng Dehuai and Lin Biao. According to an authoritative oral source, this would play a significant role during the next major leadership crisis at the 1959 Lushan meetings. While clearly Mao's implacable opposition to Peng Dehuai during and after Lushan was decisive, this source believes that memories of 1953 influenced not only Liu's support of Mao at Lushan but also his 1962 position that while others sharing Peng's opinions could be rehabilitated, Peng Dehuai himself could not.[90] Whatever the motives of Liu, Peng's involvement with Gao Gang in 1953 was now resurrected and used against him. While Peng's role had been minimized in 1953–54 in the interests of Party unity, in the context of Mao's seething anger over Peng's critique of the Great Leap Forward,[91] Peng's participation was arguably now exaggerated as he was declared an important member of the "Gao-Rao anti-Party alliance."[92] Considerations of unity were no longer determining in the face of the Chairman's fury.

A second and considerably stranger case linking Gao Gang to leadership turmoil took place three years later, centering on the then vice-premier and State Council secretary-general, Xi Zhongxun. Xi had been an old colleague of Gao Gang and of the preeminent local revolutionary leader of the Shaanxi base area, Liu Zhidan.[93] In the early 1960s Liu's sister-in-law wrote a novel about his revolutionary career and referred to other key figures including Gao by pseudonyms. Xi proofread and corrected the manuscript of his dead comrade's relative. When the manuscript was submitted to the central propaganda department, Kang Sheng read it and decided it was an attempt to reverse the verdict on Gao Gang. This came at the same time Peng Dehuai was seeking to have *his* verdict reversed in 1962, and when Kang, joined by Jiang Qing, reported his suspicions Mao reportedly exploded in anger, saying that first there was an effort to reverse the verdict on Peng and now a novel trying to do the same for Gao. Mao's anger was further stimulated by the actions of Gao's widow, who now reported that Xi had visited Gao after he had fallen and assertedly misrepresented the incident, which in fact was an attempt on Xi's part to forestall Gao's suicide, as something more sinister. The matter came to a quasi-comic, quasi-tragic denouement at the Tenth Plenum of the Eighth Central Committee in September 1962 when suddenly, out of the blue, "all hell broke loose around [Xi]," who was branded a "big anti-Party plotter and schemer." In the course of the plenum, Mao was handed and read out a note from Kang that "It is a remarkable invention, using a novel to attack the Party," and this subsequently came to be regarded as "a quotation from Chairman Mao." Xi was duly removed from his posts and reportedly "had a rough time" after his dismissal.[94]

These events concerning Peng Dehuai and Xi Zhongxun in the 1959–1962 period stand in stark contrast to the efforts of 1954–1956. If anything, the leadership tensions caused by the Gao Gang affair should have been less salient in 1959–1962 given the passage of time, but in fact they were more explosive. The reason, ironically, involves an important similarity between the two periods—leadership tensions that had previously been submerged in the name of a larger Party unity came to the surface because of the actions of Mao. In 1953 this may have been unwitting; and even if Mao had been intentionally seeking to play on leadership differences, he ultimately and firmly came down on the side of Party unity. By the late 1950s, however, in the midst of soul searching over the failures of the Great Leap, the Chairman placed far less priority on unity and willfully exacerbated existing differences, as with Peng Dehuai, and even created conflict where it hardly existed, as with Xi Zhongxun. Moreover, in 1953 and 1954 there ostensibly was a way out for those who "erred"; as late as 1957 Mao expressed remorse that he had not done more to point out that way to Gao Gang. But no way out of a similar nature was offered to Peng or Xi.[95] While a golden age may not have existed in the early 1950s, by the end of the decade the vestiges of the Party unity, which had been maintained earlier, were now severely disrupted.

6
CONCLUSION
Politics at Mao's Court

THE ONE indisputable conclusion to emerge from this study is the central role of Mao Zedong. In a classic case of an unchallenged authoritarian leader surrounded by deferential subordinates, Mao's words and actions shaped the Gao Gang–Rao Shushi affair from start to finish. Other leaders on all sides of the conflict reacted to Mao, hung on his often ambiguous words, and anticipated his moves and objectives. Mao's initial private talks with Gao clearly sparked the effort to displace Liu Shaoqi as the successor. Mao's backing of criticism of Bo Yibo at the Financial and Economic Conference facilitated Gao's harsh attacks and brought intense pressures on the Minister of Finance, but when Mao endorsed Chen Yun's more moderate view of Bo's errors those pressures eased. Meanwhile, Mao's backing of Li Weihan's proposals for the peaceful transformation of the national bourgeoisie not only saw those proposals adopted, but resulted in Gao stifling his sharply critical views of them.

At the same time or shortly thereafter, when Lin Biao and Peng Dehuai were approached by Gao Gang, Gao's claims that he spoke for the Chairman were undoubtedly crucial in their cautious support. Later their defense that they had been cheated into believing Mao had indeed backed Gao was deemed sufficient to declare their cases closed. While Deng Xiaoping seemingly did not accept Gao's entreaties, the possibility that Gao might in fact have the Chairman's blessing led to pronounced circumspection in his handling of the situation. Moreover, Deng and also Chen Yun may have delayed as much as two months or more after being approached by Gao before going to see Mao, given their apparent uncertainty concerning the Chairman's true attitude. Finally, when Mao made his first direct criticism of Gao Gang on December 24, 1953, the "conspiracy" collapsed like a house of cards.

Mao's dominant role not only in the Gao-Rao affair but also in the politics of the early 1950s generally made him at once the lynchpin of Party unity and the greatest threat to elite solidarity. There were major structural and situational factors conducive to a high degree of unity throughout this period. An unchallenged leader, a broad policy consensus on the Soviet model, a wide sharing out of leading positions to representative figures of major groups within the CCP, a sensitive recognition of the revolutionary contributions and Party status of individuals in that share out, and an awareness of the importance of Party unity to the incredible accomplishments achieved under Mao all supported solidarity.

This did not mean the absence of conflict; significant tensions based on past disputes, personality clashes, current policy debates, the moral-ideological nature of the system, and conflicting loyalties of different groups were an ongoing feature of inner-Party life. Moreover, the seriousness of the divisions sparked by Gao's manipulation of An Ziwen's list and the ability of Gao and Rao to conduct their subterranean activities involving high-ranking CCP leaders over a period of months without detection suggest an atmosphere where there were clear limits to trust and open communication. In the future, most notably during the Cultural Revolution, similar factors would produce intense conflict and major leadership schisms, but in the initial post-1949 period Mao's emphasis on Party unity—together with the structural and situational factors supporting solidarity—served to suppress differences in the name of the greater good.

But the clear implication of the Gao Gang case is that Mao's commitment to unity and leadership stability, as strong as it appeared overall until the late 1950s, was not sufficient to eliminate tensions or erase doubts in the minds of others that he might opt for a more conflictual style of leadership. The Chairman was the lynchpin of Party unity not simply because of the strength of his own position but because he supported a stable hierarchy of power below himself. If he was—or could be portrayed to be—dissatisfied with that hierarchy, then all bets were off; there was no doubt about his right to shuffle the mandarins at his court if it suited him. In such a situation, tensions that had previously been contained not only due to a common commitment to the greater good but also because Mao's leadership style gave individual leaders little incentive to rock the boat could easily become unmanageable.

In this context of a broadly based but nevertheless fragile Party unity, the Gao-Rao affair introduced factionalism in several senses. In the official sense, Gao and Rao carried out illegitimate factional activities designed to further the power interests of a particular group within the Party at the expense of others in the leadership. The members of Gao's "clique" as officially defined were of two types—close subordinates of Gao and Rao whose current careers and future prospects were closely tied to those leaders, and the two principals themselves, who were assertedly joined by opportunism. There undoubtedly was opportunism; moreover, any alignment between Gao and Rao appears to have been tacit and certainly was not based on shared career experience. By the logic of common experience Rao should have backed Liu Shaoqi, under whom he had worked in the "white areas" and in the New Fourth Army, who had promoted him earlier in his career, and for whom—if Red Guard sources are to be believed—Rao's wife had worked as a secretary.[1]

But if the ties of revolutionary experience were not a key factor linking the leaders of the "conspiracy," they played a central role in Gao's attempt to split "army and base area" cadres from those who had worked in the "white areas." This type of "factionalism"—the common identification of different revolutionary groups—was deeply felt and, moreover, legitimate as long as it did not result in excessive demands on the Party as a whole. Indeed, Mao himself spoke of the revolution being made up of many "mountaintops." The key to these factions had little to do with policy and everything to do with position—it was necessary that the different career groups be recognized in the post-1949 allocation of office and power. Furthermore, it was essential for elite harmony that the allocation create a factional balance that would both be perceived as just and be secure against any sudden disturbance. As argued in the preceding chapters, this was done with great skill from the Seventh Congress onward, but An Ziwen's list as probably misrepresented and certainly exploited by Gao Gang made it seem the accepted arrangements were about to be violated, and factional tensions resulted.

The importance of faction and the lesser role of policy are suggested by the design of Gao Gang's attack on Liu Shaoqi. Not only was the issue of factionalism—that is, the strong group loyalty of the "white area" cadres who had served under Liu—a central argument used against him, but the logic of Gao's actions implied that such ties were more important than formal claims of bureaucratic command and resultant responsibility for policy. Of course, at one level, attacking Bo Yibo was doing no more than giving voice to Mao's known displeasure with the new tax system. But for Gao, attacking Bo Yibo was primarily a way to get at Liu Shaoqi. Bo's immediate bureaucratic superior, Chen Yun, on the available evidence not only was not a target of Gao's attack, he was in fact one of the key leaders Gao sought to win over in his effort to displace Liu. And while Zhou Enlai was vulnerable on policy/bureaucratic grounds and Liu had seemingly given general approval to Bo's tax policy, the emphasis on the Liu-Bo link (as well as on that of An Ziwen to both men) strongly suggests that historical rather than policy ties were the underlying rationale in the way Gao handled the issue.

The way factionalism manifested itself pointed to another basic feature of the new Chinese regime repeatedly in evidence throughout the Gao-Rao affair—the great sensitivity of CCP leaders to Party and revolutionary status. This, of course, was the fundamental reason that maintaining the existing factional balance was such a delicate issue. That balance reflected the contributions of different segments of the elite to revolutionary victory, and to upset it was equivalent to denying the accomplishments achieved by each group over decades of struggle. Moreover, particular instances of extreme sensitivity to status abound in this story. Thus, Zhou Enlai intervened to prevent open criticism of Rao Shushi at the Organization Conference as it would not do to wash dirty leadership linen in front of lower-ranking cadres, while Deng Xiaoping assertedly deflected Gao's advances with the observation that Liu Shaoqi's position had been confirmed by history. Meanwhile, the relatively low status of such figures as Ma Hong left them virtually defenseless against being drawn into Gao Gang's activities. Perhaps most dramatic, Lin Biao could be credibly promoted by Gao as Mao's successor despite poor health because of the high prestige gained by his revolutionary accomplishments.

In one way, however, the demands of status contributed to the dilution of revolutionary ties. Since relatively equal posts had to be distributed to the regional leaders moving to Beijing in 1952-53, new work ties were often formed that cut across old associations. Thus, Xi Zhongxun, an old North Shaanxi comrade of Gao Gang, assumed a high-ranking GAC post that was to lead to extremely close ties to Zhou Enlai.[2] Also, by fall 1953 at the latest, Deng Xiaoping's economic responsibilities produced close working relations with Chen Yun, whose earlier career had been quite distinct from Deng's. A less successful case of previously distant leaders establishing work ties, of course, was that of Rao and An Ziwen within the organization department. But in general, people from different backgrounds who were drawn together in new bureaucratic units were not necessarily in conflict—a phenomenon even more dramatically illustrated by the ironic example of Bo Yibo subsequently promoting Ma Hong, who had apparently drafted Gao's 1953 speeches which so wounded Bo.[3] Nevertheless, in the immediate post-1949 period, revolutionary ties remained strong even as new postings placed old comrades in new situations.[4] While he may have underestimated the strength of the new relationships forming at the Center, it was Gao's apparent belief that old revolutionary ties, together with the lure of enhanced power and position, were more important as wellsprings of political action than alignments based on particular policy issues or bureaucratic responsibilities.

Policy, of course, was a central aspect of the political process in the early 1950s regardless of whether Gao Gang was ultimately right about the overriding significance of revolutionary career ties. Policy was, moreover, used by Gao, and there is little reason to doubt the sincerity of his comparatively leftist orientation. But in general terms the policy process throughout the Gao-Rao affair was of the consensual mode typical of the general period. Mao was a forceful actor—and the dominant one—but he worked through an extended and broadly based airing of views. In 1953 Mao clearly set the agenda of the general line and himself laid down its precise formulation even though others participated in the process; in this he shifted the emphasis of policy in virtually all spheres from economic recovery and political consolidation to planned development and socialist transformation. But the specific policies under the general line involved extensive discussion by concerned bureaucratic actors,[5] especially at the Financial and Economic Conference. At that conference the new policy on the national bourgeoisie grew out of careful investigations by the appropriate organ—Li Weihan's united front department. In addition, the overall economic policy laid down during the summer meetings affirmed the cautious approach associated with Zhou Enlai and Chen Yun. In this area, where Mao's confidence and competence were comparatively limited, he accepted the consensus of responsible economic officials on the need to curb "rash advance." Even on the tax issue, with its sensitive ideological aspect, Mao was content to accept a denunciation of the equal treatment of public and private *principle* together with the minimal practical measures deemed prudent by his specialist colleagues.

The process was similar yet different in important ways where Mao was more confident concerning his own expertise. Thus, on the one hand, the evolution of policy toward agricultural mutual aid and cooperativization incorporated the concerns of specialist bureaucracies, and a national conference was convened in October–November where these bureaucracies could express their views. The policy that emerged, moreover, married Mao's political preoccupations with the more economic concerns of his old close comrade, Deng Zihui. Yet the conference not only produced a pointed if implicit criticism of Deng Zihui, the developing policy pushed the cooperativization process faster than Deng considered wise to the extent that he seemingly stayed away as a result. In this area where Mao's confidence was high, the Chairman was willing to push his preferences on a somewhat reluctant bureaucracy, but even here he accommodated the specialists' concerns to a not insignificant degree.

Overall, the consensual process was aided immeasurably by Mao's relatively gradualist policy orientation. On all issues, including cooperativization, he warned against the "left" as well as the "right" and took account of real-world obstacles to his objectives. While he successfully moved the regime's overall course somewhat more to the "left" than some other leaders may have wished, the changes were, in broad terms, moderate and easily embraced by consensual politics.

An understanding of the Gao-Rao affair must come to grips with the personalities of Gao Gang and others involved on various sides of the events in question. Here the task is perilous particularly with regard to Gao; attacks on his ambition and conceit must be seen in the light of the tradition of denigrating defeated leaders. Nevertheless, charges that Gao was particularly dictatorial in his work relationships gain credence from his unusual reliance on much lower-ranking officials within the Northeast Bureau, and a close supporter has attested to his explosive temperament.[6] In any case, Gao was a singularly error-prone politician throughout 1953. Even if one assumes that Gao did not, as oral sources believe, "miscalculate completely" the meaning of Mao's private criticisms of Liu and Zhou and that the Chairman was leaving open the possibility of a leadership struggle, his persistence in pushing ahead despite various conflicting signals from Mao lends credibility to the view that he was indeed a "fierce and daring" high-risk player.[7] Whether blinded by an uncontrollable ambition or falling prey to a peasant mentality, which, having a simple faith in Mao's trust, could not sort out more complex motives on the Chairman's part, Gao failed to heed Mao's call for unity at the Financial and Economic Conference, his rejection of Stalinist methods of transforming the bourgeoisie at the same meetings, his apparent unwillingness to intercede on behalf of Rao Shushi, and finally the Chairman's putting forward the traditional proposal that Liu take over during his holiday. Given that so much depended on Mao's ultimate backing, the willingness to plunge ahead despite such signals seems foolhardy at best.

Other major flaws are apparent in Gao's strategy. First, he was poorly placed to present himself as a representative of the army and base areas. Although holding the top military post in the Northeast, Gao was by no means one of the great generals of the Chinese revolution. Nor did he play any part in the pre-1935 southern phase of the revolution, where major base areas were first established, the PLA's top elite cut its teeth, and the key military units that later won the crucial battles of the Anti-Japanese and civil wars first took shape. A second error was to attack Zhou Enlai, even given Mao's apparent early 1953 dissatisfaction with Zhou. Toppling Liu Shaoqi was the main objective, and there was no point in taking on the popular Zhou with his extensive military contacts as well. If Gao had been successful in the improbable project of supplanting Liu as the successor,[8] he would have automatically jumped over Zhou in the process. In addition, the attempt to portray himself as representing a fit younger generation in contrast to the "old" Liu and Zhou was silly. Liu and Zhou were vigorous men in their mid-fifties in a culture that hardly denigrated age in any case. While the generational issue had a real, if difficult to assess, social basis a dozen years later on the eve of the Cultural Revolution, in 1953 it hardly existed as a genuine problem. Moreover, in raising it Gao revealed another fundamental flaw of his endeavor. In a system where status was so important he threatened one of the most reliable guides to status—length of service to the revolution. Indeed, Gao's whole effort was paradoxical in that he sought to mobilize resentment against a purported threat to the existing factional balance in order to pose a much more radical challenge to that balance. Such an undertaking could only produce a profound anxiety within the CCP leadership.

Finally, the adoption of a quasi-Stalinist policy orientation was hardly likely to win support from key officials such as Chen Yun who were identified with the gradualist cause, or for that matter from Mao himself. Chen, who was a key target of Gao's effort to win over a "younger" generation of leaders, took clearly different positions from Gao on the national bourgeoisie and the new tax system as well as developing (albeit limited) reservations on the applicability of the Soviet model to China. That Gao pursued Chen at or after the Financial and Economic Conference is further testimony that policy was not the driving force of his activities. As for Mao, I will argue below that his ideological affinity to Gao did not extend to a consistent leftist policy advocacy.

In short, Gao's various tactics did not make for a coherent, winning strategy. The only way he could have succeeded in overcoming the enormous strength of Liu and Zhou, given his lesser status in the Party and the relative weakness of his particular "mountaintop," was through the direct intervention of Mao. If Mao's original talks in late 1952 or early 1953 had left Gao with the impression this was possible, as 1953 enfolded it became less and less likely, making Gao's stratagems increasingly counterproductive.

Weaknesses in terms of personality and strategy are also apparent with regard to Rao Shushi. While the same caveats concerning information on discredited leaders apply to Rao as to Gao, and even less hard information is available in his case, it does appear that Rao was a particularly prickly individual who generated an excessive degree of conflict with such diverse associates as Chen Yi and Pan Hannian in East China and An Ziwen in the central organization department. Moreover, if there is any truth to the story of Rao's middle-of-the-night visit to Mao to seek reassurance that his work was viewed favorably, it reveals a striking degree of insecurity, which would have also fed into his relations with colleagues and subordinates. Concerning strategy, Gao's asserted attempt to gain the backing of East China through Rao was somewhat misconceived given the greater divisions within that area than in any of the other large regions as a result of the Rao–Chen Yi feud, and the fact that Rao's support was presumably creating in Chen Yi an unsympathetic force of roughly equal status. Furthermore, Gao gained in Rao an ally with no particular personal ties to or influence with Mao; in contrast, Rao's East China colleague Tan Zhenlin had the closest historical links to Mao but seemingly, although the evidence is inconclusive,[9] managed to stay aloof from the affair. Moreover, Rao's own actions revealed a poor strategic and tactical sense. His direct attack on An Ziwen at the July organization department meeting in front of lower-ranking officials offended status and caused great consternation within the department. And in pursuing An openly at the September–October conference, he left himself vulnerable in that he had no cover from Mao's known views; the case was quite different from Gao's attack on Bo Yibo, where the Chairman's anger over Bo's tax system was well understood.

In contrast to the apparently impetuous actions of Gao and Rao, the models of successful behavior at Mao's court were Deng Xiaoping and Chen Yun. While there is a risk of circularity in the argument, oral sources believe that both these leaders had a subtle understanding of Mao. Equally important, the balance of evidence suggests they held back on the crucial political question of Gao Gang's approaches when uncertain of Mao's intent—they apparently were on the outlook for telltale signals but did not rush ahead as long as the Chairman's true feelings remained opaque. As we shall see, this was not the whole story, at least as it applied to Chen Yun in the policy realm. But the cautious sensitivity to Mao's cues seemingly was a crucial aspect of their respective modus operandi; moreover, in this case it dovetailed with their respect for existing status and fear of any disruption of that status.[10] Both Chen and particularly Deng would benefit substantially as a result of the Gao-Rao affair, but their enhanced power and prestige resulted from offering cautious support to the status quo once it seemed safe to do so rather than grasping for greater authority. Their role was to a significant extent, although not completely, reactive to the presumed desires and attitudes of Mao Zedong. At this stage of Mao's leadership, unlike later periods, a cautious commitment to Party unity plus personal loyalty to Mao outweighed any strident ideological commitment in securing the Chairman's favor.

This leaves us with Mao himself. It is, of course, impossible to know his motives. My reasons for rejecting on balance the likelihood that the Chairman was indeed seeking to displace Liu Shaoqi as his successor are to a large extent contextual. Liu had been an able deputy and the Party's most capable theorist after Mao; no one else—certainly not the crude Gao Gang—would be an obvious replacement. Moreover, the differences between Mao and Liu were not great in this period and Liu, however persistent or otherwise he might have been in putting his views, in the end always bowed to the Chairman's wishes. And the great emphasis Mao placed on Party unity, which had proved so important in achieving the victory of 1949, was not something the Chairman would casually throw away over the type of incremental policy issues that faced the leadership in 1953.

The conclusion concerning Liu also draws force from the events of 1953 themselves. While Mao did express discontent with Liu on a variety of matters—the unauthorized issuing of documents, the slogan "firmly establish the New Democratic social order," and past policy toward agricultural cooperatives—he at no time took decisive action to demote Liu. In the end, Mao saved Bo Yibo and supported An Ziwen as well. Moreover, when he raised the question of arrangements for his holiday by proposing that Liu take over and Gao—supported undoubtedly innocently by the respected Zhu De—proposed leadership by rotation, the Chairman took it as a sign of unacceptable behavior rather than using the discussion of this novel idea as a way of undercutting Liu. While Mao's intentions cannot be known, the Chairman's actions are consistent with pressuring Liu into changing his views or warning him of displeasure from on high, but not with removing Liu as the successor. Indeed, this explanation is consistent with Mao's own subsequent criticism of Gao Gang for seeking to knock over those who made mistakes rather than encouraging them to mend their ways.[11] The logic is clear: while it was acceptable to criticize Liu or Zhou for their errors, it was impermissible to seek their removal from office. But in 1953 those directly involved found it credible that Mao might be entertaining ideas of a leadership reshuffle.

Leaving aside issues of precise motivation, the Gao-Rao affair sheds light on a number of features of Mao's political style and what can only be termed life at Mao's court. First, despite being heavily involved in various policy areas and maintaining a detailed oversight over the entire range of policy, Mao was frequently distant and elusive—particularly on crucial political matters. While one cannot be certain, it would appear that he did little more than indicate to Gao displeasure at certain tendencies and past actions of Liu and Zhou. When Gao was odd man out on the peaceful transformation of capitalists, the Chairman sent an emissary in preference to direct talks. In the same period the Chairman let Bo Yibo off the hook by declaring his problem was not one of line, but at the same time he indicated that

Bo's mistakes involved a serious matter of principle and reflected the corruption of bourgeois thought.

Whether such ambiguity and indirectness on Mao's part was a deliberate ploy to keep his subordinates off balance or simply reflected his own ambivalence about the individuals and issues involved, the actions of other leaders indicated considerable uncertainty over Mao's intentions. In certain cases this probably reflected limited access to the Chairman. The willingness of the ill Lin Biao and Peng Dehuai, who had been occupied in Korea, to accept Gao Gang's account of Mao's views may have reflected their lack of recent access to the Chairman. But even those who had observed Mao closely during summer 1953 and most likely had special access based on old ties (Deng Xiaoping) or Secretariat membership (Chen Yun) could not be sure of Mao's aims. Although both went to Mao individually to expose Gao Gang, Deng had carefully held "formal negotiations" with Gao while Chen checked things out with Zhou Enlai first, not to mention that both seemingly delayed their reports by anything up to two months or more. That no one else went to Mao is also suggestive, as is the apparent tongue-tied response of Luo Ruiqing when confronted by Mao on the Gao Gang question. While Mao's aloof style kept people uncertain and at arm's length, many leaders in turn kept their distance from the awesome ruler of China.[12]

Although often distant and frequently noncommittal, Mao could also be bitingly critical. The Chairman's criticisms, whether indirect as in the case of Liu Shaoqi or bluntly personal as with Bo Yibo, naturally left uncertainty as to where the individuals concerned stood. While this may have been a deliberate device to cause anxiety among his subordinates, it was justified by Mao as the type of principled criticism that was necessary for the health of the Party.[13] In this Mao demonstrated an unusual sensitivity to theory, a sensitivity that sometimes set him at odds with his own specific policy positions and political practice. On the one hand, as one oral source put it, under specific circumstances Mao would agree to the ideas of others, such as using the national bourgeoisie, which were in tension with his general theoretical orientation of speeding up the process of transformation. But from another perspective, Mao often seemed more preoccupied with ideological correctness than with policy content. In this regard it is instructive that one of Mao's main sources of discontent with Liu, which surfaced in 1953, concerned the latter's Tianjin talks where he brilliantly realized the Chairman's purpose but erred with some ideologically unacceptable formulations concerning the merits of exploitation. Similarly, the Chairman's displeasure with Liu's use of the term "agrarian socialist thought" concerning the Shanxi cooperatives and his "firmly establish the New Democratic social order" slogan reflected the same concern for theoretical niceties.

While such "incorrect" formulations arguably affected the policy issues facing the CCP in 1953, the dwelling on such matters ripped out of historical context was hardly essential to the task at hand. Nevertheless, such a preoccupation reflected more than Mao's personal idiosyncrasy. Given an ideology where policy was presumed to be guided by a correct political line, and a political culture emphasizing moral virtue, high-ranking leaders as a group were predisposed to viewing Party affairs in terms of ideological correctness and accepted the legitimacy of intraelite criticism on theoretical issues. This tradition, in turn, opened the possibility of escalating leadership tensions over what could easily become questions of theoretical fidelity and moral worth. The net effect of Mao's leadership up to the early 1950s had been to blunt the harsher edges of this phenomenon,[14] but the basic condition remained a structural feature of the system.

As the Gao-Rao affair unfolded there was also a peculiar contradiction between Mao's broad policy orientation, which was largely gradualist, and his weakness for Stalinist theory. Despite his endorsement of a non-Stalinist peaceful transformation of the national bourgeoisie, Mao apparently was initially impressed by Gao's critique of Bo's tax policy using Soviet theoretical argumentation. Later Mao directed Party leaders at the Organization Conference to study the conclusions of Stalin's *Short Course*, which called for Party unity by weeding out opportunists, while at that very time endorsing efforts to bolster Party unity by stopping criticism of An Ziwen for, among other things, inadequate vigilance against alien elements who snuck into the organization. Finally, at the very time a lenient approach was adopted toward those involved in the Gao-Rao case, the Chairman's resolution on strengthening Party unity in its final version contained harsh Stalinist rhetoric linking Party splits to "imperialist encirclement."[15]

In ideological terms, I believe, these developments reflect Mao's lack of confidence on fundamental theoretical questions as well as the Moscow-centered nature of the international Communist movement in the early 1950s. For all his national pride, innovativeness as a revolutionary strategist, and occasional ideological assertiveness, Mao was still groping his way toward a better grasp of Marxism-Leninism at a time when Stalinist canon shaped basic theoretical understanding. Together with Mao's general ideological sensitivity, this added another uncertainty for the Chairman's colleagues. As Bo Yibo found out, he was vulnerable not only to Mao discovering a Party line on taxation where no concrete guidelines existed, but also to the Chairman's seeming enthusiasm for Gao's adaptation of Stalinist analysis. And by raising the issue to the ideological level, Mao created an atmosphere of tension typical of Stalinist practice and that of the CCP before his leadership, which led even a (partially) exonerated Bo to seek a rest cure.

Finally, notwithstanding Mao's previous practice of limiting ideological conflict, this forceful injection of theoretical issues in 1953 also enhanced the potential for abuse by the ambitious Gao Gang. Such phenomena as attacks by proxy, vague politically loaded accusations, exaggerating past "errors" without regard for historical circumstance, and collecting material on political enemies, which would become such a feature of the Cultural Revolution, were already present in the

Gao-Rao affair. The difference was that in 1953, for all his ideological preoccupations, Mao ultimately recoiled from such excesses in the name of Party unity.

In this context politics at Mao's court was played out. The authoritarian ruler was the pivot, the final word on all matters. But this did not mean that he exercised uniform control across the whole range of political activity. Rather, Mao's power in the immediate sense ebbed and flowed according to his interests, the strength of his convictions, what was placed on the agenda by events, and what caught his attention more generally. As we have seen, in some areas, most notably economic construction in the modern sector, he was content, not to ignore the issues, but in the last analysis to be guided by those with greater expertise. In others, like rural social change, he was much more in the forefront.[16] But beyond this there would always be uncertainty concerning Mao's preferences, and other leaders could only advance their interests by testing the water. Their task was not simply to maneuver in response to Mao's actions but to take tentative steps to see what scope for action existed. Given the responsibilities of such leaders as well as the general consensual style of the period, they could not simply sit back and wait for Mao. They would promote their agendas and seek to nudge the Chairman toward their solutions. On the available evidence, the master of this approach in 1953 was Chen Yun. While Chen seemingly held back on the crucial political question of Gao Gang's approach, within his own economic sphere his hand was seen in winning Mao's backing concerning the fixing of bureaucratic responsibility for transforming the national bourgeoisie, in limiting the fallout of the tax issue on both his subordinate Bo Yibo and tax policy generally, and in producing a more moderate policy toward the commercial bourgeoisie. Leaving Mao out of the picture—whether for administrative convenience, as a deliberate tactic, or even out of consideration for the Chairman's health—could have unpleasant repercussions, as Liu Shaoqi discovered both with regard to the Shanxi cooperatives in 1951 and concerning the issuing of documents generally. But seeking to set the agenda and persuade the Chairman always ran the risk of being at cross purposes with him.

What made this situation tolerable was that up until the Gao Gang affair the uncertainties largely involved policy rather than power. Leaders from Liu Shaoqi down might receive oblique but clearly understood criticism from the Chairman, but acceptance of Mao's views together with the ritual of self-criticism was sufficient to maintain one's standing. In the decade since the consolidation of his leadership in the early 1940s, Mao had been a sometimes stern but generally forgiving ruler, and others could draw comfort from that as they sought to advance their interests.[17] Intimately related to this was the fact that individual leaders pushed agendas largely concerned with their bureaucratic responsibilities and policy views. Success in these ventures naturally enhanced their influence, yet such efforts did not aim to upset the existing Party hierarchy. But when Mao's attitude was perceived to be uncertain regarding the makeup of the leadership itself, the danger of things getting out of hand was real. Then the inherent fault lines in the system, most notably the jealous concern of each revolutionary "faction" over its place in the leadership and the moral-ideological tradition that could easily exaggerate limited differences into matters of great principle, could suddenly give rise to intense conflict. Under such circumstances in 1953, the efforts of Gao and Rao threatened to exacerbate the usual contained conflict at Mao's court into something far more disruptive.

If Mao had actually toyed with the idea of a leadership shakeup, then he, too, was directly culpable for the severe threat to Party unity represented by Gao Gang; as matters unfolded he must bear some responsibility even under the most generous interpretation. But in the end, whatever his motives may have been at different times in 1953, Mao opted for Party unity and a reaffirmation of the existing leadership structure. While apparently led by theoretical concerns to adopt what was, up to that point, a rather unusually provocative political posture well into the summer, the Chairman came back to the theme of Party unity, perhaps halfheartedly at the end of the Financial and Economic Conference but decisively by the end of the year. Perhaps the best interpretation of the Gao-Rao drama is that developments went against Mao's expectations as they unfolded in 1953 not because he had a specific aim in mind, such as removing Liu Shaoqi, but because he pursued a potentially incompatible mix of goals, including expressing his dissatisfaction with Liu and Zhou, enhancing Gao Gang's status within the leadership, underlining his theoretical concerns, which included vaguely Stalinist elements, putting in place a forward-looking but still moderate set of policies, *and* at the same time maintaining leadership cohesion and the existing distribution of power.

From the long historical view, the Gao Gang affair may indeed have been an aberration in the general high level of Party unity in the early and mid-1950s. But it was an aberration rooted in court politics where final power was in the hands of one man[18] and other leaders sought to divine his intent. While there may be some justice in the current view of the Gao Gang affair as a passing blight on an otherwise golden age, the relatively benign nature of leadership politics in that age had far less to do with "inner-Party democracy" per se than with Mao's continuing attachment to a leadership style that had mightily contributed to the success of the Chinese revolution. In fact, the Gao-Rao affair is perhaps more important historically for bringing clearly into view the nature of court politics under Mao in the early 1950s, when the successful functioning of the system was so dependent on one man's opinions, and one man's self-restraint. The Party survived the threat of Gao and Rao, but their case shows that the preconditions for 1959 and 1966 were already in place in 1953, if not earlier. All that remained was for Mao to change his mind.

Appendices

I
AN OVERVIEW OF THE GAO-RAO AFFAIR

[A comprehensive, if still incomplete, account of the Gao Gang–Rao Shushi affair did not appear until after Mao's death. Even in this period Party histories generally gave only brief, stilted accounts of the case. The major exception, which is presented here, appeared in an internal publication of the Anhui provincial Party school. Written by a professional Party historian, Chen Shihui, it appeared in 1980, the year Deng Xiaoping referred to the Gao-Rao affair in his comments on drafts of the CCP's official historical resolution on the post-1949 period (see appendix V-1). Chen's account draws on a variety of sources, including major unpublished documents from 1954–55 (see appendices III–3A, VII-2A and 2B, and VIII-1) and the recollections of Party leaders (see appendix VI-1). It provides the clearest available written discussion of such key events as Mao's efforts to absolve Bo Yibo of line errors at the end of the Financial and Economic Conference and Gao Gang's effort to use An Ziwen's draft Politburo list against Liu Shaoqi. Chen's analysis, however, avoids the key event that apparently set the affair in motion, Mao's late 1952–early 1953 private conversations with Gao, where the Chairman was critical of Liu and Zhou Enlai.]

>Source: Chen Shihui, "Guanyu fandui Gao Gang, Rao Shushi Fandang Yinmou Huodong de Wenti" [Questions Concerning Opposition to the Anti-Party Conspiratorial Activities of Gao Gang and Rao Shushi], *Jiaoxue Cankao* [Teaching Reference] (Zhonggong Anhui shengwei dangxiao tushu ziliaoshi, December 1980), pp. 95–106.

IN 1953, at a crucial historical turning point when the whole nation entered into large-scale socialist transformation and planned socialist construction, the Gao Gang–Rao Shushi anti-Party affair emerged in our Party. The Party Center discovered this in time and led the whole unified Party to carry out an important struggle against the wildly ambitious Gao Gang and Rao Shushi [who sought] to split the Party and usurp power and position in the Party and the state. That struggle was necessary, and the guiding principles and methods adopted in the struggle were correct. This was an inner-Party struggle after our Party became the ruling party which was carried out comparatively well according to the basic principles of Marxism-Leninism and the Party's fine traditions. Today, after the

Party and the people have been through ten years of turmoil, and have suffered bitterly from excessive class struggle and excessive inner-Party struggle, to turn back and conduct research into the Party's struggle with Gao and Rao and the experiences and lessons [drawn from it] is significant and beneficial for reviving and developing the Party's fine traditions, for furthering Party unity and socialist modernization.

1. The Circumstances of and Reasons for the Gao-Rao Affair

Two explanations are usually given for the Gao-Rao affair: one is to emphasize or merely state that it was a reflection of sharp, deep, and complex class struggle; the other is to emphasize and point out that it was because Gao Gang and Rao Shushi were people of bad character, and to attribute the affair to individual wrongdoing. Neither of these is sufficiently comprehensive. I think that when considering the emergence of the Gao-Rao affair we must first of all see the historical change of our Party [having achieved] power. Starting with the new problems met by the Party in government, we can analyze the circumstances and conditions of the historical turning point of 1953, and the reasons and processes for Gao Gang's and Rao Shushi's own ideological change, and from this draw conclusions that are relatively in keeping with historical reality.

When they summarized the experiences of the Paris Commune, Marx and Engels said: "After the proletariat has grasped governing power and established its own country, it should prevent its work personnel from chasing after higher positions and more benefits, and prevent the nation's governing organs from becoming the master of the society instead of being the servant of society." When the CCP established the proletarian regime through the democratic revolution, it met with this inevitable new problem. Particularly in a country like China which has had thousands of years of feudal rule and which was economically and culturally extremely backward, a party like ours in which a large proportion of its members are from petty bourgeois families was bound to experience a severe testing. On the eve of Liberation, the Second Plenum of the Seventh Central Committee warned the entire Party, sharply pointing out: we must be alert for arrogance and claiming credit for victory; we must guard against "sugarcoated bullets"; we must prevent the tragedy of repeating the failure of peasant uprisings. The Party Center and Mao Zedong were very clear about the problem that was facing the governing Party and had foresight. After undergoing the Party consolidation and rectification campaign of the recovery period and the "Three-Anti" campaign, the majority of Party members were able to keep up the fine tradition of being modest and prudent and guard against conceit and arrogance. However, some Party members who held a great deal of political and economic power and who were surrounded and corrupted by strong feudal consciousness and bourgeois ideas gradually developed the arrogance and greed of self-styled heroes. Normally concealed desires of "winning promotion and getting rich" became inflated, which quickened the pace of political decadence. A small minority, including certain leading cadres, could not pass the new test of victory and governing power. They fell victim to the material and spiritual temptations of power and even went down the road of splitting and ruining the Party for their own ends. This is the objective social reason for the occurrence of Gao-Rao anti-Party affair.

Gao and Rao also had personal reasons of their own for moving down the anti-Party road. The process leading to their wrongdoings was a gradually developing one. In the past Gao Gang and Rao Shushi did some work for the revolution, but they started to show individualist and factional tendencies in the early revolutionary period. Later they did not pay attention to reforming their nonproletarian ideas during this long period of work, and especially after nationwide victory they gave themselves the air of heroes. They could not accept criticism and supervision from the organization and their comrades. Thus their extreme bourgeois individualism (which included strong feudal ways of thinking) developed more and more seriously. Their personal ambitions rose higher and higher, and the negative side of their thinking developed so swiftly that step by step they became bourgeois careerists and plotters.

Gao Gang joined the Party in 1926. He was one of the founders of the Shaan-Gan [Shaanxi-Gansu] revolutionary base area. From 1935 to 1945, under the direct leadership of the Central Committee of the Party, he was in charge of the work in the Northwest region and was the secretary of the CCP Central Committee's Northwest Bureau. He was elected as one of the members of the Party Central Committee at the Seventh Congress of the CCP, and at its First Plenum he was elected one of the members of the Politburo. In 1945 he was assigned to work in the Northeast region after the victory of the resistance war. Both before and after the Liberation of the whole country, Gao Gang gave great consideration to his future position. He told some people that after the revolutionary victory he might be minister in charge of agriculture or forestry. When Lin Biao [was transferred southward], the Central Committee of the Party appointed [Gao] secretary of the Northeast Bureau and concurrently chairman of the Northeast People's Government and commander and political commissar of the Northeast Military Region. He thus monopolized Party, government, and military power in the Northeast region. When the New China was founded, [Gao] was elected a vice-chairman of the Central People's Government. The more power he got the more he desired, and he gradually became more and more dissatisfied with his positions. He wanted the highest positions in the Party and government. From 1949 he engaged in many factional activities to split the Party and destroy its political and organizational principles. Gao Gang considered comrades Liu Shaoqi and Zhou Enlai to be his main obstacles to seizing the power of the central leadership. Therefore, he trumped up charges and spread rumors and slander to attack them, aiming to make certain cadres dissatisfied with the Center. Gao Gang disobeyed Party rules and discipline and carried out an unprincipled, factional cadre policy. He tempted cadres with promises of power and position to try to increase his influence and deceive certain people into supporting him. Gao Gang used the area that he was in charge of as a base for carrying out his own ambitions. He often put himself above the organization and did not respect its principle of unified leadership. Again and again he asserted that "the Northeast is unique," "the Northeast has always been advanced," and "the Northeast is ever correct." In the media he exaggerated and emphasized the importance of his individual role. To his superiors, he only reported his achievements, not his problems and mistakes. To those under him, he suppressed democracy while ruling like a patriarch, and he did not allow Northeast Party members to disclose any shortcomings and mistakes in the work of the Northeast to the Party Center. When he was transferred to work at the Center [Gao] thought it was "to lure the tiger out of the mountains" [an attempt to lure him away from his power base in the Northeast]. Therefore, he would not accept the position, and it was only when he was able to hold concurrently his position as secretary of the Northeast Bureau that he relaxed. But he was unwilling to allow Comrade Lin Feng to have full power over the routine work of the Northeast Bureau, something for which Comrade Mao Zedong criticized Gao Gang. Gao Gang behind the back of the Party Center privately told some of the Soviet Union's Communist leaders of the internal affairs of the CCP. He told tales and lies, promoted himself, denigrated leading comrades of the Center, and damaged Sino-Soviet unity. Furthermore, his private life was very decadent, and he totally lost all virtue as a Party member, which is not permitted by Party discipline and national law. Such a decadent private life is an example of the way in which the bourgeoisie erodes the Party. Gao Gang's extreme moral decline was one of the indications of his political degeneration.

Gao Gang's ally, Rao Shushi, joined the Party in 1925 and for a long time was engaged in underground revolutionary work. During the Anti-Japanese war Rao was appointed deputy secretary of the Southeast Bureau and Central China Bureau of the CCP Central Committee. In 1942 he was the political commissar of the New Fourth Army. Rao Shushi tried many times to seize power for himself during the decade from 1943 to 1953. To seize control of the New Fourth Army, in autumn 1943 he launched a completely wrong struggle against Comrade Chen Yi, who was the acting commander of the New Fourth Army, by mounting a surprise attack. Before launching this struggle he did not talk with Comrade Chen Yi or ask the Central Committee for instructions. He arbitrarily undertook factional activities among the leading cadres of the New Fourth Army units to attack and exclude Comrade Chen Yi. He trumped up a false charge that Comrade Chen Yi was against Comrade Mao Zedong and against the system of political commissars, and that he wanted to drive Rao away. [Rao] deceived a group of cadres [with these trumped up charges]. Then he telegraphed the Central Committee [in the manner of] the guilty party filing suit first. Rao smeared

Comrade Chen Yi and asked the Central Committee to send someone else to replace Chen Yi in order to be rid of him. In 1944 a telegram from the Central Committee ordered Comrade Chen Yi's transfer to Yan'an. Comrade Chen Yi sent the Central China Bureau a self-criticism concerning his liberalism on the question of unity in the Central China Bureau. Chairman Mao telegraphed the Central China Bureau and pointed out that the mistake Comrade Chen Yi made at the Seventh Representative Congress of the Fourth Red Army in West Fujian in the controversy over [who] was in charge was not a mistake of Party line, that this mistake had already been rectified, and that it should not be raised again.[1] [Chairman Mao] also pointed out that Comrade Chen Yi had made contributions in the civil war period; the argument between Chen and Rao at Huanghua Pond (where the New Fourth Army was stationed) was of the nature of a working relationship; [and] the Central China Bureau should stop the argument and move on to unity. But Rao incited some people to telegraph the Center jointly and put forward an opposing attitude. Rao Shushi was the type of person who organized inner-Party struggle by using the tactics of the exploiting classes of the old society to sow dissension for his own purposes, namely, to seize power. In 1949 he achieved the position of chairman of the East China Military and Administrative Committee by deceiving his superiors and deluding his subordinates. When he was secretary of the East China Bureau he made very serious right-deviationist mistakes. For example, on the question of suppressing counterrevolutionaries, he refused to make serious efforts to mobilize the masses but instead adopted the ridiculous policy of "using spies against spies." He went so far as to put forward the incorrect suggestion of "changing large numbers of counterrevolutionary cadres into our cadres," which resulted in serious consequences.

At the end of 1952 and the beginning of 1953 Gao Gang and Rao Shushi were transferred to work at the Center. Gao was appointed chairman of the State Planning Commission. Rao was appointed head of the organization department of the CCP Central Committee. They used each other, for their individual ambitions and desire for power linked them together. Originally Rao was comparatively close to Comrade Liu Shaoqi because of their work relationship. With his opportunistic approach and distorted idea of political life at the Center, [Rao] wrongly judged that Gao Gang's increasing status meant that Gao Gang had already replaced Comrade Liu Shaoqi as Chairman Mao's successor. [Rao] feared that if he again followed Comrade Liu Shaoqi he would suffer a loss in status; therefore he drew close to Gao Gang. At the same time, he thought Gao Gang was about to be successful in seizing the highest power and [decided] he would take a risk and cooperate. Gao Gang wanted to control Party personnel by using Rao Shushi in order to increase his influence. From the words and deeds of Gao and Rao during the period they worked at the Center we can see that they took mutual concerted action and carried out many anti-Party plots.

[1] At this 1929 meeting Chen was elected to replace Mao as Party secretary of the military front in Fujian after he and Zhu De separately argued with Mao over Party-army relations.

The Gao-Rao affair occurred in 1953. We should analyze the objective circumstances and concrete historical conditions at that time. Along with the deepening socialist transformation, the Party was situated in an environment where class relationships were undergoing sharp changes and class struggle was relatively tense. Internationally, imperialist encirclement still existed; internally, the bourgeoisie both in the cities and countryside constantly resisted the socialist transformation pursued by the working class and the Party. This struggle existed in both the political and economic spheres, sometimes overtly and sometimes covertly. The bourgeoisie not only had real economic strength and widespread social influence, but they also had a weapon that could not be ignored: that is, the ideology of the exploiting classes, the exploiting class style, sinister and swindling tactics for struggle, and degenerate lifestyles that remained from thousands of years of an exploiting system, which surrounded and eroded the Party. As Lenin said, "When the old society died its dead body could not be put into the coffin and buried in the grave, hence it would decay and stink right amid us and further poison us" (*Collected Works of Lenin*, 27:407). These things certainly must be reflected within the Party and spread to the weaker parts of the Party.

In 1953, to fit the needs of planned economic construction, the Center considered reforming the state system. Within a small circle there were preliminary discussions on whether to adopt a Council of Ministers system and whether the Party Center should add the positions of vice-chairman and general secretary. Comrade Mao Zedong put forward the suggestion of dividing the leadership into a first front and a second front. At the same time the Center was considering holding the National People's Congress and Eighth Congress of the Party. At every turning point in history when organizations at all levels need to adjust and change their personnel, big or small careerists will take advantage of such opportunities to seize power and speed up their own promotion. Careerists hide themselves very well in normal times; they will not unmask themselves until an opportunity arises. They can make excuses in normal times, but when there is a certain political climate they will stretch out their hands at a critical moment. This can be regarded as a general rule, and Gao and Rao were no exceptions. They capitalized on their contributions to the revolution and believed that this was an extremely good opportunity to seize power. Moreover, at the same time there were certain conditions that could be used as an excuse for their attack, that is, the Party was criticizing the incorrect ideology of departing from the general line and was correcting mistakes and shortcomings in work. Gao and Rao, then, were extremely anxious to push to the limit their plot of splitting the Party.

2. The Main Facts of the Gao-Rao Anti-Party Conspiratorial Activities

The Party-splitting conspiratorial activities of Gao Gang and Rao Shushi became noticeable before, during, and after the National Financial and Economic Work

Conference held in the summer of 1953 and the Second National Organization Conference in the autumn of the same year. Between June and December 1953, the Central Committee's Secretariat gradually discovered the anti-Party activities of Gao and Rao. In the winter of 1953 the Party Center, after gathering facts about Gao and Rao's attempt to seize leadership power, decided to act to resolve their case.

From June to August 1953 the Party Center convened the National Financial and Economic Work Conference. The main themes of this conference were to unify understanding within the Party of the general line for the transition period, to correct ideological mistakes deviating from the general line which existed among certain cadres, and to criticize the mistakes and shortcomings in taxation policy committed in the preceding six months by some comrades in charge of financial work. For example, after revising a "new tax system," they proposed the slogan "equal taxation for public and private [enterprises]." This violated the principled stipulations of the [March 1949] Second Plenum of the Seventh Central Committee to restrict capitalist economic development in the aspect of taxation policy. [The "new tax system,"] in fact, gave the advantage to the private capitalist economy while disadvantaging the development of the socialist and semisocialist economy. Comrade Bo Yibo, then deputy director of the Financial and Economic Committee and minister of finance, had some degree of responsibility with regard to this question. Normally, to sum up and draw lessons from experience and to criticize shortcomings in work are routine matters in the Party's political life. However, the motives of Gao Gang and Rao Shushi were not honorable. They diligently made use of the opportunity of the Party correcting its own shortcomings to create an atmosphere of tension to intensify inner-Party struggle. Their aim was not only to seize financial power, but more importantly also to mount an attack against comrades Liu Shaoqi and Zhou Enlai. They insisted that the mistakes in the work of the Finance Ministry were mistakes of principle and were related to comrades Liu Shaoqi and Zhou Enlai. At the conference the Gao Gang group gave several speeches which, under the guise of criticizing Comrade Bo Yibo, carried out an attack on and incited dissatisfaction with [Liu Shaoqi] by cleverly quoting words from previous speeches of Comrade Liu Shaoqi. For those who understood this situation, the moment they heard [the critique] they immediately knew that it was an attack by innuendo, [i.e.,] "openly speaking of Bo, secretly shooting at Liu."

Outside the conference they wantonly spread slanderous rumors and misinterpreted political life at the Center. They even mentioned the names of central leaders and attempted to damage their prestige. They used the method of "attacking a single fault without considering the other [good] aspects," and they insisted that Comrade Liu Shaoqi's isolated mistakes on some questions were systematic mistakes and ordinary mistakes were mistakes in line. They represented questions that had already been corrected or self-examined as current serious problems. For example, Comrade Liu Shaoqi's "Tianjin Talks" and his opinion on how to handle rich peasant Party members were both correct, no matter whether judged by the general spirit or principle or by the concrete method of application. But they exaggerated and distorted isolated inappropriate expressions [that Liu] made carelessly and moreover criticized [these expressions] from the higher level of principle as surrendering to the bourgeoisie and the rich peasants. They also collected some of Comrade Liu Shaoqi's speeches and comments on documents (for example, concerning the question of the new stage of peace and democracy, concerning the question of left-deviationist mistakes in the 1947 land reform, and concerning the question of [Liu's] comments on the Shanxi Provincial Party Committee's "Raising Higher Mutual Aid Organizations in Old Liberated Areas," etc.) and wrote them up as a file with a view to using them as ammunition for an attack.[2]

They insisted that there were factions at the Center and slandered Comrade Liu Shaoqi as having his own "circle" and Comrade Zhou Enlai his own "stall." They seized upon a "name list" of members of the [projected new] Politburo prepared by the deputy director of the central organization department, Comrade An Ziwen, and made insinuations about it. As a matter of fact, Gao Gang had discussed this "name list" with Comrade An Ziwen, but Gao and Rao made an unfounded accusation that this "name list" originated from Comrade Liu Shaoqi. The names of Comrade Bo Yibo and Lin Biao were clearly written on the "name list," but Gao and Rao said [the list] "includes Bo but not Lin." Rao also said in an instigating manner that this "name list" contained a "circle," that Comrade Bo Yibo was a member of this "circle" who had been struggled against at the Financial and Economic Conference, and in the future other conferences would be held to struggle against other members of this "circle." [Rao] sowed dissension everywhere and attempted to create disharmony within the Party.

Gao Gang attempted to deceive some of the Party cadres working in the army and win their support. [To this end,] he deliberately created and spread the fallacious viewpoint of "the theory of two parties" and the "military party theory." He divided the unified Party organization into two: one was the so-called party of the base areas and army, the other was the so-called party of the white areas. He said the Party was created by the army and made himself the representative of the "party of the base areas and army." He did his utmost to use these fallacies to give theoretical justification for his seizing the highest leadership authority. He made use of these bourgeois viewpoints which distorted the Party's character and history to insist that the leadership power of the Party and state was in the hands of the "party of the white areas" and because of this [argued] that it should be "thoroughly reorganized." He counted on Chairman Mao's "trust" in him and assumed he had organized an "economic cabinet" and had gathered a great deal of the power of the Government Administration Council. At the same

[2] For discussions of the above issues raised by Gao and Rao, see above, pp. 41–43 and 72–73.

time he subjectively thought he could probably get support from four of the six large administrative areas.³ He felt that seizing the leadership power of the Party and state was already quite within his grasp. Consequently, his activities were extremely unrestrained and incessant. He even used various opportunities, including dancing parties and dinner parties, to establish alliances and incite dissatisfaction in many ways.

At the time the Center still did not understand the ultimate aim of Gao and Rao's activities, but it already paid attention to some abnormal aspects of [their] activities and took steps to rectify in good time some improper opinions that developed due to their influence. Thus the conference attained its expected results. Comrades Mao Zedong and Zhou Enlai both had a clear attitude and conclusion about [Gao and Rao's] exaggeration of the mistakes in financial and economic work as mistakes in line. Comrade Mao Zedong, using pen on paper, drew a vivid geometric illustration to clarify to everyone [the nature of these mistakes]. [He said] that two points join a line, but the problem of the "new taxation system" is only one point, and one point doesn't make a line. The mistakes in previous financial and economic work were serious, but they were not mistakes in line. Comrade Zhou Enlai pointed out when making his summary that the mistakes in financial and economic work have not become a system; therefore, it should not be spoken of as a mistake of line. Directed against the splittist activities of Gao and Rao, the conference emphasized unity. Comrade Mao Zedong in his speech at the Financial and Economic Work Conference pointed out: "If there are any opinions, please raise them openly. To damage Party unity is the most shameful thing." "Only by relying on the political experience of the collective and the wisdom of the collective can we guarantee the correct leadership of the Party and state as well as the unshakable unity of the ranks of the Party as a whole." During the conference Comrade Mao Zedong invited comrades from every section [of the Party] to talk, and all [he] talked about was the need for unity, destroying cliques and leveling mountaintops. Comrade Zhou Enlai also stressed the significance of unity.

Gao Gang, however, ignored this completely. After the Financial and Economic Conference, in the name of going on holiday, he purposely went to East and Central-South China to "lobby"—he not only spread such reactionary theories as "the Party was created by the army" and "the history of the Party should be reassessed," but also attacked leading central comrades through all kinds of exaggerations, distortions, and even fabrications. He broadcast an illicitly drawn up name list of supplementary candidates for Central Committee members and alternate members and promoted his plan, among a number of high-ranking officials, to "reorganize" the Party and state leadership, in a secret attempt to put together his team to usurp Party and state power. In Hangzhou, Gao Gang discussed with Lin Biao a name list for an "election of the Center."

During the same period, Rao Shushi and Gao Gang cooperated under a tacit

³See below, Appendix V-1, p. 222.

understanding. Before the Financial and Economic Conference ended, Rao, without the knowledge or consent of anybody in the Central Committee, found pretexts to start a savage struggle against Comrade An Ziwen, deputy director of the central organization department. He deliberately leaked out the fact that Comrade An Ziwen had drafted a "name list" and had been given disciplinary punishment. He accused Comrade An Ziwen of being antagonistic to the Financial and Economic Conference, using this to insinuate that Comrade Liu Shaoqi's attitude toward the conference was problematic. In this way, Rao actively colluded with, supported, and participated in Gao Gang's splittist activities. Subsequently, during the Second National Conference on Organization Work held in September and October, in the name of criticizing Comrade An Ziwen's problems, Rao pointed the spearhead at Comrade Liu Shaoqi, directing a farce of "condemning An to knock down Liu." At this conference, the director of the organization department under the former Northeast Bureau made a fully prepared address. He criticized the central organization department for its use of cadres because it "blurred the distinction between enemies and friends, and was lacking sufficient vigilance against bad people," which showed the "right-leaning thought" of the leadership, who failed to ensure the implementation of a correct political line. Though talking about Comrade An Ziwen, he was actually hitting out at Comrade Liu Shaoqi's handling of certain problems. The director of the former Shandong Subbureau, on the other hand, attacked the Center from the angle of the Party rectification campaign. They did all they could to incite and coerce inside and outside of the meetings in their effort to seize power over personnel and reorganize the leadership of the central organization department. They also planned to denounce Comrade Liu Shaoqi by name and have a public "showdown."

To put a stop to Rao Shushi's activities, the Central Committee called a temporary halt to the conference and instead convened a meeting of the leadership group to expose and criticize contradictions openly. Comrades Liu Shaoqi, Zhu De, and Deng Xiaoping took part and spoke at the meetings of the leading group, stressing the importance of Party-wide unity to the implementation of the general line. At the closing meeting of the conference on October 27, central leading comrades reaffirmed, in no uncertain terms, that the central organization department had carried out the correct Party line in the past and had great achievements to its credit. They reiterated the need for Party unity. The conference entrusted every delegate to relay the Center's call for unity to all organizations of the Party upon their return to their posts. These measures of the Center fouled Rao's plot to split the Party during that conference.

Despite all this, Gao and Rao still did not realize their mistakes. After returning to Beijing from the South, Gao Gang stepped up activities to usurp Party and state power. In December 1953, Comrade Mao Zedong, according to precedent, proposed that Comrade Liu Shaoqi be entrusted to act for him in his leading work in the Central Committee while he was on holiday. Gao Gang immediately voiced his opposition and carried out a series of covert activities to get the post of the general secretary or vice-chairman of the Party. He told one responsible comrade of the Center: The Central Committee should set up vice-chairmen, and who should be elected? "One for you and one for me." He also demanded an election to replace the premier of the Government Administration Council, indicating that he should get the position. This fully revealed his extreme personal ambitions. [However,] he completely miscalculated. At this time, many comrades who had heard him make his anti-Party propaganda had already exposed them to the Central Committee. After hearing about them, Comrade Mao Zedong made certain investigations into the situation and talked to different people to learn the facts. One time, when talking to Comrade Luo Ruiqing, Comrade Mao Zedong humorously made a remark about getting a political cold and stuffed noses. He said: There are two types of sleep. One is to sleep on a bed, another is to sleep in a drum [i.e., in the dark]. If comrades had not informed me about the problems of Gao and Rao, I would still be sleeping inside the drum! Then he made further inquiries into the relevant circumstances. Based upon findings of its investigations, the central Secretariat, with the full support of all Central Committee members in Beijing with the exception of Gao and Rao, resolutely put a stop to the latter's anti-Party schemes.

Summing up the above, from the Financial and Economic Conference, Gao Gang's trip to the South, the Organization Work Conference, to December, Gao and Rao did collude in a series of systematic activities to split the Party. They were identical in the target of their attacks, the talk they spread, and their mode of operation. They had completely violated the standpoint, principles, and discipline of the Party and became bourgeois politicians and careerists.

Politically, Gao and Rao attempted to oust comrades Liu Shaoqi and Zhou Enlai from the Party Center and the government. They hoped first to control power on the first front, making Comrade Mao Zedong a mere figurehead. Comrades Liu Shaoqi and Zhou Enlai were our Party's most outstanding and long-tested leaders. They had been, for many years, secretaries of the central Secretariat and were in charge of important leading work in the Party and government. When Comrade Mao Zedong was absent from the Center, the Politburo always appointed Comrade Liu Shaoqi acting chairman of the Central Committee. That is precisely why Gao and Rao made Comrade Liu Shaoqi their particular target. Their blatant plan to "reorganize" the central leadership and openly demand to have themselves installed is a revelation of how blinded they were by their lust for power. Gao and Rao held nothing back in their insatiable appetite and quest for power; they revealed everything about their designs and no longer attempted to cover them up. From this and from Lin Biao and the "Gang of Four's" later counterrevolutionary attempts to usurp Party and state power, one can see how the word "power" epitomizes the most reactionary essence of all schemers and plotters.

In their mode of operation, Gao Gang and Rao Shushi adopted the usual tactic of the exploiting classes—that of covert subversion. They were double-dealers, acting one way to your face and another behind your back; they camouflaged themselves with the cover of supporting the Party and Comrade Mao Zedong while engaging in subversive activities against the Party and the Central Committee. They knew that they had no cause to oppose [the relevant] leading central comrades, so they never openly or formally voiced their opinions at meetings of the Center, but secretly invented materials and distorted facts, directing charges of exaggerated or falsified "mistakes" against leading central comrades, which they spread among many people. When Comrade Mao Zedong suggested increasing the number of Politburo members, the question was discussed within a limited circle. This was normal Party procedure. [Gao Gang and Rao Shushi,] however, flatly accused Comrade Liu Shaoqi of having asked Comrade An Ziwen to draw up his "name list." Actually, Comrade Liu Shaoqi did not even know that Comrade An Ziwen and Gao Gang had talked about the "name list." At the same time, [Gao and Rao] widely disseminated talk about the "name list" inside and outside the conference and from the north to the south of the country. They were masters at making things up out of thin air; it was no wonder, then, that, when they discovered isolated defects and mistakes some comrades had made in work, they took up the position of representatives of the "correct line" and [exploited these defects and mistakes] to attack viciously the people concerned and elevate their own status.

Organizationally, Gao Gang and Rao Shushi engaged in sectarian activities. Like all careerists, they tried to form factions, set up "mountaintops," and establish their own power. To do so, they aped the political maneuvering tactics of the feudal classes in carrying out anti-organizational activities inside the Party. They collected a group of people to attack another group of people, or struck some people down first to afterwards drag them in, and made people who were on hand to give in and fall into the plot. Rao Shushi had declared that his attitude to people is "to be mean first and gentlemanly afterwards." What this meant was to find an opportunity to deal the other side a harsh blow first, then when they were "subdued," to rope them in in order to use them. This was entirely the power tactics of the officialdom of exploiting classes.

The exposure of and struggle against the Gao-Rao anti-Party plot constitutes a major struggle in the Party after the founding of the People's Republic of China. Both Gao and Rao were careerists out to usurp Party and state power. Their criminal activities were, however, both without a program and without policies. That is to say, they did not put forward a line and a political platform in opposition to the Party's general line in the period of transition. Theoretically, they did not put forward a set of political views concerning the situation of the revolution, the target of the revolution, the motive force and tasks of the revolution, and so on. They had no policies and systems of their own concerning practical work. Therefore, this struggle against them is not a struggle of political line. Naturally, in order to split the Party, they had disseminated such fallacies as "the party of the army" and "the theory of two parties." At the same time, since they had engaged in splittist activities and undermined Party unity and affected and impeded the implementation of the general line for the transition period, they had to be resolutely stopped and struggled against. Organizationally, their sectarian activities violated Party organizational principles, but they had not openly declared a political line or a theoretical program because of differences with the Party on the general line for the transition period, therefore, it did not constitute a struggle of political line. Before the "Cultural Revolution," official Party resolutions and documents had never called the Gao-Rao struggle a line struggle. During the "Cultural Revolution," the "Gang of Four," quoting inappropriate words by Comrade Mao Zedong spoken at various times, made much of it with the purpose of using the issue of Gao-Rao to attack a large number of veteran cadres. My opinion is that, in inner-Party struggle, we should view a problem in its true light, neither exaggerating nor understating it. We must seek truth from facts. This struggle should be characterized as a struggle against the schemes of careerists to split the Party and one which will enhance Party unity and unification. Naturally, we can continue to discuss this viewpoint.

3. The Circumstances of the Struggle Against the Gao-Rao Anti-Party Conspiratorial Activities

Gao Gang and Rao Shushi's conspiratorial activities severely threatened Party unity, damaging the Party's cause. To arouse all our comrades to maintain and protect unity and oppose a split, the Politburo adopted a series of measures. From the Center to the local organizations, from within the Party to outside the Party, we exposed, criticized, and settled accounts with Gao and Rao, which greatly educated the whole Party and united the majority of cadres including those who committed mistakes.

At first they were exposed and criticized among the high-ranking cadres of the Center. At the central Politburo meeting of December 24, 1953, where Gao Gang's problem was revealed, Comrade Mao Zedong pointed out that Gao Gang [and his accomplices] "blew a type of wind [and] lit a type of fire," [and] called it "blowing a sinister wind [and] lighting a sinister fire," [i.e.,] "their purpose was to overwhelm the positive wind and to put out the positive fire in order to overthrow a group of people." At this meeting, Comrade Mao Zedong also put forward a proposal concerning strengthening Party unity. The Politburo unanimously agreed with this proposal, and the draft "Resolution on Strengthening Party Unity" was drawn up and transmitted to the Fourth Plenum of the Seventh Central Committee for discussion. [This plenum] was held on February 6–10, 1954. Comrade Mao Zedong did not attend the meeting because of his holidays. Entrusted by the Politburo, Comrade Liu Shaoqi made [the report to the plenum]....[4]

---

[4] The remainder of this paragraph and the following deleted paragraphs deal with the agenda of the plenum and the content of the resolution on Party unity. These matters are covered in greater detail below, Appendix VII-1, pp. 236–40.

. . .

The Fourth Plenum was a meeting of great historic importance in the history of the Party that exposed and opposed the conspiratorial activities of Gao Gang and Rao Shushi, protected the Party Center, and maintained Party unity and a unified [outlook]. It also provided the basic assurance for fulfilling the Party's general task and the general line for the transition period.

Before the Fourth Plenum of the Seventh Central Committee the Party pointed out to Gao Gang the seriousness of his mistakes and demanded he make a self-examination and put a stop to any bad intentions and actions in order not to add more mistakes to the former ones which might lead to his severance from the Party. At the plenum, although Gao Gang made a superficial self-criticism and Rao Shushi a general [unspecific] self-examination, they did not express any genuine repentance. According to the decision of the central Secretariat in mid-February 1954, two separate discussion meetings on the Gao Gang question and the Rao Shushi question were held at which thirty-seven members and alternate members of the Central Committee and forty important work personnel were present. At these two meetings many facts concerning the conspiratorial activities of Gao and Rao were further exposed, checked, and verified. At the discussion meeting on the Gao Gang question, Comrade Zhou Enlai made a summing-up speech revealing the main facts of Gao Gang's Party splitting and his attempt to seize the power of the central leadership, analyzing the causes that made Gao Gang step onto the anti-Party road, and pointing out the lessons that we should learn. In accordance with the evidence revealed at the discussion meeting on the question of Rao Shushi, comrades Deng Xiaoping, Chen Yi, and Tan Zhenlin reported to the central Politburo exposing Rao Shushi's characteristics as a hypocrite and a careerist and the fact that he acted as Gao Gang's accomplice in splitting activities. They also pointed out the lessons that should be learned. At the discussion meeting on Gao Gang, forty-three participants made speeches revealing his crimes. Facing these indisputable facts, Gao Gang not only refused to confess the most wicked and essential aspects of his crimes to the Party, but he also resisted exposure and criticism of him by (unsuccessfully) attempting suicide. In his self-criticism on February 24, he only admitted that he was against certain leading comrades of the Center, that he carried out factional and illicit activities, and he touched lightly on the fact that his mistakes might split the Party if they were further developed. In this way he tried to cover the conspiratorial activities to split the Party in order to seize the power of the Party and state which he had already carried out. He made the excuse that he was momentarily muddled in his thinking and engaged in sophistry over his despairing suicide attempt which reflected his deeper hatred of the Party and its comrades after the exposure of his conspiracy. Although at the Fourth Plenum the guiding principle of curing the sickness to save the patient and being patient in order to awaken consciousness was adopted, Gao Gang still refused to be educated and saved by the Party, and he eventually managed to commit suicide in August 1954. On the last day of the discussion meeting on Rao Shushi, sixty-six comrades from the large regions and various central departments attended. Rao made a preliminary self-criticism at the discussion meeting touching on the light points but dodging the serious problems, basically denying [all charges]. After the meeting Rao made a written self-criticism in which he admitted to some already exposed individual facts but avoided many crucial problems.

Under the leadership of the central Politburo, in April 1954 the Northeast Bureau convened a meeting of high-ranking Party cadres in the Northeast region. Comrade Zhou Enlai attended the meeting and transmitted a report "On the Resolution of the Fourth Plenum of the Seventh Central Committee and the Question of Gao Gang and Rao Shushi." The meeting seriously and sharply exposed and criticized Gao Gang's anti-Party activities, and also exposed and criticized the serious errors of some comrades who had committed mistakes in following Gao Gang. In the same month the East China Bureau convened a Party representatives meeting. In May–June an enlarged meeting was held by the Shandong Subbureau. In June an enlarged meeting was held by the Shanghai Municipal Party Committee. In August a Party representatives meeting was held in Shandong province further exposing and criticizing Rao Sushi's anti-Party activities and criticizing the problems of some comrades who had followed Rao Shushi in committing serious mistakes. The above-mentioned meetings positively improved the work of the Party organizations in Northeast and East China.

After the Fourth Plenum, on February 12 the Party Center issued "A Notice on Transmitting and Studying the Documents of the Fourth Plenum of the Seventh Central Committee." It demanded that Party organizations at different levels circulate and organize study of the Fourth Plenum documents among cadres and Party members. On February 18 the *People's Daily* published the "Communiqué of the Fourth Plenum of the Seventh Central Committee," which publicized the main contents of the "Resolution on Strengthening Party Unity." The central Politburo's disclosure of the question of Gao and Rao's anti-Party conspiratorial activities was first transmitted to the level of special district Party secretaries and above. On August 17 the Center issued the "Directive Concerning Relaying the Gao-Rao Question to All Party Members and Youth League Members." According to this directive, all Party and Youth League members were informed, as were some democratic personages outside the Party. Party organizations and CCP and Youth League members at different levels deeply studied and researched the documents of the Fourth Plenum. They firmly supported the Party Center's decision, were indignant at the conspiratorial activities of Gao and Rao, and heightened the strengthening of Party unity and unification of consciousness.

From March 21 to 31, 1955, the Central Committee held the National Party Conference. Comrade Mao Zedong was in charge of the conference and made an important speech. Comrade Chen Yun made a report about the First Five-Year Plan for developing the national economy. Comrade Deng Xiaoping made a special report "Concerning the Gao Gang, Rao Shushi Anti-Party Alliance." The conference passed a resolution "On the Anti-Party Alliance of Gao Gang and Rao Shushi" and decided to expel Gao Gang and Rao Shushi from the Party. A "Resolution on Establishing the Party's Central and Local Control Committees" was passed. Dong Biwu was elected secretary of the Central Control Committee. The Conference also passed the "Resolution Concerning the Draft of the First Five-Year Plan for the Development of the National Economy." On April 4, 1955, the above-mentioned three resolutions were approved at the Fifth Plenum of the Seventh Central Committee, and the members of the Central Control Committee were elected.

The practice of our Party's struggle against Gao and Rao demonstrated that this inner-Party struggle was fairly successful. To examine whether or not an inner-Party struggle was properly conducted we first have to ask whether it was truly necessary, whether there existed objectively a crucial inner-Party contradiction that had to be resolved. To expose and solve the inner-Party contradiction appropriately without enlarging or lessening it is the basic materialist requirement so far as inner-Party struggle is concerned. It is also the premise on which such a struggle can be correctly carried out. Our Party's struggle against Gao and Rao started from the fact that [they] carried out anti-Party conspiratorial activities, and the decision [to fight against them] was made under circumstances where their activities had already damaged our Party and faced it with the danger of a split. Such a struggle had a definite object in view. The facts were there, the people concerned were there. It was neither fictitious nor artificial.

Secondly, the reason why the struggle against Gao and Rao's conspiratorial activities was relatively successful was that this struggle embodied comparatively well our Party's principle and tradition of "seeking truth from facts," and also the correct guiding principles, policies, and methods for inner-Party struggle were adopted. There was always leadership, order, and restraint throughout the whole struggle. The struggle was resolute yet prudent. While no principles were dealt with perfunctorily, no comrades were harmed excessively. No mistakes of "broadening the scope" occurred. In general, the development was sound, and the effect was relatively good.

Relative attention was paid to investigation and research throughout this struggle, [and] the nature and the scope of the problem were made clear. Methods and steps in conformity with our Party's organizational principles were adopted. The Center discovered the problems in a comparatively timely manner. When the Secretariat discovered the splitting activities of Gao and Rao, comrades Mao Zedong, Zhou Enlai, Deng Xiaoping, and Chen Yun personally sought out people for talks, and separately investigated, carried out work, and examined circumstances to make the truth clear. When the Center got hold of Gao and Rao's essential problem of usurping Party [leadership] and seizing power, the Party without hesitation immediately exposed and resolutely stopped them so that their influence could no longer spread. Thus no more people were involved. The whole struggle developed comparatively smoothly, in a well-planned, step-by-step manner from the upper level to the lower level, from within the Party to outside the Party. It emphasized ideological education, focusing on the conceit that widely existed after coming to power, and the problem of insufficient recognition of the importance of Party unity. [In this way,] the struggle improved the whole Party's political and ideological consciousness. At this time, [the exposure of the Gao-Rao affair] was a very big shock and very deep education [to all our comrades] no matter whether they were high-ranking cadres or ordinary cadres, old Party members or new ones. While this inner-Party struggle firmly clung to our Party's principled stand and seriously dealt with the question of Gao Gang and Rao Shushi, the guiding principle of "learning from past mistakes to avoid future ones [and] curing the sickness to save the patient" was applied to those comrades who were influenced by Gao and Rao or those who even participated to some extent in these anti-Party activities. This was done according to the facts of their mistakes and how well they recognized them. On the basis of clearing up ideology, only very few comrades among them received organizational discipline and at the same time were transferred to work in other positions. These comrades were tested later, learned their lessons, and did very beneficial work for the people. [Still,] there were some shortcomings in this inner-Party struggle. For instance, some ideological criticism could have been more careful. Less severe disciplinary action could have been taken against some of the comrades. The scope of demotion and salary reduction for some individuals could have been a bit smaller. All these questions were far from the important aspect, yet attention should be paid to them. Generally speaking, however, this inner-Party struggle was effective. It not only thoroughly exposed Gao Gang and Rao Shushi but also saved comrades who had made mistakes, greatly educated the whole Party, and strengthened Party unity. In addition, at the right moment it mobilized the whole Party to aim actively at the goal of fulfilling and overfulfilling the First Five-Year Plan, thus guaranteeing the successful realization of the general line for the transition period. But unfortunately we subsequently did not sufficiently apply and develop this experience of seeking truth from facts in carrying out inner-Party struggle. Comparing this with subsequent bitter lessons, these experiences seem all the more valuable. We should make active efforts in order to restore and develop this excellent tradition in the life of our Party.

4. Lessons from Experience

More than twenty years have passed since the Gao-Rao affair. With the passing of time and the testing of practice, we can now see how the affair developed in the light of history. Comrades Mao Zedong, Zhou Enlai, [and] Deng Xiaoping all made penetrating summaries of the lessons from the experience of this inner-Party struggle and raised a series of important principles for strengthening the construction of a party in power. For example, politically it is necessary to prevent careerists from usurping power; ideologically the emphasis is on strengthening Marxist-Leninist education, opposing individualism, arrogance, and complacency, and opposing all exploiting class ideology. Organizationally it is necessary to have a sound system of democratic centralism, to persist in the principle of collective leadership and oppose the patriarchal style of arbitrary rule. Consistent, strict, systematic supervision is to be exercised over any Party member. These principles remain valid to this very day.

The negative lessons we can draw from the Gao-Rao affair show us that a victorious party, a party in power, must always be vigilant and oppose arrogance and complacency. In the history of our Party, every time we were comparatively modest and sober the Party's cause developed smoothly and its advance was quicker. On the contrary, when we were arrogant and complacent the revolutionary cause was rebuffed and suffered losses. With the victory of the democratic revolution and our Party exercising power, the people would rely upon us and be grateful, different types of people would flatter us, and in this way objective conditions gave rise to claiming credit for oneself and arrogance emerged. And as they had power, this type of mood had every possibility of developing among some Party cadres to the dangerous situation where some people would place themselves above the Party and above the people. Because of this, guarding against and opposing arrogance cannot but become a major task in the construction of a party in power. One of the factors that took Gao and Rao onto the anti-Party road was the pernicious development of their arrogance, while the fact that their illicit activities had a definite market was due to arrogance existing among some cadres to varying degrees. With the development of this mood the system of collective leadership broke down so that liberalism developed, and this gave careerists like Gao and Rao their opportunity to act. After the Fourth Plenum this dangerous mood was vigorously overcome, and many Party members and especially high-ranking cadres consciously made self-examinations that were relevant to their work and practical thinking. We were able to prevent pride and rashness and act in unity, and very quickly realized victory in the socialist transformation of the system of ownership of the means of production and overfulfilled the First Five-Year Plan. However, as Marshal Ye Jianying said in his speech celebrating the thirtieth anniversary of the People's Republic of China, "In the face of great victories we began to lack prudence," that is, we began to be so arrogant that it caused our country's socialist cause to travel a tortuous path for which we have paid bitterly. The lesson is a deep one.

The Party's struggle against Gao and Rao profoundly educated us: it is necessary to do everything to strengthen Party unity. It is the sacred responsibility of every Party member to safeguard Party unity and integration. The anti-Party, anti-Center splittist activities carried out by Gao and Rao had placed our Party in serious danger. The Fourth Plenum of the Seventh Central Committee and the National Party

Conference made a profound summary of the experiences of the Party in the struggle against Gao and Rao, it raised consolidating the Party's unification and safeguarding Party unity to the level of principle concerning the life and death of the Party, [and] it greatly raised the political consciousness of Party members and cadres. It strengthened their sense of organization and therefore made a new contribution to the theory of Party construction. Today, after having been through the unprecedented splitting activities and destruction of the Party by Lin Biao and the "Gang of Four," we realize even more how precious Party unity is and that Party unity is truly the Party's life.

The struggle against the anti-Party conspiratorial activities of Gao Gang and Rao Shushi also reveals to us that in the situation where the Party is in power, we must be especially vigilant and prevent the emergence of big and little careerists, and we must master how to see through and resist various types of conspiratorial activities. As our Party has high prestige among the people and its organization is strict, in such a situation those careerists generally do not dare to reveal their flag by openly carrying out activities but will always resort to the stratagems of politicians of the exploiting classes, carry out intrigues and plots, and engage in splitting activities and secret schemes. This is not only proven by the Gao-Rao affair, it has also been borne out by the criminal activities carried out on an even greater scale by Lin Biao and the "Gang of Four." Not only have such struggles emerged repeatedly in the history of the CCP, but similar incidents have also incessantly occurred in the history of the Communist Party of the Soviet Union. So from this we can see that preventing careerists and conspirators from usurping Party power is a general and long-term problem for proletarian parties in power. Those countries that have had a long period of feudal rule and that are comparatively backward economically and culturally must particularly pay attention to solving this problem. At the National Party Conference, in view of the conspiratorial activities of Gao and Rao, Comrade Mao Zedong pointed out sharply: Communists must be politically above board and must never learn the conspiratorial tricks of Gao Gang and Rao Shushi. At the time he also emphasized that the study of Marxism-Leninism must be strengthened, that we must learn to distinguish between appearances and reality, and we must not be confused by false appearances. We must always distance ourselves from talk and action that violates Party principles. And whatever happens we must not become tangled up with careerists. These points are undoubtedly of extreme importance for a healthy inner-Party life and for distinguishing conspiratorial activities. At the same time, we should also consider the problem from the point of view of continuing to reform and perfect the system. We should correct the malpractice of too much power being concentrated in the hands of one person, persist in the system of collective leadership, and create a robust socialist democracy and legal system. In this way the people will really be able to exercise supervision over the leading organs and leading cadres, and thus promote the healthy advancement of the socialist cause.

(In addition, [I] attach a few sentences about Rao Shushi's commonplace circumstances: as a result of discovering that he had serious political problems such as shielding counterrevolutionaries, the National Party Conference decided to expel him from the Party. After this, on April 1, 1955, public security forces arrested Rao Shushi according to legal procedures. On August 30, 1965, the Supreme People's Court sentenced him to fourteen years imprisonment and the loss of his political rights for ten years. On September 23, 1965, he was paroled. In 1967 he was again placed under supervision and examined. He died of pneumonia on March 2, 1975.)

II
THE TAX ISSUE AND OTHER DEVELOPMENTS
January–May 1953

[In the half year before the activities of Gao Gang and Rao Shushi first surfaced at the summer 1953 Financial and Economic Conference, a number of developments set the stage for those later events. Item 1 below deals with the most important of those developments, Bo Yibo's revised tax system, which both angered Mao and became a main feature of Gao's attack on Liu Shaoqi through Bo at the conference. This selection also deals with Bo's early 1953 "errors" in the commercial field. Item 2, Bo's 1981 recollection of a spring 1953 encounter with Mao, also seemingly relates to these issues. The third selection, an account of the May 1953 assignment of economic responsibilities, provides evidence of Gao's increasing prominence at the time. The final item, a May 1953 directive critical of Liu Shaoqi on the question of issuing Central Committee documents, points to another of the key factors in the period preceding the Financial and Economic Conference—Mao's dissatisfaction with aspects of the performance of his designated successor.]

1. The New Tax System and Early 1953 Commercial Work

[This summary of the new tax system introduced by Bo Yibo and the early 1953 commercial policy, taken from a post-Mao chronology, treats these developments in terms that are less severe than but similar to contemporary evaluations (see the relevant items under appendices III-3A and 3B). While the principle of equal treatment of public and private enterprises, which so upset Mao at the time, is judged erroneous in the following excerpt, the summary focuses on the practical effects of the policies in question on state industry, state commerce, goods available on the market, and price fluctuation; cf. Appendix III-3C(1). The italicized passages highlight adverse effects on Gao Gang's Northeast and Rao Shushi's East China.]

Source: Fang Weizhong, ed., *Zhonghua Renmin Gongheguo Jingji Dashiji (1949–1980 nian)* [Economic Chronology of the PRC, 1949–1980] (Beijing: Zhongguo shehui kexue chubanshe, 1984), pp. 88, 90–91.

[JANUARY] 1, [1953:] The Central Financial and Economic Committee's "Announcement Concerning Certain Revisions of the Tax System and the Date of Its Implementation" and "Trial Measures for the Commodity Circulation Tax" were published and put into practice nationwide. This revision of the tax system was intended to ensure taxation revenue and to simplify taxpaying procedures. However, it erroneously put forward the principle of "equal taxation of public and private [enterprises]." It also implemented the policy of "public [enterprises] pay more than private [enterprises and] industry pays more than commerce." [By doing so,] it deprived the state-run economy and the cooperative economy of various privileges and conveniences. For example, the allocation of goods among head offices and their branches in all state-run industry and commerce previously was not regarded as business activity [and thus] not susceptible to a transactions tax.

Under the present regulations, [however,] in the industrial sector among head offices and branches a threefold transactions tax was imposed in the process from production (i.e., product manufacture) to wholesale and retail trade. [Similarly,] in the state-run commerce sector among head offices and branches a twofold transactions tax was imposed in the process from wholesale to retail trade. As for cooperatives, which formerly received the preferential treatment of a 20 percent discount in the transactions tax and a provision exempting them from income tax in their first year of operation, now such privileges were completely removed and resulted in the equal treatment of cooperatives and private commerce. The consequence of the implementation of this revised tax system was that, on the one hand, the state-run economy and cooperative economy suffered a heavy blow, especially state industry [where] the tax burden increased while profit decreased. To mention only the heavy-industry departments, all affiliated enterprises had to pay in that year a few tens of millions of yuan in extra tax. *In the Northeast, the profit from local industries decreased by about 20 million yuan* [emphasis added]. On the other hand, the capitalist economy, especially the big private wholesalers, was provided advantageous conditions for competing with the state-run economy and scrambling for markets. They competed for sales by means of an industry-commerce alliance, giving discounts and offering credit. As a result of this, the position occupied by state-run wholesalers gradually shrank even to the extent that some local state-run commercial [enterprises] still had to buy wholesale from private commerce. Precisely because of this, price fluctuation started to occur in certain industrial cities not long after the announcement of the new tax system. *To take Shanghai as an example, the index of living costs for staff and workers rose by 4.3 percent* [emphasis added]. [These] mistakes of the revised tax system were corrected when the Financial and Economic Conference was convened in June [1953] by the CCP Central Committee.

...

[January] 31, [1953:] In January the Ministry of Commerce of the Central People's Government convened the National Conference of Heads of Commercial

Departments and Bureaus. This conference, due to the underestimation of the needs and development of the market, insufficient knowledge of the negative impact of capitalist industry and commerce on the market, the lack of a correct understanding concerning the tasks of state-run commerce in the period of large-scale economic construction, the inability to accumulate capital for the state by means of expanding the circulation of commodities, accelerating capital turnover and economizing on circulation costs but instead [having] a one-sided understanding of economic accounting, wrongly affirmed the guiding principle of "loosening one's bowels" and "retreating from the front," [i.e.,] reducing stockpiles and squeezing out capital. Under the guidance of such an erroneous principle, state-run commerce in many regions only emphasized sales to the neglect of purchasing, and even resorted to the mistaken practices of reducing purchases and sales or refusing to buy and sell light industrial goods from a part of the state-run and local state-run sectors, and not allowing the latter to sell by themselves. Consequently, this not only caused state industry to overstock certain goods in huge quantities, which surely affected production and capital turnover, it also resulted in state commerce suffering a large reduction in the variety of goods it handled, which further affected the exchange of goods and materials and supplies for the market. *For example, in the first quarter [of the financial year,] the total value of overstocked goods manufactured in Northeast factories amounted in value to 120 million yuan. At the same time, the Shenyang Municipal Department Store reduced its range of goods by more than 2,000 varieties* [emphasis added], while in the Shijiazhuang Department Store, the initial 2,000-plus varieties were decreased to 1,200 plus. What was worse was the emergence of the abnormal phenomenon of "the public retreats and the private advances" in the wholesale markets of certain large cities. The above-mentioned erroneous guiding principle was rectified during the June [1953] CCP Central Committee's Financial and Economic Conference.

2. Bo Yibo Recalls a Spring 1953 Meeting with Mao

[The following is excerpted from Bo Yibo's July 1981 article commemorating the sixtieth anniversary of the CCP, "Respect and Remembrance." Almost certainly Bo's new tax system, and perhaps his commercial policies as well, caused the apparently mild rebuke by the Chairman described here. This account thus implies limits to how far Mao was inclined to go in criticizing Bo before the Financial and Economic Conference. The second incident Bo refers to was the discussions preceding Mao's 1956 speech "On the Ten Great Relationships"; concerning that case, Bo emphasised Mao's prudent willingness to listen to the views of others.]

Source: *Hongqi* [Red Flag], no. 13 (1981): 64.
Available translation: Foreign Broadcast Information Service, *Daily Report: People's Republic of China*, July 29, 1981, p. K31.

OUR Party is a Party of innovators. As a leader of such a Party, Comrade Mao Zedong was a firm explorer of truth. To find the path of the New Democratic revolution suitable to the conditions of China, he expended the energies of more than half his life, finally achieving great historical success.... After the establishment of People's China, he continued to explore the path for building socialism in a vast country such as ours.

Two incidents have left me with an unforgettable impression.

The first one: One day in spring 1953, Comrade Mao Zedong arranged that I talk with him. He wanted me to read some books carefully, to read some philosophy, to learn some dialectics and materialism, and also to learn some logic. Then he said to me in a serious and sincere way: You say the reason you make mistakes is that you are always busy with your work. It's incorrect to say that! In Russia at the time of the October Revolution wasn't Lenin busy? Nonetheless, Lenin was able to unravel the main threads of the complicated situation that existed in Russia. The reason you make mistakes is that you lack something consistent that runs through everything. Since our Party was founded in 1921, it has dynamically undertaken an earth-shaking cause and won great achievements. In its early years, however, because it lacked experience, the Party made many mistakes. In 1942 the entire Party carried out a rectification, and it was only then that it found basic guiding principles that can be said to have been the road to the victory of the Chinese revolution, and that was the identity of the subjective with the objective. As he spoke these words, Comrade Mao Zedong repeated himself: It was twenty years before we found out that the identity of the subjective with the objective was the road to the victory of China's revolution!

3. The May 1953 Assignment of Economic Responsibilities

[This item from a post-Mao source records the division of economic responsibilities among top Party leaders in spring 1953. It indicates Gao Gang's growing importance in the economic sphere quite apart from his duties as head of the State Planning Commission; here Gao gained the authority to oversee the crucial heavy industrial sector. Also of interest are the fact that Zhou Enlai was given overall responsibility to coordinate the various sectors, and the indication of Chen Yun's poor health.]

> **Source:** "Dangdai Zhongguo de Jingji Guanli" Bianjibu ["Contemporary China Economy" Editorial Department], *Zhonghua Renmin Gongheguo Jingji Guanli Dashiji* [Chronology of PRC Economic Management] (Beijing: Zhongguo jingji chubanshe, 1986), p. 41.

[MAY] 15, [1953:] The Government Administration Council issued a "Circular on Leadership over the Work of Financial and Economic Departments under the Central People's Government." The important contents are:

1. Leadership over the work of financial and economic departments under the Central People's Government is assigned to the following five areas:

   a. The Ministry of Heavy Industry, the First and Second ministries of Machine-Building, and the ministries of the Fuel Industry, Building Construction, Geology, Light Industry, and Textile Industry are put under the leadership of Gao Gang, chairman of the State Planning Commission;

   b. The ministries of Railways, Communications, and Posts and Telecommunications are put under the leadership of Deng Xiaoping, vice-premier of the Government Administration Council;

   c. The ministries of Agriculture, Forestry, and Water Conservation are put under the leadership of Deng Zihui, vice-chairman of the Financial [and Economic] Committee;

   d. The Ministry of Labor is put under the leadership of Rao Shushi, member of the State Planning Commission;

   e. The ministries of Finance, Food, Commerce, and Foreign Trade and the People's Bank continue to be under the leadership of Chen Yun, chairman of the Financial [and Economic] Committee; in the period of Chen Yun's recovery [from illness], they are to be put under the leadership of Committee Vice-Chairman Bo Yibo.

2. To facilitate work, after leadership over the financial and economic departments has been thus assigned, offices should be set up under the chief leader in each field, to be called the Financial [and Economic] Committee's No. 1 Office (Industry), No. 2 Office (Finance), No. 3 Office (Communications), No. 4 Office (Agriculture), and No. 5 Office (Labor). Liaison among the five areas will be undertaken by the Office of the Premier of the Government Administration Council.

4. Mao's May 1953 Criticism of Liu Shaoqi and Yang Shangkun Concerning the Handling of Central Documents

[This May 19, 1953, criticism from volume 5 of Mao's *Selected Works* indicates the Chairman's displeasure with Liu Shaoqi shortly before the Financial and Economic Conference. While the title of the document, "Liu Shaoqi and Yang Shangkun Criticized for Breach of Discipline in Issuing Documents in the Name of the Central Committee without Authorization," was apparently provided by the editors of volume 5, there is no reason to doubt that Liu and Yang (the head of the CCP's general office) were the (or at least among the) targets of Mao's criticism. Note that the period to be checked covered the issuing of Bo Yibo's new tax system, which Mao had not seen beforehand.]

Source: Michael Y. M. Kau and John K. Leung, eds., *The Writings of Mao Zedong, 1949–1974*, vol. 1: *September 1949–December 1955* (Armonk, N.Y.: M. E. Sharpe, 1986), p. 346.

Chinese text: *Mao Zedong Xuanji* [Selected Works of Mao Zedong] (Beijing: Renmin chubanshe, 1977), 5:80.
Additional translation: *Selected Works of Mao Tsetung* (Peking: Foreign Languages Press, 1977), p. 92.

I. FROM now on, all documents and telegrams issued in the name of the [Party] Center must be inspected by me before they can be dispatched; *otherwise they will be invalid* [emphasis in original]. Please pay attention to this.

II. (1) Please assume responsibility for inspecting all telegrams and documents issued in the name of the [Party] Center or the Military Affairs Committee between August 1 of last year and May 5 of this year (inspection has already been made of those [issued] prior to August 1) to see if there are any—and if so, how many—that were not inspected by myself (excluding those [issued] while I was on an inspection tour or on sick leave). Then let me know the results.

II. (2) It is an error, a breach of discipline, for the resolutions of the past several meetings at the Center to have been issued on [someone else's] authority without having passed my inspection.

III
THE NATIONAL CONFERENCE ON FINANCIAL AND ECONOMIC WORK
June–August 1953

[The National Financial and Economic Conference in summer 1953 was clearly the occasion on which the activities of Gao Gang and Rao Shushi directed at Liu Shaoqi and Zhou Enlai first developed to any significant extent. The major vehicle of the attack was through criticism of Bo Yibo, especially his new tax system. The items collected in section 3 below deal more generally with Bo Yibo and the tax issue at and after the conference; for Gao's use of the issue, see Appendix I. Among the other major issues discussed at the conference were the formulation of the general line for the transition period (see section 1) and the socialist transformation of private capitalists (section 2). In both cases the items collected here deal both with the implications for Liu, Gao, and other leaders, and with leadership interaction more broadly on these issues.]

1. The General Line

[The central task of the conference was to bring financial and economic work into line with the emerging general line for the transition from New Democracy to socialism. Item 1A is Mao's initial statement of the general line together with his criticism of views deviating from it, which was delivered at the very outset of the conference, albeit to a Politburo meeting rather than to the conference itself. This statement had negative implications for Liu Shaoqi especially through the criticism of the New Democracy slogan associated with Liu. Item 1B is a letter from Zhou Enlai to Mao and Gao Gang almost two weeks after the Chairman's initial statement. This letter at once indicates Zhou's willingness to engage in discussions on the general line, although well within the parameters set by Mao, and his respectful attitude toward Gao. Finally, items 1C (1) and (2) present two subsequent formulations of the general line as determined by Mao in August and December 1953, which slightly modify that contained in 1A. The italicized portions of these items indicate the successive changes from June to August to December.]

1A. Mao on Rightist Views Departing from the General Line, June 1953

> **Source:** "Criticize the Right-Deviationist Viewpoints that Depart from the General Line" (June 15, 1953), in *The Writings of Mao Zedong*, 1:347–49, as amended.
> **Chinese text:** *Mao Zedong Xuanji*, 5:81–82.
> **Additional translation:** *Selected Works of Mao Zedong*, 5:93–94.

THE general line and the overall task of the Party during the period of transition is basically to complete national industrialization and the socialist transformation of agriculture, handicraft industries, and capitalist industry and commerce within a period of ten to fifteen years or a bit longer. This general line is a beacon illuminating every task we undertake. One must not deviate from this general line. If one is divorced from this general line, errors either of "left" deviation or of right deviation will occur.

There are people who think the period of transition is too long. Consequently they have developed a mood of impatience. This will [lead them to] commit the error of "left" deviation. After the success of the democratic revolution, some people still remained where they were. They did not understand the nature of the revolution; [they] are still continuing to carry out their "New Democracy" and have not moved [on to] carrying out socialist transformation. This is liable to lead them to commit errors of right deviation. Speaking of agriculture, the road of socialism is the only road for our country's agriculture. The heart of the Party's work in the countryside is the development of the mutual aid and cooperativization movement and the continuous growth of the forces of production in agriculture.

Right deviation is manifested in these three sentences: "Firmly establish the New Democratic social order." This proposition is harmful. In the period of transition [things] are changing every day; every day socialist elements come into being. How could this so-called New Democratic social order be "firmly established"? It is really difficult to have it "firmly established"! For example, private industry and commerce are being transformed right now. If a type of order is "established" in the latter half of this year, it will no longer be "firm" next year. [The situation of the] mutual aid and cooperativization [movement] in agriculture is also changing from year to year. The period of transition is full of contradictions and struggles. Our present revolutionary struggle goes even deeper than the armed revolutionary struggle of the past. This is a revolution that will thoroughly bury the capitalist system and all other exploitative systems. The idea of "firmly establishing the New Democratic social order" does not conform to the actual situation in the struggle and impedes the development of the socialist cause.

"Go from New Democracy toward socialism." This proposition is [too] vague. [All it says is] go in a certain direction and that's it. If we go in a direction year after year, in fifteen years can we still say [that we are simply] going in that direction? Going in a direction means that [the goal] has not yet been reached. At first glance this proposition looks acceptable, but after detailed analysis [one can see] it is not a sound one.

"Firmly protect private property." Because the middle peasants were afraid of "becoming too conspicuous" and of "communization," some people put forward this slogan to calm them down. In fact, this is wrong.

We propose a gradual transition to socialism. This is better. By gradual we mean dividing [the process into] fifteen years and each year again into twelve months. Going too fast results in being too much to the "left"; standing still results in being too much to the right. We must oppose both "left" and right, make the transition gradually, and finally complete the entire transition.

1B. Zhou Enlai's Letter to Mao Zedong to Be Passed on to Gao Gang (June 28, 1953)

> Source: "Fundamental Tasks of the Period of Transition," in *Zhou Enlai Shuxin Xuanji* [Selected Letters of Zhou Enlai] (Beijing: Zhongyang wenxian chubanshe, 1988), pp. 491–92.

FOR the Chairman to read, and pass on to Comrade Gao Gang:

I have nothing new to add concerning the draft report, "Opinions on Some Questions Concerning the Drawing Up of the Five-Year Plan," which Comrade Gao Gang did a fine job of revising. However, I still think that the initial paragraph was written in a more appropriate and comprehensive manner in the first draft, more appropriate than the revised version's "For a considerable period in the future, our goal is to realize socialist industrialization in a steady way. This will be a new historical period of our country, i.e., the new period of transition to socialism. . . ." When Comrade Jia Tuofu [then vice-chairman of the Financial and Economic Committee under the Government Administration Council] made his report to the National Labor Conference, he also used the slogan "realize socialist industrialization" in an isolated way. It was changed at my suggestion, because to raise this slogan as the only goal during our transition period is not complete; the collectivization of agriculture and the utilization and reform of capitalist industry have not been included. It would be better to rewrite the first paragraph the way it was in the first draft:

"The Chinese people, under the wise leadership of Chairman Mao and the Party's Central Committee, have already won complete victory in the New Democratic revolution and, in the past three years and more, have achieved tremendous success in economic restoration and transformation. After the victory of the New Democratic revolution, our country has already entered a new historical period, the new period of gradual transition to socialism. Over a considerably long period of time in the future, the basic tasks of the Party are: To realize steadily the industrialization of the country and step by step promote the collectivization of agriculture, so that we can change from a backward agricultural country into an advanced industrialized one, and at the same time as we develop the economy, constantly expand the economic foundations of socialism, so as to enable our country gradually to make the transition to a socialist society."

I don't know if my opinion on this matter and the phrasing are appropriate or not, and ask the Chairman and Comrade Gao Gang to consider it and decide. If feasible, then the first sentence in the last paragraph on page 18 of the draft report should also be revised; also, the gradual transition to socialism started from the time of the victory of the revolution, not this year.

In addition, in the first line on page 8, the sentence "construction of water power stations and shipbuilding industry" should be changed to "the construction of water resources, electrification, and shipbuilding industry," to avoid being misunderstood as "hydroelectric power stations."

Zhou Enlai
Morning, June 28

1C. Additional Formulations of the General Line, August and December 1953

(1) The August Formulation

> **Source:** "On the General Line of the Party During the Period of Transition" (August 1953), in *The Writings of Mao Zedong*, 1:380–81, as amended.
> **Chinese text:** *Mao Zedong Xuanji*, 5:89.
> **Additional translation:** *Selected Works of Mao Tsetung*, 5:102.

[THE PERIOD] *from the founding of the People's Republic of China to the fundamental completion of the socialist transformation is a period of transition.* During this period of transition the general line and overall task of the Party is basically *to realize, over a considerably long period of time*, national industrialization and the socialist transformation of agriculture, handicraft industries, and capitalist industry and commerce. This general line *ought to be* a beacon illuminating every task we undertake. *If we should depart from it in any facet of our work, we will be committing* errors of either *right* or *"left"* deviation [emphasis added].

Many of the principles and policies in this general line were already proposed in the resolutions of the Second Plenum of the Party's [Seventh] Central Committee in March 1949, and solutions in the area of principles have already been reached. Nevertheless, many comrades are reluctant to do their work in accordance with the stipulations of the Second Plenum and on certain problems prefer [instead] to work up another set of things that do not conform to the stipulations of the Second Plenum, or that even publicly violate the principles of the Second Plenum.

(2) The December Formulation

Source: "On the General Line of the Party during the Period of Transition" (December 1953), in *Mao Zedong Zhuzuo Xuandu* [Selected Readings from Mao Zedong's Writings] (Beijing: Renmin chubanshe, 1986), 2:704 (excerpt).

[THE PERIOD] from the founding of the People's Republic of China to the fundamental completion of the socialist transformation is a period of transition. During this period of transition the general line and overall task of the Party is *gradually* to realize, over a considerably long period of time, the *socialist* industrialization of the nation and *gradually to realize the state's* socialist transformation of agriculture, handicraft industries, and capitalist industry and commerce [emphasis added]. This general line ought to be a beacon illuminating every task we undertake. If we should depart from it in any facet of our work, we will be committing errors of either right or "left" deviation.

2. The Transformation of Capitalist Industry and Commerce

2A. Xu Dixin's Recollections

[Policy toward the transformation of capitalist industry and commerce was a major practical issue at the Financial and Economic Conference. Xu Dixin, as deputy head of the central united front work department, participated in many of the key discussions. In recent years his recollections have provided details on the roles of various leaders. In the first of three excerpts from separate sources below, Xu highlights the role of Liu Shaoqi among others; the second excerpt focuses on Zhou Enlai. The final and most interesting excerpt provides particular insight in to the role of Chen Yun and demonstrates how Gao Gang was the odd man out in this discussion.]

(1)

Source: *Dangshi Yanjiu* [Research on Party History], no. 4 (1980): 23.

THE GUIDING principles of socialist transformation toward capitalist industry and commerce were put forth in June 1953. The united front work department of the Central Committee had conducted investigation and research on capitalist industry and commerce in Shanghai during March–April of the same year. As a result, a report was drafted regarding existing problems in the placing of orders by the state with private enterprises for processing materials or supplying manufactured goods, as well as the proposal for changing private enterprises into joint state-private ownership. This report was first presented to Comrade Liu Shaoqi. Comrade Shaoqi considered such an issue so important that it warranted a full discussion by a

Politburo meeting. Both comrades Mao Zedong and Zhou Enlai took this issue very seriously. After the discussion the report was approved. It was during this meeting that Comrade Mao Zedong brought up the general line and the general task for the Party in the transition period. He pointed out that in ten to fifteen years or a bit longer national industrialization and the socialist transformation of agriculture, handicrafts, and capitalist industry and commerce should be basically completed. In the same meeting the united front work department was put in charge of the task of transforming capitalist industry and commerce by the Central Committee. In accord with the previous instructions received from the Central Committee, the united front work department summed up the guiding principles toward capitalist industry and commerce in terms of utilization, restriction, and transformation. Furthermore, the policy toward all the entrepreneurs in capitalist industry and commerce was summed up in terms of uniting, educating, and remolding.

Comrade Liu Shaoqi attached great importance to the issue of transforming capitalist industry and commerce. In the Politburo meeting of June 1953, he gave strong backing to Comrade Mao Zedong's idea that all capitalists would be ultimately remolded into working-class people instead of being peasants or petty bourgeois [elements]. Following this at the National United Front Work Conference he stressed that under the proletarian dictatorship, using the peaceful buying-out method, that is, the united front method to transform the national bourgeoisie, was not only imperative but also feasible. Comrade Shaoqi criticized the "leftist" view which maintained that to transform capitalists peacefully was "class conciliation."

Comrade Zhou Enlai also took [the issue] seriously. He emphasized that the historical mission of transforming capitalist industry and commerce could not be smoothly realized if the task of uniting, educating, and remolding members of the capitalist class was not carried out well. In the several Politburo meetings held during the summer of 1953, he repeatedly explained how important such an issue was, and further pointed out that the effort to unite, educate, and remold capitalists was not to be relaxed even after achieving the socialist transformation of capitalist industry and commerce. It goes without saying that unity should be combined with struggle. Comrade Zhou Enlai pointed out: toward the nationalist capitalist class, "the main task is to unite; struggle is for the sake of unity." It was therefore our task to convert them from exploiters into self-supporting laborers through the process of unifying, educating, and remolding.

(2)

> Source: *Bujin de Sinian* [Endless Remembrance] (Beijing: Zhongyang wenxian chubanshe, 1987), pp. 502–503.

BECAUSE my work dealt with the national bourgeoisie I was sometimes asked to attend Politburo meetings. In summer 1953 Comrade Mao Zedong proposed that our Party and nation realize the general line of "one change and three transformations" in the transition to socialism, that is, to achieve industrialization and the transformation of agriculture, handicrafts, and capitalist industry and commerce. At the time everybody agreed, but how long should it take? Comrade Zhou Enlai supported the general line but maintained that the transformation of capitalism must not be too fast; to act too quickly could only hurt the country and the national economy. According to the premier's view, fifteen years possibly was not enough—it would take a bit longer. It is a pity that due to the "leftist" tendency of seeking quick results, which prevailed at the time, the whole process from the announcement of the general line to the high tide of joint public-private ownership in all trades took less than four years!

(3)

Source: *Dangshi Tongxun* [Party History Newsletter], no. 1 (1986): 45–46.

IN THE SPRING of 1953, Li Weihan led an investigation group to the various places of Wuhan, Shanghai, Nanjing, and Jinan to carry out investigations of privately run industry and commerce. This resulted in the submission of two reports: the first was about how to deal with the problem of the public-private relationship; the second was on how to deal with the problem of the labor-capital relationship. It was Liu Shaoqi who first received the briefing from the investigation group. Li Weihan, as head of the united front work department, and the deputy heads were all present. I can still recall that during that afternoon's briefing, the issue of the state placing orders with private enterprises for processing materials or supplying manufactured goods dominated the agenda. Li Weihan proposed that these issues must be solved by the Party's unified leadership. The achievement of this investigation was that it not only discovered those problems existing in placing orders for processing materials and supplying manufactured goods but also made some breakthroughs in theory and policy concerning the transformation of capitalist industry and commerce. Li Weihan proposed that [nonmonopoly] purchase [of private enterprise goods] was the lowest form of state capitalism; the state placing orders for processing and supplying, unified purchase, and exclusive selling rights [for the output of private enterprises] were the middle forms of state capitalism; while joint public-private ownership was the higher form of state capitalism, which was thereby the important form in the transition to socialism.

During the following summer, the Politburo held quite a few meetings discussing this issue of the transformation of capitalist industry and commerce. The various leaders who attended these meetings all agreed to adopting the forms of state capitalism by which capitalist industry and commerce would be transformed step by step into socialist enterprises. Given the increasing shrinking of the purchase [method], the leaders pointed out that purchase should no longer be considered as one form. As such, state capitalism would include only the lower forms of the state placing orders for processing and supplying, unified purchase, and exclusive selling rights, and the higher form of joint ownership. During the discussion, Zhou Enlai and Chen Yun proposed that the government's policy on the transformation of capitalist industry and commerce should not remain in the stage of placing orders, instead it should be expanded to achieve gradually joint public-private ownership. Mao Zedong in the discussion proposed the general line of the Party during the transition period and pointed out that this general line and overall task was "basically to realize, over a considerably long period of time, national industrialization and the socialist transformation of agriculture, handicraft industries, and capitalist industry and commerce."

To achieve the socialist transformation of capitalist industry and commerce, both Mao Zedong and Zhou Enlai considered it necessary to have a body to assume unified responsibility. Chen Yun thought that the State Planning Commission already had too much to do. He feared that if the SPC were to be assigned the work of transforming capitalism, it might not be able to perform well. The result of the discussion was to decide that the central united front department would be in charge of the task, and Li Weihan would be concurrently a deputy head of the Central Financial and Economic Committee. A sixth office was accordingly set up under the FEC, and Xu Dixin was appointed its head, while Sha Qianli, Sun Qimeng, and Zheng Xinru served as deputies.

When the Center decided on peacefully transforming capitalist industry and commerce through the forms of state capitalism, everyone agreed. Only Gao Gang was opposed. During the several Politburo meetings he didn't utter a word. Chairman Mao therefore asked Li Weihan to talk to Gao. So at adjournment Li approached Gao, inquirying about his opinion. Gao replied: "Have you ever read *On the Opposition* by Stalin?" "Yes," said Li. Gao immediately said in a sarcastic tone: "Didn't Bukharin also advocate a peaceful entry into socialism?" Another point of discrepancy that occurred in the meetings concerned what type of people the capitalists would be transformed into. Li Weihan proposed to transform them into socialist citizens, but Lin Boqu disagreed. Regarding this dispute, Mao Zedong clearly pointed out: We must transform the capitalists into workers. Otherwise, what else can they be transformed into? Could they be landlords? No! Could they be peasants? Again no! We can only transform them into self-supporting workers.

At the Politburo meeting Mao Zedong assigned Li Weihan the job of drafting a report to the Center on policies toward capitalist industry and commerce. This report was intitially entitled "Report Concerning the Utilization, Restriction, and Reorganization of Capitalist Industry and Commerce" (the term "reorganization" was originally based on Chairman Mao's idea of "economic reorganization" raised in the Third Plenum of the Seventh Central Committee). In the Politburo discussions, Hu Qiaomu proposed to change "reorganization" to "transformation," for such a new term would be more precise and more scientific. Comrades such as Mao Zedong, Zhou Enlai, and Liu Shaoqi all agreed with Hu's opinion.

Hence we have the policy of utilize, restrict, and transform capitalist industry and commerce expressed in the present terms.

2B. The Development of Policy toward the Transformation of Capitalist Commerce, 1952–1953

[The following account from a Party history journal traces evolving policy toward the commercial sector in the transformation of capitalist industry and commerce. Relying on an interview with Li Weihan in addition to documentary materials, the author jumps from the simplistic anticommercial bias of 1952 to the changes in policy emerging during and following the Financial and Economic Conference. The crucial role of Chen Yun is highlighted in this account.]

> Source: Zhang Kai, "Zibenzhuyi Shangye de Shehuizhuyi Gaizao Fangzhen de Tichu Guocheng Chutan" [Preliminary Explorations into the Process of Proposing Guiding Principles for the Socialist Transformation of Capitalist Commerce], *Dangshi Yanjiu*, no. 3 (1986): 21–22.

... In his speech to the enlarged session of the second general meeting of the Chinese Democratic National Construction Association,[1] Huang Yanpei [recalled] his conversation with Mao Zedong on March 15, 1952, when [Mao] said: "In Beijing there are fifty thousand industry and commerce households and forty thousand street peddlers." Mao Zedong also advocated "channeling step by step commercial capital to industry according to the needs of the state." By the end of the conversation Huang Yanpei checked his own summary with Mao to make sure he had understood the spirit of Mao's talk correctly. He summed up in four points: the first was that "the Democratic Construction Association should henceforth continue recruiting new members from big industrial and commercial entrepreneurs with greater emphasis on the industrial sector." Mao replied, "correct." Such an idea was commonly shared among leaders in the Party Center at that time. So far I [the author] have yet to see or hear any account of different views at the time.

But in less than two months after the June 15, [1953,] Politburo meeting, although the guiding principle of elimination [of capitalist commerce] had not changed, there was already somebody starting to notice the other side of the question, i.e., the problems of the policy of elimination. On August 6, [1953,] Chen Yun had the following to say: "Do not blindly eliminate private businessmen," "Be attentive, do not think the 'left' is better than the right, hence committing the mistake of leftist deviation." "We should only elbow out those private businessmen who have stepped onto our front when we should not have withdrawn in the first place. But even in doing so, we must distinguish according to which trade and how many to crowd out; moreover, we must advance step by step. Only sound preparation can prevent us from the situation in which the

---

[1] A small "democratic party" representing private capitalists which was allowed to exist and was used by the CCP. Huang Yanpei was the association's chairman.

support given to one side [public-run business] is followed immediately by the collapse at the other side. . . . In a nutshell, given the immense strength of the state, to crowd out private merchants is not difficult at all. We must therefore be all the more circumspect" (*Selected Works of Chen Yun [1949–1956]*, p. 195).

The materials seen so far indicate that the guiding principle of elimination still had not completely changed as late as September 4. On September 4, [1953], the responsible leaders of the Party Center invited Huang Yanpei, Chen Shutong, and Li Zhuchen[2] for an informal discussion. Chen Shutong reflected afterward: "The number of commercial enterprises is very large, hence the most difficult to handle. I believe that we should openly make clear to them [the Party's policy regarding] the direction, future, difficulties, and methods of private business. We should tell them that [private] commerce must be swept away and replaced by state-run trade and cooperatives." What is put here, the "liquidation of commerce" (i.e., a less precise expression of "eliminating" capitalist commerce), should not be understood as merely Chen Shutong's personal view.

After a few days the situation started to change. On September 7, after having talked to some representatives from the democratic parties and industrial and commercial circles, Mao Zedong formally announced that "private commerce can also carry out state capitalism, we cannot dismiss it simply by saying 'eliminate it'" (*Selected Works of Mao Zedong*, 5:99). At the same time he continued to say: "We are short of experience in this aspect, further research is in order." Apparently, in the course of eighty-four days of serious exploration and research from June 15 to September 7, our Party finally began to realize that it could not simply follow the guiding principle of elimination to deal with capitalist commerce. Instead, the forms of state capitalism were to be adopted to achieve the socialist transformation of capitalist commerce.

On the next day, Zhou Enlai reaffirmed Mao Zedong's viewpoint at the meeting of the Standing Committee of the Chinese People's Political Consultative Committee. Moreover, Zhou further made some concrete proposals regarding how to practice state capitalism in the process of managing commerce. He said: "Those big private commercial companies that genuinely affect the national economy and the people's livelihood can practice joint public-private ownership. . . . In addition, private commerce can carry out wholesale trade for the state at the price set by the state, or they can be a purchasing and marketing agency [for the state]" (*Selected Works of Zhou Enlai*, 2:113).

3. The Attack on the Revised Tax System

3A. *Zhou Enlai's Summary Report to the Financial and Economic Conference (August 11, 1953)*

[While it is clear that the new tax system was subjected to major criticism at the

---

[2] Chen and Li, like Huang, were leading non-Party figures in private industrial and commercial circles.

Financial and Economic Conference, sources differ on how seriously the issue, and by extension Bo Yibo, was treated by the end of the conference. Zhou Enlai's report on the penultimate day of the meetings is clearly crucial in this regard, but it has only become available in recent years. Below is first a summary of the overall content of Zhou's report from a post-Mao chronology, followed by extensive excerpts from the report itself, which relate directly to Bo Yibo and also Gao Gang.]

(1)

Source: *Zhonghua Renmin Gongheguo Jingji Guanli Dashiji*, pp. 44–45.

[AUGUST] 10 [*sic*], [1953:] Premier Zhou Enlai made the summing-up report at the summer 1953 National Financial and Economic Conference.

1. In discussing certain questions in China's economic construction, Zhou Enlai said that the following points deserve our greatest attention:

First, we must go all-out to develop production and gradually satisfy demand, plan well, and avoid blind action;

Second, our unshakable policy is to ensure keypoint construction and make steady progress;

Third, under the principle of centralized and unified leadership, we must at the same time give motivation to local authorities and the masses;

Fourth, the principle of persisting in the unified leadership of the Party must be followed at all times;

Fifth, to avoid blind action and make fewer mistakes, we must study and learn honestly.

2. In discussing certain mistakes made in taxation, trade, and finance in the past half year and more, Zhou Enlai pointed out that: In the nearly four years of financial and economic work since the founding of the People's Republic of China, the first three years were marked by achievements, which were the main aspect of work. Though defects and mistakes also occurred, they were isolated cases. In the past half year and more, however, it should be said that the financial, commercial, and banking departments also did a lot of work and made some achievements, but the mistakes, too, were conspicuous, the major manifestations of which are as follows:

a. The mistakes in revising the tax system were obvious. As a consequence of its implementation, the public sector had to bear a heavier tax burden than the private sector and than commerce. This was a blow to industry, especially the backward [branches of] industry, and benefited private commerce, especially large wholesalers. It created for a time chaos in the market and roused popular discontent. It gave the advantage to the capitalist economic sector over the socialist and semisocialist economic sectors.

b. In levying agricultural tax, the peasants' share was on an average about 15 percent, resulting in an unbalanced tax burden on the peasants of the country.

c. In commercial work, the meeting of bureau heads under the [provincial]

Departments of Commerce in January this year resulted in the shrinking of the market of state commerce and some goods being sold out, and this was favorable to the development of the private economic sector and unfavorable to the development of the state and cooperative economic sectors.

d. Some comrades from financial departments worked from a mistaken view in implementing the unification of finance, that is, the view of "finance for finance's sake," which is divorced from Party policy. This view actually put finance above all else, and is a reflection of bourgeois thinking in the Party.

e. In banking work, it was correct, up until the end of June last year, to carry out a policy of gradually lowering interest rates. The mistake is in not having studied in time the question of adjusting the rates during the past year. The chief responsibility for this rests with the banks. It was also wrong, in the past, for banks to stress "guaranteed loans and guaranteed repayment" and rigidly restrict "special funds for special use" in agricultural loans. This was rectified only in March this year, after the Central leadership issued instructions about it.

f. In the financial, banking, and trading systems, political work and Party life are weak, especially in leading departments.

3. In discussing future policy, Zhou Enlai pointed out:

a. Regarding financial work. The task of financial work is to increase resources rationally through developing production and expanding exchange; to economize and accumulate more capital to ensure keypoint construction projects; to strengthen national defense; and to improve gradually the life of the working people. The financial structure should be determined under the unified leadership and planning of the central authorities. Functions and powers should be defined, management exercised at different levels, and accountability of each level to the next higher level established. In financial management, we must change from supply finance to construction finance. There should be priorities in work, changing the past mistake of grasping the trivial things instead of important things, focusing on revenues but not expenditure, and managing administration rather than construction. Regarding the national budget, we shall, within the unified plan of the national budget, implement a three-level budget system (at the central, provincial and municipal, and county levels). Limits of central and local revenues and expenditures should be defined. There should be a rough central-local ratio in accordance with priorities and nonpriorities, degree of urgency, and centralization and decentralization. Localities should handle about 20 percent.

b. Regarding taxation work. The task of taxation is to ensure and develop socialist and semisocialist industry and commerce and use, restrict, and reform capitalist industry and commerce in a step-by-step, conditional, and case-by-case way, so that, on the one hand, more capital can accrue and benefit keypoint construction projects of the country and, on the other hand, the revenues of different classes are adjusted so as to be advantageous to the worker-peasant alliance. Our tax policy is to handle public and private enterprises differently and in accordance with the complexity of the situation; the degree of control by the state over joint state-private enterprises should gradually increase to the degree exercised over state enterprises. Agricultural tax, under the policy of less acquisition and more purchase, should resolutely implement the policy of "fixing the output of grain according to the size of the land tilled; state acquisition according to a fixed ratio and reduction and exemption according to law, so that there will be no increase of tax when outputs increase."

c. Regarding commercial work. The task of commerce is to increase city-country mutual aid, domestic-foreign exchange, stabilize the market, promote development of industry and commerce, increase state tax revenues and rational profits, so as to accrue capital for the state to ensure keypoint construction projects, gradually ensure the people's needs, and consolidate the worker-peasant alliance. The policy in commerce is to go all-out to consolidate state commerce and develop it in a planned and step-by-step way, i.e., first we must study market development and the people's needs, and in accordance with this, correctly control price policy, improve management, increase return on capital, and expand the scope of manufacturing according to orders and the scope of purchase and sales in a planned and step-by-step way, so as to increase the total turnover.

d. Regarding grain management work. The task is to go all-out to increase outputs, fulfill purchasing plans, correctly control the price, exercise strict supervision over the market, improve grain transportation and storage, and practice thrift, so as to keep up with the tendency of increased demand for commodity grain in large and medium cities, mining areas, and farming areas that produce only cash crops.

In addition, Zhou Enlai spoke about questions to pay attention to regarding bank interest rates, agricultural loans, and financial, banking, and trade work.

(2)

> **Source**: *Zhonggong Dangshi Jiaoxue Cankao Ziliao* [CCP History Teaching Reference Materials] (Zhongguo Jiefangjun Guofang Daxue dangshi dangjian zhenggong jiaoyanshi, April 1986), 20:133, 134, 135, 136–37, 138, 139, 142–43.

. . .

AT this conference, in response to the call of the Central Committee and Comrade Mao Zedong and at the participants' urging, thorough exposure and criticism of certain serious mistakes that have occurred in the recent period in the work of taxation, commerce, finance, and banking were made; concentrated criticism was also made of Comrade Bo Yibo, who is chiefly responsible for these serious mistakes. At the same time, many constructive suggestions were put forward in regard to policies in finance, taxation, commerce, grain, and banking. All this will enable us to take a big stride forward in work in areas concerned.

. . .

The Second Plenum [of the Seventh Central Committee held in March 1949] also pointed out: "The policy of restricting private capitalism will inevitably meet with the resistance of the capitalist class to different extents and in different forms. This will be especially true of the big entrepreneurs of private enterprises, i.e., the big capitalists. Restriction and counterrestriction will be the main form of class struggle inside a New Democratic country." Such class struggle inside our country cannot but be reflected in the ideological struggle within our Party. The many mistaken views and the working style as represented by Comrade Bo Yibo are precisely the reflection of bourgeois ideas in the Party.

...

In accordance with the spirit of the Party Center's instructions, I basically agree with the report made by Comrade Gao Gang, [that is,] the fundamental tasks of our country's First Five-Year Plan of construction should be: To concentrate our primary effort on developing heavy industry and establishing the foundations for national industrialization and modernization of national defense; train corresponding personnel for construction and develop transportation and communications, light industry, agriculture, and commerce; in a step-by-step way promote the cooperative movement in agriculture and handicrafts and continue to reform private industry and commerce, while bringing into play the proper role of individual farming, the handicrafts industry, and private industry and commerce. All this is to ensure the stable increase of the proportion of the socialist sector in the national economy and to ensure that, on the basis of developing production, the people's material and cultural life will steadily improve.

...

... the principle of the Party's unified leadership must be strictly observed at all times. The Party Center and Comrade Mao Zedong have always stressed the Party's unified leadership and opposed individual Party organizations and Party members trying to assert their own "independence," opposed the erroneous tendencies of anarchism and lack of discipline, and opposed decentralism. This is not accidental. The many mistakes that occurred recently in taxation, commerce, finance, and banking are inseparable from attempts to assert "independence" from the Party, from the erroneous tendencies of anarchism and lack of discipline, and from decentralism. The revision of the tax system and many other measures contrary to Party principles were taken arbitrarily without reporting to the Party Center or consulting the local Party committees, and by ignoring the opinions of relevant departments concerned. Instead, prior consultations were made with representatives of the bourgeoisie on the question of revising the tax system; this is a departure from the position of the Party. All these are inevitable consequences of the development of decentralism. At a time when our Party, in the period of transition, is both cooperating with and struggling against the bourgeoisie, we must keep up our vigilance and strengthen and obey the Party's unified leadership in trying to reach the aim of gradually transforming capitalist industry and commerce without being corrupted by bourgeois ideology. Comrades working for the government at all levels must obey the leadership of the Party; comrades of Party committees at all local levels must keep a tight check on government work, especially financial work; subordinate Party organizations must obey the Party's Central Committee. Only so can we reduce or avoid possible mistakes.

. . .

It is not yet possible at this conference to make an overall summary of the financial and economic work of the country in the four years since the founding of the People's Republic of China. Many facts, however, point to the remarkable results achieved. In principle, I agree with the basic analysis made by Comrade Li Fuchun, that is, due to the concerted efforts of the people of the nation and the whole Party, financial and economic work basically implemented the resolutions of the Party's Second and Third plenums and the instructions of the Party Center and Comrade Mao Zedong and has accomplished a great deal. That is, production has resumed, exchange of commodities expanded, prices stabilized, and national revenue and expenditure balanced. All this has given strong support to the movement to oppose U.S. aggression and aid Korea, enabled the nation to overcome many difficulties, initially improved the people's livelihood, and effected a fundamental turn for the better in the financial and economic situation, thus helping the country to enter the stage of planned construction. In the first three years, our accomplishments were the main thing; although there were also shortcomings and mistakes, they were of an isolated nature. However, in the past six months and more, although financial, commercial, and banking departments also did a lot of work and made some achievements, mistakes made by the leadership of these departments were conspicuous, and these mistakes are the subject of our present discussion. We shall now analyze these mistakes:

The mistake in revising the tax system. This mistake is obvious. The result of the tax revision is that the public sector is paying higher taxes than the private sector; industry is paying more than commerce, which is a blow to industry, with the result that industry has become backward while private commerce, especially large distributors, held the advantage. The market was at one time in confusion, causing dissatisfaction among the population. This was favorable to the capitalist economic sector and unfavorable to the socialist and semisocialist economic sectors. Originally, according to the resolution of the Party's Second Plenum, the tax policy should have been one of the ways to restrict private capitalism, and different treatment should have been accorded to the private capitalist economic sector and to the state and cooperative sectors. The tax revision, however, advanced the slogan of "equal taxation of public and private [enterprises]." It abolished tax advantages and favorable treatment formerly given to the state and cooperative sectors and instead gave them to the private capitalist sector in the name of "simplifying taxes." This was precisely the aspect which won the enthusiastic support of the Preparatory Committee of the National Federation of Industry and

Commerce. Talking only about "protecting tax revenues" in violation of Party policy, without taking into account the development of this year's market and the ill effects of heavier taxes upon state enterprises and cooperatives, and maintaining that "tax revenues have increased in amount" is a manifestation of a lack of understanding or an unwillingness to understand the essence of the mistake. We must point out once again that the mistake made in the current tax revision is a mistake in violation of the relevant stipulated principles set down by the Party's Second Plenum. It is a major issue affecting state policy, affecting the interests of the people of the nation, and leading to adjustments in the revenues of different classes. Toward such a major issue, the Ministry of Finance, especially Comrade Bo Yibo who is chiefly responsible, failed to study earnestly beforehand the relevant principles of the Second Plenum or report to and ask the Central Committee for instructions, but carelessly put it into the form of a circular of the Central Financial and Economic Committee which was submitted to the Government Administration Council for approval while asking the *People's Daily* to publish an editorial on "equal taxation of public and private [enterprises]." Afterward, no serious self-criticism was made for a long time. This mistake is a mistake of the gravest nature.

. . .

In drawing up this year's budget, the Ministry of Finance also committed a relatively serious mistake. In the section on revenues, a relatively large proportion of the items were either made up, exaggerated, or not entirely reliable. These misleading facts were the basis on which expenditures were considered. Comparing the net revenues of 1952 and 1953, this year's increase is only 20 percent over last year's, but expenditure increased by over 40 percent. This is an enormous discrepancy. With expenditure greatly expanded, the policy of keypoint construction and stable advance was violated. At the same time, reserves were smaller and would not have been enough to meet expected and unexpected contingencies. Moreover, due to the unified handling of national revenue and expenditure, too much was centralized and allocations to lower levels were too tight and rigidly restricted to specific purposes. Local authorities lost the power and initiative to handle funds flexibly within their regions. Therefore, not long after the announcement of the budget, the balance was upset. This budget had been approved by the Party Center, but in reality it did not conform to the instructions of the Party Center and Comrade Mao Zedong on setting up three lines of defense in drawing up budgets, [that is,] increasing production, saving, and keeping large reserves. As far as the government is concerned, I and Comrade Chen Yun failed to study the issue earnestly and must be held responsible to some extent. On the drawing up of the budget, however, Comrade Bo Yibo must take the major responsibility. It is still not entirely possible to avoid exaggeration and unreliability in revenue items due to changes in the situation, lack of experience, and the effect of other mistakes. But falsifying items can and must be prevented in the coming year.

. . .

Many of the above mistakes are serious, and some are in violation of the principles set down by the Second Plenum. As they have not yet formed into a system, we are not calling them mistakes of line. However, if they had not been constantly corrected under the leadership of the Party Center and Comrade Mao Zedong, if they had not met with the protests of local Party committees, and if they had not been thoroughly criticized during this conference but had been allowed to develop unchecked, the work of these departments would be in danger of completely departing from the line of the Party.

Although these mistakes are different in nature and extent and can also be traced to certain objective causes, their consequences and influence are to different extents detrimental to the socialist and semisocialist economic sectors and to the worker-peasant alliance and favorable to capitalism in the towns and countryside. They reflect right-opportunist thought in the economic realm and are precisely the manifestation of bourgeois thought in the Party. We must point out that in government work, especially in that of the financial, banking, and trade systems, there really exist some bourgeois viewpoints. We must examine ourselves for not having paid enough attention to them and not carrying out the necessary struggle against them.

The chief responsibility for these mistakes lies with Comrade Bo Yibo. Confronted with criticism, supervision, and help from everyone, Comrade Bo Yibo has already made two self-criticisms. In the second self-criticism, Comrade Bo Yibo has shown increased realization of his mistakes but has not been able to expose the roots of his mistakes. We must point out that the mistakes made by Comrade Bo Yibo in financial and economic work are not accidental but stem from his ideological, social, and historical roots. The ideological root of Comrade Bo Yibo's right opportunist mistakes lies in his not having started out from Marxism-Leninism and from Party policy and the interests of the laboring people, but consciously or unconsciously reflecting his many bourgeois viewpoints, sentiments, and working styles. In the transition period, when our Party has to both cooperate and struggle against capitalist elements of town and country while at the same time gradually carrying out socialist transformation of them, this type of class struggle will inevitably be reflected in inner-Party ideological struggle. Comrade Bo Yibo himself admits that his feelings for the working class have become remote. To whom, then, has he become closer? It has to be the capitalist class. This is the social root of his mistakes. Comrade Bo Yibo said that he came from a petty-bourgeois class background, but he had forgotten the fact that, if the petty-bourgeoisie does not surrender to the proletariat, it would inevitably fall under the influence of the capitalist class. I agree with the opinion expressed by Comrade Gao Gang and others that the most conspicuous problem with Comrade Bo Yibo's bourgeois individualism is in having wrongly placed his personal position [above] that of the Party, in not having been honest to the Party, and in his lack of democracy in working style and his feelings of guildism. He has committed mistakes of a similar nature in his past work, and these mistakes, due to complacency and arrogance, have exposed themselves in a concentrated manner in the past six months. The bourgeois individualist ideas and working style of Comrade Bo Yibo are all the more damaging to the Party and to the laboring people because of his high position as a leader in the Party. Therefore, Comrade Bo Yibo should realize that the crux of correcting his mistakes lies in studying Marxism-Leninism harder and linking it with his work, in being concerned with the interests of the laboring people, and in firmly eliminating his bourgeois individualist ideas and guildist feelings, honestly obeying the unified command of the Party, listening to the opinions of the masses, and earnestly serving the people. It must also be pointed out that Comrade Bo Yibo has fought valiantly against the enemy in the past, and in different periods in the past when he correctly carried out the Party line he made relatively major achievements in his work. The question now is whether Comrade Bo Yibo can modestly accept the correct criticism of various comrades and firmly rectify his mistakes. We hope that he can modestly accept the correct criticism of his comrades and resolutely rectify his mistakes so that, under the Party's leadership, he could continue to do work beneficial to the Party and the people.

. . .

This conference has also proved that the series of mistakes committed by Comrade Bo Yibo in financial and economic work is related to his erroneous working methods. Instead of relying on collective experience and wisdom, instead of following what Comrade Mao Zedong has always stressed, that we must concentrate the experience of the masses, Comrade Bo Yibo likes to make decisions arbitrarily. Mistakes in his work inevitably follow, resulting in dire consequences. In the future, we must always remember to implement Comrade Mao Zedong's important injunction to concentrate the experience of the masses in order that we can do our work well. To be able to carry out this injunction, every responsible comrade must maintain links with the masses, be highly concerned and have enthusiasm for the interests of the people and the nation, and always listen to the opinions of the masses and study and analyze them earnestly.

Comrades! Our Party is the party in power throughout the nation. The correctness or incorrectness (as exemplified by the revised taxation system) of each Party policy will have wide repercussions. There are many things we do not yet understand and much knowledge that we do not yet possess; moreover, our understanding of Marxism-Leninism is not adequate. Therefore, every comrade, especially responsible comrades, must always be prudent and cautious in his work to reduce mistakes. We also need to learn through mistakes to avoid deviations. We must all take warning from Comrade Bo Yibo's mistakes, guard against arrogance and rashness, and, under the leadership of the Party Center and Comrade Mao Zedong, obey the Party's highest principle—collective leadership. We must subject ourselves to the interests of the laboring people, put our best efforts into the construction of the country, and overcome all difficulties. Only so can we do our work well and advance our cause.

3B. Mao's Criticisms of Bo Yibo

[Another, even more significant indication of the heavy criticism of Bo Yibo during the Financial and Economic Conference were Mao's harsh comments during his speech on the last day of the meetings. The only available (partial) text of this speech, extensive portions of which are reproduced in item 1 below, is from volume 5 of Mao's *Selected Works*. This version, however, distorts Mao's overall position by highlighting his negative comments and deleting his conclusion that Bo's mistakes were not mistakes of line; cf. above, Appendix I, p. 165. The brief italicized passage concerning Party unity in this item is the same passage referred to in Appendix I, but here it is implied that the offender is Bo, while in Chen Shihui's account the target is given as Gao Gang. The short excerpt from Mao's early November 1953 remarks in item 2 briefly illustrates the apparent distortions in volume 5 by comparing its rendition of Mao's renewed criticism of Bo Yibo with a Cultural Revolution version of the same text. The differences are highlighted by italics.]

(1) "Oppose the Bourgeois Ideology in the Party"
(excerpts) (August 12, 1953)

> **Source**: *The Writings of Mao Zedong*, 1:364–70, as amended.
> **Chinese text**: *Mao Zedong Xuanji*, 5:90–96.
> **Additional translation**: *Selected Works of Mao Tsetung*, 5:103–10.

THIS conference has been a very good conference, and Premier Zhou's conclusions were also very good. We can now see that after the "Three-Anti" and "Five-Anti" campaigns, there remain two types of errors in the Party. One type consists of general mistakes, such as the "five excesses," which anybody can commit and which can be committed at any time. "Five excesses" mistakes can also turn into "five deficiencies" mistakes. Another type [of mistake] consists of mistakes of principle, such as the deviation toward capitalism. This is a reflection of bourgeois ideology within the Party and a question of a standpoint that violates Marxism-Leninism.

The "Three-Anti" and "Five-Anti" campaigns were a very severe attack on bourgeois ideology in the Party. However, at that time only the bourgeois ideology related to corruption and waste got a good thrashing, while [the problem of] the bourgeois ideology reflected in the question of line was not resolved. This type of bourgeois ideology exists not only in financial and economic work but also in political and legal work, in cultural and educational work, and in other areas of work as well. It also exists both among the comrades at the Center and among the comrades at the localities.

As far as mistakes in [our] financial and economic work are concerned, since last December—when Comrade Bo Yibo proposed the new taxation system of "equality between public and private [enterprises]"—and up to this conference, [these mistakes] have been seriously criticized. If the new tax system develops further, it will inevitably become divorced from Marxism-Leninism and from the Party's general line for the period of transition and will develop toward capitalism.

Is the period of transition to lead toward socialism or toward capitalism? According to the Party's general line, it is to be a transition to socialism. This requires a rather long period of struggle. The mistake in the new tax system is different from the problem of Zhang Zishan;[1] it is a problem of ideology, a problem of having deviated from the Party's general line. We must launch a struggle against bourgeois ideology in the Party. In terms of [its] ideological condition the Party has three types of people in it. Some comrades are steadfast and have not wavered; they have Marxist-Leninist thought. Some comrades are basically Marxist-Leninist, but they have mingled in [with their other thoughts] some non-Marxist-Leninist thought. A small number of people are no good; their thought is non-Marxist-Leninist. In the criticism of Bo Yibo's ideological mistake some people say that Bo Yibo's mistake is that of petty bourgeois individualism. This is not appropriate. The main thing for which he ought to be criticized is his bourgeois thought, which is beneficial to capitalism and harmful to socialism. Only such a criticism is correct. We've said that "left" opportunist mistakes are a reflection of petty bourgeois fanaticism in the Party. Such [mistakes] occurred at times when we were splitting away from the bourgeoisie. [But] during during the three periods when we cooperated with the bourgeoisie, that is, during the first period of cooperation between the Guomindang and the CCP, the period of the war of resistance against Japan, and the current period, it was always bourgeois ideology that influenced some people in the Party and caused them to waver. Bo Yibo's mistake was committed under such circumstances.

Bo Yibo's mistake is not an isolated one. It exists not only at the Center but at two [other] levels, [the level of] the greater administrative regions and [the level of] the provinces and municipalities as well. Each of the greater administrative regions, the provinces, and the municipalities must call a meeting to inspect its own work in accordance with the resolution of the Second Plenum of the Seventh Central Committee and the conclusion of this conference in order to educate the cadres.

. . .

Bo Yibo's mistake is a reflection of bourgeois ideology. It is beneficial to capitalism and harmful to socialism and semisocialism; it has violated the resolution of the Second Plenum of the Seventh Central Committee.

[1]Zhang Zishan was executed for embezzlement during the Three-Anti campaign.

On whom do we rely? Do we rely on the working class, or do we rely on the bourgeoisie? Early on, the resolution of the Second Plenum of the Seventh Central Committee had already made it clear that "we must wholeheartedly rely on the working class." As to the problem of rehabilitating and developing production, the resolution also states that we must affirm that "production in state industries comes first, production in private industries second, and production in handicraft industries third." The emphasis is on industry, and within industry, the emphasis is on heavy industry, which is state-run. Among the five sectors of the economy[2] in our country at present, the state-run [sector of the] economy is the leading factor. Capitalist industrial and commercial enterprises must gradually be led toward state capitalism.

The resolution of the Second Plenum states that on the basis of developing production [we must] improve the living standards of the workers and the laboring people. [However,] people with bourgeois thought do not pay attention to this point, as Bo Yibo has demonstrated. Our emphasis must be placed on developing production, but we must give due consideration to both developing production and improving the people's lives. An effort must be made [to improve the people's] well-being; it cannot be too big an effort, but we cannot ignore it altogether. At present there are still quite a few cadres who disregard the people's livelihood and don't care whether they live or die. In Guizhou there was a regiment that at one time occupied a great deal of the peasants' land. This was an act of severe encroachment on the people's interests. It is wrong not to be concerned with the people's livelihood, but nevertheless, the emphasis must still be put on production and construction.

With regard to the problem of utilizing, restricting, and transforming the capitalist [sector of the] economy, the Second Plenum also made that very clear. The resolution [it adopted] stated that the private capitalist [sector of the] economy must not be left uncurbed and unrestricted; we must restrict it in terms of its sphere of operation, the taxation policy [as it applies to this sector], market pricing, and labor conditions. The relationship between the socialist economy and the capitalist economy is one of leader and led. Restriction and opposition to restriction constitute the primary form of class struggle within the New Democratic state. At present, to talk about "equality between public and private [enterprises]," as the new tax system does, is at variance with the line that [accepts] the state economy as the leading sector.

As for the problem of carrying out the cooperativization of the agricultural economy that is based on individual [peasants' production], and the handicraft industry [sector] of the economy, the resolution of the Second Plenum stated very clearly that "these types of cooperatives are organizations of the collective econ-

[2] The five economic sectors were the state-run economy, the semisocialist cooperative economy, the semisocialist state capitalist economy, the individual economy of peasants and handicraft workers, and the private capitalist economy.

omy of the masses of the laboring people that are based on the system of private ownership but are under the management of the state power led by the proletariat. The fact that the Chinese people are culturally backward and do not have a tradition of cooperativization makes expanding and developing the cooperativization campaign quite difficult for us. Nevertheless, it can still be organized, and must be organized; it must be expanded and developed. If we had only the state economy and no cooperative economy, we would not be able to lead [that sector of] the economy based on the individual [production] of the laboring people gradually onto the path of collectivization, we would not be able to develop from a New Democratic country into a socialist country of the future, and we would not be able to consolidate the proletariat's leadership in the state power." This resolution dates from March 1949, but quite a few comrades have not paid any attention to it; they regard it as news [when] actually it is old news. Bo Yibo wrote the article "Strengthen the Party's Political Work in the Rural Areas" in which he said that for the individual peasants to take the path [of achieving] collectivization through mutual aid and cooperativization "is pure illusion because the present mutual aid teams are based on the individual economy, and on such a basis they cannot gradually develop into collective farms, much less achieve agricultural collectivization on an overall scale by taking such a path." This is in violation of the Party's resolution.

At present there are two united fronts, two alliances. One is the alliance between the working class and the peasants, which is the foundation. Another is the alliance of the working class and the national bourgeoisie. The peasants are laborers and not exploiters, [so] the alliance of the working class and the peasants is a long-term one. Nevertheless, there are contradictions between the working class and the peasants. In accordance with the principle of voluntary [participation] we should gradually lead the peasants from the system of individual ownership toward the system of collective ownership. In the future, there will also be contradictions between the system of state ownership and the system of collective ownership. These are all nonantagonistic contradictions. [On the other hand,] the contradictions between the working class and the bourgeoisie are antagonistic contradictions.

The bourgeoisie is bound to corrupt people and bombard them with sugarcoated bullets. The sugarcoated bullets of the bourgeoisie are both material ones and spiritual ones. A spiritual sugarcoated bullet has hit the mark in Bo Yibo. His mistake is [a result of] his being influenced by bourgeois thought. The bourgeoisie applauded the editorial that propagandized the new tax system, and Bo Yibo was happy. He sought the opinion of the bourgeoisie regarding the new tax system beforehand and made a gentlemen's agreement with the bourgeoisie, but he did not report to the Central Committee. At that time, neither the Ministry of Commerce nor the [All-China] Federation of Supply and Marketing Cooperatives approved [of the new tax system], and the Ministry of Light Industry was not satisfied either.

Of the 1.1 million cadres and personnel in the financial, economic, and commercial system [of the nation], the overwhelming majority are good; a small minority are not good. These bad people can be further divided into two parts; one part consists of counterrevolutionaries who ought to be swept away; another part consists of revolutionaries who have made mistakes, including Party members and non-Party personnel. We should use the method of criticism and education in order to transform them.

...

To guarantee the success of the socialist cause, we must exercise collective leadership and oppose excessive decentralism and subjectivism.

At present we must oppose subjectivism; we must oppose not only the subjectivism of blind adventurist advances, but also the subjectivism of being conservative. In the past, in the period of the New Democratic revolution, [our Party] made mistakes of subjectivism, some of which were "rightist" and some "leftist." [The errors of] Chen Duxiu and Zhang Guotao were "rightist," and in Wang Ming's case they were "leftist" [errors] at first and later "rightist." At the time of the rectification at Yan'an, efforts were concentrated on opposing dogmatism and, on the side, opposing empiricism; both were [manifestations of] subjectivism. If theory is not integrated with reality, the revolution cannot be triumphant. Rectification resolved this problem. We adopted the policy of learning from past mistakes in order to avoid future ones, and curing the sickness in order to save the patient. This was correct. This time, when we carry out a resolute and thorough criticism of Bo Yibo, we are doing it so that people who have committed mistakes can correct them and so that the triumphant progress of socialism will be guaranteed. The present is a period of socialist revolution, but there is [still] subjectivism. Neither impetuous rash advance nor conservatism acts in accordance with reality; both are subjectivism. If subjectivism is not opposed and removed, the revolution and construction cannot succeed. During the period of the democratic revolution, we used the method of rectification to resolve [the problem of] subjectivist mistakes throughout the whole Party, and we united those comrades who upheld the correct line and those who had made mistakes. [These comrades] proceeded on from Yan'an to the various theaters of war, and the entire Party, exerting its efforts in unison, achieved victory thoughout the country. Now the cadres are more mature and the level [of their political consciousness] has been raised; we hope before too long to rid ourselves basically of subjectivism in our leadership work, and strive to make the subjective correspond to the objective.

The key to resolving all these problems lies in strengthening collective leadership and opposing decentralism.... On March 10, 1953, to avoid the danger of the various departments of the government becoming divorced from the leadership of the Party Central Committee, the Central Committee passed the resolution to strengthen [Party] leadership over government work.

Centralization and decentralization are constantly in contradiction with each other. Since we entered the cities, decentralization has developed further. To solve this contradiction, all major and important issues must first be discussed and decided by the Party committees before [the decisions] are carried out by the government. For instance, such major issues as erecting the Monument to the People's Heroes in Tiananmen [Square] and dismantling the city walls of Beijing were decided by the Center and then carried out by the government. Problems of secondary importance can be taken care of by the leading Party groups in the departments of the government. It just won't do for all problems to be monopolized by the Center. To oppose decentralism [is a measure] that will best win the hearts of the people because the majority of the comrades in the Party are concerned about collective leadership. In terms of their attitude toward collective leadership, people inside the Party can be classified into three types. People of the first type are concerned about the collective leadership. People of the second type are indifferent and believe that it would be best if the Party committee didn't interfere with [their affairs] but that if it did interfere, that's all right too. [The attitude that] "it's best if they do not interfere" shows a lack of Party spirit, whereas [the attitude that] "interference is all right too" [shows that they] still retain [a measure of] Party spirit. We must take hold of [their attitude that] "inteference is all right" and conduct persuasion and education [to overcome] the lack of Party spirit. Otherwise, each ministry would do its own thing and the Center would not be able to exercise control over them. The ministers would not be able to manage the department and bureau heads, the division heads would not be able to manage section chiefs, and nobody would be able to manage anybody else. [Consequently] there would be a large number of kingdoms, [like the] eight hundred feudal lords. The third type is made up of an extreme minority; they resolutely oppose collective leadership and believe that it is best never to interfere with anything. In the resolution on strengthening Party spirit, it was emphasized that the discipline of democratic centralism must be strictly enforced; the minority must submit to the Central Committee (in this case the majority must submit to the minority, [but] this minority represents the majority). *If there are any opinions, please raise them openly. To damage Party unity is the most shameful thing. Only by relying on the political experience of the collective and the wisdom of the collective can we guarantee the correct leadership of the Party and state as well as the unshakable unity of the ranks of the Party as a whole* [emphasis added].

At this conference, Liu Shaoqi said he had made some mistakes, and Comrade [Deng] Xiaoping also said he had made some mistakes. No matter who they are, people who have made mistakes must examine [their mistakes] and accept the supervision of the Party and the leadership of the Party committees at the various levels. This is a major condition for accomplishing the Party's task. Throughout the country there are a lot of people who rely on the anarchistic situation to survive. Bo Yibo is such a person. Politically and ideologically, he is somewhat corrupted, [so] it is absolutely necessary to criticize him.

...

(2) Excerpts from Two Versions of Remarks Regarding Bo Yibo (November 4, 1953)

>(i) **Source**: Volume 5 of Mao's *Selected Works*, in The Writings of Mao Zedong, 1:428.
>**Chinese text**: *Mao Zedong Xuanji*, 5:122.
>**Additional translation**: *Selected Works of Mao Tsetung*, 5:138.

WITHOUT the Conference on Financial and Economic [Work] held in July and August, the problem of the general line would not have been solved for many of our comrades. The main [accomplishment of] the Conference on Financial and Economic [Work] in July and August was primarily the resolution of this problem. *The criticism of Bo Yibo was precisely for his error in deviating from the general line* [emphasis added].

>(ii) **Source**: *Mao Zedong Sixiang Wansui, 1949.9–1957.12* [Long Live Mao Zedong Thought, September 1949–December 1957] (n.p., n.d.), p. 42.

WITHOUT the Conference on Financial and Economic [Work] held in July and August, the problem of the general line would not have been solved. The main [accomplishment of] the Conference on Financial and Economic [Work] in July and August was primarily the resolution of the general line problem. *The criticism of Bo Yibo's mistakes also concerned the general line problem* [emphasis added].

3C. Adjustments in Tax Policy

[While Bo Yibo's new tax system was heavily criticized at the Financial and Economic Conference, it is unclear precisely what was done to rectify the situation. Item 1 below is excerpted from the only available portions of Chen Yun's report to the Central People's Government Council a month after the conclusion of the conference. Although Chen treats the tax system and also mistakes in commercial work (cf. Appendix II-1) as errors of principle, his analysis is cautiously pragmatic rather than ideological in approach. Moreover, Chen implies that only limited practical measures were taken, notably the reimposition of "one set of taxes" (see the italicized section). Item 2, from a post-Mao chronology, gives specific information concerning the restoration of this business tax, which had been eliminated under Bo's system.]

(1) Excerpts from Chen Yun's Report after the Conference

>**Source**: "Overcome Defects and Mistakes in Financial and Economic Work"

(September 14, 1953), in *Chen Yun Wenxuan (1949–1956)* [Selected works of Chen Yun, 1949–1956] (Beijing: Renmin chubanshe, 1984), pp. 196–99, 201.

IN THE first half of this year the situation of the national economy was stable and on the rise. It would seem now that apart from agricultural production, which has met with natural disasters and will have difficulty in fulfilling plans, the situation in other areas is good. Our overall economic work has made achievements. Work in finance and commerce from the main aspects has scored successes.

At present, I will speak mainly about the defects and mistakes in financial and economic work.

Let me first speak about work in tax revenue.

In the first half of this year the achievements in tax revenue are: First, the year's plan for tax revenue has been 43 percent completed. According to the experience of a number of years, tax revenue is usually collected by "four in the first and six in the second," that is, 40 percent is collected in the first half of the year and 60 percent in the second half. The first half of this year is rather good in that we have already collected 43 percent. Second, the task is stipulated according to policy; policy and task are identical, and this has also been well carried out. Third, the style and attitude of people working in taxation has improved compared to the past. In the past half year, however, work in taxation has registered a serious mistake, that is, the mistake of revising the taxation system.

Since Liberation and up until last year, the proportion of orders placed by the state with private enterprises for processing materials or supplying manufactured goods, purchasing, and marketing has gradually increased. In this way business relationships have decreased relatively, and with this so has taxation. It is necessary to make this up. With such a situation there was reason to suggest a revision of the taxation system. But consideration should be given as to what method to adopt. According to the revised tax system, orders placed by the state with private enterprises for processing materials or supplying manufactured goods, purchasing, and marketing are not taxed, while a transactions tax is made on business relationships. It is said that doing it this way means "equality between public and private [enterprises]." This so-called equality between public and private [enterprises] actually means adding taxes to state commercial enterprises and cooperatives. From this the corollary follows that it is proposed the tax for wholesale enterprises is shifted to the factories to pay, and a large number of wholesale merchants do not pay tax, in this way changing the links in tax payment. Thus, the error in revising the taxation system is, to sum up, twofold: One is "equality between public and private [enterprises]," the other is the change in the link of tax payment.

Can public and private [enterprises] be treated equally? They cannot. The formulation "equality between public and private [enterprises]" is wrong. This is because of the different nature of both state and private enterprises. First of all, the entire profits of a state enterprise must be handed over to the state, while private enterprises only pay income tax to the state. Furthermore, the responsibilities borne by private commercial enterprises and the state are different. Private commercial enterprises just do business and make money, and of course provide the needs of the market. The state commercial enterprises not only do business and make money, more importantly they maintain production and stabilize the market. State commercial enterprises, in order to maintain production in the factories, must place orders for processed goods, be it the peak season or the slack season. When agricultural products are ready they must be purchased, even if they can only be retailed half a year later, or if it takes a year when they can be exchanged for goods with foreign countries, otherwise agricultural products would be unmarketable. To stabilize the market, it is necessary to have an adequate stockpile of goods. If there is no such accumulation, the speculative activities of private businessmen could not be put down. With accumulation, commercial enterprises bear the responsibility of bank interest. Not only that, sometimes they have to do business that sustains losses. Using steamships and naval vessels to transport grain from Sichuan to Wuhan and Shanghai to sell is an example of doing business that sustains losses because the cost of transportation is very high. Would it be possible to mark [goods] in the markets of Wuhan and Shanghai: "This rice is from Sichuan, transport costs are very high so an amount for transport will be added, thus the price is high"? (Laughter.) The price cannot be raised for selling; we can only sustain losses. From the point of view of the state, this is completely necessary. If the people's government does not adopt such measures, then it will make a big mistake. Would private business adopt such measures? They definitely would not. So we say the nature of private commerce and state commerce is different. The cooperatives are about the same as state-operated commerce, they have similar tasks. Thus to say of state run commercial enterprises, cooperative commercial enterprises, and privately owned commercial enterprises that there is "equality between public and private" appears fair and reasonable. Actually it is not fair. Consequently, the formulation "equality between public and private [enterprises]" is wrong.

Where is the error in changing the link in tax payment? The error lies in that the tax on wholesale business is moved to the factories to pay, exempting the wholesale merchant from taxation, and then he can attack state commerce. Why? Because the price he pays is the same as that of state commercial enterprises, but in the sale price he can be lower than that of state commercial enterprises. At present, the wholesale merchant does not mind having a big volume of trade. The bigger the volume, the faster the capital turnover, and the more money that can be made. In this way, private commerce will develop greatly, which would be a big blow to state commerce. At the same time it would be a blow to industry in the hinterland. Take, for instance, industry in the areas of Chongqing and Xi'an; originally they had two sets of taxes, that is, a commodity tax and a turnover tax on products leaving the factory. Many commodities are bought directly from the factory, and it has not been necessary to pay a wholesale business tax. But now, adding a wholesale business tax will create great difficulties for industries in the hinterland, and it will also stimulate the blind development of industry in coastal cities like Shanghai and Tianjin. The first half of this year saw the phenomenon of "big fish eating little fish," and this was where it came from. This does not conform with state policy.

We are a country led by the working class and the state-owned economy. In a country like ours, the error of revising the tax system as described above is an error of principle. *The mistake has been made, what do we do? In my opinion the new tax system is already being carried out. If the new arrangements have not been made well and it is immediately changed back, this will cause chaos for a while, so any change must not be made hastily. Exactly how we solve this problem must be studied well. We have already restored one set of taxes on those wholesalers who were exempted, in this way constraining them somewhat* [emphasis added].

To sum up, to change the tax system it is necessary to act with caution as it involves the various aspects of economic life.

Let us now speak of commerce.

For some years, the state-owned commercial enterprises have organized an interflow between the cities and the countryside, [and] domestic and international exchange which has promoted the restoration and development of industry and agriculture, established the national market, and played an important role in restoring the economy. In the first quarter of this year, however, the business turnover of state-owned commercial enterprises decreased; that is no good. There were many reasons for the decrease in the volume of business, the most important being insufficient estimation of the quantities demanded by the market this year, an overestimation of stockpiled commodities, considering wrongly that there were too many things in the warehouses, which was called "too big a bellyful," and proposing a slogan of "loosening one's bowels." Moreover, placing orders for processing goods was decreased. In this way the phenomenon of being out of stock appeared very quickly in the market. This is an error in our work.

Another error is in purchasing products to buy less from state factories and more from privately owned factories. This is also because of the underestimation of the market, so that state-owned enterprises were asked not to produce so much. But state-owned enterprises still produced because the workers are working there and output cannot be reduced. The state-owned factories wanted the state commerce units to purchase the goods they had produced, but the commerce units would not. The state-owned enterprises said, "You won't purchase our goods, we'll sell them ourselves," but the state commerce units would not permit them to do this. Consequently, state-owned factories are very dissatisfied with the state commerce units. Adopting this type of attitude toward state-owned factories is also an error of principle.

. . .

I have spoken above of the defects and errors in the aspects of tax, commerce, and finance. The Central Financial and Economic Committee and the various bodies in charge are all responsible for this. I am the chairman of the Central

Financial and Economic Committee, and I should first of all be responsible for these problems.

...

(2) The Restoration of the Wholesale Business Tax

Source: *Zhonghua Renmin Gongheguo Jingji Guanli Dashiji,* pp. 45–46.

[AUGUST] 22, [1953:] The Ministry of Commerce submitted to the Financial [and Economic] Committee and the Central Committee of the Communist Party a "Report on Market Conditions after Resumption of Taxation of Wholesalers, and Measures to Be Adopted." The important contents are:

1. Most private wholesalers learned about the August 1 resumption of taxation on July 27 or 28. Thus, starting July 27, there was a rush among private businesses everywhere to sell inventories, in an effort to evade taxation. They lied to retailers that they better stock up as there would soon be a price hike.

2. Developments in wholesale commerce after the August 1 resumption of taxation include the following:

   a. Some wholesalers were in business as usual; some planned to close down temporarily.

   b. Part of the wholesalers have independently or collectively raised wholesale prices.

   c. Wholesalers have begun to curtail or stop charge accounts.

   d. Wholesalers protested to government personnel: "Are state businesses paying taxes? If not, isn't that a violation of the principle of equality between public and private [enterprises]?" "The government in the past proposed that the principle was to maintain present taxes and make no increases. This new measure is an increase and doesn't conform to the goverment's original principle, etc." They asked that they be permitted to raise prices in accordance with the rate of tax increase.

   e. Retailers generally support this measure, so do wholesale-retail businesses. They indicated that past taxes were unbalanced; now there is balance.

   f. Clerks working in wholesale businesses generally indicated that the increase was reasonable, but part of them are apprehensive about the capitalists closing down and hence losing their jobs.

3. Wholesale volume of state businesses went up sharply from August 1 to 5. The Taiyuan Cotton Cloth Company, for instance, had a daily sale of 1,400 bolts before. On August 5, the volume went up to 4,600 bolts. The early August daily sales of soap at the Shanghai Department Store went up three to four times as compared to the end of July.

4. Measures we plan to take in the future:

   a. We plan to adopt the policy of resolutely eliminating large wholesalers of cloth and daily goods, especially in the large cities as a start. State commerce should stop supplying them and prohibit them from raising prices, and try to make them turn to other trades voluntarily.

b. As for medium and small wholesalers of cloth and daily goods, we plan to give them some room for the time being. Those that get their supplies from state companies and distribute to village peddlers should be allowed to continue temporarily. After giving the priority to cooperatives and state retailers in supplies, they should get a small amount of supplies.

IV
THE STRUGGLE IN THE CENTRAL ORGANIZATION DEPARTMENT AND THE NATIONAL CONFERENCE ON ORGANIZATION WORK
July–October 1953

[The organizational sphere became enmeshed in the Gao-Rao affair as a result of Rao Shushi's efforts from mid-1953 to assert his authority as head of the Central Committee's organization department, and in the same process to undermine Liu Shaoqi through attacks on An Ziwen. An overview of Rao's activities in this respect and their background is given in item 1. The conflict on the organization front came to a head at the September–October National Conference on Organization Work where Rao was firmly rebuffed. At that conference, however, Mao left an ambiguous message, which is indicated by items 2A and 2B.]

1. Rao Shushi's Struggle against An Ziwen

[As surrogate for Liu Shaoqi in the organization department, deputy department head An Ziwen became a key figure in the Gao-Rao affair. This account describes the conflict in the organizational sphere in late 1953 from An's perspective.]

> Source: Chen Yeping and Han Jingcao, eds., *An Ziwen Zhuanlüe* [A Short Biography of An Ziwen] (Taiyuan: Shanxi remin chubanshe, 1985), pp. 99–104.

IN 1953, Gao Gang and Rao Shushi carried out their conspiratorial activities to split the Party and usurp the supreme leadership of Party and state power. Gao Gang first of all got the support of Lin Biao so as to shoulder out Comrade Liu Shaoqi. The activities of Gao and Rao were abnormal in that they used barter tactics, schemes, and intrigues. An Ziwen actively took part in this struggle against these bourgeois individualist careerists and went through a severe test.

Rao Shushi Causes Chaos in the Central Committee's Organization Department

In the spring of 1953 Rao Shushi became the head of the organization department of the Central Committee.

Prior to the exposure of the anti-Party activities of Gao and Rao, An Ziwen did not see through their conspiracy and made a mistake for which he received the Central Committee's criticism and disciplinary warning. When he perceived the anti-Party conspiracy of Gao Gang and Rao Shushi, in order to preserve the unity of the Party he carried out resolute struggle against their conspiracy.

In mid-July 1953, at a department heads meeting[1] of the central organization department, Rao Shushi made a sudden attack on An Ziwen for an entire morning. One minute he was sitting, the next minute standing, rudely and unreasonably censuring An Ziwen. Now and then he pointed rudely at him, demanding to know why it was that he had not reported certain problems to him but instead [reported] first to Liu Shaoqi and Premier Zhou. In a loud, formidable tone, Rao Shushi shouted, "Wang Fu (at that time section head of the Party members administration section), Zhao Han (at the time head of the general office) are new recruits. When they hear guns, they can't help being tense. But you, An Ziwen, you are an old soldier, hearing a gun firing you shouldn't have [felt tense]...."[2]

In the face of this sudden attack, An Ziwen remained calm and almost didn't answer.

What was it all about?

Just prior to this Wang Fu and Zhao Han had taken some comrades to observe the developing situation of the New Three-Anti campaign and Party rectification in the countryside in Shandong province and had met with obstruction from the local Party organization. Wang Fu and Zhao Han went to seek out the leaders of the Shandong Subbureau of the CCP Central Committee to discuss this problem but could not get their point through. Then, as they were unable to continue working there, Wang Fu and Zhao Han returned to Beijing. An Ziwen reported this incident to comrades Liu Shaoqi and Zhou Enlai.

After this department heads meeting Rao Shushi held a number of further meetings to criticize An Ziwen, groundlessly accusing him of supporting the "branches against the areas," and even distorted the fact that Wang Fu and Zhao Han had to leave Shandong as "a protest against the Central Committee bureau and subbureau." He also used the fact that An Ziwen was not actively taking part in the National Financial and Economic Conference as a pretext to accuse him of "not being clear on demarcation lines and not having a good [political] sense of smell." Particularly disgraceful was that Rao Shushi fabricated a report to the Center libeling An Ziwen as having accepted his "criticism."

This behavior of Rao Shushi caused strong dissatisfaction among the comrades

---

[1] *Buwu huiyi*—this would include the head of the organization department, the deputy heads, and the heads of the various sections. It would have been very unusual for Rao Shushi to have spoken in such a way to An Ziwen in front of lower-ranking cadres.

[2] The apparent meaning is that he should not have overreacted and reported this incident to Liu Shaoqi and Zhou Enlai.

of the central organization department who took part in the meeting.

From this time, the normal order of the central organization department was disrupted and work became semiparalyzed.

Afterward Chairman Mao criticized Rao Shushi, saying: Don't think you know everything because you've been first [Party] secretary of a large region. You still haven't worked at the Center. Why is it that you carried out a struggle against "a high mandarin of the Ministry of Official Personnel Affairs" (meaning An Ziwen) and didn't even notify the Center!

Resolute Resistance to the Attack Against the Party by Gao and Rao at the National Financial and Economic Conference

In June 1953 the Center convened the National Financial and Economic Conference. The meeting was presided over by Premier Zhou, and a core small group was set up. Gao and Rao used this meeting to launch an attack on the Party.

The meeting was originally to discuss financial and economic work. But as a result of the interference of Gao and Rao, its original direction could not be carried out and it became a big inner-Party struggle meeting. An Ziwen, Gao Gang, and Rao Shushi were all members of the core small group of the conference. During the conference, both Gao and Rao acted with arrogant bossiness, with an imperiousness as though they considered themselves quite unexcelled. An Ziwen saw soberly the seriousness of the situation. At this meeting Gao and Rao condemned the central organization department on the question of its appointment of cadres and certain problems of Party construction. The situation was quite clear, "the drinker's heart was not in the cup of wine" [meaning Gao and Rao had ulterior motives]. They spoke of the central organization department but their spearhead was directed at Liu Shaoqi and Zhou Enlai, against the Central Committee of the Party headed by Chairman Mao. As some people at the meeting condemned the appointments of certain people by name, An Ziwen directed his secretary, (deputy head of the general office) Comrade Han Jingcao, to look up the files of those comrades one by one. On the face of it, those few comrades who had been named did have a "complicated" history, but conclusions had been made on the important questions that were clear. The reason the history of these cadres was "complicated" was the Party's struggle against the Guomindang reactionaries. They had carried out many different kinds of complex struggle, open or secret, legal or illegal, against the enemy under the instructions of the Party. Their history was clear and they had made contributions in the struggle against the enemy, and some had made outstanding contributions. The "complicated" nature of their history, from an important aspect, reflected the harshness of the democratic revolution in China, its tortuous path, and its complexity. After the national victory, the Party's appointment of these comrades was correct, and there was nothing to dispute. Acting as they did, Gao and Rao clearly had ulterior motives.

At the Financial and Economic Conference, Rao Shushi put pressure on An Ziwen to force him to speak, saying, "in a big inner-Party struggle like this you should make your position clear." An Ziwen adopted the struggle method of "at this time silence is better than sound" and resolutely refused to speak, thus showing this attitude. He said to Han Jingcao: "I've thought it over and over again and decided not to speak. If doing this is wrong, then let history make the conclusion!" During the meeting he said nothing that was harmful to Party unity and did nothing to harm Party unity, [thus] resolutely resisting the attack against the Party by Gao and Rao.

Normally speaking, An Ziwen was a very lively person, and working day and night meant nothing. At that time the leading comrades of the Center were accustomed to working at night. Even on a freezing winter night when he was already asleep, if any leading comrade of the Center phoned, he would get up and go. Nor was such a situation rare, it occurred often. An Ziwen always completed every kind of duty given him by the Center with vigorous energy. There were a number of matters that were not strictly part of the professional area of the organization department, but he always actively carried these out and never shifted responsibility onto others. Outside of work he would talk cheerfully and humorously. But during these days of the Gao-Rao events he became silent and morose. He could not sleep nor eat; sometimes he would pace up and down in the courtyard, seriously considering how to struggle with the anti-Party conspiratorial activities of Gao and Rao.

*Before and After the Second National
Organization Work Conference*

In September 1953 the Party Center took charge of convening the Second National Organization Work Conference. Gao and Rao used that meeting to continue to attack the Party and to vilify and censure the central organization department as well as An Ziwen.

During the preparations for the Second National Organization Work Conference, there initially had been no decision for the central organization department to make a work report to the conference. At a critical moment, when it was almost time for the conference, Rao Shushi told An Ziwen that as he had worked in the central organization department for many years, he should make a report on its work to the conference. Undoubtedly this was designed to put An Ziwen in a difficult position. Forced by Rao and despite the pressure of time, An Ziwen organized some people to work day and night to write the report. In the report he insisted on the principle of being realistic, to confirm work achievements and at the same time to make an examination of faults and errors.

Chairman Mao entrusted Liu Shaoqi with presiding personally over the meeting of the leading group of the Organization Work Conference. Those taking part in the leading group meeting were Zhu De, Li Fuchun, Hu Qiaomu, Xi Zhongxun, Yang Shangkun, Qian Ying, and the organization department heads of the six Central Committee [regional] bureaus, and Rao Shushi and An Ziwen. Presided over by Liu Shaoqi, the leading group held many meetings. The plenary meetings of the Second National Organization Work Conference were divided by regions to discuss general organization work, while the meetings of the leading group were mainly to solve the so-called problem of the contradiction between Rao and An. At these meetings Liu Shaoqi, with the sharp observance of a statesman, was severe in exposing the lies of Rao Shushi. Liu Shaoqi said solemnly: Chairman Mao instructed me to bring the struggle within the organization department out into the open and solve it, and he pointed out clearly, "in the past the central organization department has made achievements and [it] has carried out the correct line in its work." As to the errors and mistakes of the organization department, with the breadth of a proletarian revolutionary Liu Shaoqi took responsibility. The comrades at the meeting were extremely moved. Finally Liu Shaoqi said: Our organization work must serve well the general line of the transition period. I am sure comrades are happy and can shoulder the responsibility of this task.

In his speech to the Second National Organization Work Conference, Deng Xiaoping said: The work of the central organization department has made achievements and has carried out the line of the Central Committee. He emphasized: "This is indivisible from the leadership of Chairman Mao and especially of Comrade Shaoqi. However, Comrade Ziwen also has achievements, one cannot consider that only the leadership is good, that it could produce achievements if the work was badly carried out."

2. Mao's Letter to the Leaders of the Organization Conference

[Toward the latter part of the Organization Conference Mao moved to rebuke Rao Shushi, affirm the contributions of An Ziwen, and emphasize Party unity. At the same time, however, he sent a letter to the conference leaders (item 2A) that called for study of the concluding section of the Stalinist *Short Course* (item 2B), a text that presented a very different view of Party unity.]

2A. "Letter to Yang Shangkun" (October 22, 1953)

> Source: *The Writings of Mao Zedong*, 1:421–22.
> Chinese text: *Mao Zedong Shuxin Xuanji* [Selected Letters of Mao Zedong] (Beijing: Renmin chubanshe, 1983), pp. 469–70.

COMRADE Shangkun:
   Please take the six points in the conclusion of [the book] *Liangong Dangshi*

[History of the Communist Party of the Soviet Union][1] and print them as a single leaflet to be sent tonight or tomorrow to the various comrades attending the organizational meeting. Please ask them to make use of the two or three days recess in the meeting to read, study, and, where possible, even discuss [these points] so that when Comrade Liu Shaoqi and others reach this issue in their speeches in the conference, they [the attending comrades] may already have some understanding of this matter. When the leading group meets this afternoon, please notify Comrades Liu [Shaoqi], Rao [Shushi], and Hu Qiaomu of this matter (i.e., the matter of printing and distributing the concluding points [of the book]). While you are at it, you may print some extra copies (you may print one or two thousand copies) and distribute [the surplus] to cadres in Beijing, and charge the General Party Committee[2] with notifying the various departments and Party groups, urging them to read and discuss [the subject].

Mao Zedong
2 [P.M.]
October 22

2B. Excerpts from the "Conclusion" to the Stalinist Short Course *Recommended for Study by Mao*

> Source: *History of the Communist Party of the Soviet Union (Bolsheviks): Short Course* (London: Cobbett Publishing Co., 1939), pp. 323ff.

WHAT are the chief conclusions to be drawn from the historical path traversed by the Bolshevik Party? What does the history of the CPSU(B) teach us?

1. The history of the Party teaches us, first of all, that the victory of the proletarian revolution, the victory of the dictatorship of the proletariat, is impossible without a revolutionary party of the proletariat, a party free from opportunism, irreconcilable toward compromisers and capitulators, and revolutionary in its attitude toward the bourgeoisie and its state power....

2. The history of the Party further teaches us that a party of the working class cannot perform the role of leader of its class, cannot perform the role of organizer and leader of the proletarian revolution, unless it has mastered the advanced theory of the working class movement, the Marxist-Leninist theory....

3. The history of the Party further teaches us that unless the petty bourgeois parties that are active within the ranks of the working class and that push the

---

[1] This surely refers to the 1938 Stalinist text, *History of the Communist Party of the Soviet Union (Bolsheviks): Short Course.*

[2] This refers to the general Party committee of the various organs directly subordinate to or affiliated with the Central Committee of the CCP at the time. It was the general Party leadership organ for the organs directly under the Central Committee, the Central People's Government, and the Military Affairs Committee as well as the people's organizations at the central level.

backward sections of the working class are smashed, the victory of the proletarian revolution is impossible. . . .

4. The history of the Party further teaches us that unless the Party of the working class wages an uncompromising struggle against the opportunists within its own ranks, unless it smashes the capitulators in its own midst, it cannot preserve unity and discipline within its ranks, it cannot perform its role of organizer and leader of the proletarian revolution, nor its role as the builder of the new, socialist society.

The history of the development of the internal life of our Party is the history of the struggle against the opportunist groups within the Party—the "Economists," Mensheviks, Trotskyites, Bukharinites, and nationalist deviators—and of the utter defeat of these groups.

The history of our Party teaches us that all these groups of capitulators were in fact agents of Menshevism within our Party, the lees and dregs of Menshevism, the continuers of Menshevism. Like the Mensheviks, they acted as vehicles of bourgeois influence among the working class and in the Party. The struggle for the liquidation of these groups within the Party was therefore a continuation of the struggle for the liquidation of Menshevism.

If we had not defeated the "Economists" and the Mensheviks, we could not have built the Party and led the working class to the proletarian revolution.

If we had not defeated the Trotskyites and Bukharinites, we could not have brought about the conditions that are essential for the building of socialism.

If we had not defeated the nationalist deviators of all shades and colors, we could not have educated the people in the spirit of internationalism, we could not have safeguarded the banner of the great amity of the nations of the USSR, and we could not have built up the Union of Soviet Socialist Republics.

It may seem to some that the Bolsheviks devoted far too much time to this struggle against the opportunist elements within the Party, that they overrated their importance. But that is altogether wrong. Opportunism in our midst is like an ulcer in a healthy organism, and must not be tolerated. The Party is the leading detachment of the working class, its advanced fortress, its general staff. Skeptics, opportunists, capitulators, and traitors cannot be tolerated on the directing staff of the working class. If, while it is carrying on a life-and-death fight against the bourgeoisie, there are capitulators and traitors on its own staff, within its own fortress, the working class will be caught between two fires, from the front and the rear. Clearly, such a struggle can only end in defeat. The easiest way to capture a fortress is from within. To attain victory, the Party of the working class, its directing staff, its advanced fortress, must first be purged of capitulators, deserters, scabs, and traitors.

It cannot be regarded as an accident that the Trotskyites, Bukharinites, and nationalist deviators who fought Lenin and the Party ended just as the Menshevik and Socialist-Revolutionary parties did, namely, by becoming agents of fascist espionage services, by turning spies, wreckers, assassins, diversionists, and traitors to the country.

> "With reformists, Mensheviks, in our ranks," Lenin said, "it is *impossible* to achieve victory in the proletarian revolution, it is *impossible* to retain it. That is obvious in principle, and it has been strikingly confirmed by the experience both of Russia and Hungary.... In Russia, difficult situations have arisen *many times*, when the Soviet regime would *most certainly* have been overthrown had Mensheviks, reformists and petty bourgeois democrats remained in our Party...." (Lenin, *Selected Works*, English. ed., 10:256–57)
>
> "Our Party," Comrade Stalin says, "succeeded in creating internal unity and unexampled cohesion of its ranks primarily because it was able in good time to purge itself of the opportunist pollution, because it was able to rid its ranks of the Liquidators, the Mensheviks. Proletarian parties develop and become strong by purging themselves of opportunists and reformists, social-imperialists and social-chauvinists, social-patriots and social-pacifists. The Party becomes strong by purging itself of opportunist elements." (Stalin, *Leninism*, English ed., p. 83)[1]

5. The history of the Party further teaches us that a party cannot perform its role as leader of the working class if, carried away by success, it begins to grow conceited, ceases to observe the defects in its work, and fears to acknowledge its mistakes and frankly and honestly to correct them in good time....

6. Lastly, the history of the Party teaches us that unless it has wide connections with the masses, unless it constantly strengthens these connections, unless it knows how to hearken to the voice of the masses and understands their urgent needs, unless it is prepared not only to teach the masses, but to learn from the masses, a party of the working class cannot be a real mass party capable of leading the working class millions and all the laboring people....

Such are the chief lessons to be drawn from the historical path traversed by the Bolshevik Party.

[1] Emphasis and excerpting in the *Short Course*.

V
GAO GANG'S APPROACHES TO OTHER LEADERS

[From mid-1953 to the end of the year, Gao Gang engaged in extensive lobbying of Party and military leaders. While Party histories give a general indication of the appeals used by Gao in these contacts—fanning the resentment of army leaders at alleged favoritism to "white area" cadres, denigrating the performance of Liu Shaoqi and Zhou Enlai, and offering positions in a Gao-led administration (see Appendix I)—only fragmentary evidence exists of the concrete approaches themselves. The following items, together with Appendix VI–1, are the only accounts of Gao's lobbying that have been uncovered. They recount approaches made to three of the Party's highest-ranking and most prestigious figures, Chen Yun, Deng Xiaoping, and Lin Biao; another high-ranking military leader, Luo Ronghuan; and South China Party leader Tao Zhu.]

1. Deng Xiaoping's Account of Gao's Approach to Chen Yun and Himself

[This excerpt from Deng Xiaoping's March 19, 1980, comments on a draft of the CCP's historical resolution for the post-1949 period has become the basis for virtually all accounts touching on Gao Gang's approach to Secretariat member Chen Yun and himself, then a vice-premier. Deng's version is notable for conveying, perhaps unintentionally, the caution with which he responded to Gao. On the other hand, it asserts an immediate reporting of the incidents by Chen and Deng to Mao which, on balance, is difficult to credit. Deng also points out a number of other important aspects of Gao's activities including his effort to secure regional backing through a few key figures, and claims that policy (Gao's "real line") played a minor role. The latter point, however, must be qualified by the fact that one of the main objectives of the historical resolution was to discredit the Cultural Revolution concept of "two-line struggle."]

Source: *Deng Xiaoping Wenxuan (1975–1982)* [Selected Works of Deng Xiaoping, 1975–1982] (Beijing: Renmin chubanshe, 1983), pp. 257–58.

Available translation: *Selected Works of Deng Xiaoping (1975–1982)* (Beijing: Foreign Languages Press, 1984), pp. 278–79.

IT was correct to expose Gao Gang and Rao Shushi. Whether this struggle can be regarded as one between two lines is something that can be looked into further. I am quite clear on the whole story. After Comrade Mao Zedong proposed at the end of 1953 that the work of the Central Committee be divided into a "first front" and a "second front," Gao Gang became very active. He first gained the support of Lin Biao, which was what emboldened him to go ahead full steam. At the time, he was in charge in Northeast China, while Lin Biao was in charge in Central-South China and Rao Shushi in East China. So far as Southwest China was concerned,[1] he tried to win me over and had formal negotiations[2] with me in which he said that Comrade Liu Shaoqi was immature. He was trying to persuade me to join in his effort to topple Comrade Liu Shaoqi. I made my attitude clear, saying that Comrade Liu Shaoqi's position in the Party was the outcome of historical development, that he was a good comrade on the whole, and that it was inappropriate to try to oust him from such a position. Gao Gang also approached Comrade Chen Yun for formal negotiations and told him that a few [Party] vice-chairmanships should be instituted, with himself and Chen each holding one of them. At this point, Comrade Chen Yun and I realized the gravity of the matter and immediately brought it to Comrade Mao Zedong's attention. It was highly irregular for Gao Gang to engage in behind-the-scenes deals and conspiracies in his attempt to bring Comrade Liu Shaoqi down. Therefore, we should reaffirm that it was correct to struggle against Gao Gang. The Gao-Rao case was handled rather leniently. Hardly anyone was hurt. In fact, care was taken to protect a number of cadres. All in all, we had no choice but to expose Gao Gang and Rao Shushi and deal with their case as we did. Our handling of it was correct from the present perspective as well. But so far as Gao Gang's real line is concerned, actually, I can't see that he had one, so it's hard to say whether we should call it a struggle between two lines. Please discuss this further.

2. An Account of Gao's Dealings with Lin Biao

[This excerpt from a 1987 article by a Party historian specializing on Lin Biao was, according to oral sources, based on a c. 1965 letter from an old Fourth Field Army subordinate of Lin's, Liu Yalou, who was to die shortly thereafter. The letter, which recounted what Lin had revealed to Liu at the time about his relations with Gao, reportedly enraged Lin, who crumpled it up and threw it into a spitoon, from which it was later surreptitiously retrieved by one of Lin's secretaries. Given Lin's

---

[1] Deng's account ignores Gao's approach to Peng Dehuai in which he attempted to secure the backing of the Northwest.

[2] *Zhengshi tanpan.* The official translation, in *Selected Works of Deng Xiaoping*, p. 278, rendered this phrase as "serious talks," a milder and less accurate translation.

disgrace in 1971, the article understandably places a negative gloss on his role, one that may overstate his actual cooperation with Gao. It is of particular interest for its focus on personnel appointments as a major element in Gao Gang's strategy, and also for its indication of the key role played by Chen Yun in hosing down the affair after Mao had been informed of Gao's activities by Chen and Deng Xiaoping.]

> **Source**: Yu Nan, "Lin Biao Jituan Xingwang Chutan" [Preliminary Exploration of the Rise and Fall of the Lin Biao Clique], in *Shinianhou de Pingshuo—Wenhua Dageming Shilunji* [Reviews and Comments after Ten Years—Collection of Historical Essays on the Cultural Revolution], ed. Tan Zhongji, Zheng Shui, et al. (Beijing: Zhonggong dangshi ziliao chubanshe, 1987), p. 61.

AFTER the founding of the PRC, Lin Biao was on sick leave and didn't do much work. In 1953 when he was recuperating in Beijing and Hangzhou, he was on very close terms with Gao Gang and, moreover, participated in Gao's anti-Party conspiracy. In October 1953 Gao made a special trip to Hangzhou to consult Lin many times regarding a list of candidates for the Party Center as well as a list of militiary representatives for the Eighth Party Congress, etc. [Lin's wife,] Ye Qun, also frequented Gao Gang's lodge on Lin Biao's behalf discussing political matters. Lin Biao flatteringly claimed that Gao Gang was politically very strong and would have a remarkable future in the Party.

At the end of November Lin Biao handed a letter to Gao Gang's wife and asked her to ensure that the letter was passed to Gao Gang personally—don't lose it and don't tell anybody else about it. Regarding such a letter, once in 1962 when the Gao Gang affair had long been exposed, Ye Qun made up a story to Gao Gang's wife, saying it was written by Lin Biao to criticize and warn Gao Gang about the danger of the latter's underground activities; as for the secrecy of the letter, it was meant to exhort Gao to rectify privately his mistakes [before they became noticeable]. [Ye also attempted to explain away the fact that in 1953] in Hangzhou Lin Biao saw [Gao's] list for central personnel by claiming that at the time Lin criticized Gao Gang concerning the illegitimacy of such activities. All these claims are in fact Ye Qun's fabrication to deceive the Center and to cover up Lin Biao's involvement in Gao Gang's anti-Party conspiratorial activities for fear that the Center might pursue further the matter of the Gao-Lin relationship.

Our Party Center and Mao Zedong were then aware, to some extent, of Lin Biao's involvement in certain of Gao Gang's activities and therefore made the effort of sending Chen Yun to win over Lin Biao. But Lin Biao concealed many crucial details concerning his illicit relations with Gao Gang. Therefore he was able to get away with the matter because the Center did not pursue it further. Lin Biao's involvement in Gao Gang's anti-Party conspiratorial activities indicates that he harbored great political ambitions.

3. Gao's Approach to Tao Zhu

[The incident described in the following account undoubtedly took place during Gao Gang's "holiday" in East and Central-South China after the Financial and Economic Conference. This Red Guard source is of particular interest for its focus on Gao's use of prospective appointments to gather support. Other points of interest are the references to earlier career links to Gao in the Northeast just after Liberation, and the description of the successive self-examinations Tao was required to undertake after the defeat of Gao and Rao. As with the great bulk of Cultural Revolution sources, the events discussed have been placed in the context of alleged opposition to Mao by Liu Shaoqi and Deng Xiaoping, even though in this case Liu was actually the main target of the Gao-Rao affair. While Red Guard sources should be treated with considerable skepticism, in this case both post-Mao documentary materials and oral sources affirm Tao's involvement in Gao's activities. This is the only item in the appendices where the original Chinese text has not been sighted.]

Source: *Pi Tao Zhanbao* [Criticize Tao Combat Bulletin] (Beijing), April 10, 1967, in *Survey of China Mainland Press*, no. 3962, pp. 9–10.

TAO ZHU was an important member of the anti-Party clique of Gao Gang and Rao Shushi. Yet in the more than ten years after the crushing of that anti-Party clique, Tao Zhu was not only able to remain free from the punishment of the law, but rose steadily in rank and position. That was indivisible from the protection afforded him by Liu Shaoqi and Deng Xiaoping on many occasions. Irrefutable facts show that, being on the same bourgeois reactionary stand, the three have formed an alliance long ago.

While Tao Zhu was still working in the Northeast, he already joined Gao Gang's anti-Party clique. Someone disclosed in 1950 that Zhang Wentian, Kai Feng, Yang Shangkun, and others were still opposed to the struggle against the Wang Ming line led by Chairman Mao and the Party Center, that they, in conspiracy with Zhang Xiushan (Gao Gang's close associate) and others, had formed a small group and were energetically promoting Gao Gang, and that Tao Zhu also belonged to the small group. Tao Zhu knows how to sail with the wind. When you want "left," he would go to an appalling extent to the "left." When you want right, he would show you how rightist he is. Gao Gang was very much impressed with his "ability."

In the second half of 1951, Tao Zhu was transferred to Guangzhou to serve as the fourth secretary of the South China Subbureau, and later he became first secretary. In 1953 Gao Gang and Rao Shushi rabidly turned against the Party. Gao Gang went to Guangzhou with his close associate Zhang Xiushan and personally had secret talks with Tao Zhu. Gao said to Tao: They (meaning members of the anti-Party clique) all agree that I should be vice-chairman of the Party. What do you think? Tao replied: "You are most experienced in practical work." Gao also promised Tao a high position in the government, saying, "If you come to the

Center, you may be a vice-premier." He then told Tao Zhu the names of several persons whom he wanted to appoint to positions in the Center.

Not long after Gao Gang returned to Beijing, his anti-Party scheme was exposed, and two members of the anti-Party clique were compelled to make a confession. Seeing that the situation was unfavorable, Tao Zhu hurriedly made a false confession. He said that Gao Gang came to him to sound him out, that having heard Gao's words, he thought Gao was merely indulging in idle gossip, and that he thought Gao was not serious and therefore did not expose his designs promptly. After the exposure and failure of the Gao-Rao scheme, Tao Zhu did his best to please Liu Shaoqi and went over to Liu Shaoqi's side. Liu was also impressed with Tao, and the two men made use of each other. In a self-examination that he made before the CCP Guangdong Provincial Committee, Tao Zhu said: "In the past I had some critical views of Comrade Liu Shaoqi's work in the land reform. Now I have none. Comrade Shaoqi has always been correct. Opposition to Comrade Liu Shaoqi is tantamount to opposition to the Party and Chairman Mao." At once he exalted Liu Shaoqi to the skies.

Such a false confession by Tao Zhu concerning the Gao-Rao anti-Party alliance could of course not convince anyone. If Gao Gang told Tao such secrets, how could their relations be ordinary relations? Gao Gang said that he himself would be vice-chairman and Tao would be a vice-premier. How could such words be a mere attempt to sound out Tao? Someone reported to the Party Center, warning it not to believe Tao's false confession. As a result, Tao Zhu hated that comrade to the bone. In 1955, when Deng Xiaoping was in Guangzhou, Tao Zhu called a meeting, ostensibly for the purpose of solving the problem of unity of the Party Provincial Committee, but actually to attack those comrades who made reports on the situation to the Party Center. Deng Xiaoping also attended the meeting and gave Tao his support, saying that Tao Zhu was right and urging all comrades of the committee to rally around him. The comrade who reported the facts again reported to the Party Center and Liu Shaoqi, saying that Tao was hatching a secret scheme and that he was a member of the Gao Gang anti-Party clique. However, Liu Shaoqi blamed him, saying that he had "grown antlers on his head" and that he was too fond of fighting.

In 1957 the Party Center again investigated Tao Zhu's relations with Gao Gang. Tao Zhu made a statement, but it was not approved. His second statement was barely passed.

In 1962, under the pretext of opposing regionalism, Tao Zhu again attacked the comrade who informed against him to the Party Center. Liu Shaoqi actively supported Tao Zhu. He said to that comrade: "You have been given your position. That is very good. You should devote yourself to your job for the rest of your life." Liu Shaoqi also warned him not to say "strange things." He wanted him to unite himself with the local comrades, and rally with them around Tao Zhu and around the Provincial Committee headed by Tao Zhu.

Tao Zhu energetically exalted Liu and Deng, while Liu and Deng in return did all they could to protect Tao Zhu. That was no accident at all. They were leaders of the same black headquarters. They were confederates on the common basis of opposition to the Party and to Chairman Mao.

4. Gao's Visit to Luo Ronghuan

[This account excerpted from a 1978 journal article reports on Gao's approach to a leading military figure, Luo Ronghuan, who was to become one of China's ten PLA marshals in 1955. It is particularly notable for Luo's care to determine Mao's attitude. Other points of interest are Luo's apparent sensitivity to the need to balance the interests of different military groups although he himself was a leading cadre of Lin Biao's Fourth Field Army, and the reference to Gao's proposal to place Lin at the head of a Soviet-style Council of Ministers (cf. Appendix VI–1). It is also of note that the article appearing three months before the landmark Third Plenum still used the Cultural Revolution demonology, which assigned Peng Dehuai an anti-Party role. Since Luo died many years earlier, in 1963, it is likely that the account is based either on his oral revelations to close associates or on his written report after Gao's disgrace.]

> Source: Zong Zhengzhibu Lilunzu [General Political Department Theory Group], "Zai Mao Zhuxi Weida Qizhi xia Zhandou de Guanghui Yisheng" [A Brilliant Life of Battle under Chairman Mao's Great Banner], *Lishi Yanjiu* [Historical Research], no. 9 (1978): 8.

AFTER the founding of the PRC, Comrade Luo Ronghuan was a resolute defender of Chairman Mao's revolutionary line during our Party's struggles against the anti-Party cliques of Gao Gang, Rao Shushi, and Peng Dehuai.

In the early years after Liberation Gao, due to his individualistic ambition, formed an illicit mutual connection with Lin Biao. He advocated that Lin be the chairman of the Council of Ministers, while at the same time he himself be the Party vice-chairman or general secretary, in order to seize the highest leadership of both the Party and state. One evening in 1953 Gao Gang quite unexpectedly paid a visit to Comrade Luo's residence, asking [Luo] straight away whether the CCP should also follow the [Soviet] Council of Ministers system of which Lin Biao would be the chairman. Astonished by what he had just heard, Comrade Luo Ronghuan hastened to ask: "Has this question been discussed by the Center? Is this Chairman Mao's intention?" Gao Gang initially thought he could win over a vote from Comrade Luo Ronghuan by relying on the close working relationship previously established between them during the [pre-Liberation] period in the Northeast. However, it was not to be the case. Facing such a string of questions he could only reply with embarrassment: "The Center hasn't discussed it, neither is Chairman Mao aware of this. But I think we should have a discussion first."

Comrade Luo Ronghuan immediately pointed out in a very serious manner: "It is not appropriate for us to discuss such a great issue. Neither is it appropriate to let Lin Biao be what you call chairman of the Council of Ministers. In our troops there are the First, Second, and Fourth Front Armies, and also the 15th Army Group. Which leader of these groups should assume what new post should be settled collectively by Chairman Mao and the Party Center." Crestfallen, Gao Gang walked away as such a conversation had laid bare his conspiracy. After the exposure of the Gao-Rao anti-Party clique, Comrade Luo Ronghuan enthusiastically participated in the struggle by presenting a written report although he could not attend the meetings of the Center due to sickness.

VI
MAO'S REACTION TO GAO GANG'S ACTIVITIES

[Once Chen Yun and Deng Xiaoping informed Mao of Gao Gang's approaches to them, the Chairman's attitude toward Gao underwent a major change, even if the motivation for that change is open to question. The following two selections provide very different types of evidence concerning Mao's views and activities at this juncture and subsequently. The first item, an excerpt from the recollections of Public Security Minister Luo Ruiqing's daughter concerning her father's career, recounts a conversation where Mao revealed to Luo his understanding of the "conspiracy" and the subsequent coordination of his activities concerning Gao Gang with the public security chief. The second item is excerpted from a section from Mao's concluding remarks to the March 1955 National Party Conference, which formally disposed of the Gao-Rao case (see Appendix VIII). Although clearly reflecting developments over the entire period since Gao's exposure, these remarks also provide clues to the Chairman's reaction and activities at the time, including at the crucial December 24, 1953, Politburo meeting.]

1. Mao's Conversation with Luo Ruiqing and Subsequent Developments

[This memoir account is most probably valid in broad terms, but undoubted or likely inaccuracies (see notes 1 and 4) indicate the general problem with the reliability of such materials. In this case the fact that Luo Ruiqing himself had been dead for nine years at the time his daughter's recollections were published doubly underscores the issue of fallible memories. In any case, the account is notable for the further evidence it provides of leadership equivocation in the face of uncertainty about Mao's position, confirmation of Gao pushing Lin Biao for a key state post (cf. Appendix V-4), and information on Gao's activities during and outside of the December Politburo meetings.]

Source: [Luo] Diandian, *Feifan de Niandai* [Extraordinary Times] (Shanghai: Shanghai wenyi chubanshe, 1987), pp. 149–51.
Additional Chinese text: *Wenhui Yuekan* [Wenhui Monthly Review], no. 2 (1987): 25–26.

ONE day in 1954,[1] the Chairman and father had a special conversation. Chairman Mao asked father: What would happen if I retired to the second front? Who would take charge of the first front? Father said: If the Chairman retires to the second front, of course it should be Comrade Shaoqi who would preside over the first front. However . . . (indicating the rumors that were aimed at lowering Comrade Shaoqi's prestige). Chairman Mao didn't wait for father to finish. He immediately criticized him, saying: Your nose doesn't work, neither does your sense of smell. He also said: In this world when people sleep, there are some who sleep on beds and some who sleep in a drum [i.e., in the dark]. I can see you're in the dark. Do you know there are people carrying out conspiracies, organizing an underground headquarters in Beijing? You say you support my flag, why is it when you hear certain things you don't question if they're true or false? Then the Chairman told father: The one who is conspiring, organizing an underground headquarters, is Gao Gang. When I retreat to the second front, he wants to be a Party vice-chairman. He told x x[2] you will be a vice-chairman of the Party and so will I. You think he supports Lin Biao? This time there's no Lin Biao here.[3] Chairman Mao said: He (meaning Gao Gang) will not only strike down Liu Shaoqi, he will strike me down and he will strike down Lin Biao. For father listening to Chairman Mao, this was a great shock. The Chairman finally said: This man has deceived some cadres and we must win them back.

After that talk, Chairman Mao went to Hangzhou and father also went with him. Prior to leaving, Chairman Mao held a meeting.[4] Father attended. Gao Gang was also present. The Chairman explained that while he was away from Beijing, Comrade Liu Shaoqi would act on his behalf. Chairman Mao nodded his head and said: In Beijing there are now those fomenting trouble, carrying out underground activities. Chairman Mao gesticulated upwards and downwards saying: the wind spread by the Central Committee goes this way (he gesticulated upwards), the wind he is blowing goes this way (he gesticulated downwards). All of us must pay attention. The Chairman went on: Do you agree or not? As father recalled, Gao Gang's face went quite red and he said unnaturally, "Agree." In the evening Gao Gang suddenly phoned father, saying he would like to come and visit him. Father replied asking him not to come; if there was anything to say, father would go to his place to talk. He agreed and said there was something he wanted to talk about. Putting down the telephone, father immediately phoned Chairman Mao, telling him of this incident. The Chairman

[1] *Sic*. It is extremely unlikely that the conversation took place in 1954 in view of Gao's "exposure" on December 24, 1953 (cf. the following item). The best estimate would be that the conversation occurred in November 1953, while early December would also be possible.
[2] Undoubtedly Chen Yun; see above, Appendix V-1, p. 222.
[3] Meaning obscure; one possibility is that Gao Gang did not nominate Lin Biao as a vice-chairman.
[4] Here Luo Diandian apparently conflates several Politburo meetings into one session; see chapter 5, n. 21.

said: Go quickly, see what he has to say. Father went to Gao Gang's home. Gao Gang told him he should pay attention to the Chairman's health. When Chairman Mao went for a physical examination he must remain in the vicinity, looking carefully, left and right. He repeatedly said father must pay attention and not be careless. He also said: If a Council of Ministers is set up, I agree to Lin Biao. As he said this, Gao Gang's manner seemed ill at ease, even a little panicky. Father said: I will pay attention to the Chairman's health, and I will not be careless when he goes for an examination. He also said: As to the Council of Ministers, the Chairman would possibly not agree with your opinion. He also told Gao Gang that Lin Biao was then not in the best of health. There was nothing more to say, and father took his leave.

. . .

. . . From the beginning to the end of the Gao Gang events, father came to understand Chairman Mao more deeply. In the struggle against Gao Gang, he saw how Chairman Mao devised strategies without revealing himself, how there was strength in his gentleness. By remaining calm and collected he forced his opponent into an obvious disadvantage. At the same time father came to understand deeply that there were definitely hostile elements in the Party, and that inner-Party struggle was extremely complicated and harsh. . . .

2. Mao's Review of the Gao Gang Affair at the National Party Conference (March 31, 1955)

[The following excerpt from Mao's concluding speech to the 1955 National Party Conference presents the Chairman's reflections on the Gao-Rao affair well after the fact. Mao's remarks reveal some unfortunately limited details of the events of 1953 and his own role; of particular interest is the brief italicized passage, which is the most authoritative source on the decisive Politburo meeting of December 24, 1953. More broadly, the item is noteworthy for Mao's insistence that a Gao-Rao alliance actually existed, his discriminating and generally lenient posture toward those involved in the affair, and his continuing adherence to a centrist policy orientation.]

> **Source:** *The Writings of Mao Zedong*, 1:534–39, as amended.
> **Chinese text:** *Mao Zedong Xuanji*, 5:146–52.
> **Additional translation:** *Selected Works of Mao Tsetung*, 5:161–67.

Concerning the Gao Gang-Rao Shushi Anti-Party Alliance

THE first point: Some people ask: Is there, after all, such an alliance? Or perhaps it is not really an alliance, but rather two separate independent kingdoms, two go-it-aloners? Some comrades say that they have not seen any documents, and that if they were an alliance, they should have had an agreement of some sort and with the agreement there would be documents. Indeed, there were no written agreements; we were not able to discover any. We say, [however], that Gao Gang and Rao Shushi did form an alliance. From what can we see this? It can be seen, first, in the joint activities of Gao Gang and Rao Shushi at the time of the Conference on Financial and Economic Work; second, from the collaboration between Rao Shushi and Zhang Xiushan in carrying out anti-Party activities at the time of the Conference on Organization Work; and third, from Rao Shushi's own words. Rao Shushi said, "From now on the Center's organization department should have Guo Feng as its core." The organization department had Rao Shushi as its director, and [then] Guo Feng, Gao Gang's confidant, was made its core. Now isn't that just fine! What solid unity! Fourth, we can see it from the fact that Gao Gang and Rao Shushi distributed everywhere a slate of candidates for the Politiburo illicitly put together by An Ziwen. An Ziwen was given a disciplinary warning for this. Gao Gang, Rao Shushi, and their people distributed this list of names to everybody who attended the Conference on Organization Work and to each of the southern provinces. What was their motive for distributing this thing everywhere? Fifth, [we can see it] from Gao Gang's expression to me on two occasions of his [desire to] protect Rao Shushi, and Rao Shushi's insistence on protecting Gao Gang to the very last. Gao Gang told me that Rao Shushi was in big trouble and asked me to bail him out. I said to him, why are you speaking on Rao Shushi's behalf? I'm in Beijing, so is Rao Shushi; why should he want you to represent him and not come directly to me [himself]? Even if he were in Tibet he could send a telegram, but he is in Beijing! He has legs, doesn't he? The second time was on the day before Gao Gang was exposed.[1] Gao Gang was still expressing his desire to protect Rao Shushi. To the very last, Rao Shushi wanted to protect Gao Gang; he wanted to redress the injustice against Gao Gang. *At the meeting of the Center at which Gao Gang was exposed, I said that there were two headquarters in Beijing. One was a headquarters led by me; we blew a positive (yang) wind and lit a positive fire. The other was a headquarters commanded by someone else; it blew a sinister (yin) wind and lit a sinister fire, and was operating underground* [emphasis added]. After all, should government come from one source, or should it come from many sources? From the many things mentioned above, it can be seen that they [Gao and Rao] had an anti-Party alliance and were not two unrelated independent kingdoms or "go-it-aloners."

As for the doubts that some comrades have because there are no written agreements, and the question that it may not have been an alliance, this would be to equate anti-Party alliances formed by conspirators with other usual open and formal political and economic alliances, and to see them as similar things. These people were engaging in a conspiracy! Do you need a written agreement when you

---

[1] In other words, December 23, 1953, the day before the December 24 Politburo meeting here referred to as "the meeting of the Center."

are forming a conspiracy? If you say that it was not an alliance because it did not have any written agreements, then how about the internal [structure] of each of the two anti-Party cliques of Gao Gang and Rao Shushi? Gao Gang did not have any agreements with Zhang Xiushan, Zhang Mingyuan, Zhao Dezun, Ma Hong, and Guo Feng either. We haven't seen their written agreements either. Then again, we haven't seen any pact between Rao Shushi and people like Xiang Ming and Yang Fan. Therefore, the idea that you cannot consider something an alliance if you have not found a written agreement for it is wrong.

The second point: What attitude should be adopted by comrades who have been influenced by Gao and Rao and by those who were able to avoid their influence? Among those who have been influenced, some were more deeply influenced and some less so. Some have been influenced generally and have merely been brushed by their wings. A few comrades have been more deeply influenced; they have talked with them about many questions, and carried on clandestine activities doing propaganda for them. These two [groups] are different. Nevertheless, at this conference, regardless of whether the influence on them was slight or deep, most of these comrades have already indicated their attitudes. Some gave a very clear expression [of their attitudes] and have made supplementary [remarks] today. Some delivered speeches that were on the whole quite good, but were not quite right in certain parts. No matter how they did it, these types of people all have already made some expression [of their attitudes]. We ought to welcome them one and all; after all, they have each made some sort of a statement! There were also some individuals who requested to speak but who were not given the floor because of the lack of time; they can submit a written report to the [Party] Center. The problem with those who have not yet spoken is not a serious one. They were just brushed by [the conspirators'] wings; they know something but did not speak out about it. As for those who spoke, aren't there some who still retain a tail? Therefore, we have now decided that all speeches and reports, whether they concern the Five-Year Plan or the problem of the Gao-Rao anti-Party alliance, can be taken back and revised. Pay attention to each word, phrase, and sentence, and within five days revise all those parts that are incomplete or incorrect. We must not grab people's little queues just because they did not give a correct account of themselves at this conference, and then make it difficult for them to acquit themselves in the future. You can make revisions, and only the revised final draft will count.

With regard to these comrades, we should adopt this type of attitude, that is, hoping that they will correct their mistakes. We must not only observe but should also help. That is to say, we must not only observe to see whether or not they change, but must also help them to make the change. People need help. Even though the lotus flower is pretty, it needs green leaves to enhance its beauty. A fence has to be propped up by three stakes; a stout-hearted man needs the help of three other people. It's not good for people to go it alone; help is always needed, especially with problems of this nature. Observing is necessary. Observe to see if they change or not, but merely watching is passive. We must also help them. We welcome the reform of all those who were influenced [by Gao and Rao], no matter whether deeply or slightly influenced; we must not only observe, but must also help. This is the positive attitude that we must take toward comrades who have made mistakes.

Comrades who have not been influenced must not be arrogant and should take serious precautions to guard against [this] disease. This is an extremely important matter. Some of the comrades we mentioned above may have been duped, some others have been more deeply entrapped, but because they have committed a mistake their vigilance may have been heightened so that they will not commit mistakes of this sort again in the future. After being sick once, one becomes immune; getting a vaccination has a preventive effect. Nevertheless, nothing can be guaranteed; it's still possible to catch smallpox. Therefore, it would be best to have another vaccination in three or five years' time, that is, to hold a meeting like this one. Other comrades should not be arrogant, and should be very cautious to avoid committing mistakes. Why did Gao Gang and Rao Shushi not touch people like these? There are various possibilities. The first is that they are people whom they [Gao and Rao] considered enemies; naturally, therefore, they did not go among them to propagandize [their cause]. The second type are those they looked down on and considered to be people of no major consequence. They thought that it was not necessary to propagandize among these people then [and] that later, when "the major affair of state was settled," [these people] would naturally go over to their side. The third type are people they did not dare touch. These people probably had stronger immunity, and one look told [Gao and Rao] that they were not [people whom they could easily influence]. Although these comrades were not considered to be their enemies, nor were they people of no major consequence, [Gao and Rao] did not dare touch [them]. The fourth type are those whom they did not have time [to reach]. It took time even for this epidemic to spread. If it had not been exposed for another year, it would be hard to say where some people would stand. Therefore let us not thumb our noses, [or say:] "Look, weren't you contaminated all over? I am clean!" If it had not been exposed, I am sure that in another year many people would have been influenced.

I think what we've just said are precisely the things to which both those comrades who have been influenced by Gao and Rao and those who have not been influenced by them should pay attention.

The third point: Over issues of principle, we should always carefully keep our distance from the comrades whose arguments and activities are in violation of the Party's principles. . . . You must not fail to keep a distance [between yourselves and these people] just because they are old friends, old bosses, old subordinates, old colleagues, old schoolmates, or because they are from your native village. In this Gao-Rao anti-Party affair, as well as in two line struggles within the Party in the past, we've often had the experience in which people found it difficult to speak [frankly] and could not maintain a distance because they felt that the [personal] relationship was too longstanding and too deep, and so they did not repulse them or draw clear distinctions. Consequently they were trapped more and more deeply, and they got tangled up with those "ghosts" [who violate Party principles]. Therefore we should make our attitudes public and should adhere to the principles.

The fourth point: Some comrades say, "We know some bad things about Gao and Rao, but we can't see that they have a conspiracy." I say that there are two types of situations. One type is where people heard Gao Gang and Rao Shushi say many things that were in violation of the Party's principles, or even [some cases] in which Gao Gang and Rao Shushi discussed some matters of anti-Party activity with them. In these cases [our comrades] should have been able to see [that there was a conspiracy]. The other type [of situation] is where people knew some bad things in general about them but did not recognize [the existence of] the conspiracy. This is understandable because [the conspiracy] was difficult to see. Even the Party Center did not discover their anti-Party conspiracy until 1953. It was through [the events at] the Financial and Economic Work Conference, the Conference on Organization Work, and the various problems prior to the Financial and Economic Conference that one could see that they were abnormal. At the time of the Financial and Economic Work Conference their abnormal activities were discovered, and each time [they did something abnormal] they were rebuffed. Therefore they later turned completely to secret activities. We didn't discover this conspiracy, these conspirators, and the conspiratorial cliques until the autumn and winter of 1953. For a long time we didn't see that Gao Gang and Rao Shushi were bad people. Such things have happened before. During the Jinggangshan period there were a few traitors whom we never thought would have become traitors. I believe every one of you must have had this experience.

...

The fifth point: The danger of having an arrogant mind....

The sixth point: Refrain from being "left," and refrain from being right. Some people say, "It's better to be 'left' than to be right." Many comrades also say this. In fact many people may say in their hearts, "It's better to be right than 'left,'" but they just don't say it aloud. Only honest people would say it aloud. There are two kinds of opinions. What is "left"? Running ahead of the times and running ahead of the present circumstances, being an adventurist in orientation, policy, and action, and engaging in undisciplined struggle on questions that are being struggled over and on controversial matters is "left." This is not good. To be right is to lag behind the times and behind the present circumstances and to lack the spirit of struggle. This is no good either. In our Party there are not only people who like to be "left," but also quite a few people who like to be right or right-of-center. All these are no good. We must struggle on both fronts and oppose both "left" and right.

I'll say only this much about the question of the Gao Gang-Rao Shushi anti-Party alliance.

VII
THE FOURTH PLENUM AND SUBSEQUENT MEETINGS, 1954

[Following Mao's decisive rebuff to Gao Gang in December 1953, the Fourth Plenum was convened in February 1954 to deal with, among other matters, the Gao-Rao affair. The first item below, an excerpt from the communique of the plenum, publicly canvassed the issue of Party unity but without providing specific details or even identifying Gao and Rao by name. The plenum was followed in the same month by two special discussion meetings designed to investigate the activities of Gao and Rao separately and to undercut their prestige among those with whom they had worked. These meetings and their findings were not publicized outside the Party at the time, but important documents from them have become available in the post-Mao period. Item 2A below is the outline of Zhou Enlai's speech to the discussion meeting on Gao, while selection 2B is a written report by the convenors of the meeting dealing with Rao. Both documents provide some detail concerning the alleged sins of the two principals. Finally, from March to mid-summer 1954 various regional and local meetings were held to expose further Gao and Rao; item 3 contains brief excerpts from the report of a May 1954 East China meeting that bear on the issue of whether an alliance between Gao and Rao actually existed.]

1. Excerpt from the Communiqué of the Fourth Plenum (February 18, 1954)

[The main feature of this excerpt from the Fourth Plenum's communique is its paraphrase of the "Resolution on Strengthening Party Unity" originally proposed by Mao at the decisive December 24, 1953, Politburo meeting. While it is not known precisely what Mao proposed on December 24, the italicized passage below corresponds to Mao's draft as recorded in a Cultural Revolution text dated February 1954 in *Mao Zedong Sixiang Wansui (1949.9–1957.12)*, p. 43. The only difference is that the order of problems to be dealt with has been reversed. In the Cultural Revolution text and the resolution as actually passed on February 10 (see *Zhonggong Dangshi Jiaoxue Cankao Ziliao*, 20:261–63), references to comrades "[who] are still able to place the Party's interest above their personal interests" take precedence over those to people who "deliberately undermine Party unity, . . . persist in refusing to correct their errors, or even carry out factional splitting or other dangerous activities within the Party." In the communiqué, which was issued a week later, the latter is dealt with first, perhaps reflecting what was deemed inadequate repentance on the part of Gao and Rao during the plenum and the initial stages of the discussion meetings. In addition, there are passages in the resolution, both as passed on February 10 and as paraphrased in the communiqué, that were not included in the brief Cultural Revolution text. These are of particular note for their harsh Stalinist tone (cf. Appendix IV-2B) and for their implicit comparison of Gao and Rao to major "renegades" in both Soviet and CCP history, viz., Chen Duxiu, Zhang Guotao, and Beria.]

> Source: New China News Agency, Beijing, February 18, 1954, in *Survey of China Mainland Press*, no. 751, pp. 1, 3–5, as amended.
> Chinese text: *Renmin Ribao* [People's Daily], February 18, 1954, p. 1.

THE Central Committee of the CCP elected by the Seventh Party Congress held its Fourth Plenum from February 6 to 10, 1954.

Attending the plenary session were thirty-five members and twenty-six alternate members of the Central Committee. Nine members and alternate members were absent for reasons of health or because [they were] otherwise engaged. Present at the session, too, were fifty-two leading members of the Party, government, army, and people's organizations.

Comrade Mao Zedong was away on holiday and so was not present. Comrade Liu Shaoqi, secretary of the Secretariat of the Central Committee of the CCP, delivered the "Report of the Politburo of the Central Committee of the CCP to the Fourth Plenum of the Seventh Central Committee" on behalf of the Politburo and Comrade Mao Zedong. Important speeches were made at the session by comrades Zhu De, Zhou Enlai, and forty-two others.

After detailed discussion, the session unanimously adopted a "Resolution on Strengthening Party Unity," which was put forward on the recommendation of Comrade Mao Zedong. It also adopted unanimously a resolution approving the work of the Central Committee's Politburo in the period following the Third Plenum and a resolution on convening a Party conference in 1954.

Here are the main points of the "Report of the Politburo of the Central Committee of the CCP to the Fourth Plenum of Seventh Central Committee," which was made by Comrade Liu Shaoqi as entrusted to him by the Politburo and Comrade Mao Zedong, and the "Resolution on Strengthening Party Unity," which was passed at the session.

The *Report by Comrade Liu Shaoqi* is in three parts: (1) Work of the Politburo of the Central Committee since the Third Plenum; (2) Concerning the convening of a Party conference; and (3) The fight to strengthen Party unity.

...

Coming to *the struggle for strengthening Party unity*, Comrade Liu Shaoqi said that Comrade Mao Zedong had put forward a proposal for strengthening Party unity at the meeting of the Politburo of the Party's Central Committee on December 24, 1953. The Politburo unanimously endorsed the proposal submitted by Comrade Mao Zedong and, on the basis of this proposal, formulated a draft "Resolution on Strengthening Party Unity" for discussion by the Fourth Plenum of the Seventh Central Committee.

The *Resolution on Strengthening Party Unity*, which was adopted by the Fourth Plenum, points out that the unity of the Party, the unity of the working class, the unity of the laboring people, and the unity of the people of the whole country are the fundamental guarantee for the victory of the revolution. This is one of the most fundamental theses of Marxism-Leninism. Relying on its unity, the CCP has led the people of the whole country to the accomplishment of the New Democratic revolution and the founding of the People's Republic of China. However, the revolutionary cause in China has not yet come to [its] final completion. The enemies of the people within the country have not yet been completely eliminated, and outside the country imperialist encirclement still exists. China is now in the stage of the socialist revolution or socialist transformation. We must, step by step, carry through socialist industrialization and the socialist transformation of agriculture, handicrafts, and capitalist industry and commerce, and build our country into a great socialist country. This revolution is even more far-reaching and broader than the revolution against imperialism, feudalism, and bureaucratic capitalism. It involves extremely complex and acute struggle. In this struggle, foreign imperialism, on the one hand, will not sit idly by and simply watch us; and on the other hand, those classes within the country that have already been overthrown will not willingly reconcile themselves to extinction, while those classes that are to be eliminated will not give up without resistance. Inveterate counterrevolutionary elements among them will undoubtedly collude with foreign imperialists to seize every opportunity to undermine the cause of our Party and people in their attempt to defeat the Chinese revolution and restore reactionary rule in China. One of the most important methods of the imperialists and counterrevolutionaries for sabotaging our cause is, first and foremost, to undermine the unity of the Party and to look for agents within our Party. In our Party, we have had Chen Duxiu and Zhang Guotao; and in the [Communist] Party of the Soviet Union there was Beria. These are momentous historical lessons that show that the enemy not only will always seek agents within our Party but in the past has found them, and it may be in the future, too, he will find vacillating and disloyal elements and those who join the Party with ulterior motives to act as his agents.

Comrade Liu Shaoqi said in his report that the Politburo of the Central Committee considers that serious attention should be drawn to the following point. The greatest danger to the Party is the danger of the enemy creating divisions and causing sectarian activities inside the Party, and making use of a faction in the Party (if the enemy can really create such a faction) to act as his agent. This is because the enemy knows as well as we do that a fortress can most easily be taken from within. No member of the Party should therefore think it strange that the imperialists who are trying to stage a comeback and the bourgeois elements who are resolutely resisting socialist reformation create divisions and look for agents inside the Party. There is nothing strange in this. It would indeed be strange if the enemy did not try to cause a split among us, did not try to capitalize on differences in our ranks or make use of disloyal and vacillating elements and those who join the Party with ulterior motives as his agents. Our duty, therefore, is decidedly not to allow the Party's vigilance to become completely relaxed in the spirit of everything being perfect; but on the contrary to raise its vigilance through the realities of the class struggle and the lessons of history. Our duty is to keep the whole Party level-headed and counter the enemy's schemes by action to strengthen Party unity.

The "Resolution on Strengthening Party Unity" as adopted by the plenum makes a comprehensive analysis of the situation within our Party. It shows that the CCP, on the basis of Marxism-Leninism and a correct political and organizational line, having gone through all kinds of sacrifices and struggles, has built up the unified leadership of the Central Committee headed by Comrade Mao Zedong and brought about a monolithic unity of the whole Party. With the timely overcoming of hostile activities and wrong tendencies dangerous to the unity of the Party, this unity has grown increasingly stronger and has thus made the Party invincible. Nevertheless, our Party still has a policy of alliance with the bourgeoisie. Petty bourgeois encirclement is like a vast ocean. Our Party is a very big one, and education in Marxism-Leninism within the Party is still inadequate. The ideological and political makeup of some of the cadres is still rather complex. At the same time, among some of our cadres, even certain high-ranking cadres within our Party, there is still a lack of understanding of the importance of Party unity, of the importance of collective leadership, of the importance of consolidating and enhancing the prestige of the Central Committee. In particular, since the victory of China's New Democratic revolution, there has grown up among some of the cadres within the Party a most dangerous kind of conceit. They lose their heads over certain achievements they have made in their work, forgetting the modest attitude and spirit of self-criticism which should animate a Communist Party member. They exaggerate the role of the individual and emphasize individual prestige. They think there is no one equal to them in the wide world. They listen only to others' flattery and praise but cannot accept others' criticism and supervision; they suppress and revenge themselves against those who criticize them. They even regard the region or department under their leadership as their individual inheritance or independent kingdom. All this shows it is of paramount necessity that at this crucial historical stage, when our country is carrying out socialist transformation, all comrades in the Party must heighten their revolutionary vigilance and strengthen Party unity. Party unity is the life of the Party. This is a fundamental principle of Marxism-Leninism. To undermine Party unity is to go directly contrary to the fundamental principles of Marxism-Leninism. It amounts to helping the enemy to endanger the life of the Party. The resolution requires all Party comrades to raise the most conscious and loving attention toward Party unity and to work to strengthen Party unity. This is especially true for the responsible comrades of the Central Committee and committees above the provincial (municipal) level and the high-ranking, responsible comrades in the armed forces. They must have the highest awareness of the necessity of Party unity and the measure of their own responsibility. They must make very great efforts and do whatever necessary within the Party in this connection.

To this end, concrete measures for strengthening Party unity are formulated in the "Resolution on Strengthening Party Unity" adopted by the plenum. At the same time, it points out that *Party unity must be and can only be unity based on Marxism-Leninism, on correct political and correct organizational principles. To strengthen Party unity, it is impermissible to restrict democracy within the Party or criticism and self-criticism within the Party; on the contrary, the full development of democracy within the Party and the full development of criticism and self-criticism within the Party must be safeguarded to avoid, in every way possible, all shortcomings and errors which can possibly be avoided, and so help the Party's cause to advance smoothly. In criticizing shortcomings or errors of Party members, different approaches should be adopted according to different circumstances. The Party must wage unrelenting struggle against those who deliberately undermine Party unity, stand up against the Party, persist in refusing to correct their errors, or even carry out factional splitting or other dangerous activities within the Party. The Party must take strict disciplinary action against them or even expel them from the Party when necessary. Only so can Party unity and the interests of the revolution and the people be safeguarded. However, as to comrades whose shortcomings or errors are comparatively unimportant, or comrades who have serious or comparatively serious shortcomings or have committed serious or comparatively serious errors, but, having been helped by criticism, are still able to place the Party's interest above their personal interests, and are willing to mend their ways and actually make amends, the policy of "helping a man with goodwill" and "curing the sickness to save the patient" should be adopted. Serious criticism must be applied and necessary struggle waged against their shortcomings or errors, according to the specific circumstances. But in making the criticism and waging the struggle, the directives of the Central Committee and Comrade Mao Zedong should be applied. These are: "Starting out from unity, to attain unity through criticism or struggle." The comrades concerned should not be shut off from the chance of making amends. Moreover, their individual, partial, temporary, comparatively unimportant shortcomings or errors should not be exaggerated into systematic, serious ones; to do so is not to start out from unity and in this way the aim of unity cannot be attained. Therefore, it is not in the interest of the Party* [emphasis added].

The "Resolution on Strengthening the Party Unity" as adopted by the plenum finally points out that the unity of the responsible comrades of the Central Committee and the committees above provincial (municipal) level and the high-ranking, responsible comrades in the armed forces is the key to the unity of the whole Party. In the cause of strengthening Party unity, these responsible comrades shoulder the greatest responsibility. The resolution calls on these comrades to set an example themselves and to educate the cadres of the whole Party to do the same and, with one heart and purpose, to "consolidate the entire Party membership on the ideological basis of Marxism-Leninism and unite it like a harmonious family and [with] steel-like solidity" so as to rally around it the entire working class, the entire laboring people, and the people of the whole country in the struggle to defeat any subversive schemes of the enemy both at home and abroad and ensure the victory of the great cause of socialist construction and socialist transformation.

2. The Discussion Meetings Concerning Gao and Rao

2A. "Comrade Zhou Enlai's Speech Outline at the Discussion Meeting on the Gao Gang Question" (February 1954)

[This outline of Zhou Enlai's speech summing up the meeting dealing with Gao Gang was the first known inner-Party document to deal with Gao's "errors" in a relatively detailed fashion. It is of particular note for its seeming references to Gao's purported misrepresentation of Mao's views presumably as expressed by the Chairman in their late 1952–early 1953 private conversations (points 6 and 9). Also of interest are its carefully restricted treatement of any Soviet factor in the Gao-Rao affair (point 8), and its picture of Gao as someone of very limited theoretical abilities who relied on the contributions of surbordinates in this regard (point 7). In addition, Zhou notes Gao's first, unsuccessful suicide attempt during the discussion meeting.]

Source: *Zhonggong Dangshi Jiaoxue Cankao Ziliao*, 20:267–69.

AT this discussion meeting on the question of Gao Gang, in accordance with Gao Gang's own address to the meeting and with his unsuccessful suicide attempt and summing up the addresses and exposés made by forty-three comrades, we can arrive at the following understanding, that is, Gao Gang's mistake of extreme individualism has already progressed to the stage of engaging in schemes to split the Party so as to achieve his unbridled personal ambition of seizing leadership in the Party and state. Upon exposure of his personal ambitions and the failure of his schemes, he embarked, in despair, on the road of suicide, thereby cutting himself off from the Party and the people.

The following are the facts about Gao Gang's schemes to split the Party and seize power in the Party and state:

1. He disseminated in the Party such absurdities as "the Communist Party grew out of the barrel of a gun" and "the Party was created by the army" in order to support his fallacy that the Party was a "party of the military," which he used as his weapon to split the Party and seize leadership. Gao Gang insisted that within the CCP there exists a dualist outlook on Party history: that Comrade Mao Zedong represented the red areas, while Comrade Liu Shaoqi represented the white areas. He alleged that the mainstays of the Chinese Party were trained in the army, and that the cadres of the white areas were now attempting to seize Party power. Therefore, (1) he declared that in compiling Party history, revision should be made of the "Resolution on Certain Questions in the History of the Party" and new conclusions drawn, and (2) he tried to incite and influence high-ranking cadres in the army with his fallacies while preparing to form a group of deputies to the Eighth Party Congress in order to seize Party leadership.

2. He engaged in sectarian activities and opposed comrades of the central leadership. Since 1949, Gao Gang has been deliberately spreading talk among many people about isolated defects and mistakes of certain central leading comrades. Later on, he further spread the talk that these isolated and temporary defects and mistakes, which had already been rectified, were systematic mistakes. Some of this he even had copied onto files as material to support his attacks. At the same time, he actually resorted to lying. Gao Gang vilified central leading comrades for being sectarian to cover up his own sectarian activities. He did so to attack leading central comrades concerned so as to gain leadership over the Party and the state.

3. He resorted to lies and fomented discord at every opportunity in order to sow dissension in the Party. Gao Gang spread lies about such and such people being on, or left out of, the "list" of candidates suggested by leading central comrades for membership in the Politburo or Secretariat. He alleged that leading central comrades disagreed with the choice of a certain comrade to head the work of a certain department at the central level, or did not support a certain comrade's correct leadership in a certain province, and so forth, so as to sow discord. He utilized the erroneous personal opinion of one comrade that a list of candidates be drawn up for the Politburo and various central ministries and departments to spread rumors everywhere. Using his own position of power, he searched for contradictions and talked to A about B, C about D, seeking either to create bad blood or to win support for himself, or sometimes using both tactics at the same time.

4. He implemented a factional cadre policy, thereby undermining unity inside the Party. He was especially free in making promises of promotion and other favors to certain cadres in an effort to widen his influence and win personal support. Gao Gang's cadre policy is unprincipled and factionalist. He frequently tried to draw a

group around him in order to attack another group, thus creating factions within the Party and disrupting unity. His promises included promoting so and so to be an alternate member of the Central Committee, so and so to be Politburo member, so and so to be minister of a certain central ministry, and so on. This is definitely not permitted by the Party Constitution and Party discipline.

5. He regarded the region under his leadership as personal capital and, in fact, his independent kingdom. As secretary of the Northeast Bureau, Gao Gang reported only good news while suppressing the bad. He never made self-criticisms and would not take criticism from others. When he was transferred to the central level, he said that it was like "luring the tiger out of the mountains." This worry was put to rest only when he found out that he concurrently retained the post of secretary of the Northeast Bureau. Gao Gang never wanted the central leadership and central departments and ministries to inspect the work of the Northeast Bureau. Whenever inspectors came, he would viciously attack certain weaknesses he found in them as a warning for them to lay off.

6. He falsely used the name of the Center [which] did great damage to its prestige. Gao Gang distorted many things in the political life of the Center and spread many lies and rumors, attacking others and glorifying himself. This resulted in some comrades forming a mistaken impression of him, and undermined the prestige of leading central comrades.

7. He plagiarized others' works to elevate himself and impress and cheat the Center. To seize power, he spent much thought on showing off, not by studying hard but through taking over others' viewpoints. In discussing Malenkov's report, Gao Gang's address to the meeting on the question of commerce was not his own viewpoint at all but stolen entirely from others in order to hoodwink the Center. Many of his addresses to central meetings not only were written by others but were not even based upon his suggestions. He seldom read them carefully before presenting them. However, Gao used them time and again to win the trust of the Center. Gao knows next to nothing of Marxism-Leninism, and in action, has actually gone to the reverse of Marxism-Leninism, but he often bragged about how hard he studied Marxism-Leninism in order to gain influence.

8. On the question of Sino-Soviet relations, he sowed discord and behaved in a way detrimental to Sino-Soviet unity. While in the Northeast, Gao Gang, without reporting his intentions to the Center and getting its approval, talked indiscreetly to certain comrades of the Soviet Union about problems inside the Chinese Party. Upon returning to China after a visit to the Soviet Union, he also made many provocative remarks and again used the occasion to brag about himself. He also made many remarks that were obviously disruptive to Sino-Soviet unity.

9. He engaged in schemes to seize Party and state power. Before and after the Conference on Financial and Economic Work and since the central leadership raised the question of whether China, too, should adopt the state structure of the Council of Ministers [as instituted in the Soviet Union] and whether the Party's

Central Committee should add a vice-chairman or a general secretary, Gao Gang had urgently and actively engaged in activities to get a position of power in the Party and state. Pretending to wave the banner of Comrade Mao Zedong, he fabricated words that Comrade Mao Zedong was supposed to have used and actively opposed two leading central comrades while pretending to support two other leading central comrades. At the same time, he demanded to be made vice-chairman of the Central Committee. Actually, he did not really support the comrades he feigned he did, but was trying to get their patronage and use them as his springboard to power. It is precisely on this question that the essence of Gao Gang's conspiracy was most clearly revealed.

In addition to the above activities to split the Party and seize power, according to the latest revelations made by comrades, Gao Gang led a dissolute life completely contrary to the moral standard of a Communist. We must point out that the decadence of his personal life is one manifestation of the corrosive influence of bourgeois thought on our Party, and that we must oppose and resolutely resist such corrosion. From Gao Gang's major activities cited above, we can see that Gao Gang, a Party member with two decades of revolutionary history, has hopelessly sunk into the quagmire of bourgeois individualist careerism and has shamefully attempted to remold the Party and the country in his own bourgeois individualist image.

The Politburo of the Central Committee of the Party, to preserve unification and unity in the Party and in accordance with Comrade Mao Zedong's suggestion, called the Fourth Plenum to warn the entire Party and to point out to Gao Gang the gravity of his mistakes, to demand that he make a thorough examination of his mistakes and stop harboring bad thoughts and engaging in bad actions, so that he would not continue to make mistakes and alienate himself further from the Party.

Despite this policy adopted by the Fourth Plenum of "curing the sickness to save the patient" and waiting for Gao Gang to realize his mistakes, despite the two superficial self-examinations he made at the session and at the subsequent discussion, Gao Gang in truth resisted self-examination. He hated the Party and the help of comrades in exposing his mistakes and refused to reveal his most ugly, most essential things. Finally, in disregard of repeated warnings from the Party and comrades, he shamefully attempted to commit suicide and thus completely alienated himself from the Party and the people. Although his suicide attempt failed due to the obstruction of comrades, it constituted a flagrant betrayal of the Party, a fact that he cannot deny.

There are ideological, social, and historical roots for Gao Gang's schemes to split the Party and seize Party and state power. Throughout the long years of revolutionary struggles, Gao Gang did show a side that was correct and did make contributions to the revolution. That was why he had won the trust of the Party. However, his individualist ideas (demonstrated by his arrogance and unbridled ambition when things were going smoothly and his passivity and worry over personal loss when things were not going well) and the decadence of his lifestyle continued unchecked for a long time. They actually got worse after nationwide victory. This was his dark side. The progressive worsening of his dark side turned him, step by step, into a de facto agent of the bourgeoisie within our Party. Gao Gang's recent anti-Party activities are the inevitable culmination of the development of his dark side; they are at the same time a reflection of the bourgeoisie's attempts to split, undermine, and corrupt our Party in the period of the transition to socialism. His serious criminal activities, if they had not met with the resolute and forceful check of the Center, would have brought serious damage to the cause of the Party and the people. His crimes have canceled out the partial contributions he had made to the revolution; they prove that his motives in taking part in the revolution were impure. For Gao Gang, bourgeois personal ambition has completely overruled loyalty to serving the people that Communist Party members must preserve.

Up to the present time, Gao Gang is still trying to gloss over his mistakes. In his self-examination of February 24, 1954, he confessed only to opposing individual comrades of the central leadership that led to sectarian and illicit activities, and that this mistake, if it continued to develop, would split the Party. His confession was an attempt to cover up his total scheme of splitting the Party and seizing Party and state power. He also tried to cover up the seriousness of his attempted suicide as a momentary impulse for self-destruction while in actual fact it reflected his intense hatred for the Party and its comrades after his schemes had been exposed. Therefore, we must not lightly believe Gao Gang's somewhat penitent remarks at the present time. We must put him under supervised education for a long time to come. If Gao Gang is really repentant, then he should submit to the Party's supervised education, genuinely confess and admit to his crimes. Without long-term testing, we will never believe that he is ready to reform his extremely individualistic thoughts and actions, which have developed for a long time.

Developments in the Gao Gang case show that it was entirely necessary and correct for the Party's Central Committee to have called the Fourth Plenum and passed a resolution to enhance the unity of the Party, and to have patiently reasoned with Gao Gang so that he could realize and correct his mistakes, up until the time he attempted suicide. The Central Committee hereby resolves to make public his crimes to high-ranking Party cadres throughout the nation, make public the resolution on strengthening Party unity to the whole Party, and publish in the press the major contents of the resolution. This is necessary to enable the Party's high-ranking cadres, comrades of the entire Party, and people of the whole nation to understand what they should respectively know about the true situation so that they are mentally prepared to strengthen their struggle to safeguard the interests of the Party and the people.

From Gao Gang's case, we should draw the following lesson: all conceit, liberalism, individualism, sectarianism, cliquism, decentralism, localism, and departmentalism must be criticized. The fallacy of the "party of the military" must be criticized. Individualistic careerists must be guarded against. Illicit activities in the Party must be prohibited. Factionalist cadre policy must be opposed. The idea of establishing independent kingdoms must be eliminated. Unified leadership of the Party and collective leadership must be upheld. Inner-Party democracy and criticism and self-criticism must be practiced. All cadres of the Party, without exception, must be subject to the supervision of the Party organization and the masses of the people. A communist outlook on life must be established. Education in Marxism-Leninism must be reinforced.

(Adopted by the Politburo of the Central Committee on March 1, 1954)

2B. "Report of Deng Xiaoping, Chen Yi, and Tan Zhenlin Concerning the Discussion Meeting on the Rao Shushi Question" (March 1, 1954)

[This written report on the meeting dealing with Rao is of special interest for the light it sheds on the issue of whether in fact a Gao-Rao "alliance" ever existed. While the report claims that Gao and Rao worked together to split the Party in 1953, the great bulk of the discussion deals with specific events *before* 1953 and generalized assertions concerning Rao's disputatious and insecure personality. Beyond this, the report records Rao's flat denial of any explicit coordination of activities with Gao and indicates the inability of the meeting to provide any convincing evidence to the contrary.]

Source: *Zhonggong Dangshi Jiaoxue Cankao Ziliao*, 20:272-76.

TO the Central Committee:

The following is a report on the results of the series of discussions on the question of Rao Shushi called by the decision of the Secretariat of the Central Committee.

A total of seven meetings were held. The first four meetings focused on the facts of the mistakes committed by Comrade Rao Shushi. At the fifth and sixth meetings, many comrades spoke and continued to expose his mistakes. Rao spoke at the seventh meeting, making a self-criticism. Comrades Deng Xiaoping and Chen Yi then made addresses to the meeting, thereby concluding the discussions.

The meetings were attended by twenty-six comrades including some from East China who were in Beijing or who had been transferred to Beijing, as well as comrades of central departments and ministries who had work relations with Rao. At the concluding meeting on the seventh day, sixty-six comrades from the large administrative regions and from central departments and ministries came to listen to Rao's self-criticism.

The discussions earnestly verified and exposed the concrete facts of the mistakes committed by Comrade Rao Shushi. Rao often dodged and hedged, hence the importance of verification. In the process of verification, Comrade Rao admitted some and denied some of his mistakes. After various comrades spoke on the fifth and sixth meetings, Rao was still quibbling on important issues.

The discussions drew the following conclusions on the question of Comrade Rao Shushi:

I. According to the facts as verified by the discussions, Comrade Rao Shushi has been shown to be an extremely individualistic bourgeois careerist. His personal ambitions were constantly on the ascendant. His most glaring crime was his and Gao Gang's activities in 1953 to split the Party.

1. The discussions examined the question of how Comrade Rao Shushi undermined the prestige of the central leadership and disrupted Party unity in 1953 from the time of the National Conference on Financial and Economic Work to the National Conference on Organization Work. During this period, Rao Shushi's activities completely exposed him as a sinister careerist and that, in fact, he had already formed an anti-Party alliance with Gao Gang.

After he was appointed director of the central organization department in February 1953, to achieve his infamous aim of climbing step by step to a higher position, Rao, starting out from his own ugly thoughts of sectarian power struggle, began to distort political life within the central leadership. He erroneously estimated that certain comrades were on their way out and certain others were on their way up. Based on these ridiculous speculations, he energetically stirred up dissension inside the Party. He and Gao Gang, making use of Comrade An Ziwen's erroneous proposal about candidates for central organizations which was An's personal opinion, fabricated and widely spread talk that certain comrades formed a faction, a "circle," and that a certain leading central comrade was a supporter of this faction or circle. He told people that the Financial and Economic Work Conference had already carried out struggle against so and so of the "circle," and that another person of the "circle" would be struggled against after the conference. This talk proves that he and Gao Gang were together trying to create chaos and split the Party. Subsequently, before the Financial and Economic Conference had even ended, without prior knowledge and consent from anyone in the central leadership, he baselessly made up all kinds of pretexts to instigate a struggle against Comrade An Ziwen inside the organization department, because he thought An was a member of what they called the "circle." The struggle Rao instigated was, on the one hand, to achieve his aim, by the most ruthless means possible, of cowing or squeezing out Comrade An Ziwen and others, but more importantly, he was utilizing this struggle to demonstrate his utmost eagerness in support of and participation in Gao Gang's struggle to split the Party and seize the supreme power of the Party and state. Rao's struggle against Comrade An Ziwen not only was not reported to the Center beforehand and naturally did not get its approval, but after the Center discovered his mistake and put a halt to it, Rao was not at all repentant.

He openly rejected the Center's intervention and continued with the struggle. In his struggle against Comrade An Ziwen, Rao alleged that one of An's mistakes was his resentment of the Financial and Economic Conference. But when Rao's ignominious activities and manipulations were exposed among the leading cadres at the National Organization Work Conference, Rao shamelessly told Comrade An Ziwen that he did not say it was An who resented the Financial and Economic Conference but some other leading comrade of the Center. That is to say, his struggle was not really targeted at Comrade An Ziwen, but at the other leading central comrade. These facts prove that it was no coincidence that Rao instigated the struggle, but that it was fully planned. He was determined, by hook or by crook, to damage the prestige of the Party Center, oppose central leading comrades, participate in Gao Gang's anti-Party activities, and engage in political speculation to achieve his futile ambition of climbing to a higher position after he succeeded and in an effort to consolidate and develop his despicable goal of personal power. In his actions, Rao has completely violated the Party's standpoint, principles, and discipline.

Rao Shushi, in following the anti-Party activities of Gao Gang, is actually demonstrating the attempt of the bourgeoisie to corrupt, subvert, and split our Party.

2. The discussions examined the behavior of Comrade Rao Shushi over many years in the past and proved that his and Gao Gang's 1953 activities to split the Party were the outcome of the development of their unbridled personal ambitions, which they had harbored for a long time. They were not random acts of Rao's but were rooted in his personal history. The following three incidents can be cited.

    a. Comrade Rao Shushi's autumn 1943 struggle against Comrade Chen Yi at Huanghuatang, the site of the New Fourth Army headquarters. According to exposés by comrades Zeng Shan, Lai Bozhu, Zhang Yunyi, Liu Xiao, Liu Changsheng, and Chen Yi, and the facts admitted to by Rao himself during the discussions, particularly in view of the cable Rao sent to the Center at the time regarding the struggle against Comrade Chen Yi and Comrade Mao Zedong's return cable, the incident can be characterized as an out-and-out sectarian activity by Rao Shushi to squeeze out Comrade Chen Yi by utilizing certain isolated defects and mistakes of Chen's. Rao neither consulted Comrade Chen Yi before he started the struggle nor asked the Center for permission, but took the action arbitrarily. He organized a struggle among the leading officers of the units directly under the New Fourth Army's command and charged Comrade Chen Yi, entirely erroneously, with so-called opposition to Comrade Mao Zedong, opposition to the system of political commissars in the army, as well as with the crime of trying to drive out Rao. He thus hoodwinked a part of the officers in order to hit at and squeeze out Comrade Chen Yi. In his cable to the Center, Rao invented lies about Chen Yi being irresponsible in work. At the same time, he also lied that he had given well-intentioned help to Chen Yi but got no results, and hence he had to ask the Center to send a replacement who was strong in both ethics and capability for Chen Yi. Rao did all this to reach his aim of kicking out Comrade Chen Yi.

In 1944, Comrade Chen Yi, in accordance with a cable from the Center, was transferred to Yan'an. In a cable to the Central China Bureau, Comrade Chen Yi made a self-criticism of certain mistakes of liberalism that he had committed on the question of unity in the Central China Bureau. Comrade Mao Zedong also sent a cable to the Central China Bureau pointing out that the nature of Comrade Chen Yi's past mistake in chairing a debate at the Seventh Congress of the Red Fourth Army in western Fujian [in 1929] was not that of the general line, and that it had been resolved long since, and therefore should not be brought up again. Comrade Mao Zedong also pointed out that Comrade Chen Yi had performed many meritorious deeds in the periods of the civil war and the Anti-Japanese war. The conflict between Chen and Rao at Huanghuatang, Comrade Mao Zedong further stated, was of the nature of work relations. He finally instructed the Central China Bureau to end the debate and restore unity. In a return cable, Comrade Rao Shushi continued to maintain an attitude of opposition to Comrade Mao Zedong's cable and Comrade Chen Yi's self-criticism. He again incited several leading cadres to send a joint telegram to the Center maintaining the same hostile stand.

From the struggle against Comrade Chen Yi at Huanghuatang, it can be seen that Rao Shushi, in complete violation of the instructions of the Center, resorted to methods employed by the exploiting classes of the old society in organizing inner-Party struggles. He also invented lies to dupe the Center, so as to reach his shameful aim of achieving personal power.

b. The incident in 1949 when Comrade Rao Shushi did his best to get the position of chairman of the East China Military and Administrative Committee. After the conclusion of the People's Political Consultative Committee in 1949, the Center had called responsible comrades of the large administrative regions together to discuss the list of candidates for corresponding Military and Administrative Committees. It was decided that the commanders of each field army would concurrently be the chairmen of the Military and Administrative Committees. When the Center dealt with the question, all administrative regions except the East China region offered no obstruction. The East China region, because Comrade Rao Shushi was not in Beijing, could not reach a final decision. At the time, Comrade Mao Zedong had personally told Comrade Chen Yi that he wanted Chen to be the chairman of the East China Military and Administrative Committee. Comrade Chen Yi declined on the grounds that he was too busy in Shanghai and proposed Comrade Rao Shushi for the post. Comrade Mao Zedong insisted, however, that Chen was more suitable, but indicated that the matter could be given to the East China Bureau for discussion, and its decision reported to the Center for approval. Chen relayed Comrade Mao Zedong's instructions to Rao after returning to Shanghai, whereupon Rao immediately decided that he would assume the post. He gave no consideration at all to the Center's opinion and did not formally put the question to the East China Bureau for decision. Later, when Rao came to the Center,

Comrade Mao Zedong again explained to Rao that in all large administrative regions the field army commanders were concurrently made chairmen of the Military and Administrative Committees. At this, Rao made the excuse that several comrades in the East China Bureau disagreed with Chen Yi becoming chairman of its Military and Administrative Committee, with the aim of getting himself appointed by the Center. On this question, Rao admitted that he "started out entirely from bourgeois individualism, not from the requirements of the Party and the interests of the people." He further admitted that he "did not respect and was dishonest to Chairman Mao and the Party Center."

c. The rest cure taken by Comrade Rao Shushi in Beijing in February 1952. During the "Three-Anti" and "Five-Anti" movements, Comrade Rao Shushi, due to convulsions of his eye nerves, was unable to work. Comrade Su Yu suggested to the Center that Rao should take a rest cure. The Center agreed and, out of solicitude for Rao, appointed Comrade Su Yu to accompany him to Beijing for his treatment and recuperation. Rao was suspicious upon receiving the cable asking him to go to Beijing. After arriving in Beijing, when he heard that the Center planned to send such and such comrade to Shanghai to help in leading the "Three-Anti" and "Five-Anti" [movements], he became even more suspicious. In Beijing, when he was under treatment in hospital, he indicated his dissatisfaction, based upon his suspicions, to comrades who were in the same hospital. After leaving hospital, his dissatisfaction with the Center had grown to such uncontrollable proportions to the point where, one night about 3 A.M., he made a big scene and repeatedly asked to talk to Comrade Mao Zedong. In three hours of talk, he expressed doubt about the Center's trust in him. He demanded of Comrade Mao Zedong answers to the three questions: (1) Was he brave in fighting the enemy? (2) Did he commit any mistakes of line while working in East China? (3) Why was he transferred to Beijing under the escort of Comrade Su Yu? Despite Comrade Mao Zedong's explanations on the three points, Rao was still not satisfied. Finally, Comrade Mao Zedong answered that if you (Rao) yourself feel well enough, you can return immediately to East China to resume work. Only then did Rao realize how unreasonable his suspicions were. Reassured that the Center had no other intention, he took leave. Thereafter, Rao went into long-term recuperation. While recuperating in Dalian, he heard that the Secretariat of the Central Committee had decided to transfer him to Beijing, and this rekindled his dissatisfaction.

At the discussions, Rao confessed to his suspicions and the fact that he had probed the question and found that the Center had no other intention than his welfare. The discussions also verified that, although Rao professed to have got rid of his suspicions of the Center, he did not really understand his own problems or make a self-examination of it, but tried his best to mend his slip and cover up his dissatisfaction with the Center.

The discussions uncovered many other instances, major and minor, demonstrating Comrade Rao Shushi's mistakes, which we will not go into here.

II. The unanimous opinion of the meetings was that the extreme bourgeois individualism revealed in the person of Comrade Rao Shushi was not of an ordinary nature but had its special features. Rao was adept at camouflaging his essential character. For many years he had shown himself to the world as a person of discipline and self-control. In his schemes inside the Party for power, he never showed his hand until the crucial moment. Even when he did show his hand, he still covered up his true intentions and used others to achieve his aim. Rao Shushi is a hypocrite rarely found in the Party.

The discussions pointed out that although Comrade Rao Shushi did not advance any new theories, his basic thinking consisted of a denial of the Communist Party as a unified, revolutionary, Marxist-Leninist party. He regarded the Party as a clique made up of many factions. He thought that opportunist maneuvers could make his star rise. When he was working in one region, he never wanted central departments to examine his work, never made a self-criticism, but always covered up his defects. He often adopted an attitude of attack and resistance to central departments and even leading central comrades. He regarded the area under his leadership as his "independent kingdom." After coming to work at the Center, in line with his speculative nature he threw his lot in with Gao Gang, who was scheming to seize the supreme power of the Party and the government, to wage a struggle to seize power and position. This was the political essence of the bourgeois individualist speculator Rao.

III. The discussions pointed out that Comrade Rao Shushi adopted a series of measures that were entirely contrary to the working style of the Party in his struggle to gain Party power—that of "power play." Comrade Rao Shushi had an unsavory personal style, which can be summed up as follows: (1) Rumormongering, hookwinking superiors and subordinates alike; (2) making promises of promotion to gain support alternating with attacks against those who would not toe his line, or using a combination of both—attacking first then giving favors later; (3) grasping the "pigtails" of comrades—finding others' weaknesses and faults to use as a handle for attack or blackmail; (4) deliberately planting "nails" to be used when necessary to launch sudden attacks against others; (5) when arriving at a new position, employing a series of stratagems to pressure and cow others, to establish "who's boss"; (6) fabricating excuses to attack people he did not like—he admitted that he often used different occasions to launch his own attacks; (7) lying and denying what he had just said; (8) presenting a modest and respectful demeanor while actually boosting his own image.

The major incidents enumerated above—[Rao] and Gao Gang's anti-Party activities in 1953, the struggle Rao instigated against Chen Yi at Huanghuatang in 1943, his efforts to gain the post of chairman of the East China Military and Administrative Committee in 1949, and his rest cure in Beijing in 1952—represent Rao's devious manipulations and unscrupulous personal style. His underhanded behavior cannot be easily detected and proved without examination and verification. Sometimes, he gave people the impression that he was a man of honesty and integrity. But after verifying the facts, he was completely exposed. Some of the comrades said during the meetings that [their attitude] toward Rao changed from respect to suspicion, then to rage. This is a natural reflection of the exposure of a hypocrite.

In short, Comrade Rao Shushi is a past master at the sort of power play that is typical among the exploiting classes in the old society. He had brought these abilities into the Party. This was a common conclusion arrived at in the discussions.

IV. Up to the present, Comrade Rao Shushi has not entirely admitted his mistakes. In his self-criticism, he admitted that he had never experienced the tempering of a rectification campaign, that he was arrogant and complacent, that he was wont to exaggerate his contributions, that he was dishonest, had an unscrupulous style, used some tactics in political speculative activities inside the Party that should only have been employed against the enemy, that the nature of his mistakes was bourgeois individualism, that in certain specific instances his bourgeois individualism had already grown to the proportions of careerism, etc. The above illustrates that he had admitted to some mistakes superficially, but is still not sincere or thoroughgoing. He is unwilling to probe at the roots of his mistakes. On the questions of Huanghuatang and the position of chairman of the East China Military and Administrative Committee, although he admitted to a little more of the facts, he still had some reservations. On the question of his rest cure in Beijing, although he admitted to part of the problem, he also put up a lot of arguments and refused to probe the roots. On the crucial question of his direct opposition to leading central comrades and his participation in the splittist activities of Gao Gang from the period of the Financial and Economic Work Conference to the Organization Work Conference, he admitted only to the lighter charges and tried to deny the heart of the problem. This shows that Rao is still maintaining a dishonest attitude toward his own mistakes.

During the discussions, some comrades raised the question as to why Gao Gang and Rao Shushi carried out such major anti-Party activities at the same time and what the relationship between the two was. On this question, Rao alleged that [he and Gao] "agreed without prior consultation and happened to have the same view." Due to lack of time, this question was not pursued, but Rao owes it to the Center to make an honest confession in the future. The discussions also demanded that Comrade Rao Shushi reflect deeply and honestly confess to the Central leadership the ideological and social roots of his serious mistakes. Whether Rao can thoroughly admit and rectify his mistakes rests with Rao himself.

The discussions also pointed out that, in long years of work in the past, Comrade Rao Shushi had followed normal procedure. He usually did not reveal his schemes to gain power until the crucial moments. Although he had made some accomplishments in his work, in the past ten years or more he had always committed serious mistakes at critical junctures. This reveals a most ugly side of his nature, and it in effect cancels out his good side. Rao, if he wishes to continue to be a Communist Party member, must probe into his problems and confess them, he must temper himself in future tests and completely discard his extreme individualistic thoughts and behavior which have existed in his person for a long time.

V. The discussions finally pointed out that the Party, in exposing the mistakes of Comrade Rao Shushi, should at the same time learn a lesson. This is that the unified leadership of the Party and the Party's principle of collective leadership must be firmly adhered to; inner-Party democracy must be advocated and developed; criticism and self-criticism inside the Party, especially among high-ranking cadres, must be enhanced; the Party must hone its proletarian senses and be on guard; Party unity must be strengthened so as not to give the enemy the opportunity to disrupt it; every cadre must establish a communist outlook on life; [and] Marxist-Leninist education of the whole Party must be reinforced. Only so can the Party make progress and lead the people in completing the great historical tasks in the period of transition.

Deng Xiaoping, Chen Yi, Tan Zhenlin
March 1, 1954

(Approved by the Politburo of the Central Committee on March 15, 1954)

3. Excerpts from East China Bureau Report on Expanded Meeting Concerning the Fourth Plenum (May 10, 1954)

[The East China meeting was one of various regional and local meetings convened to review the results of the Fourth Plenum and the subsequent discussion meetings. Given the locale it naturally focused on Rao Shushi. The first two of the three excerpts presented here point to doubts harbored by East China cadres concerning the charges laid against Rao. The second excerpt is of particular relevance for its bearing on the questionable nature of the official 1954–55 assertion of an explicit Gao-Rao "alliance." The final excerpt suggests that the 1954 criticism of East China leader Tan Zhenlin, who was alleged by Cultural Revolution sources (see chapter 2, n. 124) to have been an active participant in Rao's activities, had nothing to do with the Gao-Rao "conspiracy." It also indicates that Chen Yi, despite his high status and past disputes with Rao, treated Rao with great caution during the period before his disgrace.]

Source: *Zhonggong Dangshi Jiaoxue Cankao Ziliao*, 20:312, 314, 315.

. . .
. . . Some people voiced suspicion as to whether or not Gao and Rao may have already established organizational links with the enemy. Judging from certain questionable points in Rao Shushi's historical data, there is absolute need to examine this question carefully. The meeting is of the view, however, that the

question of organizational links, whether they actually existed or not, should not be the only one under consideration when looked at from the viewpoint of drawing lessons therefrom. All anti-Party elements, whatever form their activities take, are actually working for the same end from the point of view of being agents of the bourgeoisie who seek to undermine the Party from within and implement the bourgeoisie's reactionary tasks. Politically, this is the essence of the matter, and should be grasped in organizing our counterattack against the anti-Party clique. Only so can we deal the anti-Party clique a fatal blow and defend the Party's interests. If we regard the Gao Gang–Rao Shushi problem as merely a problem outside the Party, the matter would in effect be oversimplified and would prevent us from understanding with greater depth and in an all-round way the essence of class struggle, and hence from drawing necessary lessons.

...

... Cadres of the East China Bureau did not have many contacts with Gao Gang. Last year, when he visited Shanghai, Nanjing, and Hangzhou, he did carry out certain activities, but in a covert manner. The meeting criticized the saying that "Gao Gang had no influence in East China, all we need to do is to expose Rao Shushi." As Gao Gang is the chief of this anti-Party alliance, and subsequently "opened fire on the Party," his crime is especially serious. Our exposure of him, therefore, can by no means be relaxed. In essence, Gao and Rao come from the same mold. Their difference is in the extent of their crimes and the different forms their activities manifested. We must criticize Gao Gang and Rao Shushi together as agents of the bourgeoisie for us to be able to understand the resolution of the Fourth Plenum, heighten our vigilance, and enhance our ability to expose hypocrites and schemers.

...

The meeting is of the opinion that, as far as comrades Chen Yi, Tan Zhenlin, and Shu Tong are concerned, their merits form their primary and basic side. They are capable of leading all the work in East China. They have some shortcomings, which they are in the process of correcting. Besides agreeing with the self-examinations of the three comrades, the meeting would like to stress their following shortcomings: (1) Regarding Comrade Chen Yi: He had some misgivings on the question of struggling against Rao Shushi, with the result that he did not expose Rao's activities earlier to the Center; he is capable in grasping major issues but lacks in-depth and systematic study of the specific circumstances and problems involved; and he didn't do enough in taking the initiative to get close to and listen to the opinions of [subordinate] cadres. (2) Regarding Comrade Tan Zhenlin: He has not been able to get rid of completely his sense of complacency and subjective one-sidedness in his way of thinking; he rushes into decisions impetuously without careful thought; he speaks impulsively without consideration of the occasion and weighing his words, resulting in many comrades' misunderstanding about him. (3) Regarding Comrade Shu Tong: His fighting will is not sufficiently strong; in work, he is more cautious than innovative; in working style, he has some measure of routinism.

VIII
THE 1955 NATIONAL PARTY CONFERENCE

[The National Conference of the CCP was held from March 21 to 31, 1955. The "Gao Gang–Rao Sushi anti-Party alliance" was one of the three items on the agenda along with the First Five-Year Plan and the establishment of a Party Central Control Committee. The latter item was also related to the Gao–Rao affair since, in the official interpretation, weaknesses in existing inner-Party supervisory mechanisms contributed to the "conspiracy." The result of the conference was an official verdict on the case expelling Gao (posthumously) and Rao from the Party and disciplining several lower-ranking members of their "clique." At the conclusion of the conference a resolution on the affair was passed and made public, thus marking the first time that Gao and Rao had been openly denounced by name. A translation of this resolution appears in *Current Background*, no. 324, April 5, 1955, pp. 4–6. While the resolution gave the first concrete public description of the "crimes" of Gao and Rao, a much more extensive account was provided by a report given by Deng Xiaoping during the conference. This was the most extensive review of the case prior to Chen Shihui's article translated in Appendix I. It was not made public, however, and has only come to light in a post-Mao documentary collection; it is translated for the first time below.]

1. Deng Xiaoping, "Report on the Gao Gang, Rao Shushi Anti-Party Alliance" (March 21, 1955)

Source: *Zhonggong Dangshi Jiaoxue Cankao Ziliao*, 20:512–25.

COMRADES! On behalf of the Central Committee, I shall now report to the National Party Conference on the question of the Gao Gang–Rao Shushi anti-Party alliance.

I

The Party, under the leadership of the Central Committee headed by Comrade Mao Zedong, has thoroughly fouled the intrigues of the Gao Gang–Rao Shushi anti-Party alliance. This marks a new victory of great significance in the history of our Party.

Our Party throughout its history has many times triumphed over renegades and anti-Party elements. In 1927, the Party carried out the struggle against the renegade Chen Duxiu and his followers, later purging these elements. It was this that enabled the Party, in the grave situation following the defeat of the revolution, to enter victoriously a new period of struggle with the rural areas as revolutionary bases. During the Long March of the Red Army in 1935, the Party smashed the renegade Zhang Guotao's conspiracy to split the Party, and was thereby able to complete successfully the great Long March and await the new situation of the Anti-Japanese war. Both these incidents occurred in historical periods when class relations were undergoing drastic changes and class struggle was at white heat, or at crucial junctures of the revolution. The attempts of both the Chen Duxiu elements and Zhang Guotao to sabotage the Party reflected the fierce attacks against the Party of class enemies outside the Party. Historical experience has shown that, had not the Party carried out determined struggle against these renegades until they were ousted, the Party and the revolution would have suffered crushing defeats. The fact that our Party was able to purge renegades and capitulators from its ranks enabled it to weather severe storms and go forward successfully.

Naturally, the current situation of our Party is fundamentally different from the time of the two instances cited above. The revolution has won an unprecedented victory. However, we are situated in a similarly tense period of drastic change in class relations and class struggle; we are at another crucial juncture of revolutionary development. As everybody knows, in the period of transition from the stage of New Democratic revolution to that of socialist revolution, class struggles will not become more relaxed, but, on the contrary, will become more complicated and acute. Our Party is leading the broad masses of the laboring people in the struggle to build socialism and carry out socialist transformation in order to build our country into a great socialist country. This is a revolution deeper and broader in nature than the New Democratic revolution to oppose imperialism, feudalism, and bureaucratic capitalism. Our Party has become the party in power in the nation. This does not mean that class enemies at home and abroad who hate our socialist cause will cease their attacks against us. On the contrary, they will concentrate more strength to attack our Party with every means.

The imperialists, particularly the American imperialists, are doing their best to encircle us and constantly attempting to sabotage our country. The U.S. imperialists are not only occupying Japan and South Korea, they have not only formed the so-called SEATO, they are not only disrupting the peace in Indochina, but they are also entrenched on China's territory Taiwan together with their henchmen the Chiang Kai-shek renegade clique and actively preparing to start a direct aggressive war against the Chinese mainland. Counterrevolutionary subversive activities directed by the U.S. imperialists and the Chiang Kai-shek traitor clique are daily increasing in intensity along with the development of socialist construction and transformation in the country.

Socialist transformation calls for the elimination of all exploiting classes. In China's transition period, although we still have the need as well as the possibility to form a united front with the national bourgeoisie, we would be falling into dangerous delusions if we think that the industrial and commercial capitalists and rich peasants would not rise in opposition while their financial position is increasingly weakened and they are being squeezed out. As a matter of fact, the capitalist class of town and country are constantly carrying out struggles against the working class, the Communist Party, and the People's Government. These struggles are sometimes of a political nature, sometimes of an economic nature, sometimes overt, and sometimes covert. They not only still possess substantial financial strength as well as wide connections in social life, but also possess weapons that should not be ignored, and that is the ideology, working style, sly tactics of struggle, and corrupt and decadent way of life of the exploiting classes formed in the course of the centuries-old rule of the system of exploitation. All these things are constantly encircling and corrupting the working class and the laboring people.

Both foreign imperialists and domestic counterrevolutionaries know that, in order to attack the Chinese people, they must first strike at its most vital spot—the Chinese Communist Party, which is the leading force of the people and working class of China. The easiest way to storm a fortress is from within. That is why they are always trying to make use of the vacillating and most unreliable elements in the Communist Party and, through them, to split, corrupt, and disintegrate the Party, so as to accomplish their design of making a counterrevolutionary comeback.

For this reason, we must regard the building of socialism as a serious class struggle. The Resolution of the Fourth Plenum of the Party's Seventh Central Committee said: "In this struggle, foreign imperialism, on the one hand, will not sit idly by and simply watch us; and on the other hand, those classes within the country that have already been overthrown will not willingly reconcile themselves to extinction, while those classes that are to be eliminated will not give up without resistance. Inveterate counterrevolutionary elements among them will undoubtedly collude with foreigners in an attempt to defeat the revolutionary cause and restore reactionary rule in China. One of the most important methods of the imperialists and counterrevolutionaries for sabotaging our cause is, first and foremost, to undermine the unity of the Party and to look for agents within our Party."

It is by no means an accident that the Gao Gang–Rao Shushi anti-Party alliance should emerge at this juncture of class struggle.

The Gao Gang–Rao Shushi anti-Party alliance aimed to usurp the supreme power of the Party and state by means of a conspiracy. This is their hallmark and program. Why did they want to overthrow the central leadership? They had no reasons that they could make public. They never openly proposed any political program or principles that were different from those of the central authorities. On the contrary, at every official occasion, they repeatedly voiced support for the central leadership. Since they dared not propose any political program and principles in opposition to those of the central leadership but had to overthrow the central leadership to achieve their unbridled personal ambitions, they could only resort to intrigues such as organizing secret factions, spreading rumors and slander, sowing discord, spreading untruths, and never revealing to the Party organization at Party meetings what they really had in mind. They were an unprincipled and unscrupulous inner-Party conspiratorial clique that plotted to usurp the supreme power of the Party and state. Obviously, our Party can never tolerate such intrigues. If we tolerated such intrigues, it would mean abandonment of the Party's political and organizational principles. It would mean the Party's extinction.

Let us ask: How can such attempts to seize the power of the Party and the state by conspiracy have anything in common with the interests of the Party, the working class, and patriotic people? If this is not meeting the needs of the imperialists and bourgeois counterrevolutionaries, what else can it be?

The anti-Party activities of Gao Gang and Rao Shushi showed that they were not merely influenced by bourgeois ideology on isolated questions at different times. They were in a deliberate plot to split the Party and seize the supreme power of the Party and state to serve the interests of imperialism and the bourgeoisie, and they became, in effect, bourgeois agents in the Party.

The CCP is the vanguard of the Chinese working class and is in command of guiding the cause of socialism. If the power of Party leadership falls into the hands of schemers and renegades, and if the Party as the fighting command post is disintegrated and corrupted from within, what will result is definitely not socialist victory; it can only be bourgeois victory and a comeback by imperialism and all counterrevolutionary forces.

Without doubt, if our Party is to lead the broad masses of the people to achieve the great goal of socialism, it must wage resolute and unrelenting struggle against class enemies outside the Party, and it must, first of all, wage resolute and unrelenting struggle against class enemies who have wormed their way into the Party.

Between June and December 1953, prior to the Fourth Plenum of the Party's Seventh Central Committee called by the Politburo in early February 1954, the Secretariat of the Central Committee had already begun to discover the anti-Party activities in which Gao Gang and Rao Shushi were engaged. The Secretariat held the view that such activities were not simply a manifestation of degeneration involving individual Party members, but a reflection of acute class struggle within our Party in the new period of socialist revolution in China. Following a proposal by Comrade Mao Zedong in December 1953, the Politburo drafted the "Resolution on Strengthening Party Unity" and submitted it to the Fourth Plenum for approval. The session passed the resolution and called on the entire Party membership to enhance Party unity under the unified leadership of the Central Committee headed by Comrade Mao Zedong, and to defeat the plot of foreign and domestic enemies to split our Party. It called for struggle to defeat the attack on the Party by bourgeois agents who had already emerged or who might emerge in the Party. The Gao Gang–Rao Shushi anti-Party alliance was unmasked, isolated, and thoroughly defeated at the Fourth Plenum and thereafter.

Victory in the struggle against the Gao Gang–Rao Shushi anti-Party alliance proves once again that our Party is a strong, invincible party founded on the ideological and organizational principles of Marxism-Leninism. It proves that our Party is good at purging conspirators and renegades from its ranks, and good at striving for complete victory in the working class revolution by relying on the strength of unity and unified leadership. With victory in the struggle against the Gao Gang–Rao Shushi clique, our Party has become more consolidated than ever and rallies even more closely around the Central Committee headed by Comrade Mao Zedong. Our Party is more solid and unified than before, its fighting capability is stronger than ever. These are the basic guarantees that the Chinese people will defeat foreign and domestic enemies and succeed in socialist construction and socialist transformation.

However, we should not cherish the idea that since we have won victory in the struggle against the Gao Gang–Rao Shushi anti-Party alliance, it would be smooth-sailing from now on. It is necessary to keep in mind that the struggle for socialism has just begun, and henceforth we will encounter more complex and acute struggles than those of the past few years. That is why it is an urgent political task of the Party to sum up our experience and draw necessary lessons from this struggle.

II

How were the activities of the Gao Gang–Rao Shushi anti-Party alliance uncovered? What measures were taken by the central leadership against this conspiracy?

Their conspiratorial activities came to light in the course of the National Conference on Financial and Economic Work held from June to August 1953 and the Center's Conference on Organization Work held from September to October of the same year, and in the periods before and after these conferences. Both Gao and Rao had then been newly transferred to the central level. When they were doing regional work away from Beijing, their attempts to seize central leadership were entirely covert. When Gao Gang was appointed chairman of the State Planning Commission at the central level and Rao Shushi was appointed director of the central organization department and both moved to Beijing, their conspiratorial activities escalated and the two began to collude. These activities were concentratedly expressed during the two conferences.

The central leadership called the National Conference on Financial and Economic Work in the summer of 1953. The purpose of the conference was to set down the Party's general line for the period of transition to socialism and to correct decentralism and the tendency to depart from unified central leadership, and other manifestations of bourgeois concepts in financial and economic work. While these tasks were duly fulfilled at the conference, Gao Gang also took advantage of the occasion to engage in conspiratorial activities. He and his followers made irresponsible allegations at the conference meetings to stir up inner-Party disputes. During conference recesses, they spread rumors to undermine the prestige of the central leadership, particularly against two members of the Secretariat—comrades Liu Shaoqi and Zhou Enlai—while at the same time they sang Gao Gang's praises. Gao Gang attempted to turn the conference into an attack on the Party's central leadership. Political speculator Rao Shushi rose to the occasion by siding with Gao Gang in opposing the central leadership. The central leadership was at first not fully aware of the ultimate goal of Gao Gang and Rao Shushi's conspiratorial activities, but it did take note of their abnormal attitudes, and took timely measures to correct the erroneous opinions that ensued as a result of the activities of Gao, Rao, and their followers. Consequently, the conference achieved fruitful results.

Nevertheless, Gao Gang and Rao Shushi labored under the misconception that their activities at the conference had scored initial success. They continued to make efforts to usurp central leadership.

After the National Conference on Financial and Economic Work, Gao Gang, nominally on vacation, toured East China and the Central-South [region]. Systematically and in a planned way, he spread a great many rumors among high-ranking cadres in an attempt to set them against the central leadership. To split the Party, he came up with many anti-Party fallacies such as that "the Party was created by the army" and that "a reevaluation of Party history is necessary." He invented many untruths to attack the Central Committee and leading comrades of the Central Committee. He advanced a plan to "reorganize" the Central Committee and leading organs of the state. This plan was in effect a plot to overthrow the leadership of the Central Committee and install himself as the leader.

During the same period, Gao Gang's collaborator Rao Shushi used the central organization department and the National Conference on Organization Work for new conspiratorial activities. Within the organization department, Rao arbitrarily instigated a so-called struggle against Comrade An Ziwen, then deputy director of the department. Subsequently, at the Second National Conference on Organization Work in September and October, Rao Shushi waged a direct struggle against Comrade Liu Shaoqi and the Party's Central Committee. In his address to the conference, the former director of the organization department of the Party's Northeast Bureau, Comrade Zhang Xiushan, viciously attacked the work of the central organization department before 1953. It was later discovered that the text of Zhang Xiushan's speech was prepared for him by Gao Gang's anti-Party faction long before the conference. In this inciting speech, Zhang Xiushan exaggerated the past mistakes of the central organization department, slandered the work of the department as "making no distinction between ourselves and the enemy" and as being "right-deviationist." He made oblique accusations against Comrade Liu Shaoqi. Comrade Lai Keke, former director of the organization department of the Party's Shandong Subbureau, also attacked the central authorities on the issue of Party consolidation. His speech was drafted at the suggestion of Xiang Ming, then acting Party secretary of the Shandong Subbureau. Rao Shushi was extremely gratified at these attacks against the central leadership, since his own purpose was exactly to oppose Comrade Liu Shaoqi and the Central Committee.

To stop the splittist activities of Rao Shushi and Zhang Xiushan and to help them correct their errors and realize the significance of Party unity, the central leadership stressed to the conference the significance of unity within the entire Party, and charged every conference participant with the responsibility of conveying this message to all Party organizations in the country. This thwarted the plot of the Gao Gang–Rao Shushi anti-Party alliance to use the National Organization Work Conference to oppose the Center's plans, although at the time the Center was not yet fully aware of the entire plot of the Gao-Rao clique. Later, Gao Gang's follower Zhang Xiushan confided to others: "The issue was not resolved at the Organization Conference. The opportunity was not ripe, and we had to wait."

Unrepentant, these infamous schemers still believed that their despicable activities from the time of the Financial and Economic Conference to the time of the Organization Work Conference would help them to achieve their aim in the near future. Back in Beijing after his activities in the South, Gao Gang, believing that his anti-Party propaganda had been successful, became more frantic in his plot to seize the supreme power of the Party and state. In December 1953, when Comrade Mao Zedong according to his usual practice proposed entrusting Comrade Liu Shaoqi with handling the work of the Central Committee while he was on holiday, Gao Gang came out in opposition and worked secretly to get himself appointed general secretary or vice-chairman of the Party's Central Committee. He also demanded a change of the current premier of the Government Administration Council, which meant that he himself wanted to assume the post. His ambition to seize supreme power in the Party and state was thus unmasked. However, his assessment of the situation proved entirely wrong. By this time, many comrades who had heard his anti-Party slanders had reported his intrigues to the Central leadership. The Secretariat led by Comrade Mao Zedong, with the unanimous support of all members of the Central Committee in Beijing except Gao Gang and Rao Shushi, resolutely suppressed the intrigues of the Gao Gang–Rao Shushi anti-Party alliance. In February 1954, the Fourth Plenum of the Seventh Central Committee dealt this anti-Party clique a fatal blow.

At the Fourth Plenum, Gao Gang and Rao Shushi still showed no signs of repentance. In accordance with the decision of the Secretariat, two discussion meetings were called in mid-February on the questions of Gao Gang and Rao Shushi separately. Those elected to attend the meetings included thirty-seven members and alternate members of the Central Committee and forty key working personnel. Evidence against Gao Gang and Rao Shushi was verified at the meetings. Comrade Zhou Enlai made a summing up speech at the discussion on the question of Gao Gang. Comrades Deng Xiaoping, Chen Yi, and Tan Zhenlin jointly made a report to the Politburo on the evidence submitted to the discussions on the question of Rao Shushi. The speech and report were examined and approved by the Politburo. Faced with irrefutable evidence, Gao Gang still refused to admit his guilt. He showed his hatred for the Party and his determination to betray the Party to the very end by attempting to commit suicide when the meeting was still in progress. His effort to kill himself was unsuccessful, and he maintained a hostile attitude toward the Party and the people. In August 1954, he again attempted suicide, and this time ended his life as a renegade. Rao Shushi made a self-criticism to [his] discussion meeting but was reluctant to make a clean breast of his intrigues. He denied all major charges and admitted only minor ones. After the meeting, Rao wrote a self-criticism in March 1954. He pleaded guilty to some facts which had already been exposed by others but kept silent on many crucial issues and continued his attacks on the Party.

After the Fourth Plenum, the entire membership of the Party discussed the documents issued by the session. The Politburo first conveyed to cadres at and above the level of special district Party secretaries the truth about the Gao Gang–Rao Shushi anti-Party alliance. This was later conveyed to all members of the Party, the Youth League, and non-Party activists, while some of the non-Party democrats were given a briefing on the matter. After discussing the resolution of the Fourth Plenum and the message of the Politburo on the question of the Gao Gang–Rao Shushi anti-Party alliance, all organizations and members of the Party and the Youth League voiced warm support for the decision of the Politburo and expressed indignation at Gao and Rao for their anti-Party activities. They raised their vigilance against conspiracies and disruptive activities by foreign and domestic enemies and deepened their understanding of the importance of enhancing Party unity. Led by the Politburo, the Party's Northeast Bureau called a meeting of high-level cadres of the Northeast region in April 1954 to further expose the anti-Party activities of Gao Gang and his followers. An enlarged meeting was called by the East China Bureau in the same month, an enlarged meeting of the Shandong Subbureau was called in May, a municipal Party conference was called in Shanghai in June, and another Party Conference was called in Shandong in August. At these meetings, the anti-Party activities of Rao Shushi and his follower Xiang Ming, former acting secretary of the Shandong Subbureau, were further revealed. After the crimes of Gao Gang and Rao Shushi were made known to the entire Party, new evidence, especially that uncovered at the above meetings, showed the vicious features of Gao Gang and Rao Shushi as ambitious bourgeois careerists.

The new evidence testified that, as long ago as 1949, Gao Gang had already begun to engage in systematic anti-Party activities. Since then, in order to overthrow the central leadership, he had fabricated and spread absurd rumors to undermine its prestige, undermine Party unity, exaggerate his own ability, and secretly scraped together a group of people to support his seizure of power and form his anti-Party faction as a tool for his intrigues.

Gao Gang's activities were all aimed at opposing the Central Committee headed by Comrade Mao Zedong. However, the schemer knew that his plots could not stand exposure, and therefore he pretended that he had never opposed Comrade Mao Zedong but only opposed Mao's close comrades-in-arms Liu Shaoqi and Zhou Enlai. He knew that if he openly opposed Comrade Mao Zedong too early, it would be disadvantageous to his scheme. Comrades Liu Shaoqi and Zhou Enlai were the two stumbling blocks that he first had to remove on his road to seizing power. In his mind, if he succeeded in removing these two close comrades-in-arms of Mao Zedong's from the Party's Central Committee and the government and went on to replace them, then he could have more freedom to go on to oppose openly Comrade Mao Zedong. As we all know, comrades Liu Shaoqi and Zhou Enlai are [two of] our Party's most outstanding and long-tested leaders. They have been members of the Secretariat in charge of important leading work in the Central Committee for many years. Comrade Mao Zedong and the Central Committee have always appointed Comrade Liu Shaoqi acting chairman of the Central Committee in the absence of Comrade Mao Zedong. That is why when Gao Gang attacked the work of the Secretariat and the Central Committee, he concentrated his attacks on Comrade Liu Shaoqi.

What reason could Gao Gang have in opposing leaders long acknowledged by the entire Party such as comrades Liu Shaoqi and Zhou Enlai? As he had no other ammunition to attack them with, Gao fabricated lies and rumors, such as that comrades Liu Shaoqi, Zhou Enlai, and other leading comrades had committed grave mistakes. He spread such rumors in secret, to damage the prestige of Liu Shaoqi, Zhou Enlai, and other comrades. But when these rumors were exposed to light, they only served to prove that Gao Gang himself was guilty of opposing and splitting the Party in order to seize Party leadership.

Gao Gang deliberately attacked comrades of the central leadership for no other purpose than to seize power. He wanted to sweep aside obstacles on his road to seizing of power. To achieve his aim, Gao Gang was unscrupulous. Anyone who stood in his way, whatever his name, became the target of his rumors and attacks.

Gao Gang knew he could not justify his attacks on comrades of the central leadership. That was why he never openly and formally raised any opinions against Liu Shaoqi, Zhou Enlai, and other comrades at meetings of the central leadership. He dared not make public what he had in mind, so he could only sow discord secretly within the Party to hoodwink a few people with poor judgment, and bolster the courage of his followers to help him spread anti-Party rumors. These are the usual tricks and characteristics of schemers.

What showed particularly clearly the anti-Party nature of Gao Gang's activities was the absurd theory of the Party being a "party of the army," which he widely spread. He hoped, with this fallacy, to get the support of our glorious military personnel. For this purpose, he divided the Party organizations prior to the founding of the People's Republic into the "party of the base areas and the army" and the "party of the white areas." He said that the entire Party was created by the army and that, therefore, the "party of the base areas and the army"—of which he himself was the representative—was the Party's mainstay. He alleged that the present Central Committee and leading organs of the state were in the hands of people from the "party of the white areas." These organizations should, therefore, be thoroughly reorganized, so that they could come under the leadership of the "party of the base areas and the army," or, in other words, his own leadership. Obviously, this was an absurdity he fabricated for the purpose of splitting the Party and seizing Party leadership. As we all know, our glorious PLA was created and organized by the Communist Party. Without a Marxist-Leninist Communist Party and without Communist Party leadership, the creation of an army of an entirely new type such as the PLA would have been impossible. On this point, there has never been any doubt in our Party and army. Our Party is a unified one, the vanguard of the working class; it has never been and can never be divided into the "party of the base areas and the army" and the "party of the white areas." The entire PLA and Party organizations in the armed forces have always been under the unified leadership of the Party Central Committee. Gao Gang's fallacy showed that his activities were not confined to slandering a few comrades of the central leadership. He was openly slandering our Party, the Party's history, and the PLA. He vainly attempted to exert influence in the army to oppose the central leadership and to reform the Party in his image, in the image of the anti-Marxist and counterrevolutionary bourgeoisie.

To carry out his conspiracy to usurp Party leadership, Gao Gang put in important positions a group of soul mates and organized an anti-Party faction with himself as the nucleus. He gave them promotions that skipped several levels, made promises of enabling so-and-so to become a member of the Party's Central Committee, and armed them with his conspiratorial plans against the central leadership. Under Gao Gang's command, several cadres of the former Northeast Bureau actively participated in his anti-Party activities. They included comrades Zhang Xiushan, Zhang Mingyuan, Zhao Dezun, Ma Hong, Guo Feng, and Chen Bocun. To varying extents, they enthusiastically supported Gao Gang in his sectarian activities against the central leadership. Gao Gang and his sect monopolized the Northeast Bureau. They ostracized and attacked all dissidents. After Gao Gang was transferred to Beijing in 1952, the Central Committee put Comrade Lin Feng in charge of the Northeast Bureau, appointing him acting secretary. Gao Gang instructed Zhang Xiushan and Zhang Mingyuan to hold on to real power in the bureau and try to shut out Comrade Lin Feng so that he could not effectively take charge. Gao Gang and his faction regarded the Northeast region as an independent kingdom not subject to the leadership of the central authorities. They defied the central leadership and tried to establish their own prestige by spreading such ideas as "the Northeast is special" and "the Northeast is more advanced than the central level." They resisted the central leadership's correct policies with erroneous left- or right-deviationist policies of their own, to the point where they refused to implement long-standing decisions and instructions from the central leadership. They went so far as to claim that many central policies were actually initiated by the Northeast, as if the Northeast region was not led by the central leadership but vice versa. On several occasions, when Gao Gang learned about new work arrangements soon to be announced by the central leadership, he would beat them to it and start deploying those arrangements in the Northeast, so that he could later claim that he was more advanced than the central leadership. Gao Gang was hostile to and resisted all inspections and criticism of work in the Northeast by any central organization. He forbade Party members in the Northeast to reveal to the central leadership any shortcomings in the region's work. When the central leadership decided to transfer Gao Gang to Beijing, he said it was "to lure the tiger out of the mountains." Such anti-Party remarks showed that in the eyes of Gao Gang and his cronies the Northeast had long become "Gao Gang's kingdom."

After Gao Gang became chairman of the State Planning Commission, he claimed that he had formed an "economic cabinet." He challenged the Central People's Government and the Government Administration Council with his "economic cabinet," in order to split the unified state machinery under the unified leadership of the Party's Central Committee.

Gao Gang's anti-Party and anti–working class thoughts and actions have their historical roots. According to facts that have come to light, Gao Gang's role in the revolutionary struggle in the Shaanxi-Gansu-Ningxia area was exaggerated. During that period, his activities had already revealed tendencies of individualism and sectarianism. On several occasions when he had been confronted with hardships and dangers and when his personal desires had not been satisfied, Gao Gang had vacillated and become passive. He had led a decadent life for a long time. After entering the cities from the countryside [that is, when the Communist Party assumed power in 1949], Gao Gang used every despicable means to molest women and had had sexual relations with a number of women of questionable political background. Gao's extreme moral degeneration was a reflection of his complete political degeneration.

It was no coincidence that Rao Shushi should join forces with Gao Gang in 1953 to form an anti-Party alliance. Evidence shows that Rao Shushi had been a careerist and political swindler for a long time. His specialty was hypocrisy. Although his mind contained nothing but sordid ideas of personal gain, he tried his best to pretend to be a "man of principle." On the surface, he was a man who carefully implemented all instructions of the central leadership. In reality, he constantly distorted the Center's principles and policies and peddled his bourgeois wares. He posed as a man of integrity while he was really a liar and a political speculator.

In the Party, Rao Shushi often resorted to the "power politics" of the exploiting classes to achieve his individualistic ends. As far back as 1943 in the period of the Anti-Japanese war, to usurp power in the New Fourth Army, Rao instigated an entirely erroneous struggle against Comrade Chen Yi. He often told people that the way he dealt with dissenters was "by first treating them meanly before treating them like gentlemen." In other words, he would first find some opening to deal his opponents a mean blow. After the latter became subdued, he would then "treat them like gentlemen" so as to use them. This was the tactic he used when he unjustifiably attacked Comrade An Ziwen in the organization department in 1953. What kind of tactic is that? If one is honestly working for the Party and not a schemer, he would never use such tricks found only in the politics of the exploiting classes.

When Rao Shushi was working in East China, he resisted supervision by the central leadership. He often used such excuses as that Shanghai's conditions were "special," East China's were "special," or that "certain working departments of the central authorities cannot represent the Center" to reject leadership or criticism from central departments. He undermined collective leadership in East China's Party organization and tried his best to establish his own authority. To monopolize leadership in East China, he pulled the wool over the eyes of his superiors and subordinates and wrangled for himself in 1949 the position of chairman of the East China Military and Administrative Committee. He gave direct orders to his cronies on the Shanghai Municipal Party Committee to control important matters in that city. The Shanghai Municipal Party Committee was in effect unable to function as a grade–1 Party committee. In this way, Rao was, in effect, exercising one-man rule over East China and Shanghai.

Because Rao Shushi looked at things purely from an individualistic viewpoint and because he had usurped power in East China and Shanghai where he practiced a bourgeois rule, he was most apprehensive when he fell sick and the Center decided, in early 1952, to transfer him to Beijing for medical treatment and convalescence. Afraid that his wrongdoings would be discovered, he deliberately feigned madness and quarreled with Comrade Mao Zedong to test whether the Center still trusted him. Like Gao Gang, he regarded his transfer to Beijing as "a tiger being lured out of the mountains" and hated the central leadership for it. A scheming careerist just like Gao Gang, Rao at the time wrongly assessed the situation from the viewpoint of a bourgeois speculator and came to the conclusion that Gao Gang's conspiracy to usurp Party power was about to succeed. He hurriedly came out to act as Gao Gang's front-line fighter so that when the time came for the anti-Party alliance to "divide the spoils of victory," he would get a big share. He thus revealed himself as a hypocrite, careerist, and speculator.

Rao Shushi's actions in trying to establish separatist rule and resisting supervision and criticism from above while exercising patriarchal rule over his subordinates and undermining collective rule were mirrored by his follower Xiang Ming, acting secretary of the Party's Shandong Subbureau. Xiang Ming openly attacked work groups sent by the central organization department and the Central Discipline Inspection Committee to work in Shandong. He, too, practiced a patriarchal rule. Under the pretext of opposing errors of decentralism, he attacked many comrades holding different views. After Gao Gang and Rao Shushi formed their anti-Party alliance and started to attack the central leadership, Xiang Ming actively supported Rao Shushi. Both inside the central organization department and at the National Conference on Organization Work, he enthusiastically supported Rao Shushi's struggles against the central leadership. Even at the Fourth Plenum when Rao Shushi's mistakes were exposed and afterward, he tried to cover up and bolster Rao Shushi's morale. As birds of a feather flock together, bourgeois individualists always stand on the same side for the common goal of opposing the Party.

III

The above evidence shows that the most serious crime perpetrated by the Gao Gang–Rao Shushi anti-Party alliance was their conspiracy inside the Party to usurp power. This conspiracy strikes at the very life of the Party and therefore cannot be allowed. To allow it will only help the imperialists and counterrevolutionaries.

The Gao Gang–Rao Shushi anti-Party alliance conspired to overthrow the central leadership. Our Party is organized on the basis of democratic centralism. Any member of the Party who has a complaint against leading comrades of the central authorities can lodge the complaint with the Party organization through appropriate channels. But Gao Gang and Rao Shushi did not follow this practice. They did not openly propose their line and policy to challenge that of the central leadership. Instead, they carried out secret activities against the central leadership behind the back of the Party organization.

The Gao Gang–Rao Shushi anti-Party alliance plotted to overthrow the Party's Central Committee headed by Comrade Mao Zedong. They pretended to support Comrade Mao Zedong while secretly opposing Liu Shaoqi, Zhou Enlai, and other leading comrades. They pitted one person against another. In a word, what they sought was power for themselves. They changed their colors freely for the sake of seizing power.

The Party and the people can never trust conspirators, because conspirators are men with no principles. Their actions are dictated by their goal of seizing power. When necessary, they can pretend to be Communists and do useful work under the Party's leadership. But as soon as they deem it unnecessary to continue doing so and find it more advantageous to oppose communism, they will side with enemies of communism and the people. This is exactly how Gao Gang and Rao Shushi acted.

Naturally, schemers will always claim that they are correct, capable, and have a lot of achievements to their credit. First, even if all this were true, what good would it do to the Party and the people? A schemer who can pretend to be correct in both words and deeds for a time is actually more dangerous to the Party and the people by masking his true intentions.

Second, such boasts made by schemers are usually nothing but lies. If they do not lie and cannot deceive people, they would not be schemers.

Let us take a look at Gao Gang and Rao Shushi's true performance at work. Although they tried hard to cover up their intentions and dared not advocate their bourgeois line and program openly and systematically as a replacement for the Party's line and program, they did not succeed in hiding their anti-Party bourgeois character.

In his work, Gao Gang often donned a "leftist" mask to undermine the Party line. For example, during the time of land reform in the Northeast from 1946 to 1947, Gao Gang made many "leftist" proposals. As a result, grave "leftist" mistakes were made in land reform in the Hebei-Rehe-Liaoning region under Gao Gang's leadership. But when the Party's Northeast Bureau inspected and corrected the "leftist" deviations in land reform in the spring of 1948, Gao Gang countercharged that the "leftist" mistakes were made in late December 1947 after the resolutions of the National Conference on Land Reform were conveyed to the lower levels. Thus, he denied his own mistakes and at the same time attacked the National Land Reform Conference called by the Party Central Committee.

In the course of work in the Northeast after Liberation, Gao Gang voiced many "leftist" sentiments to win support. For example, he attempted to pursue a policy of immediate elimination of private capitalist industry and commerce. He set a speed for economic construction in the Northeast in disregard of actual conditions. Gao Gang also used "leftist" pretexts to resist the central leadership's policy of both uniting with and struggling against the national bourgeoisie as well as the Party's united front policy in the political power structure.

But Gao Gang's position was not "leftist" at all times. There were times when he revealed his bourgeois rightist stand. For example, for a long period after land reform, Gao Gang emphasized the role of rich peasants in increasing grain production. He was against setting up agricultural cooperatives and wished to adopt a wage system in rural mutual aid teams. Whether "leftist" or rightist in form, Gao Gang's mistakes had the same impact in undermining our socialist cause.

On the question of resisting the U.S. aggression and aiding Korea, Gao Gang was at first opposed to sending volunteers to Korea. But when the enemies crossed the 38th parallel to invade North Korea in early October 1950, he panicked and ordered evacuation at all cost. Transcripts of his speeches during the Korean war showed that he had no definite opinions on how to cope with the situation. When the Korean-Chinese side was winning battles, he became expansive and called for the "immediate liberation of all Korea." When the war was at a stalemate, he exaggerated hardships and made pessimistic forecasts. All this demonstrated his opportunistic thinking.

What commands our particular attention is Gao Gang's practice of lowering the standards of Party members and downplaying the Party's leading role. At one time, the Northeast admitted new Party members by the mistaken method of "self-assessment and public discussion, approved by the Party organization." The central leadership ordered this mistake corrected in December 1948, but Gao Gang continued with the process. Moreover, he spread many rumors to oppose the resolutions of the First National Conference on Organization Work on the question of Party building and Party consolidation because he was against setting strict standards for Party membership. He did not want collective leadership in the Party but stressed the role of the individual. This seriously damaged the Party's system. Under its influence, rural Party organizations in the Northeast were virtually incapacitated; all activities came from individual Party cadres. In industrial and mining enterprises, Gao Gang stressed the administrative leadership of one-man management. As a result, the role of Party organizations and trade unions was severely curtailed, as were the functions of Party organizations in the localities concerned. Such practices showed, in fact, his intention of abolishing the Party altogether.

If Gao Gang's mistake was vacillation between "left" and right, Rao Shushi's mistake in carrying out Party policy was out-and-out right capitulationism. This is clearly revealed in his urban and rural work as well as in his work in suppressing counterrevolutionaries.

Rao Shushi put off all urban social reforms in East China for a long time. Such reforms had not even got off the ground in Shanghai in early 1952 when Rao left East China. He never seriously implemented the instruction of the central leadership to rely on the working class in urban struggles. Alleging that workers in Shanghai were "complicated" and that "disorders might ensue," he dared not mobilize and organize workers for struggles and dared not mobilize the masses to report and accuse counterrevolutionaries. This caused the workers' movement to suffer a great setback in post-Liberation Shanghai. On the other hand, he made concessions to the bourgeoisie. In the initial stage of the "Five-Anti" movement, he was still summoning bourgeois representatives to meetings where he made arrangements for them to make "self-accusations." He several times deleted the phrase "repulse the frantic attacks of the bourgeoisie" from an editorial of the *Liberation Daily* in fear of offending the bourgeoisie.

On the question of suppressing counterrevolutionaries, Rao Shushi laid one-sided stress on leniency and did not implement the correct policy of the central leadership to rely on the masses and mobilize them to suppress counterrevolutionaries. He stressed relying on public security organs alone to make arrests, calling this "using special agents to contain enemy agents." At one time, he advocated "turning large numbers of counterrevolutionary cadres into our cadres." When the nationwide campaign to suppress counterrevolutionaries was launched, Rao Shushi had to supervise a roundup of counterrevolutionaries in Shanghai after repeated urging by the central leadership, but he soon stopped the mass struggle to expose and accuse counterrevolutionaries under the pretext that "the populace was frightened" and "production was affected."

In rural work, too, Rao Shushi did not freely mobilize the masses or seek to destroy completely the feudal order; he was protective of the interests of landlords and rich peasants. On the question of what road to take in rural development after land reform, he stressed development of the rich peasant economy and was indifferent to organizing the peasants to take the road of cooperation. He held the view that after the land reform, the Party should no longer rely on poor peasants and farm laborers, because to do so would dampen the peasants' enthusiasm for production and discourage them from trying to become rich peasants.

Rao Shushi's right capitulationist thinking seriously disrupted the Party's work in Shandong province. Xiang Ming, former acting secretary of the Party's Shandong Subbureau, actively supported Rao Shushi in his anti-Party activities and faithfully collaborated with Rao in his right deviationist mistakes. Xiang Ming also fabricated the absurdity that "Shandong is special" to resist the Center. He also defied the leaders of the Party's East China Bureau after Rao Shushi left and flaunted the province's special characteristics to turn Shandong into an independent kingdom. Like Rao Shushi, Xiang Ming followed the line of capitulation to urban capitalism. He was passive toward urban reform and wanted no restrictions against private enterprises. In rural work, he consistently resisted the Party's class policy, opposed the principle of establishing mutual aid teams and agricultural cooperatives, and advocated expansion of farm production by relying on the enthusiasm of rich peasants and spontaneous capitalist forces in the rural areas. He demanded "firm permission for a rich peasant economy to develop." Xiang Ming's capitulationist line found rampant expression in Party consolidation and the purchase of grain from the peasants and caused serious consequences. He resisted the policies of the central leadership on Party consolidation under the pretext of "opposing implementing Party consolidation in isolation." He refused to give Party members a systematic communist education and allowed spontaneous capitalist trends to develop in Party organizations. This in effect allowed capitalist ideology to corrupt our Party. In the campaign to unify grain purchase and marketing, he adopted a policy of education and negotiation with rich peasants when purchasing grain from them while coercing poor and lower-middle peasants to sell their grain. This was clearly a policy to protect the interests of rich peasants and bully the poor and lower-middle peasants, who constitute the basic masses of the Party in the rural areas. As a result, rural order was seriously disrupted and relations between the Party and the masses undermined.

It should be pointed out, however, that because of the correct leadership and high prestige of the Party's Central Committee, because instructions of the Center were conveyed directly to the provinces and municipalities, and because the majority of cadres had basically implemented the principles and policies of the central leadership, work in Shandong as a whole has advanced in the correct direction and results have been achieved. Gao Gang and Rao Shushi's mistakes were, at one stage or another, rectified by the Center. Although their covert anti-Party activities caused adverse consequences, these consequences could not offset the efforts of the majority of Party members who are loyal to the Party. Gao Gang, Rao Shushi, and others described their own mistakes as correct measures, and even attributed the achievements in these regions as a whole to their own efforts in an attempt to convince others that they were "ever correct" and "very capable." That is their big lie.

It should be understood that no Communist should regard the achievements of a locality or a department under his leadership as the results of his individual work. However wise and capable he may be, he can never achieve anything single-handedly without relying on the leadership of the Party's Central Committee and his superiors, without relying on the collective wisdom of the Party organization, without relying on the cooperation of other localities and departments, and without the strength of the broad masses of cadres and people. The wrong idea of placing one's individual role above that of the collective is incompatible with the basic principles of Marxism and the noble quality of a Communist. Gao Gang and Rao Shushi not only demonstrated their anti-Marxist thinking on the question of the role of the individual, they also tried, like all schemers, to create a myth about their own ability in order to cover up their mistakes in work.

For instance, the Northeast is our country's important industrial base and has played a big role in economic restoration and construction in the country. But it was certainly not because of Gao Gang's "ability" and "good leadership" that the Northeast region has acquired this status. From 1945 to 1948, the Center dispatched a dozen or more members of the Central Committee to supervise its work. At the time, the person chiefly in charge of the work there was Comrade Lin Biao, not Gao Gang. When Comrade Lin Biao left for China proper after the Northeast was totally liberated, the central leadership decided that the region's priority was to stabilize and restore its economy. Necessary measures were taken to ensure that its economy would not be affected by the war [to the south], and the whole nation was mobilized to support economic restoration there. Due to the leadership of the central authorities and help from the entire Party, due to Soviet aid, and because of the region's own economic resources, it was a matter of course that the Northeast should be a step ahead of the rest of the nation in achieving results and accumulating experience. In fact, the Northeast would have achieved greater results had it not been for Gao Gang's sectarian activities, which disrupted work and hampered the implementation of the policies of the Center. Gao Gang, however, has always regarded achievements in the Northeast as his personal achievement and capital. Similarly, Rao Shushi also sang his own praises and posed as a capable leader. For example, in opposing the mistakes of Comrade Li Yu in Shandong in 1947, a number of senior-ranking comrades in Shandong took a leading part in the struggle. But after the problem was resolved, Rao Shushi attributed it to himself alone in his report to the Center.

Pretending to know everything and to be capable of doing everything, posing as learned men, and attributing others' achievements to oneself—such is the self-styled "ability" of Gao Gang and Rao Shushi.

IV

How was it possible for schemers like Gao Gang and Rao Shushi to emerge in our Party?

Comrade Mao Zedong has said: The members and cadres that our Party needs are those "with a good grasp of Marxism-Leninism, political foresight, and work proficiency, who are imbued with the spirit of self-sacrifice and can solve problems independently, who remain unwavering in times of hardship, and work faithfully for the nation, the proletariat, and the Party. The Party relies on them to forge ties with Party members and the broad masses of the people, to exercise strong leadership over the masses for the goal of defeating the enemy. They should reject self-interest, individual heroism, and showing off. They are not lazy or passive, and they should reject arrogant sectarianism. They are selfless heroes of their nation and class. These are the qualities and styles worthy of members, cadres, and leaders of the Communist Party." It should be pointed out that all outstanding members and cadres of our Party are like this. By relying on them, the Party achieved great victory in the Chinese people's revolution and is striving to build our country into a great, socialist power.

At a time when our Party is leading the people of the nation in entering the first year of our First Five-Year Plan for socialist construction, i.e., 1953, there emerged in our Party the plot by the Gao Gang–Rao Shushi anti-Party alliance to overthrow the Party's Central Committee. What grave dangers are entailed in the conspiracy to seize the headquarters of China's socialist cause at this crucial juncture in class struggle! Is it possible that Gao Gang, Rao Shushi, and their like are unaware of the implications of their intrigue? Can it be a mere caper without evil intentions on their part after they have long plotted their activities at their own risk and at the risk of the Party and the country? Of course not. As we have pointed out, the emergence of such intriguers can only be a reflection of contemporary class struggle within our Party.

When the entire Party learned the truth of the Gao Gang–Rao Shushi anti-Party alliance in the course of studying the resolutions of the Fourth Plenum of the Party's Seventh Central Committee, most comrades indicated that they had gained a deeper understanding of the nature and extreme danger of such anti-Party activities. However, there were also some comrades who were politically inexperienced or not too good at observing things through class analysis, who became bewildered. How could such "big cadres" commit mistakes? Was it possible? They failed to understand it because they did not know how to look at the question against the overall background of class struggle. It should be understood that, as our country draws step by step closer to its goal of building a socialist society, contradictions between capitalist factors and socialist factors become increasingly sharp. Under the circumstances, any member of our Party who departs from the leadership and principles of the Party, persists in the bourgeois individualistic way of thinking, and guides his actions by the goal of personal power, will inevitably slide to the side of the enemies of socialism, and even become schemers like Gao Gang and Rao Shushi. The emergence of the Gao Gang–Rao Shushi anti-Party alliance is not an inexplicable event beyond the laws of class struggle. We can understand such anti-Party activities in the light of the laws of class struggle, after which we can wage a correct and effective struggle against the anti-Party elements involved. Notorious renegades such as Chen Duxiu and Zhang Guotao emerged in our Party as agents of class enemies. We have waged relentless struggles to expel such renegades. The reason some comrades found the Gao-Rao anti-Party alliance inexplicable is that they do not understand the history of the Party and class struggles in the past and at the present stage.

Some other Party members have thought that, since our Party was a long-tested party, there should have been no anti-Party schemers in our midst. This view will prevent them from acquiring a correct understanding of the Gao Gang–Rao Shushi anti-Party alliance. It should be pointed out that, on the one hand, since our Party is situated in an environment of complex class struggles and has countless ties with social forces outside the Party, it would be unrealistic to think that it can be free of renegades and degenerates. On the other hand, precisely because our Party is long-tested and under the correct leadership of the Central Committee headed by Comrade Mao Zedong and enjoys a high prestige among the people, anti-Party elements dare not openly advocate their anti-Party programs and can only engage in unprincipled and illicit activities. For the same reason, any intrigues engaged in by anti-Party elements cannot succeed or harm the foundations of our Party. On the contrary, our Party can successfully unmask and defeat these intrigues. This shows that our Party can defeat all class and national enemies and proves that our Party is a great and glorious party.

A very small number of comrades regarded the mistakes of Gao Gang and Rao Shushi as common inner-Party mistakes, not anti-Party activities. Naturally, we must, in waging struggle against mistakes, make a clear distinction between the two cases and employ correspondingly different measures. As stated in the Resolution of the Fourth Plenum of the Seventh Central Committee, in one situation, "for comrades whose shortcomings or errors are comparatively unimportant, or comrades who have serious or comparatively serious shortcomings or have committed serious or comparatively serious errors, but, having been helped by criticism, are still able to place the Party's interest above their personal interests and are willing to mend their ways and actually make amends, the policy of curing the sickness to save the patient should be adopted." In the second situation, "the Party must wage unrelenting struggle against those elements who stand up against the Party, persist in refusing to correct their errors, or even carry out factional splitting or other dangerous activities within the Party, including taking strict disciplinary action against them or even expelling them from the Party when necessary." Which category do Gao Gang and Rao Shushi's activities fall under—the first or the second? Since their anti-Party alliance has engaged in systematic activities to split the Party and overthrow the Central Committee, and they have revealed their goal of usurping the leadership of the Party and state, transforming the Party and state according to their bourgeois individualist view, and since, if their intrigues had succeeded, both our Party and state would have perished, can we still claim that their mistakes were common inner-Party mistakes? In the case of Gao Gang, who committed suicide in open defiance of the Party after his whole intrigue came to light, we cannot but consider him a despicable renegade!

V

The Central Committee holds that, to enforce Party discipline, it is necessary to expel from the Party Gao Gang, the ringleader of the anti-Party intrigue and diehard renegade, and Rao Shushi, the other ringleader of the anti-Party intrigue, and remove them from all their posts within and and outside of the Party.

In accordance with decisions of the Shandong Provincial Party Conference and the conference of senior cadres of the Northeast region, the Politburo of the Party's Central Committee has already dismissed comrades Xiang Ming, Zhang Xiushan, Zhang Mingyuan, Zhao Dezun, Ma Hong, Guo Feng, and Chen Bocun from their posts.

The Central Committee holds that the entire Party should draw a profound lesson from this struggle to defeat the Gao Gang–Rao Shushi anti-Party alliance.

To enhance Party unity as called for in the Resolution of the Fourth Plenum of the Seventh Central Committee is the basic lesson to be learned in the struggle to defeat the Gao-Rao anti-Party alliance. The whole Party must fully realize that we are now in the midst of an environment of complex and acute class struggle whether viewed in the light of the international or national situation. The Resolution of the Fourth Plenum said: "One of the most important methods of the imperialists and counterrevolutionaries for sabotaging our cause is, first and foremost, to undermine the unity of the Party and to look for agents within our Party." The entire Party, particularly high-ranking cadres of the Party, must strictly follow the provisions of the Resolution of the Fourth Plenum and strive to enhance constantly Party unity and consolidate Party unification.

In the struggle against the Gao Gang–Rao Shushi anti-Party alliance, our vigilance should be alerted by the fact that inner-Party disputes must be carried out openly and legally in the Party organization; we must strictly prohibit sectarian, splittist, and conspiratorial activities. Our Party requires all members to carry out faithfully all the decisions and instructions of the Party and, at the same time, allows contention among different opinions at Party meetings so as to distinguish right and wrong and reach correct conclusions. The Party absolutely forbids intrigues to oppose this or that person behind the back of the Party organization, such as that carried out by the schemers Gao Gang and Rao Shushi. Such activities are directly in violation of Party discipline and endanger Party unification, and are therefore anti-Party in nature. There are instances of comrades who, having heard anti-Party talk from Gao Gang, Rao Shushi, and others, failed to report them to the Party organization or ask them to voice their opinions formally in the Party organization. Such an attitude is absolutely wrong. Liberal attitudes are harmful to Party unity and helpful to the activities of anti-Party elements.

The Resolution of the Fourth Plenum said: "To strengthen Party unity, it is impermissible to restrict democracy within the Party or criticism and self-criticism within the Party; on the contrary, the full development of democracy within the Party and the full development of criticism and self-criticism within the Party must be safeguarded to avoid, in every way possible, all shortcomings and errors which can possibly be avoided, and so help the Party's cause to advance smoothly." In the organizational life of the Party, careerists like Gao Gang and Rao Shushi always try to act independently of their superiors, while establishing patriarchal rule in undertakings under their charge. They reject collective leadership, suppress democracy and criticism, and dare not engage in criticism and self-criticism in accordance with legitimate, inner-Party democratic practice. These schemers will take advantage of any lack of democracy in inner-Party life. Therefore, we must correctly promote inner-Party democracy, resolutely implement the principle of collective leadership, and develop inner-Party criticism and self-criticism, to give careerists no opportunity to carry out covert anti-Party activities.

The struggle against the Gao Gang–Rao Shushi anti-Party alliance has also enabled us to see the harmful effect of complacency and the cult of the individual. The fact that Gao Gang, Rao Shushi, and their like embarked on an anti-Party road is inseparable from their complacency in work and their reluctance to recognize their own drawbacks and mistakes and their aversion to supervision and criticism. They set themselves up as idols and promoted blind worship among their followers. All those who are conceited and cultivate the cult of the individual will always deny the collective strength and wisdom of the masses and place themselves above the masses and the Party organization, and thereby cause the revolutionary cause to suffer losses and defeats. In places where self-complacency and the cult of the individual have emerged, the principled stand of the Party will be weakened and may even completely disappear. Comrades and particularly high-ranking cadres of the whole Party must keep this lesson firmly in mind.

Without doubt, our Party encourages every member to develop fully his talent and wisdom and constantly raise it to higher levels. But, at the same time, our Party must exercise strict and systematic supervision over every member (even the most responsible members of the Party) through appropriate organizations of the Party. Without supervision from above or below, even the best members of the Party can make grave mistakes and degenerate. We Communists must follow the principle of faithfully placing our work under the supervision of the Party organization and never placing ourselves above it. In our Party, not all Party committees at every level are conscientiously implementing the system of collective leadership; supervision over Party cadres, particularly high-ranking cadres, and over Party organizations, particularly high-level Party organizations, is not frequent or strict enough. This leaves loopholes for schemers like Gao Gang and Rao Shushi to take advantage of. That is why, for a period of time, the Center was unaware of their intrigues. We must draw a serious lesson from this and perfect all necessary systems, primarily the establishment and strengthening of a system of inspection tours of the central leaders to supervise all localities in the country, for organizations at a higher level to supervise organizations at a lower level, for appropriate Party departments to supervise relevant departments of the state, and for personnel departments of cadre management to examine the performance of the cadres, to ensure that all Party members are under Party supervision. At the same time, it is necessary to establish immediately a central supervisory commission and local supervisory committees at every level to examine regularly and deal with cases of violation of rules and discipline by Party members, and wage constant and resolute struggle against elements who violate the Party Constitution and discipline, the laws and regulations of the state, and particularly to prevent the recurrence of events gravely detrimental to the Party's interests such as the case of Gao Gang and Rao Shushi.

The struggle against the Gao Gang–Rao Shushi anti-Party alliance indicates to us once again the major significance of promoting education in Marxism-Leninism and Communist ideology. It is a basic task of our Party to strengthen ideological work and wage constant struggle against all kinds of bourgeois ideas that corrupt our Party. Any weakening of work in this area is detrimental to the Party. All members of the Party must raise their level of understanding of Marxism-Leninism, sharpen their "senses" as Communists so that they can sharply and correctly distinguish between Communist and bourgeois things, and advocate and develop the former while opposing and eliminating the latter. The Party must, at the same time as it systematically transforms capitalist industry and commerce in the economic realm, systematically criticize and defeat the influence of bourgeois ideology in the ideological realm. It is particularly important for high-ranking cadres of the Party to raise their theoretical level of Marxism-Leninism; whether we do well in this study or not is the key to whether we can perform well as leaders and stand the test of rigorous class struggle. The Party requires every high-ranking cadre to study constantly and conscientiously. It will institute a rotation system of sending Party cadres at different levels to study at Party schools.

At a crucial juncture in our country's socialist development, our Party has shattered the Gao Gang–Rao Shushi anti-Party alliance. This is a historic victory for our Party and the people of our country. With the elimination of corrosive factors from within, the strengthened and consolidated Chinese Communist Party under the leadership of the Central Committee headed by Comrade Mao Zedong will constantly strengthen Party unity and more effectively rally the working class and all laboring people around itself to achieve complete victory in the great goal of socialist construction and socialist transformation of our country.

NOTES

Introduction

1. For another critique questioning this official view, see Lawrence R. Sullivan, "Leadership and Authority in the Chinese Communist Party: Perspectives from the 1950s," *Pacific Affairs* (Winter 1986–87). While sharing my skepticism, Sullivan's analysis differs significantly from mine in its belief that a "fundamental 'constitutional' conflict over the role of the leader" (p. 607) was played out in these years. In contrast, my interpretation is that there was no argument over Mao's role, only a clear disparity between that role and official "democratic" norms.

2. Cf. the assertions in the authoritative "Resolution on Certain Questions in the History of Our Party since the Founding of the People's Republic of China" that "for various historical reasons, we failed to institutionalize and legalize inner-Party democracy . . . , or we drew up the relevant laws but they lacked due authority"; *Beijing Review*, no. 27 (1981): 25–26.

3. The importance of military "factions" has been most systematically argued in William Whitson, "The Field Army in Chinese Communist Military Politics," *The China Quarterly* (*CQ*), no. 37 (1969). The present study confirms the significance of these groupings but does not support many of Whitson's assertions concerning their political and policy implications.

4. A brief overview of the Gao Gang affair based on these sources is in Frederick C. Teiwes, "Establishment and Consolidation of the New Regime," *The Cambridge History of China* (Cambridge: Cambridge University Press, 1987), 14:97–103. A further brief discussion of aspects of the case is in Frederick C. Teiwes, "Mao and His Lieutenants," *Australian Journal of Chinese Affairs* (*AJCA*), no. 19–20 (1988): 26–27.

5. E.g., see Harold C. Hinton, *The "Unprincipled Dispute" Within the Chinese Communist Top Leadership*, U.S. Information Agency IRI Intelligence Summary, no. LS-98-55, July 1955 (on agricultural cooperativization); Franz Schurmann, *Ideology and Organization in Communist China* (Berkeley: University of California Press, 1966), chap. 4 (on industrial management); and John Wilson Lewis, "Revolutionary Struggle and the Second Generation in Communist China," *CQ*, no. 21 (1965): 126–32 (on strategies of social control).

6. In this view, the case reflected a situation where the pre-1954 large administrative region had become "a camouflaged power center beyond the effective control of [Beijing]"; John Wilson Lewis, *Chinese Communist Party Leadership and the Succession to Mao Tse-tung: An Appraisal of Tensions*, U.S. Department of State Policy Research Study, January 1964, p. 9.

7. For an extreme statement of Gao as Stalin's "tool" in extending a "Soviet organizational foothold" in China, see H. F. Schurmann, "Organizational Contrasts Between

Communist China and the Soviet Union," in *Unity and Contradiction*, ed. Kurt London (New York: Frederick A. Praeger, 1962), pp. 73–74.

8. An exception is Peter S. H. Tang, "Power Struggle in the Chinese CP: The Kao-Jao Purge," *Problems of Communism* (November–December 1955). For a review of some relevant Hong Kong analyses, see Mineo Nakajima, "The Kao Kang Affair and Sino-Soviet Relations," *Review: The Study of Communism and Communist Countries in Japan* (March 1977): 16–17.

9. See Philip Bridgham, "Factionalism in the Central Committee," in *Party Leadership and Revolutionary Power in China*, ed. John Wilson Lewis (Cambridge: Cambridge University Press, 1970), pp. 205–11; Roy Franklin Grow, "The Politics of Industrial Development in China and the Soviet Union: Organizational Strategy as a Linkage Between National and World Politics," Ph.D. dissertation, University of Michigan, 1973; and Nakajima, "Kao Kang Affair."

10. Bridgham, "Factionalism," p. 206; and Frederick C. Teiwes, "The Evolution of Leadership Purges in Communist China," *CQ*, no. 41 (1970): 125.

11. Frederick C. Teiwes, *Politics and Purges in China: Rectification and the Decline of Party Norms 1950–1965* (White Plains: M. E. Sharpe, 1979), chap. 5.

12. While hardly anything was openly said about the Gao-Rao affair from 1955 to the Cultural Revolution, the case did have repercussions on the subsequent fall of several other top leaders, most notably Peng Dehuai in 1959 and Xi Zhongxun in 1962. See below, pp. 140–41.

13. The basic themes were laid down in the communiqué of the Fourth Plenum and an accompanying *Renmin Ribao (RMRB)* [People's Daily] editorial, in New China News Agency (NCNA), Beijing, February 18, 1954, in *Survey of China Mainland Press (SCMP)*, no. 751, pp. 1–8. See appendix VII-1 for excerpts from the communiqué.

14. The authoritative contemporary public statement on the case against Gao and Rao is "Resolution on the Kao Kang–Jao Shu-shih Anti-Party Alliance," NCNA, Beijing, April 4, 1955, in *Current Background (CB)*, no. 324, pp. 4–6.

15. E.g., a passing reference in the April 5, 1956, *RMRB* editorial, "On the Historical Experience of the Dictatorship of the Proletariat," in *Communist China 1955–1959: Policy Documents with Analysis*, ed. Robert K. Bowie and John K. Fairbank (Cambridge: Harvard University Press, 1965), p. 150; and a summary of the affair in Teng Hsiao-ping (Deng Xiaoping), "Report on the Revision of the Constitution of the Communist Party of China," *Eighth National Congress of the Communist Party of China* (Peking: Foreign Languages Press, 1956), 1:203–205.

16. Most notably Peng Dehuai (see *The Case of Peng Teh-huai 1959–1968* [Hong Kong: Union Research Institute, 1968], pp. 41–43); Tao Zhu (see *Pi Tao Zhanbao* [Criticize Tao Combat Bulletin] [Beijing], April 10, 1967, in *SCMP*, no. 3962, pp. 9–10); and Tan Zhenlin (see *Wenhui Bao* [Wen Hui Daily], May 20, 1968, in *SCMP*, no. 4205, pp. 4–7).

17. E.g., *RMRB*, April 18, 1968, in *SCMP*, no. 4176, pp. 5–7.

18. A case in point is the accusations of Tan Zhenlin's involvement in the affair; see chapter 2, n. 124.

19. Initially the two best-known volumes were *Mao Zedong Sixiang Wansui (WS)* [Long Live Mao Zedong Thought], 2 vols. (Taibei, 1967, 1969). By the late 1980s nearly two dozen previously unavailable volumes of Mao's talks and writings had appeared in the West. For a listing and analysis, see Timothy Cheek, "The 'Genius' Mao: A Treasure Trove of 23 Newly Available Volumes of Post-1949 Mao Zedong Texts," *AJCA*, no. 19–20 (1988): 314–15 and passim.

20. See the evaluation of the initial *Wansui* and other Mao collections in Stuart Schram, ed., *Mao Tse-tung Unrehearsed, Talks and Letters: 1956–71* (Harmondsworth: Penguin Books, 1974), pp. 49–57. See also Cheek, "The 'Genius' Mao," pp. 327–28, 332–34.

21. *Selected Works of Mao Tsetung* (*SW*), vol. 5 (Peking: Foreign Languages Press, 1977). For an overall analysis of this collection, see Stuart R. Schram, "The Origins of the Chinese Road: New Perspectives in the Light of Volume V," *CQ*, no. 74 (1978).

22. E.g., see the account in *Peking Review*, no. 51 (1977): 10–11, which places Bo Yibo's new tax system in the context of Liu Shaoqi's "counterrevolutionary revisionist line" while ignoring Zhou Enlai's role.

23. *SW*, 5:103–11. See appendix III-3B(1).

24. See appendix III-3B(2). While there is no inherent reason to assume that *Wansui* or other unofficial texts are necessarily more accurate in this regard given that they were often based on notes or transcriptions (see Schram, *Mao Unrehearsed*, p. 50), the evidence of bias in the deletions suggests that differences in wording, seemingly reflecting the same bias, may have been deliberately provided by the editors of volume 5.

A careful comparison of volume 5 to one of the *Wansui* volumes, *Mao Zedong Sixiang Wansui 1949.9–1957.12* [Long Live Mao Zedong Thought, September 1949–December 1957] (*WS 1949–1957*) (n.p., n.d.), reveals some variations in the words used but more frequently the deletion of crucial phrases or paragraphs. Perhaps the most blatant case concerned the deletion from Mao's November 15, 1956, speech to the Central Committee of remarks harshly critical of Stalin to leave a much more favorable view in volume 5; compare *WS 1949–1957*, pp. 115–16, and *SW*, 5:341–42. But more significant for the events at hand were the deletion of mitigating phrases in Mao's 1953 criticisms of Liu Shaoqi and others. See, e.g., below, p. 58. Another factor to consider is the possibility that Mao himself may have doctored these texts. As is well known, the earlier volumes of Mao's *Selected Works* were subjected to heavy editing, with Mao himself retaining the final word. See the account of this process for volume 4 in *RMRB*, October 22, 1987, in Foreign Broadcast Information Service, *Daily Report: People's Republic of China* (FBIS), October 27, 1987, p. 22; and, more generally, Cheek, "The 'Genius' Mao," pp. 322–26. According to oral sources, Mao retained similar authority over the process of editing volume 5, which began in 1961. Thus it is conceivable that Mao's original words were altered by the Chairman himself or others involved in the editorial process subject to his approval, in contexts quite different from the situation prevailing when volume 5 was published. That is, the texts may reflect Mao's meaning but not his meaning at the time they were originally delivered.

25. Cf. Cheek, "The 'Genius' Mao," p. 334.

26. *SW*, 5:106–107.

27. Ibid., p. 386.

28. The revival of Party history is analyzed in Susanne Weigelin-Schwiedrzik, "Party Historiography in the People's Republic of China," *AJCA*, no. 17 (1987).

29. For typical examples, see *Zhonggong Dangshi 170 ti Wenda* [Questions and Answers on 170 Topics in CCP History] (Shenyang: Liaoning renmin chubanshe, 1984), pp. 260–62; and Zhonggong Jiangxi Shengwei Dangxiao Dangshi Jiaoyanshi [Jiangxi Province CCP Party School Party History Teaching and Research Office], *Zhonggong Dangshi Baiti Jieda* [Answers on 100 Topics in CCP History] (Nanchang: Jiangxi renmin chubanshe, 1984), pp. 303–306.

30. "Resolution on Questions in History," p. 17; and Zhongong Zhongyang Wenxian Yanjiushi [CCP Central Committee Documents Research Office], *Guanyu Jianguo yilai Dang de Ruogan Lishi Wenti de Jueyi Zhuyiben (xiuding)* [Revised Notes on the Resolution on Certain Questions in the History of Our Party since the Founding of the People's Republic of China] (Beijing: Renmin chubanshe, 1985).

31. E.g., Zhonggong Dangshi Yanjiushi [CCP Central Committee Party History Research Office], *Zhonggong Dangshi Nianbiao* [Chronology of Major Events in CCP History] (Beijing: Renmin chubanshe, 1987), p. 259, makes no mention of the crucial December 24,

1953, Politburo meeting where Gao Gang's efforts were comprehensively rebuffed.

32. See appendices III-2A(1-3), IV-1, V-4, and VI-1. While some of these accounts are not strictly memoirs, they clearly draw on the memories of the concerned leaders. Note also that appendix V-5 appeared before the 1978 plenum; however, the real explosion of memoir and related literature came from 1979.

33. *Liu Shaoqi Xuanji* [Selected Works of Liu Shaoqi] (Beijing: Renmin chubanshe, 1985), 2:125–31; *Zhou Enlai Xuanji* [Selected Works of Zhou Enlai] (Beijing: Renmin chubanshe, 1984), 2:119–28; and *Chen Yun Wenxuan (1949–1956)* [Selected Works of Chen Yun, 1949–1956] (Beijing: Renmin chubanshe, 1984), pp. 229–33.

34. *Selected Works of Deng Xiaoping (1975–1982)* (Beijing: Foreign Languages Press, 1984), pp. 278–79.

35. Ibid., pp. 278–79, 293–94.

36. Strictly speaking, there is considerable overlap of internal publications and these materials since many chronologies and memoirs that are readily available in bookstores have routinely been classified as *neibu*. The usage here refers especially to materials that are generally tightly held within Chinese work units.

37. Chen Shihui, "Guanyu fandui Gao Gang, Rao Shushi Fandang Yinmou Huodong de Wenti" [Questions Concerning Opposition to the Anti-Party Conspiratorial Activities of Gao Gang and Rao Shushi], *Jiaoxue Cankao* [Teaching Reference] (Zhonggong Anhui shengwei dangxiao tushu ziliaoshi, December 1980), pp. 95–106. Chen has also published two open articles jointly with other scholars dealing with the case in less detail in *Xinshiqi* [New Period], no. 8 (1981): 16–17; and *Dangshi Yanjiu* [Research on Party History] (*DSYJ*), no. 4 (1982): 21–27.

38. *Zhonggong Dangshi Jiaoxue Cankao Ziliao* [CCP History Teaching Reference Materials] (*ZDJCZ*), vols. 19 and 20 (Zhongguo Jiefangjun Guofang Daxue dangshi dangjian zhenggong jiaoyanshi, March and April 1986). Five of the seven documents in question are translated in full or part in appendixes III-3A, VII-2A and 2B, VII-3, and VIII-1. The remaining documents are Rao Shushi's October 27, 1953, concluding speech to the Organization Conference and an April 24, 1954, Northeast Bureau decision on the Gao-Rao issue.

39. Ma Hong served as president of the Chinese Academy of Social Sciences from 1982 to 1986, while Guo Feng served as first secretary of Liaoning province from 1983 until retirement in 1985.

40. The Hong Kong journal *Zhengming* [Contention] (September 1980): 40, in an otherwise well-informed article (see below, n. 46), stated that some Central Committee members wanted to resolve the Gao Gang question, but only Ma Hong and Guo Feng—neither of whom was a Central Committee member at the time—were mentioned by name.

41. *Zhengming* (November 1980): 18 claims that Deng Xiaoping issued a directive concerning the Gao case stipulating that Mao's political tactics not be discussed. While I have no independent confirmation of this claim, the issue has clearly been untouchable in both open and *neibu* sources.

42. For an argument on this point, see Frederick C. Teiwes, *Leadership, Legitimacy, and Conflict in China: From a Charismatic Mao to the Politics of Succession* (Armonk: M. E. Sharpe, 1984), pp. 76ff.

43. Liao Kai-lung (Liao Gailong), "Historical Experiences and Our Road of Development" (October 25, 1980), part 2, *Issues & Studies* (November 1981): 91. In this somewhat free-wheeling internal report, Liao dealt gingerly with Mao's pre-1957 abuse of democratic procedures, such as his 1955 attack on Deng Zihui (part 1, *Issues & Studies* [October 1981]: 77), but still reached the "full play to democracy" conclusion for the entire 1935–1957 period.

44. See Li Weihan's comments on how the Gao issue adversely affected the study of

border region history; *Zhonggong Dangshi Ziliao* [CCP History Materials] (Beijing: Zhonggong dangshi ziliao chubanshe, 1985), 14:6.

45. E.g., see the usage adopted in "Resolution on Questions in History," p. 17. Cf. Hu Hua's 1981 paper at a Party history conference where a ritual listing of anti-Party schemers included such old standbys as Wang Ming, Lin Biao, and Jiang Qing, but not Gao Gang; *Chinese Law and Government* (*CLG*) (Fall 1986): 86. See also below, p. 46.

46. Apart from these sources, the only other accounts reporting Mao's discussions with Gao I am aware of are two articles in *Zhengming* (September 1980): 40–41 and (November 1980): 18–19, which themselves rely on oral sources.

This study has not relied upon Hong Kong or Taiwan sources although I have consulted them. Although some of these sources seem very well informed, many are clearly speculative and wide of the mark. For example, the account of the Gao-Rao affair in Han Shanbi, *Deng Xiaoping Pingzhuan* [Critical Biography of Deng Xiaoping], vol. 2 (1950–1970) (Hong Kong: East and West Culture Co., 1987), chap. 2, is fundamentally at variance with PRC sources. However, where such sources appear generally credible and provide potentially illuminating information, said information is included in the notes. See, e.g., above, nn. 40, 41; and below, chap. 4, nn. 51, 63.

47. See Weigelin-Schwiedrzik's discriminating analysis, "Party Historiography," pp. 83–85.

48. Only one authoritative source actually offered the information on Mao's talks with Gao. The most others would say is that Gao acted because of illusions resulting from the high esteem in which he was held by the Chairman. Nevertheless, the story was confirmed by two significant sources. First, an individual personally involved in the affair acknowledged this account after I relayed it to him. Second, a scholar specializing in the period read in Chinese translation the section of my *Cambridge History* chapter dealing with case, said it was very good, and only raised a question of evidence concerning a secondary point. In other interviews I attempted to elicit further confirmation by asking why Gao launched his activities, but, given the apparent taboo, I chose not to raise it directly.

49. For a similar judgment, see Roderick MacFarquhar, *The Origins of the Cultural Revolution*, vol. 2: *The Great Leap Forward 1958–1960* (New York: Columbia University Press, 1983), pp. 434–35.

Chapter 1

1. The following draws on Teiwes, "Establishment of the New Regime," pp. 56–57; and Teiwes, "Mao and His Lieutenants," pp. 9–15, 35–44.
2. *WS*, 1969, p. 479.
3. The "Resolution on Questions in History," p. 16, refers to this tension as an inevitable "struggle between restriction [of capitalism] and opposition to restriction."
4. For a detailed summary of this decision, see *Yan'an Zhengfeng Yundong Jishi* [Record of Events in the Yan'an Rectification Movement] (Zhangjiakou: Qiushi chubanshe, 1982), pp. 368–69.
5. See Peng Dehuai's account of this decision in *Peng Dehuai Zishu* [Peng Dehuai's Self-statement] (Beijing: Renmin chubanshe, 1981), pp. 257–58.
6. Perhaps the most important example of this came in 1956 when Mao apparently accepted the consensus of economic specialists on the need to slow down the pace of growth despite his misgivings; see Teiwes, *Politics and Purges*, pp. 213–14. It is also notable in the case at hand that although Mao was critical of other leaders in 1953 for positions impinging on the process of socialist transformation, no evidence has been found of any dissent on his part concerning the pace of economic growth per se.
7. For a more detailed analysis, see Teiwes, "Mao and His Lieutenants," pp. 35–44.

8. At the Seventh Congress and after, Zhu De as the leader of the Communist armies was sometimes listed second after Mao, but it was widely understood within the CCP that the actual order was Mao, Liu, Zhou, and Zhu. Until 1950 Ren Bishi was the fifth secretary, but after his death Chen Yun, who up to then had ranked sixth in the leadership, took over Ren's position. Cf. Teiwes, "Mao and His Lieutenants," p. 8n.; and Zhongguo Geming Bowuguan Dangshi Yanjiushi [Party History Research Office of the Museum of the Chinese Revolution], ed., *Dangshi Yanjiu Ziliao* [Party History Research Materials] (Chengdu: Sichuan renmin chubanshe, 1982), 3:659.

9. Mao's wife, Jiang Qing, described him as "the silent type [who] does not talk much"; see Roxane Witke, *Comrade Chiang Ch'ing* (Boston: Little, Brown, 1977), p. 340. For another suggestion of a somewhat standoffish personality, see the report that on the Long March, "Mao almost always stayed in a house separate from his comrades"; Harrison E. Salisbury, *The Long March: The Untold Story* (New York: Harper and Row, 1985), p. 242.

10. See Chen Yun's 1962 account of Mao's reticent style when discussing problems; *Chen Yun Wenxuan (1956–1985)* [Selected Works of Chen Yun, 1956–1985] (Beijing: Renmin chubanshe, 1986), p. 180.

11. Chang Kuo-tao (Zhang Guotao), "Mao—A New Portrait by an Old Colleague," *The New York Times Magazine*, August 2, 1953, p. 47.

12. An oral source who worked on Zhou's staff in 1949 reported almost continuous communication with Mao by phone or in person. Although, according to another oral source, only Secretariat members could phone directly at any time, Politburo member Gao Gang had no problem arranging access while Rao, who was not even of Politburo status, was able to secure a late-night audience with Mao almost immediately. See below, p. 44.

The possibility of, but also the inhibitions on, access in this period is also suggested by the post-Mao account cited in MacFarquhar, *Origins*, 2:194–95, of Peng Dehuai bursting into Mao's bedroom to argue a point during the Korean war. As MacFarquhar notes, Mao's reported comment that only Peng would do such a thing undoubtedly meant that no one else would dare approach him in such a manner.

13. E.g., in the Cultural Revolution the supersensitive Zhou Enlai realized that direct approaches to Mao were a dangerous tactic to be used sparingly; Percy Jucheng Fang and Lucy Guinong J. Fang, *Zhou Enlai—A Profile* (Beijing: Foreign Languages Press, 1986), pp. 165–66.

14. See Mao's June 4, 1950, letter to Liu in Michael Y. M. Kau and John K. Leung, eds., *The Writings of Mao Zedong, 1949–1976*, vol. 1: *September 1949–December 1955* (WM) (Armonk, N.Y.: M. E. Sharpe, 1986), pp. 95–96.

15. Oral sources. See the discussion of Mao's relations with Liu Shaoqi below, pp. 41–44. An exception from a somewhat earlier period was the 1944 criticism of Peng Dehuai. See Frederick C. Teiwes, "Peng Dehuai and Mao Zedong," *AJCA*, no. 16 (1986): 85–86; and below, p. 106. Another exception was criticism of Wang Ming at the June 1950 Central Committee plenum; *Dangshi Yanjiu Ziliao*, 3:661.

16. For an extended critique of the view that Mao consistently relied on divide-and-rule tactics, see Teiwes, "Mao and His Lieutenants," pp. 44–56.

17. E.g., Zhengzhi Xueyuan Zhonggong Dangshi Jiaoyanshi [CCP History Teaching and Research Office of the Political Academy], *Zhongguo Gongchandang Liushinian Dashi Jianjie* [Brief Introduction to Major Events in the CCP's Sixty Years] (Beijing: Jiefangjun Zhengzhi Xueyuan chubanshe, 1985), p. 405.

18. NCNA, Shenyang, December 5, 1952. Over a year later Gao was reported in the Northeast one last time by NCNA, Anshan, December 26, 1953. I am indebted to Timothy Cheek for assistance in tracing the movements of Gao, Rao, and other leaders through the biographical files of the U.S. Consulate General, Hong Kong.

19. "Deng Xiaoping, Chen Yi, Tan Zhenlin guanyu Rao Shushi Wenti Zuotanhui de Baogao" [Report by Deng Xiaoping, Chen Yi, and Tan Zhenlin on the Discussion Meeting concerning the Rao Shushi Question] (March 1, 1954), in ZDJCZ, 20:273.
20. NCNA, Shanghai, February 25, 1953, in *SCMP*, no. 519, pp. 30–31.
21. For a general discussion of these regions and their fading out, see Teiwes, "Establishment of the New Regime," pp. 79–83, 95.
22. Zhonggong Zhongyang Wenxian Yanjiushi [CCP Central Committee Documents Research Office] and Xinhua Tongxunshe [New China News Agency], eds., *Deng Xiaoping* (Beijing: Zhongyang wenxian chubanshe, 1988), p. 50; and Wolfgang Bartke, *Who's Who in the People's Republic of China* (Armonk, N.Y.: M. E. Sharpe, 1981), p. 52.
23. Donald W. Klein and Anne B. Clark, *Biographic Dictionary of Chinese Communism* (Cambridge: Harvard University Press, 1971), 1:313.
24. See Deng's biography in Hu Hua, ed., *Zhonggong Dangshi Renwu Zhuan* [Biographies of Personalities in CCP History] (*ZDRZ*) (Xi'an: Shaanxi renmin chubanshe, 1983), 7:366; and *Ta Kung Pao* [Impartial Daily] (Hong Kong), December 8, 1952, in *SCMP*, no. 468, pp. 18–19.
25. See the listing of regional officals appointed at the start of 1953 in NCNA, Beijing, January 18, 1953, in *SCMP*, no. 494, pp. 1–27.
26. These conclusions are based on a systematic reading of *SCMP* and *CB* for the period November 1952–February 1954, plus the biographical files of the U.S. Consulate General, Hong Kong. An apparent exception was Deng Xiaoping's appearance at a Southwest regional meeting in December 1952; NCNA, Chongqing, December 17, 1952, in *SCMP*, no. 475, p. 25. Oral sources in the Southwest, however, believe that Deng was basically absent from the area after his transfer to Beijing.
27. The poor state of Lin's health is confirmed by *Dangshi Yanjiu Ziliao*, 3:659; Tan Zhongji et al., eds., *Shinianhou de Pingshuo—Wenhua Dageming Shilunji* [Reviews and Comments after Ten Years—Collection of Historical Essays on the Cultural Revolution] (Beijing: Zhonggong dangshi ziliao chubanshe, 1987), p. 61; and oral sources. In addition, the appointment of Ye Jianying as acting first secretary and acting commander in the Central-South in May 1953 suggests that Lin was formally on sick leave as of that date; Junshi Kexueyuan "Ye Jianying Zhuan" Bianxiezu [Military Science Academy's "Ye Jianying Biography" Writing Group], *Ye Jianying Zhuanlüe* [Brief Biography of Ye Jianying] (Beijing: Junshi kexue chubanshe, 1987), p. 225.
28. This was particularly emphasized by an authoritative oral source. Mao also noted Deng's military accomplishments when restoring him to duty in 1973; see Teiwes, "Mao and His Lieutenants," pp. 69–70.
29. Rao assumed this post in 1942 and thus held a leading military position during the final years of the Anti-Japanese war and throughout the civil war. However, he does not figure large in accounts of the major military events of the late 1940s in East China, even where those accounts were written before his fall. Klein and Clarke, *Biographic Dictionary*, 1:409.
30. Gao's largely civilian role is relatively clear for the 1937–1945 period when he held key Party and government posts in the Northwest, but somewhat less so for the Northeast after 1945; see ibid., 1:431–32. Cf. Steven I. Levine, *Anvil of Victory: The Communist Revolution in Manchuria, 1945–1948* (New York: Columbia University Press, 1987), where there is virtually no reference to any military role on Gao's part.
31. The following is based on Chen Shihui, "Guanyu fandui Gao Gang," p. 96; ZDJCZ, 20: 268, 518; and oral sources.
32. In formal status terms, Gao clearly remained below Liu, Zhou, and Zhu De, who were the only leaders identified as Mao's "close comrades-in-arms" during this period. The case of Chen Yun is less clear since on formal occasions state rank (where Gao as a

vice-chairman of the Central People's Government Council outranked Vice-Premier Chen as well as Zhou) was normally used. In December 1953, however, when Mao and his "old comrades" voted in local elections, the order listed was Mao, Liu, Zhou, Zhu, Chen, and Gao. See NCNA, Beijing, May 1, 1952, in *SCMP*, no. 327, p. 1; ibid., October 1, 1952, in *SCMP*, no. 428, pp. 1, 3; ibid., May 1, 1953, in *SCMP*, no. 562, p. 2; *RMRB*, October 3, 1953, p. 1; and NCNA, Beijing, December 10, 1953, in *SCMP*, no. 707, p. 24. While there is some basis for arguing that Chen Yun was temporarily eclipsed by Gao Gang in the first half of 1953, this may be explained by Chen's poor health. Political reasons are also possible. See below, p. 29.

33. Deng Xiaoping, "Guanyu Gao Gang, Rao Shushi Fandang Lianmeng de Baogao" [Report on the Gao Gang–Rao Shushi Anti-Party Alliance] (March 21, 1955), in *ZDJCZ*, 20:518.

34. E.g., *Liushinian Dashi Jianjie*, p. 405. Such allegations, which are stated particularly forcefully in the 1954–55 documents collected in *ZDJCZ*, 20:269, 296–97, 518, include charges of reporting only good news to the Center, resisting investigation and criticism by the central authorities, downplaying the role of the Center, emphasizing the "special nature" of the Northeast, devising "various left or right policies" to oppose central policy, and even refusing to carry out central directives. There is little doubt that such phenomena occurred, but their significance should not be overstated. I am struck by the vague nature of most of these accusations; the more concrete ones concern Gao's effort to build up the Northeast's and his own prestige by claiming credit for the region's successes without adequately acknowledging central support. The other charges seem to amount to the inevitable exploitation of "empty spaces" in the relations of branch (central) and area (local) authorities (ibid., pp. 316–17) rather than to any systematic "opposition" to Beijing. The verdict of the April 1954 Northeast Bureau meeting that the region had basically carried out the line and policies of the Center (ibid., p. 296) is clear evidence on this point. See also below, n. 35.

35. For a comprehensive argument rejecting the view of the Northeast as an independent power center, see Teiwes, *Politics and Purges*, pp. 186–91.

36. Ma Hong, Guo Feng, Zhang Mingyuan, Zhang Xiushan, and Zhao Dezun, who all held leading posts in the Northeast Party Bureau under Gao but did not themselves have great seniority in the CCP. See *SW*, 5:168; Teiwes, *Politics and Purges*, p. 185; and below, pp. 130–32. The term "five tiger generals" in Chinese folklore refers to five famous warriors from the Three Kingdoms period.

37. Mao's criticism apparently came after Gao's transfer, but whether it was early in the piece or only after Gao's disgrace is unclear. See Chen Shihui, "Guanyu fandui Gao Gang," p. 96; and *ZDJCZ*, 20:297, 518. For further evidence of Gao shunting Lin Feng aside in the period before Gao's transfer, see Lin's biography in Klein and Clark, *Biographic Dictionary*, 1:555.

38. An oral source reports such ambivalence on the part of He Long, a figure regarded favorably in post-Mao China, concerning his assignment to central duties.

39. Rao Shushi was also accused of a similar attitude, including regarding his appointment in Beijing as "luring the tiger out of the mountains"; Deng Xiaoping, "Guanyu Gao, Rao," p. 519. This, together with other charges that Rao too set up an "independent kingdom," regarded East China as special, etc., naturally raises doubts that Rao is simply being tarred with the same brush as Gao. What is striking, however, is the specificity of allegations concerning Rao's dominance as the local king in East China, particularly that he was able to use close followers virtually to negate the function of the Shanghai Municipal Party Committee under Chen Yi; ibid. Also of interest in this regard is 1954 criticism of Chen on the grounds that he was too apprehensive in his relations with Rao and did not expose him to the Center early enough; *ZDJCZ*, 20:315. Thus, like Gao Gang, Rao's preeminent regional position involved vast powers giving pause to even so high-ranking an

5:340; and Chen Shihui, "Guanyu fandui Gao Gang," p. 96.

144. Liao Kai-lung, "Historical Experiences," *Issues & Studies* (October 1981): 79, speaks of Stalin regarding Gao as a Zhang Zuolin figure, i.e., a local warlord susceptible to foreign pressure. In fact, according to oral sources, Stalin used the Zhang Zuolin analogy openly and jokingly when Gao visited Moscow in 1949 with Liu Shaoqi.

145. In particular, according to an oral source, Gao won Soviet favor by providing the Soviet army with supplies in 1949–1950 when natural disasters caused a grain shortage.

146. According to one oral source, Alexi Kosygin, who in the early 1950s was deputy chairman of the Council of Ministers and minister of light industry, was dispatched to the Northeast on business by Stalin and held talks with Gao. Besides the discussions with Soviet officials, there are also indications of similar questionable contacts with North Korean leaders; see *ZDJCZ*, 20:296.

147. This dating is based on *Khrushchev Remembers: The Last Testament*, trans. and ed. Strobe Talbott (Boston: Little, Brown, 1974), p. 243, where Khrushchev refers to Gao's conversations with Ambassador Panyushkin; and "Chronology of Events, January–April 1953," pp. 5, 11, which gives Panyushkin's tour of duty as December 1952–March 1953.

148. *Khrushchev Remembers: The Last Testament*, pp. 243–44; and oral sources basing their information on Chinese data. The question of Stalin's motives in revealing the talks to Mao left Khrushchev mystified, while an oral source speculated that Stalin realized the danger to Sino-Soviet relations of overly intimate ties. This source further recounted another apparent act of distancing himself from Gao whereby Stalin recalled and had executed a Soviet adviser who had served Gao.

149. If we take Khrushchev literally that Stalin handed over the reports in a conversational manner (ibid., p. 243), then the incident would have taken place during their only meeting in early 1950. Oral sources also report Stalin turning over information on Gao's contacts with Soviet officials to Mao as early as 1950; however, it is unclear whether this included statements about Liu and Zhou or just referred to the passing on of materials concerning military and natural resources matters in the Northeast. The latter incident reportedly was not regarded as a significant mistake.

One oral source, a retired Party official, was the only such source to see Gao's Soviet links as a major factor in his downfall. On balance, I regard this source as less well-placed than others, and this view as not fitting the overall pattern of evidence. One should note, however, that if this indeed was the case, then the interpretation of Mao's talks with Gao as setting Gao up for a fall (see above, p. 38) becomes viable. In particular, if Mao's talks with Gao took place *after* Stalin's death, then the possibility that Mao was setting in motion an anti-Gao maneuver with his Soviet "patron" no longer on the scene would reflect a certain logic. But again, given the overall pattern of evidence, I believe this to be extremely unlikely.

150. For an earlier discussion of this factor, see Teiwes, *Politics and Purges*, p. 193.

151. See below, p. 128. All of the above explanations of Mao's possible motives in not reacting were suggested by oral sources.

152. For a subsequent expression of Mao's ambivalent feelings toward Stalin and the Soviet Union, see Schram, *Mao Unrehearsed*, pp. 96–103. An authoritative oral source states that Mao was never on really good terms with the Soviet Union, but oral sources generally emphasize the importance and respect he attached to Moscow and Stalin.

153. For example, Li Fuchun, who apparently had special responsibilities for negotiating economic matters with the Soviet Union. See *Bujin de Shinian*, pp. 416–20; Huai En, *Zhou Zongli Shengping Dashiji* [Chronology of Premier Zhou's Life] (Chengdu: Sichuan renmin chubanshe, 1986), p. 360; and NCNA, Beijing, September 15, 1953, in *SCMP*, no. 651, p. 3.

154. It is unclear from my oral source whether Mao specifically mentioned Malenkov in the Soviet context or Chen, Deng, and/or Lin in the Chinese one. Of course, what would

123. A typical example is the extensive year-by-year listing of Liu's crimes in with Liu Shao-ch'i" (Red Guard pamphlet), in *CB*, no. 834, August 17, 1967, 13. Also note the general conclusion that of all the charges laid against Liu Shao Cultural Revolution, a relatively small proportion dealt with the 1949–1953 period Dittmer, *Liu Shao-ch'i and the Chinese Cultural Revolution: The Politics of Mass C* (Berkeley: University of California Press, 1974), p. 311.

124. According to an authoritative oral source, Rao was on the list of 21 personally selected by Mao for inclusion in *The Great Soviet Encylopedia* at the r the Soviet Communist Party. See table 3.

125. For various statements concerning Rao's lust to control his units over t 1943–1953 period, his desire to be the sole power in East China, and his claims th China was special," see *Shishi Shouce* [Current Events Handbook], April 25, *SCMP*, no. 1052, p. 10; Xiao Xiaoqin and Li Liangzhi, *Zhongguo Gemingshi* Revolutionary History] (Hongqi chubanshe, 1984), 2:27; and *Zhonggong Dangs Wenda*, p. 261. Cf. above, n. 39.

126. "Deng, Chen, Tan guanyu Rao," p. 274; Deng Xiaoping, "Guanyu Ga p. 519; and oral sources.

127. Chen Shihui, "Guanyu fandui Gao Gang," p. 97; *Huiyi Chen Yi* [Remem Yi] (Beijing: Renmin chubanshe, 1980), p. 73; "Deng, Chen, Tan guanyu Rao," pp and oral source.

128. "Deng, Chen, Tan guanyu Rao," p. 274; Chen Shihui, "Guanyu fa Gang," p. 97; and oral source.

129. Cf. above, n. 39.

130. While various sources state Rao's belief in Gao's success, Chen Shihui, fandui Gao Gang," p. 97, explicitly claims he believed that Gao had displac successor.

131. The most important career links were in the late 1920s when Rao served in the Northeast underground, and when he was Liu's deputy political commissar i Fourth Army in the early 1940s. Klein and Clark, *Biographic Dictionary*, 1:408 Zhang Guangxin and Yang Shuzhen, eds., *Zhonggong Dangshi Shijian Ming Jianshi* [Brief Explanations of Events, Terms and Personalities in CCP Histor Shaanxi renmin chubanshe, 1985), pp. 377, 463.

132. Chen Shihui, "Guanyu fandui Gao Gang," p. 97.

133. *Dangshi Huiyi Baogaoji* [Collection of Reports to the Party History Co (Beijing: Zhonggong zhongyang dangxiao chubanshe, 1982), p. 85.

134. See "Resolution on Kao-Jao Alliance," p. 4; Deng Xiaoping, "Gu Rao," pp. 520–21; and *Huiyi Chen Yi*, pp. 70–71. Rao's rightist mistakes allegedl "surrender to the capitalists, landlords, and rich peasants in the cities and countr

135. Oral sources.

136. E.g., *Geming he Jianshe Wenda*, p. 86; and He Xin, Wang Jiaxun, Mingxian, *Zhongguo Gongchandang Shigang* [Outline History of the CCP Beijing Daxue chubanshe, 1986), p. 337.

137. At the May 10, 1954, East China Bureau meeting dealing with the cas 20:314.

138. Ibid., pp. 275, 314, 515; *SW*, 5:161–62; oral sources; and above, p. 12.

139. Chen Shihui, "Guanyu fandui Gao Gang," p. 97.

140. Ibid.

141. For an earlier review of the evidence on this issue, see Teiwes, *Politics c* pp. 191–94.

142. For a comprehensive review of Soviet sources, see Nakajima, "Kao Ka

143. E.g., *Hong Tianxun* [Red Dispatch], March 1968, in *SCMP*, no. 414:

played the same role under Chen in the Northeast's financial and economic committee in the late 1940s. Klein and Clark, *Biographic Dictionary*, 1:151, 495–96.

66. Cf. above, n. 56.

67. According to an authoritative oral source, immediately after Chen returned to China from the Soviet Union in the company of Wang Ming in late 1937, Mao engaged him in private conversations to determine the situation in Moscow, which had such important implications for Mao's political position vis-à-vis Wang. Thereafter, Chen worked closely with Mao in the organizational sphere and also began his career as the Chairman's most trusted economic official. Cf. Bachman, *Chen Yun*, pp. 14ff.

68. See ibid., pp. 40–41.

69. See ibid., p. 30; Deng Liqun, "Xiang Chen Yun Tongzhi Xuexi," p. 85; and NCNA, July 14, 1984, in FBIS, July 25, 1984, p. K5.

70. Cf. David Bachman's excellent statement of one of Chen's key rules of political action, "Do not argue with Mao. Try to win him over behind the scenes and defer to his wishes once he has made up his mind. Retire from political activity rather than be forced into a situation where conflict with the Chairman is inevitable"; *Chen Yun*, p. 147. Quite independently, an authoritative oral source offered an analysis of Chen along these lines.

71. See below, pp. 60–61, 67–68. A very well-placed oral source agreed to the proposition that during the events of 1953 Chen was relaxed and demonstrated a good understanding of Mao.

72. In particular, both *Selected Works of Deng Xiaoping*, p. 278; and Hu Hua, ed., *Zhongguo Shehuizhuyi Geming he Jiansheshi Jiangyi* [Lectures on the History of China's Socialist Revolution and Construction] (Beijing: Zhongguo Renmin Daxue chubanshe, 1985), p. 89, assert these developments happened at "the end of 1953," while Chen Shihui, "Guanyu fandui Gao Gang," p. 98, speaks only of those plans being made "in 1953," and Hao Mangbi and Duan Haoran, *Liushinian*, p. 424, state that several of the associated issues were under discussion in "spring 1953."

73. Documentary evidence supporting this assertion is the appearance of an article in the CCP's theoretical journal, *Xuexi* [Study], September 1, 1952, in *CB*, no. 215, reviewing the first five Party congresses. It appears, however, that a National Party Conference, initially scheduled for February 1953, was to be held first; *ZDJCZ*, 20:256.

74. "Chronology of Events in Communist China, January–April 1953," in *CB*, no. 321, March 15, 1955, p. 3.

75. Oral sources indicate that Mao's health had been periodically weak since 1946 and assert the Chairman planned a holiday partly for health reasons before the intensification of Gao Gang's activities in the latter part of the year. More problematically, Cultural Revolution sources (see chap. 2, n. 124) suggest that Mao's health was an issue by the time of the Financial and Economic Conference. Cf. below, p. 117.

76. Chen Shihui, "Guanyu fandui Gao Gang," p. 98.

77. *Guanyu Lishi Wenti Jueyi*, p. 226.

78. I have not been able to locate written references to *fan maojin* before fall 1953 (see below, pp. 89–90), but this was clearly the theme of the many attacks on "blind rash advance" (*mangmu maojin*), "adventurism" (*maoxian zhuyi*), "impetuous attitudes" (*jizao taidu*), and similar deviations.

79. Both directives appear in *RMRB*, March 26, 1953, in *CB*, no. 240, pp. 3–18.

80. NCNA, Beijing, January 13, 1953, in *SCMP*, no. 492, p. 5; and ibid., February 17, 1953, in *CB*, no. 230, p. 12.

81. E.g., see *RMRB*, November 18, 1952, in *SCMP*, no. 456, p. 10; ibid., April 28, 1953, in *SCMP*, no. 565, pp. 18–19; NCNA, Beijing, November 5, 1953, in *SCMP*, no. 689, pp. 18–20; ibid., December 29, 1953, in *SCMP*, no. 719, p. 11; Fang Weizhong, *Jingji Dashiji*, pp. 95, 107; and Zhonggong Zhongyang Wenxian Yanjiushi, *Zhu De Nianpu* [Chronicle of

Zhu De] (Beijing: Renmin chubanshe, 1986), pp. 369–70, 372.

82. See the various SPC decisions in this respect in "Dangdai Zhongguo de Jihua Gongzuo" Bangongshi ["Contemporary China Planning Work" Office], *Zhonghua Renmin Gongheguo Guomin Jingji he Shehui Fazhan Jihua Dashi Jiyao 1949–1985* [Summary of Events in PRC National Economic and Social Development Planning 1949–1985] (Beijing: Hongqi chubanshe, 1987), pp. 37–41.

83. See Thomas, *Government and Administration*, pp. 116–17; and below, pp. 54, 58–59.

84. Chen Shihui, "Guanyu fandui Gao Gang," p. 98.

85. For these developments, see Mark Selden, *The Yenan Way in Revolutionary China* (Cambridge: Harvard University Press, 1971), pp. 39–71, 200–203. According to one well-informed oral source, Mao was particularly impressed by the parallel repression suffered by himself and Gao. For an account suggesting that Gao was less than totally happy with Mao's "Party Center" over its handling of the matter, see Warren Kuo, *Analytical History of The Chinese Communist Party*, Book 3 (Taipei: Institute of International Relations, 1970), pp. 126ff.

86. "Correcting Unorthodox Tendencies in Learning, the Party, and Literature and Art" (February 1, 1942), in *A Documentary History of Chinese Communism*, ed. Conrad Brandt, Benjamin Schwartz and John K. Fairbank (New York: Atheneum, 1966), p. 387.

87. By 1952, the Northeast accounted for 52 percent of China's industrial output. The region played a model role in various movements, most notably the 1951–52 Three-Anti Campaign focusing on urban corruption. See Teiwes, "Establishment of the New Regime," pp. 82–83.

An earlier case where Mao used a regional model to push a set of policies concerned the Jin-Cha-Ji Border Region under Nie Rongzhen and Peng Zhen in 1939 and 1940. This case had a similar effect of advancing the careers of particular Party leaders, most notably Peng Zhen. Timothy Charles Cheek, "Orthodoxy and Dissent in People's China: The Life and Death of Deng Tuo (1912–1966)," Ph.D. dissertation, Harvard University, 1986, pp. 98–99; and oral source. While this is perhaps suggestive of a leadership pattern on Mao's part, my basic feeling is that given the circumstances where large-scale economic construction began first in the Northeast, some model role for the region was inevitable in the early 1950s.

88. For examples of such derision in a variety of sources, see *Zhongguo Qingnian* [China's Youth], April 16, 1955, in *SCMP*, no. 1036, p. 15; *Chen Yun Wenxuan (1949–1956)*, p. 232; and Chen Shihui, "Guanyu fandui Gao Gang," p. 96.

89. A relevant example given Cultural Revolution accusations against Liu Shaoqi in this regard is Gao's statements concerning Party members who sought individual riches. In 1950 Gao was tolerant of such Communists, but in 1952 he sharply condemned those who hired labor and lent at usurious rates. See Thomas P. Bernstein, "Problems in Village Leadership after Land Reform," *CQ*, no. 36 (1968): 5, 10; and below, pp. 72–73.

90. See *Jihua Dashi Jiyao*, p. 36.

91. See *RMRB*, October 1, 1952, in *CB*, no. 219, pp. 16–22. In this article Gao also warned against the adventurist tendency in economic construction. The view of Gao as a "rightist" on cooperativization is argued in Hinton, *Unprincipled Dispute*.

92. See *Renmin Shouce 1953*, p. 426.

93. See NCNA, Beijing, August 10, 1952, in *CB*, no. 276, pp. 9–11.

94. Deng Xiaoping, "Guanyu Gao, Rao," p. 520, also pictured Gao as often adopting a leftist posture but hastened to add that sometimes he favored rightist practices as well.

95. One oral source cites as examples of Mao's trust his role in having Gao appointed a vice-chairman of the Central People's Government in 1949 and allowing Gao to read sensitive military documents even though he was not a member of the Party's Military Affairs Committee.

96. While much of this assessment of Gao's character comes from scholarly sources who might be suspected of repeating conventional wisdom, one oral source specifically relayed such an assessment by Guo Feng, one of Gao's followers denounced in 1955. See also Chen Yun's Fourth Plenum likening of unrepentant individuals, i.e., most certainly including Gao, to a water buffalo; *Chen Yun Wenxuan (1949–1956)*, p. 230.

97. NCNA, Beijing, November 24, 1949, in *CB*, no. 163, pp. 5–11. Ironically, this article is a rather extreme statement of the position that Communists should be rewarded in status and materially for their achievements, a position attributed to Liu Shaoqi and severely criticized during the Cultural Revolution.

98. At least some indication of Mao's statements would be known within high Party circles since, according to my source, Gao reorganized Mao's words and used them in his efforts to win support. A record may exist, given the propensity for extensive note-taking at meetings of high Party leaders. See the account of the crucial 1959 meeting of Peng Dehuai, Mao, and other top leaders at Lushan, the seriousness of which was indicated by the fact that, contrary to normal practice, notes were not taken; *Baokan Wenzhai* [Selections from Newspapers and Periodicals], October 4, 1988, p. 3.

99. In "Establishment of the New Regime," p. 99, I stated on the basis of discussions with an authoritative source that Mao objected to the cautious advocacy of Liu and Zhou concerning economic construction. This appears mistaken. No evidence of such differences has been found in talks with various other oral sources, contemporary 1953 documents, or post-Mao written sources. Finally, when checking with the same authoritative source he clarified the matter by stating that the pace of transformation, not construction, was Mao's central concern.

100. No oral source suggested such a possibility. One source, however, did report that Guo Feng (see above, n. 96) claimed Mao had betrayed Gao. Even if accurate, however, this would more likely refer to Mao's turning against Gao at the end of 1953 than to an anti-Gao plot hatched from the outset.

101. For a discussion of Mao's contrasting perceptions of Liu and Zhou, see Teiwes, "Mao and His Lieutenants," pp. 56–60. Fang and Fang, Zhou Enlai, passim, offer a general view of Zhou as a loyal assistant to Mao.

102. Chen Shihui, "Guanyu fandui Gao Gang," p. 99.

103. "Liu Shao-chi and Yang Shang-kun Criticized for Breach of Discipline in Issuing Documents in the Name of the Central Committee Without Authorization" (May 19, 1953), *SW*, 5:92. The text of this brief directive does not mention any names, and its title was presumably provided by the editors. It is credible that Liu and Yang were targets, given Liu's position as the authoritative second in command and Yang's as head of Central Committee's general office, which distributed documents, but it is possible that they were not the sole targets. At the time of publication of volume 5 both Liu and Yang were still in disgrace. On the likely link to the substance of the Mao-Gao talks, see below, p. 69.

According to oral sources, this criticism was unfair since it had been established practice since 1945 that Liu had the right to issue documents in the name of the Central Committee. In addition, these sources believe that in 1952–53 Liu was taking particular care not to pass on excessive paperwork to Mao because of the Chairman's health problems; see above, p. 33. Finally, they note that as a result of Mao's criticism, Liu became especially careful about keeping Mao informed of Central Committee work; cf. below, p. 59.

104. See Levine, *Anvil of Victory*, pp. 98–101. Oral sources confirm the general accuracy of this account. One source who worked with Peng Zhen commented on the poor state of Peng-Gao relations.

105. Another oral source claims that Gao's assertion, which apparently was forcefully articulated in 1953, that Liu was biased in favor of Peng was unfair in that Liu was the first to discover and correct many of Peng's mistakes. Concerning the point at issue, however,

this still leaves the likely possibility that Gao *perceived* bias on Liu's part.

106. E.g., "Resolution on the Kao-Jao Alliance," p. 4; and Cheng Xuan et al., *Zhongguo Shehuizhuyi Geming he Shehuizhuyi Jiansheshi Wenda* [Questions and Answers on the History of China's Socialist Revolution and Socialist Construction] (Haerbin: Heilongjiang renmin chubanshe, 1986), p. 86.

107. The following is based on Gong Yuzhi, *Zai Lishi Zhuanzhe zhong* [In the Midst of Historical Change] (Beijing: Sanlian chubanshe, 1988), pp. 361–69; *Wenxian he Yanjiu* [Documents and Research], no. 6 (1985): 34–36; and oral sources.

108. Liu's article can be found in *Liu Xuanji*, 2:92–99. For a general account of conflict in the trade unions during this period, see Paul Harper, "The Party and the Unions in Communist China," *CQ*, no. 37 (1969): 89–99.

109. This account draws on Teiwes, "Mao and His Lieutenants," pp. 8–12, 56–60.

110. An example of exaggeration and distortion is Cultural Revolution claims that Liu's inclusion of the notion that the "semiproletariat" was part of the leading class in China in the 1951 criteria for Party members drew Mao's sharp rebuke; see, e.g., *Ziliao Zhuanji* [Special Collection of Materials], November 1968, in *SCMP (Supplement)*, no. 246, p. 12. According to the 1983 edition of Mao's letters, Mao only raised the issue in a polite manner in a December 1951 letter to Liu after it had been brought up by Liu's old associate, An Ziwen. Moreover, Mao himself had earlier used the concept of the semiproletariat as part of the leading class. *WM*, pp. 230–31. Of course, it is possible that Mao was critical of the formulation by 1953.

111. Teiwes, *Politics and Purges*, pp. 78–95; and oral sources. The oral sources place greater emphasis on the differences between Mao and Liu while affirming Mao's partial responsibility for the initial excesses.

112. *WM*, pp. 95, 171, 174.

113. *DSYJ*, no. 2 (1980): 25; *Lishi Yanjiu*, no. 2 (1980): 50; and oral sources. Cf. Kenneth Lieberthal, "Mao versus Liu? Policy towards Industry and Commerce: 1946–1949," *CQ*, no. 47 (1971).

114. *Dangshi Yanjiu Ziliao*, 3:662.

115. *Lishi Yanjiu*, no. 2 (1980): 51ff.; and oral sources.

116. *Dangshi Yanjiu Ziliao* (Chengdu: Sichuan renmin chubanshe, 1985), 6:717–19; the Shanxi document and Liu's comment in "Quiwen Gongxinshang, Yiyi Xiangyuxi" [Wonderful Literature Should Be Appreciated Together, Doubtful Meanings Should Be Analyzed Together] (Red Guard collection of Liu Shaoqi's writings); *SW*, 5:71; and oral sources. On the staged process of cooperativization, see "Agricultural Cooperativization in Communist China," *CB*, no. 373, January 20, 1956, pp. 4, 7.

117. Most particularly, in the course of his August 1953 criticism of Bo Yibo, Mao dredged up a July 1951 article (i.e., the same month as Liu's comment) in which Bo attacked "agrarian socialist thought"; *SW*, 5:106. Mao's comments grossly distorted the overall thrust of Bo's article, which in fact argued for strengthening political work in order to overcome rich peasant thinking and push villages further down the revolutionary path; see *Xinhua Yuebao* [New China Monthly] (July 1951): 535–37.

118. E.g., *RMRB*, March 26, 1953, in *CB*, no. 240, pp. 3, 6–7, 12, 14–15; and *DSYJ*, no. 3 (1981): 18–21. Interestingly, the latter source, which focuses on the efforts of the North China Bureau, where Liu Shaoqi's close comrades Bo Yibo and Liu Lantao held sway, to correct left deviations, also noted a similar moderate policy in Gao Gang's Northeast.

119. *SW*, 5:91.

120. *Xinhua Wenzhai* [New China Documentary Collection], no. 7 (1981): 187.

121. For other issues possibly causing Mao dissatisfaction with Liu in the first half of 1953, see above, n. 110; and below, pp. 56–58, and chap. 2, n. 33.

122. Cf. Teiwes, "Mao and His Lieutenants," p. 60.

123. A typical example is the extensive year-by-year listing of Liu's crimes in "Down with Liu Shao-ch'i" (Red Guard pamphlet), in *CB*, no. 834, August 17, 1967, pp. 12–13. Also note the general conclusion that of all the charges laid against Liu Shaoqi in the Cultural Revolution, a relatively small proportion dealt with the 1949–1953 period; Lowell Dittmer, *Liu Shao-ch'i and the Chinese Cultural Revolution: The Politics of Mass Criticism* (Berkeley: University of California Press, 1974), p. 311.

124. According to an authoritative oral source, Rao was on the list of 21 leaders personally selected by Mao for inclusion in *The Great Soviet Encyclopedia* at the request of the Soviet Communist Party. See table 3.

125. For various statements concerning Rao's lust to control his units over the entire 1943–1953 period, his desire to be the sole power in East China, and his claims that "East China was special," see *Shishi Shouce* [Current Events Handbook], April 25, 1955, in *SCMP*, no. 1052, p. 10; Xiao Xiaoqin and Li Liangzhi, *Zhongguo Gemingshi* [China's Revolutionary History] (Hongqi chubanshe, 1984), 2:27; and *Zhonggong Dangshi 170 ti Wenda*, p. 261. Cf. above, n. 39.

126. "Deng, Chen, Tan guanyu Rao," p. 274; Deng Xiaoping, "Guanyu Gao, Rao," p. 519; and oral sources.

127. Chen Shihui, "Guanyu fandui Gao Gang," p. 97; *Huiyi Chen Yi* [Remember Chen Yi] (Beijing: Renmin chubanshe, 1980), p. 73; "Deng, Chen, Tan guanyu Rao," pp. 273–74; and oral source.

128. "Deng, Chen, Tan guanyu Rao," p. 274; Chen Shihui, "Guanyu fandui Gao Gang," p. 97; and oral source.

129. Cf. above, n. 39.

130. While various sources state Rao's belief in Gao's success, Chen Shihui, "Guanyu fandui Gao Gang," p. 97, explicitly claims he believed that Gao had displaced Liu as successor.

131. The most important career links were in the late 1920s when Rao served under Liu in the Northeast underground, and when he was Liu's deputy political commissar in the New Fourth Army in the early 1940s. Klein and Clark, *Biographic Dictionary*, 1:408–409; and Zhang Guangxin and Yang Shuzhen, eds., *Zhonggong Dangshi Shijian Mingci Renwu Jianshi* [Brief Explanations of Events, Terms and Personalities in CCP History] (Xi'an: Shaanxi renmin chubanshe, 1985), pp. 377, 463.

132. Chen Shihui, "Guanyu fandui Gao Gang," p. 97.

133. *Dangshi Huiyi Baogaoji* [Collection of Reports to the Party History Conference] (Beijing: Zhonggong zhongyang dangxiao chubanshe, 1982), p. 85.

134. See "Resolution on Kao-Jao Alliance," p. 4; Deng Xiaoping, "Guanyu Gao, Rao," pp. 520–21; and *Huiyi Chen Yi*, pp. 70–71. Rao's rightist mistakes allegedly involved "surrender to the capitalists, landlords, and rich peasants in the cities and countryside."

135. Oral sources.

136. E.g., *Geming he Jianshe Wenda*, p. 86; and He Xin, Wang Jiaxun, and Chen Mingxian, *Zhongguo Gongchandang Shigang* [Outline History of the CCP] (Beijing: Beijing Daxue chubanshe, 1986), p. 337.

137. At the May 10, 1954, East China Bureau meeting dealing with the case; *ZDJCZ*, 20:314.

138. Ibid., pp. 275, 314, 515; *SW*, 5:161–62; oral sources; and above, p. 12.

139. Chen Shihui, "Guanyu fandui Gao Gang," p. 97.

140. Ibid.

141. For an earlier review of the evidence on this issue, see Teiwes, *Politics and Purges*, pp. 191–94.

142. For a comprehensive review of Soviet sources, see Nakajima, "Kao Kang Affair."

143. E.g., *Hong Tianxun* [Red Dispatch], March 1968, in *SCMP*, no. 4143, p. 2; *SW*,

5:340; and Chen Shihui, "Guanyu fandui Gao Gang," p. 96.

144. Liao Kai-lung, "Historical Experiences," *Issues & Studies* (October 1981): 79, speaks of Stalin regarding Gao as a Zhang Zuolin figure, i.e., a local warlord susceptible to foreign pressure. In fact, according to oral sources, Stalin used the Zhang Zuolin analogy openly and jokingly when Gao visited Moscow in 1949 with Liu Shaoqi.

145. In particular, according to an oral source, Gao won Soviet favor by providing the Soviet army with supplies in 1949–1950 when natural disasters caused a grain shortage.

146. According to one oral source, Alexi Kosygin, who in the early 1950s was deputy chairman of the Council of Ministers and minister of light industry, was dispatched to the Northeast on business by Stalin and held talks with Gao. Besides the discussions with Soviet officials, there are also indications of similar questionable contacts with North Korean leaders; see *ZDJCZ*, 20:296.

147. This dating is based on *Khrushchev Remembers: The Last Testament*, trans. and ed. Strobe Talbott (Boston: Little, Brown, 1974), p. 243, where Khrushchev refers to Gao's conversations with Ambassador Panyushkin; and "Chronology of Events, January–April 1953," pp. 5, 11, which gives Panyushkin's tour of duty as December 1952–March 1953.

148. *Khrushchev Remembers: The Last Testament*, pp. 243–44; and oral sources basing their information on Chinese data. The question of Stalin's motives in revealing the talks to Mao left Khrushchev mystified, while an oral source speculated that Stalin realized the danger to Sino-Soviet relations of overly intimate ties. This source further recounted another apparent act of distancing himself from Gao whereby Stalin recalled and had executed a Soviet adviser who had served Gao.

149. If we take Khrushchev literally that Stalin handed over the reports in a conversational manner (ibid., p. 243), then the incident would have taken place during their only meeting in early 1950. Oral sources also report Stalin turning over information on Gao's contacts with Soviet officials to Mao as early as 1950; however, it is unclear whether this included statements about Liu and Zhou or just referred to the passing on of materials concerning military and natural resources matters in the Northeast. The latter incident reportedly was not regarded as a significant mistake.

One oral source, a retired Party official, was the only such source to see Gao's Soviet links as a major factor in his downfall. On balance, I regard this source as less well-placed than others, and this view as not fitting the overall pattern of evidence. One should note, however, that if this indeed was the case, then the interpretation of Mao's talks with Gao as setting Gao up for a fall (see above, p. 38) becomes viable. In particular, if Mao's talks with Gao took place *after* Stalin's death, then the possibility that Mao was setting in motion an anti-Gao maneuver with his Soviet "patron" no longer on the scene would reflect a certain logic. But again, given the overall pattern of evidence, I believe this to be extremely unlikely.

150. For an earlier discussion of this factor, see Teiwes, *Politics and Purges*, p. 193.

151. See below, p. 128. All of the above explanations of Mao's possible motives in not reacting were suggested by oral sources.

152. For a subsequent expression of Mao's ambivalent feelings toward Stalin and the Soviet Union, see Schram, *Mao Unrehearsed*, pp. 96–103. An authoritative oral source states that Mao was never on really good terms with the Soviet Union, but oral sources generally emphasize the importance and respect he attached to Moscow and Stalin.

153. For example, Li Fuchun, who apparently had special responsibilities for negotiating economic matters with the Soviet Union. See *Bujin de Shinian*, pp. 416–20; Huai En, *Zhou Zongli Shengping Dashiji* [Chronology of Premier Zhou's Life] (Chengdu: Sichuan renmin chubanshe, 1986), p. 360; and NCNA, Beijing, September 15, 1953, in *SCMP*, no. 651, p. 3.

154. It is unclear from my oral source whether Mao specifically mentioned Malenkov in the Soviet context or Chen, Deng, and/or Lin in the Chinese one. Of course, what would

have been crucial in the Chinese context was his usage of "successors." Was this simply a general reference to the need to bring younger people into key posts as was then happening with the movement of regional leaders to the Center, or was he implying the need for such people to *replace* those already in the highest positions?

155. E.g., *Wen hui bao*, May 20, 1968, in *SCMP*, no. 4205, p. 5.

156. Their respective years of birth were: Rao, 1903; Chen, 1905; Deng, 1904; and Lin, 1907; Gao himself was born in 1905. Of the key individuals approached only Peng Dehuai, born 1898, was the same age as Liu and Zhou, while Lin Biao, although the youngest of all, had serious health problems, and Chen Yun's health was also questionable. See above, pp. 21, 29.

In the Soviet case the generational factor made somewhat more sense with a gap of nine to a dozen years between the 51-year-old Malenkov (b. 1902), on the one hand, and Kaganovich (b. 1893) and Molotov (b. 1890), who were in their early sixties, on the other.

157. For example, concerning the joint dictatorship of several classes as distinct from the Soviet concept of the dictatorship of the proletariat. See Benjamin Schwartz, "China and the Soviet Theory of People's Democracy," *Problems of Communism* (September–October 1954); and Arthur A. Cohen, *The Communism of Mao Tse-tung* (Chicago: University of Chicago Press, 1964), chap. 3.

158. See *Khrushchev Remembers: The Last Testament*, p. 242; and *Khrushchev Remembers*, trans. and ed. Strobe Talbott (Boston: Little, Brown, 1970), pp. 464–65.

159. *Dang de Wenxian* [Party Documents], no. 5 (1988): 53–55, 59–60; and oral sources.

160. NCNA, Beijing, April 25, 1953, in *SCMP*, no. 559, pp. 19–22.

161. See NCNA, Beijing, November 11, 1953, in *SCMP*, no. 687, p. 48; *RMRB*, November 17, 1953, in *SCMP*, no. 696, pp. 20–23; and NCNA, Wuhan, November 28, 1953, in *SCMP*, no. 698, pp. 28–29.

162. E.g., *History of the Communist Party of the Soviet Union (Bolsheviks): Short Course* (London: Corbett Publishing Co., 1938), pp. 235–36, 254, 281–83; V. I. Lenin, *Collected Works* (Moscow: Progress Publishers, 1965), 32:141–43; Lenin, *Selected Works* (Moscow: Foreign Languages Publishing House, 1951), 2-2:718, 722; J. V. Stalin, *Works* (Moscow: Foreign Languages Publishing House, 1954–55), 7:332–35, 342–46; 8:136–38, 148–49; 10:313, 319; 12:319, 337, 372; and Stalin, *Problems of Leninism* (Peking: Foreign Languages Press, 1976), pp. 298–300, 438, 491.

163. E.g., *Short Course*, pp. 239–40, 249–50; Lenin, *Selected Works*, 2-2:277–78; and Stalin, *Works*, 7:317; 10:303–307.

164. E.g., *Short Course*, pp. 252, 269, 274; Stalin, *Works*, 12:313–14; and Stalin, *Problems of Leninism*, pp. 328–35, 352–63, 418, 449–50.

165. E.g., *Short Course*, pp. 232, 243, 256, 259, 274, 285, 298–99; Stalin, *Works*, 12:282, 314; and Stalin, *Problems of Leninism*, pp. 417–18, 421–22.

Chapter 2

1. E.g., "Resolution on Kao-Jao," p. 4. Cf. above, p. 39.

2. See *RMRB*, December 16, 1985, in FBIS, December 20, 1985, p. K7. See Bachman, *Chen Yun*, p. 145, for a somewhat different view.

3. See *Liushinian Dashi Jianjie*, p. 397; and Fang Weizhong, *Jingji Dashiji*, p. 99. Slightly different dates of June 13 and August 11 are given by Teng Hsiao-ping, "Report on Revision of the Constitution," p. 197. Various sources, including Fang Weizhong, who implies a somewhat later beginning, treat the precise date of the start of the conference as unknown, but there is a general consensus that it closed on August 12; see *Jingji Guanli Dashiji*, p. 42; and *Jihua Dashi Jiyao*, p. 40.

4. See *Peking Review*, no. 51 (1977): 11; Huai En, *Zhou Dashiji*, p. 362; and Chen

Yeping and Han Jingcao, eds., *An Ziwen Zhuanlüe* [Brief Biography of An Ziwen] (Taiyuan: Shanxi renmin chubanshe, 1985), p. 101.

5. See Xiao Xiaoqin and Li Liangzhi, *Gemingshi*, p. 28; and He Xin et al., *Dangshi Jiangyi*, p. 306.

6. *Liushinian Dashi Jianjie*, p. 397; Huai En, *Zhou Dashiji*, pp. 362–63; and *Chen Yun Wenxuan (1949–1956)*, p. 201.

7. *Liushinian Dashi Jianjie*, pp. 397–98, 405; Xiao Xiaoqin and Li Liangzhi, *Gemingshi*, p. 28; Hao Mengbi and Duan Haoran, *Liushinian*, p. 425; and Shanghai shi Gaoxiao "Zhongguo Gongchandang Lishi Jiangyi" Bianxiezu [Shanghai Higher School "Lectures on CCP History" Compiling Group], *Zhongguo Gongchandang Lishi Jiangyi* [Lectures on CCP History] (Shanghai: Shanghai renmin chubanshe, 1984), p. 263. The conference also saw regional criticism of "excessive" central fianancial control, disputes on how to handle provincial grain surpluses and deficits, and ministerial complaints about the state budget; Bachman, *Chen Yun*, pp. 43–44.

8. "Resolution on Kao-Jao," p. 5.

9. *Selected Works of Deng*, p. 279.

10. Chen Shihui, "Guanyu fandui Gao Gang," p. 101.

11. *Guanyu Lishi Wenti Jueyi*, p. 226.

12. *Mao Zedong Xuanji* [Selected Works of Mao Zedong] (Beijing: Renmin chubanshe, 1977), 5:81.

13. *Liushinian Dashi Jianjie*, p. 399; and *Guanyu Lishi Wenti Jueyi*, p. 227. See appendix III-1C for Mao's successive amendments in August and December 1953.

14. Hu Hua, *Shehuizhuyi Jiangyi*, p. 83; and *People's China*, January 1, 1954, in *CB*, no. 285, p. 16.

15. *Dang de Wenxian*, no. 5 (1988): 58–60; *Zhonggong Dangshi Yanjiu* [CCP History Research], no. 1 (1988): 19; and oral sources.

16. *SW*, 5:94.

17. *Mao Xuanji*, 5:81, 89; and *Zhou Enlai Shuxin Xuanji* [Selected Letters of Zhou Enlai] (Beijing: Zhongyang wenxian chubanshe, 1988), p. 492.

Whatever Mao's intent in the vague wording concerning speed in the August formulation, in his August 12 speech the Chairman spoke of socialist transformation over "fifteen years or a bit longer" (*Mao Xuanji*, 5:97), i.e., in essentially the same terms as in June. Moreover, by December he was attaching a relatively cautious meaning of eighteen years to the vaguer formulation. Another sign of caution in December was his altering of "basically to realize" to "gradually to realize" the transition. See *Zhonggong Dangshi Yanjiu*, no. 1 (1988): 19; and *Jingji Dashidian*, p. 101.

18. This assumes that Gao's revised draft was written after June 15. My well-placed source argues that this almost certainly was the case since, given Zhou's work style, he would not have taken more than a few days to respond to Gao's document.

19. *Zhou Shuxin Xuanji*, pp. 491–92; and oral source.

20. *SW*, 5:102.

21. See *Selected Works of Mao Tse-tung* (*SW*) (Peking: Foreign Languages Press, 1961), 4:361–75; *Selected Works of Zhou Enlai* (Beijing: Foreign Languages Press, 1981), 1:397–409; and *Selected Works of Liu Shaoqi* (Beijing: Foreign Languages Press, 1984), 1:417–28.

22. For a lengthy analysis of this theoretical muddle, see Tokuda Noriyuki, "Mo Taku To 'Shin Minshushugi' gainen ni tsuite" [On Mao Zedong's Concept of "New Democracy"], in *Ajia Keizai* [Asian Economy], September 1966, pp. 100–11. For a PRC overview, see *DSYJ*, no. 3 (1982): 32–33.

23. *Mao Xuanji*, 5:81–82.

24. *Nongye Jixie Jishu* [Agricultural Machinery Technology], no. 9 (1968), in *Selections from China Mainland Magazines* (*SCMM*), no. 633, p. 4; and *SW*, 5:93n.

25. Oral sources claim that Liu did not speak of a New Democratic "social order" (*zhixu*) in public or documents but only referred to consolidating the New Democratic "system" (*zhidu*). Indeed, the only written references to *zhixu* I have seen are in the context of attacks on Liu.

26. Mao's only pre-1953 reaction to the slogan, according to Cultural Revolution sources I have seen, occurred in criticisms of the 1951 eight criteria for Party membership. This reportedly also involved rejection of the idea of a "semiproletarian" segment of the leading class, yet post-Mao sources on the latter issue depict a polite Mao forwarding the concerns of An Ziwen. Oral sources, moreover, know of no Mao statement on the New Democracy slogan before June 1953. See above, chapter 1, n. 110.

27. See Liu's May 2, 1953, address to a trade union congress, in *Collected Works of Liu Shao-chi, 1945–1957* (Hong Kong: Union Research Institute, 1969), pp. 269–70.

28. In the period up to fall 1952 both Mao and Liu depicted a relatively long period that would surely take several five-year plans before the start of the transition. Apparently the shortest time projected by either was Liu's 1950 statement envisioning a six- to nine-year period before China was "more or less on the socialist path"; ibid., p. 238.

29. *WS 1949–1957*, p. 32. This text is apparently misdated as June 25, 1953, but the relevant passages clearly correspond to the June 15 text in volume 5. There is, of course, also the possibility that Mao gave some examples of erroneous leftist ideas that were not recorded in either *Wansui* or official texts.

30. This, however, was asserted in a Cultural Revolution source; see above, n. 26.

31. NCNA, Beijing, June 11, 1953, in *SCMP*, no. 589, p. 19. Of course, if Gao and Rao had *not* established close liaison (see above, p. 46), Rao would not necessarily have been aware of Mao's views if the Chairman had expressed them to Gao.

32. For all of this, conceivably Liu may not have been overly concerned about the matter at this point given his experience in adjusting to Mao's theoretical rebukes. Indeed, a week after Mao's statement, Liu used the indefinite formula of "marching step by step from New Democracy to socialism," while for the remainder of 1953 and 1954 the same vagueness about the relationship of New Democracy to socialism and when it would be completed marked official statements without any ideological fallout. See NCNA, Beijing, June 23, 1953, in *SCMP*, no. 596, p. 12; ibid., November 22, 1953, in *CB*, no. 271, p. 2; and *DSYJ*, no. 3 (1982): 32–33. It should also be noted that while Mao's August reformulation of the general line (see above, pp. 55–56) possibly was a move to the left, in another sense it retreated into the same indefiniteness that the Chairman criticized on June 15.

33. Liu may also have been vulnerable to Mao's criticism in the June 15 document of "firmly protect[ing] private property," (*Mao Xuanji*, 5:82) a notion Mao later linked to the "four big freedoms" issue over which Liu was harshly criticized during the Cultural Revolution; see *SW*, 5:135. This issue apparently related to the period of Mao's 1950 call to maintain the "rich peasant economy" and is thus another instance of distortion; see Teiwes, *Politics and Purges*, pp. 111n, 113–14. The prime target in 1953, however, was more likely to have been Mao's old follower Deng Zihui, who was also accused of promoting the "four big freedoms" and whose February directive on mutual aid and cooperativization criticized the "premature attempt" to limit the private property of peasants in agricultural cooperatives; *RMRB*, March 26, 1953, in *CB*, no. 240, p. 6. See also below, pp. 89–91.

34. Liu himself subsequently attacked the slogan in 1954; *Collected Works of Liu 1945–57*, p. 285.

35. *SW*, 5:110. This source further noted that Deng Xiaoping also acknowledged errors. See also below, pp. 67–68, 76.

36. Oral source. Li had been a schoolmate of Mao's and worked with him in the early 1920s. Later, however, Li was aligned with other Party leaders in apparent conflict with Mao. See Klein and Clark, *Biographic Dictionary*, 1:535–37.

37. On June 6, 1952, Mao commented that "the contradiction between the working class and the national bourgeoisie has become the principal contradiction in China; therefore the national bourgeoisie should no longer be defined as an intermediate class"; *SW*, 5:77. While the first part of this quotation is comprehensible given the asserted victory over the landlords and bureaucratic capital, there is no indication in Mao's other statements of this period or general CCP policy that the national bourgeoisie was anything other than an "intermediate class" that the Party should strive to win over to its cause. According to oral sources, Mao was using the term "intermediate class" in the narrow political sense suggested above, i.e., that the bourgeoisie became the major object of struggle after land reform. This was not meant to imply any change in the vacillating class character of the capitalists, nor to propose anything other than a broadly moderate policy toward them. These sources also state that the assertion by the editors of volume 5 that Mao was criticizing Li was inappropriate since Mao approved the report Li was making as a whole, although he did cross out the reference to the bourgeoisie as an intermediate class. Cf. *DSYJ*, no. 5 (1982): 25.

38. *WM*, p. 283.

39. Ibid., p. 329.

40. *DSYJ*, no. 3 (1986): 21.

41. *Bujin de Sinian*, p. 502; *DSYJ*, no. 4 (1980): 23; ibid., no. 5 (1982): 26; *Zhonggong Dangshi Yanjiu*, no. 4 (1988): 42–43; and oral sources. One of Li's reports was written on May 27, a little over a week after Mao's statement on documents, while a second report was simply dated May 1953; see *Li Weihan Xuanji* [Selected Works of Li Weihan] (Beijing: Renmin chubanshe, 1987), pp. 263, 268.

42. *Wuxian de Huainian*, p. 502; and *DSYJ*, no. 4 (1980): 23, 28.

43. *Dangshi Tongxun* [Party History Newsletter], no. 1 (1986): 46; and NCNA, Beijing, September 18, 1953, in *SCMP*, no. 654, p. 5. Li had already been a prominent GAC official as secretary-general, a post he now relinquished. Chen's control in this area became even clearer in 1954 when Mao entrusted him with the responsibility for transformation; Chen Guanglin, *Chen Yun Jingji Gongzuo*, p. 3.

44. *DSYJ*, no. 3 (1986): 21–22; *SW*, 5:113; and *Zhonggong Dangshi Yanjiu*, no. 4 (1988): 43–44.

45. *Dangshi Tongxun*, no. 1 (1986): 45–46; Hu Hua, *Shehuizhuyi Jiangyi*, p. 82; Hao Mengbi and Duan Haoran, *Liushinian*, p. 421; *DSYJ*, no. 4 (1980): 23; ibid., no. 6 (1980): 45; and oral source.

46. *WM*, pp. 383–85.

47. See Li Weihan, *Huiyi yu Yanjiu* [Recollections and Research] (Beijing: Zhonggong dangshi ziliao chubanshe, 1986), 1:380.

48. The 1928 Stalinist collection was aimed at the earlier oppositionists, especially Trotsky, Zinoviev, and Kamenev, rather than Bukharin who actually received a friendly mention (p. 885); J. V. Stalin, *On the Opposition* (Peking: Foreign Languages Press, 1974).

A similar story has Gao, at a 1954 meeting discussing approval of Li's "use, limit, and transform policy," asking Li if he was aware of Kautsky's theory of a "peaceful march to socialism"; Liao Gailong, ed., *1984 nian Zhonggong Dangshi Wenzhai Niankan* [1984 CCP History Collection Annual] (Beijing: Zhonggong dangshi ziliao chubanshe, 1987), p. 526. While it is possible that the two stories conflate a single incident, it is also possible that the Kautsky incident took place at the February 1954 Fourth Plenum, which would have reviewed all Party policies. In any case, if this incident did take place it would seem to be yet another example of Gao's theoretical inadequacies, at least in terms of orthodox CCP understanding, since this understanding linked the notion of a "peaceful march to socialism" to Bernstein, not Kautsky. In fact, Kautsky's later thinking in this regard came close to that of Bernstein, but there is little reason to assume Gao was familiar with such details of early twentieth-century Marxist thought. What seems to have been the case was that Gao plucked the theory of a "peaceful march to socialism," of which he was vaguely aware, out of the air but got the advocate of that theory according to the official Party view wrong. See Xia Zhengnong, ed., *Shehuizhuyi Cidian* [Dictionary of Socialism] (Yanbian: Jilin renmin chubanshe, 1985), pp. 206–207, 332–33.

49. *Dangshi Tongxun*, no. 1 (1986): 46.

50. The oral source did not mention the incident at the conference, but according to *DSYJ*, no. 5 (1982): 28, when Li Weihan reported on the "use, limit, and transform" policy on July 23, due to the interference of Gao and Rao the discussion could not be developed to reach a decision.

51. NCNA, Beijing, December 31, 1952, in *SCMP*, no. 483, pp. 24–26; and *Chen Yun Wenxuan (1949–1956)*, pp. 196–97.

52. Ibid.; Fang Weizhong, *Jingji Dashiji*, p. 88; *Peking Review*, no. 51 (1977): 11; and oral source.

53. *Chen Yun Wenxuan (1949–1956)*, p. 199; Fang Weizhong, *Jingji Dashiji*, p. 90; *Peking Review*, no. 51 (1977): 11; and oral source.

54. Caizhengbu Jiaoyusi [Finance Ministry Education Office], *Zhongguo de Caizheng Gaige* [China's Financial Reform] (Beijing: Beijing Daxue chubanshe, 1986), p. 56.

55. *SW*, 5:105.

56. Ibid., p. 103. Informed oral sources claim to be unaware of any criticism before the conference.

57. *WM*, p. 329.

58. *Hongqi* [Red Flag], July 1, 1981, in FBIS, July 29, 1981, p. K31.

59. Oral sources; and Huai En, *Zhou Dashiji*, p. 362. A possible indication of Bo under attack was a reference to *Acting* Minister of Finance Rong Zihe on June 6, 1953; see *CB*, no. 277, January 30, 1954, p. 23.

60. Oral source.

61. *SW*, 5:92, 107; and oral sources. Cf. above, p. 39.

62. NCNA, Beijing, December 30, 1952, in *SCMP*, no. 487, p. 8; and Bachman, *Chen Yun*, p. 42.

63. The case is conceivably analogous to that of Zhou Enlai in that published sources make no mention of Mao's displeasure with Zhou. Oral sources, however, explicitly acknowledge such displeasure in Zhou's case.

64. See *SW*, 5:107, where Mao notes the objections of the Ministry of Commerce and Federation of Supply and Marketing Cooperatives, and the dissatisfaction of the Ministry of Light Industry.

65. Oral sources differed on the identity of Gao's ghostwriter; one identified Ma Hong (see above, p. 37) and another named Liu Mingfu. In each case there were close work ties to Gao in both the Northeast and the SPC.

66. While the instance is far from clear-cut, there is suggestive evidence that Bukharin was on the minds of Party leaders at this point in the form of Deng Zihui's reference to Stalin's critique in a late July speech as he indicated a shift in policy on mutual aid and cooperativization; *RMRB*, July 2[2], 1953, in *CB*, no. 255, p. 4. Deng's reference to the strongly anti-Bukharin 1929 text, "The Right Deviation in the CPSU(B)," was actually to a fairly mild passage concerning the superiority of collective agriculture, which made no mention of Bukharin. Moreover, Deng's reference arguably simply reflected the study campaign under way, while oral sources strongly believe, with good reason, that Deng was not the sort of person to engage in leftist posturing. Nevertheless, the citation of such a text at the time Gao was using the Bukharin analogy remains intriguing.

67. See *SW*, 5:161. An oral source noted the contributions to the criticism of Bo by Rao's two East China subordinates from Shandong, Party Secretary Xiang Ming and organization head Lai Keke. Xiang was identified as a member of the clique in 1955 but Lai

was not, apparently on the grounds that his position was too low to merit mention. Cf. below, pp. 80, 84.

68. Chen Yeping and Han Jingcao, *An Ziwen Zhuanlüe*, pp. 101–102; and oral sources. Local leaders were particularly critical of the impact of Bo's tax system on their revenues; see above, p. 63.

69. Chen Shihui, "Guanyu fandui Gao Gang," p. 98; and oral sources.

70. For Mao's initial reaction to Gao's critique I am almost exclusively reliant on an authoritative oral source, while much of what I have pieced together concerning the likely development of the Chairman's attitudes is deduction based on this source and what is known about Mao's actions at the end of the conference (see below). While it is perilous to rely so heavily on one source, on balance I have chosen to do so since the source in question is very close to one of the members of Gao Gang's group.

71. See "Zhou Enlai Tongzhi zai guanyu Gao Gang Wenti de Zuotanhui shang de Fayan Tigang" [Comrade Zhou Enlai's Speech Outline at the Discussion Meeting on the Gao Gang Question] (February 1954), in *ZDJCZ*, 20:268.

72. Oral sources with access to the (incomplete) record of the Financial and Economic Conference know of no statements by Mao prior to his speech on the final day. Note also the report that Zhou Enlai conveyed Mao's definition of the general line to the conference; above, p. 53. While several oral sources claimed that Mao did not attend the conference except to give his closing speech on August 12, a well-placed source reports that Mao was present a few days earlier while Gao addressed the meeting. See below, p. 68.

73. While able to identify some of the actors (cf. above, n. 67), given the incomplete record oral sources say they are unable to specify precisely who criticized Bo, or who defended him.

74. Deng Xiaoping, "Guanyu Gao, Rao," p. 517; and Chen Shihui, "Guanyu fandui Gao Gang," p. 98.

75. Cf. *Xinshiqi*, no. 8 (1981): 16.

76. *Chen Yun Wenxuan (1949–1956)*, p. 195.

77. See ibid., p. 201, for a September 1953 statement by Chen assuming personal responsibility.

78. *Lishinian Dashi Jianjie*, pp. 397–98. Cf. *Chen Yun Wenxuan (1949–1956)*, p. 198, for a subsequent statement to the same effect.

79. Oral source. Cf. above, p. 32.

80. Chen Shihui, "Guanyu fandui Gao Gang," p. 99; *Xinshiqi*, no. 8 (1981): 17; above, p. 67; and oral sources. A well-placed oral source agreed to the proposition that Chen had a good understanding of Mao and was relaxed at the time.

81. See above, n. 72. If Gao's talk took place, as my oral source claimed, "one or two days" before Mao's August 12 speech, then it would have come after Chen Yun's remarks *if* they were made on August 6. The evidence is not firm, however, about the dating of either Chen's or Gao's remarks; the only thing that seems relatively clear is that Chen's took place toward the end of the conference. Even if Chen's speech came first, he still could have picked up clues concerning Mao's attitude based on the Chairman's response to the briefings he received.

82. See *SW*, 5:103; and above, pp. 54–55.

83. Zhou Enlai, "Zai Yijiuwusan nian Xiaji Quanguo Caizheng Jingji Huiyi shang suozuo de Jielun" [Summary Made at the Summer 1953 National Work Conference on Financial and Economic Work] (August 11, 1953), in *ZDJCZ*, 20:133–36, 138–39. According to oral sources, this is a complete text of Zhou's report.

84. See above, p. 9.

85. Chen Shihui, "Guanyu fandui Gao Gang," p. 99.

86. Ibid.

87. *Mao Xuanji*, 5:91.
88. Ibid., p. 96.
89. Ibid., p. 90 (emphasis added).
90. Ibid., p. 94. See above, pp. 65–65.
91. See above, pp. 42–43.
92. *SW*, 5:126, 129, 138.
93. See appendix III-3B(2).
94. No written source has been found supporting this view. When Deng Xiaoping replaced Bo as minister of finance in September 1953, Bo was simply relieved of his post, i.e., there was no acting status conferred on Deng as would have been appropriate if it were a case of sick leave. NCNA, Beijing, September 18, 1953, in *SCMP*, no. 654, pp. 5, 7.
95. *Bujin de Sinian*, p. 25. This reminiscence by Bo Yibo states that this happened after the Organization Work Conference of September–October 1953.
96. *Chen Yun Wenxuan (1949–1956)*, pp. 196–98.
97. *Jingji Guanli Dashiji*, p. 45.
98. *Caizheng Gaige*, pp. 56, 61. The formula had been used as early as 1950 with reference to the relations of the public and private economies; see *ZDJCZ*, 19:128–29.
99. Huadong Shifan Daxue Lishixi [East China Normal University History Department], *Zhonghua Renmin Gongheguo Shinian Dashiji* [A Ten-Year Chronology of the PRC] (Shanghai: Huadong Shifan Daxue, 1959), p. 320; *Zhonghua Renmin Gongheguo Fagui Xuanji* [Collection of PRC Laws and Regulations] (Beijing: Falü chubanshe, 1957), pp. 359–62, 372–76; and Sifabu Fazhiju [Ministry of Justice Legal System Bureau], ed., *Zhonghua Renmin Gongheguo Fagui Mulu (1949 nian–1982 nian)* [List of PRC Laws and Regulations, 1949–1982] (Beijing: Falü chubanshe, 1984), p. 141.
100. Zhongguo Sehui Kexueyuan Jingji Yanjiusuo [Chinese Academy of Social Sciences Economic Research Institute], *Zibenzhuyi Gongshangye de Shehuizhuyi Gaizao* [The Socialist Transformation of China's Capitalist Industry and Commerce] (Beijing: Renmin chubanshe, 1978), p. 174.
101. Oral sources support the view that changes to the tax regulations were minimal.
102. E.g., *Liushinian Dashi Jianjie*, p. 405.
103. E.g., *WS*, 1969, p. 276; Chen Shihui, "Guanyu fandui Gao Gang," pp. 98–99; and oral sources.
104. Nearly all oral sources endorsed the power interpretation, although one well-informed Chinese scholar was of the opinion that policy differences were the basic cause of the affair.
105. Hu Hua, *Shehuizhuyi Jiangyi*, p. 89. This is an overall description of the activities of Gao and Rao, but it surely applies to the Financial and Economic Conference.
106. In February 1959; *WS*, 1969, p. 276.
107. Chen Shihui, "Guanyu fandui Gao Gang," p. 98; and He Xin et al., *Dangshi Jiangyi*, p. 306.
108. Chen Shihui, "Guanyu fandui Gao Gang," pp. 98–99.
109. This probably referred to what Red Guard sources claimed was Liu's late 1949 view that Party members with rich peasant origins could be retained for the time being; *Ziliao Zhuanji*, November 1968, in *SCMP (Supplement)*, no. 246, p. 12. In early 1953, however, the CCP's North China Bureau, which had strong ties to Liu through Bo Yibo, issued detailed regulations calling for the expulsion of Party members engaging in various rich-peasant and capitalist activities; *RMRB*, February 26, 1953, in *SCMP*, no. 532, pp. 19–22.
110. See above, pp. 64–65, 69–70.
111. According to oral sources, both Mao and Liu approved the policy, but Liu gave the report as Mao was not in good health; they claim to have seen no evidence of criticism of Liu on this matter by Mao. Nevertheless, these sources indicate a discrepancy in the two

men's ideas, with Mao emphasizing striving for peace but also the need to resort to fighting if efforts failed, and Liu being somewhat more sanguine about a peaceful solution.

112. Chen Shihui, "Guanyu fandui Gao Gang," pp. 98–99; *DSYJ*, no. 2 (1980): 17; and oral sources.

113. Chen Shihui, "Guanyu fandui Gao Gang," p. 99.

114. Ibid.; "Zhou Fayan Tigang," p. 267; and Hao Mengbi and Duan Haoran, *Liushinian*, p. 425. The latter two sources identify Mao as the representative of the "red areas" although not specifically in the context of the conference.

115. Oral sources. See below, pp. 102–104.

116. Chen Shihui, "Guanyu fandui Gao Gang," p. 99; and above, p. 16

117. Cf. "Zhou Fayan Tigang," p. 268, where the charge that Gao "made use of the name of the Central Committee" can be read as claiming Mao's support, and where the explicit accusation that Gao fabricated Mao's words to oppose "two leading Central Committee comrades" is laid.

118. Chen Shihui, "Guanyu fandui Gao Gang," p. 99; and oral sources.

119. *Mao Xuanji*, 5:147–48.

120. Ibid., p. 150.

121. Such was probably the case for those criticized by an *RMRB* editorial, carried by NCNA, Beijing, April 10, 1955, in *SCMP*, no. 1026, p. 5, for failing to oppose Gao and Rao's slanders or asking them to put their views formally.

122. *SW*, 5:164.

123. It should also be noted that Mao's distinctions may have been designed deliberately to play down the actual involvement of leading officials in the name of Party unity.

124. Zhou Ming, ed., *Lishi zai Zheli Chensi—1966–1976 nian Jishi* [Contemplating History—a True Record of 1966–1976] (Beijing: Huaxia chubanshe, 1986), 3:17.

With so much uncertainty surrounding the who and the what of the subterranean maneuvers during the Financial and Economic Conference, it is frustrating that the one case fairly extensively documented in Cultural Revolution materials is not supported by subsequent sources. This concerns Tan Zhenlin, at the time acting secretary of the CCP East China Bureau, and Chen Peixian, then fourth Party secretary in Shanghai. According to both official and Red Guard sources during the Cultural Revolution, Tan and Chen were deeply involved in "secret talks" with Gao and Rao at the conference. Gao assertedly went on a mission to Moscow during the conference and on his return sought Tan out for private talks rather than report to the Party Center. Tan also assertedly visited conference participants in their guesthouses at night, lobbying for the "young and capable" Gao and the "outstanding Marxist" Rao while attacking "sinister ministers around the Center." Moreover, it apparently was about this time that Tan and Chen allegedly drafted an open letter to Mao requesting that he "take a rest" and give up at least some of his posts. Chen reportedly later defended his actions by claiming they were designed to protect Mao's health by reducing his burdens. Some credibility was given to these charges by the fact that Chen was required to make a "strict self-criticism" at a Shanghai meeting in 1954, while Tan "carried out criticism and self-criticism of the work of the East China Bureau and [his] own work." For fuller discussion and documentation, see Teiwes, *Politics and Purges*, pp. 170–71, 179–81, 205–206, 210n.

While it is not surprising that Tan and Chen, old cadres who survived the events of 1953 and were later victimized during the Cultural Revolution, were not named in any post-1978 account of the Gao-Rao affair published in China, there are still reasons for doubting the above reports. Most significant is that well-informed oral sources know of no involvement on Tan's part; nor are they aware of any letter by Tan and Chen or anyone else asking Mao to take a rest. While not denying that the Cultural Revolution materials might be true, an authoritative source believes such events would not normally be excluded from archival material available to him. Furthermore, this source believes that Tan was very secure given his status as one of Mao's longest and closest supporters, that he had no particular links to Gao, and that his working relations with Rao had been relatively brief. Thus he would not seem to be a prime candidate for active involvement in the activities of Gao and Rao. In addition, a Taiwan source claims Tan and Rao could not tolerate each other; *Dalu Guancha* [Mainland Survey], no. 1 (1974): 52.

Finally, in early 1954 Tan, along with Deng Xiaoping and Rao's old enemy Chen Yi, was placed in charge of the meetings examining Rao's case. See, e.g., Xiao Xiaoqin and Li Liangzhi, *Gemingshi*, p. 30. Here, as with meetings to examine Gao's case under Zhou Enlai, those in charge were either the targets/enemies of Gao and Rao (Zhou and Chen), or had rejected their approaches (Deng). Although people who had been receptive to Gao (Peng Dehuai and Lin Biao) subsequently received key appointments, it seems unlikely that someone involved in a major way would have been given the role Tan performed in early 1954. As for Tan's 1954 self-criticism, newly available documents strongly suggest this was unrelated to the Gao-Rao affair; *ZDJCZ*, 20:312, 315. Of course, no final verdict on Tan's involvement can be offered given the conflicting information available, but on balance it is improbable that Tan participated in the Gao-Rao activities as asserted by the Cultural Revolution sources.

125. *Mao Xuanji*, 5:150. Cf. Chen Shihui, "Guanyu fandui Gao Gang," p. 99.

126. These sources include an official to whom Zhou recounted the events of 1953 and a scholar basing his conclusion on memoirs and other written materials.

127. He Xin, Wang Jiaxun, and Chen Mingxian, eds., *Zhongguo Gongchangdang Shigang* [CCP Outline History] (Beijing: Beijing Daxue chubanshe, 1986), p. 374, implies awareness of the attack on Liu and Zhou, but this seems more a loosely structured generalization than a specific assertion.

128. Chen Shihui, "Guanyu fandui Gao Gang," p. 99; and He Xin, Wang Jiaxun, and Chen Mingxian, *Zhongguo Gongchangdang Shigang*, p. 374.

129. The *Selected Works* version of Mao's speech also carries the reference to undermining Party unity being "most shameful" (p. 109), which was cited by Chen Shihui. The difference, of course, is that Chen Shihui presents Mao's remarks as directed squarely at Gao Gang, while volume 5 implies that Bo Yibo was the target.

130. Chen Shihui, "Guanyu fandui Gao Gang," p. 99.

131. *SW*, 5:108.

132. *Liushinian Dashi Jianjie*, p. 398.

133. *Mao Xuanji*, 5:95.

134. *Zhou Xuanji*, 2:108.

135. See *RMRB*, September 29, 1953, p. 1; NCNA, Beijing, November 5, 1953, in *SCMP*, no. 689, p. 18; and ibid., December 29, 1953, in *SCMP*, no. 719, pp. 11–12.

Chapter 3

1. Other work conferences held in summer and fall 1953 included those dealing with united front work, the planned purchase and marketing of grain, and handicraft cooperativization. See Kenneth G. Lieberthal and Bruce J. Dickson, *A Research Guide to Central Party and Government Meetings in China, 1949–1986* (Armonk: M. E. Sharpe, 1989), pp. 16–18; and Fang Weizhong, *Jingji Dashiji*, pp. 105–107.

2. See, e.g., *SW*, 5:161, 165.

3. See Shandong Secretary Xiang Ming's article in *RMRB*, February 27, 1953, in *SCMP*, no. 535, p. 17, which calls for carrying out the new campaign and approvingly cites Liu, Zhou, and An along with Mao; and the editorial note in ibid., April 19, 1953, in *SCMP*, no. 557, p. 22, which praised Shandong's experience in the New Three-Anti drive.

4. These officials seemingly acted as representatives of the Central Discipline Inspec-

tion Committee rather than the organization department; see *RMRB*, April 14, 1955, in *SCMP*, no. 1034, pp. 25–26. One of An Ziwen's additional posts was deputy secretary of this committee; Chen Yeping and Han Jingcao, *An Ziwen Zhuanlüe*, p. 80.

5. One of the outcomes of the Gao-Rao affair was the 1955 decision to strengthen, at least on paper, the independent role of Party disciplinary bodies. See "Resolution on Establishment of Party Control Committees," NCNA, Beijing, April 4, 1955, in *CB*, no. 324, pp. 7–9.

6. The above paragraph is based on Chen Yeping and Han Jingcao, *An Ziwen Zhuanlüe*, pp. 89, 100; and *RMRB*, April 14, 1955, in *SCMP*, no. 1034, pp. 25–26. On the New Three-Anti Campaign, see Frederick C. Teiwes, *Elite Discipline in China: Coercive and Persuasive Approaches to Rectification, 1950–1953*, Contemporary China Papers no. 12 (Canberra, 1978), chap. 5. On the "branches vs. areas" issue generally, see Jonathan Unger, "The Struggle to Dictate China's Administration: The Conflict of Branches vs Areas vs Reform," *AJCA*, no. 18 (1987). Cf. above, chapter 1, n. 34.

7. Chen Yeping and Han Jingcao, *An Ziwen Zhuanlüe*, pp. 53, 62, 66, 72–73, 76, 85; Wang Jianying, *Zuzhishi Huibian*, pp. 297, 376–77, 425, 487–88, 530, 601; oral source; above, p. 29; and below, p. 82.

8. Chen Yeping and Han Jingcao, *An Ziwen Zhuanlüe*, pp. 1–2, 83–85; oral source; and below, p. 98.

9. Chen Yeping and Han Jingcao, *An Ziwen Zhuanlüe*, pp. 100–102; "Deng, Chen, Tan guanyu Rao," p. 273; and oral source.

10. Chen Yeping and Han Jingcao, *An Ziwen Zhuanlüe*, pp. 100–102; and oral source.

11. Conceivably this was the first of two occasions on which, according to Mao in 1955 (*Mao Xuanji*, 5:147), Gao "express[ed] to me ... his [desire to] protect Rao Shushi." Of course, this first effort might have been earlier or, more likely, later at the Organization Conference. See below, p. 86.

12. Xiao Xiaoqin and Li Liangzhi, *Gemingshi*, p. 29.

13. See chapter 4. No source I am aware of actually places Gao at the conference.

14. Huai En, *Zhou Dashiji*, p. 365; and *ZDJCZ*, 20:119.

15. Chen Yeping and Han Jingcao, *An Ziwen Zhuanlüe*, p. 80.

16. Li gave a report on the FFYP to the conference; *ZDJCZ*, 20:119.

17. Chen Yeping and Han Jingcao, *An Ziwen Zhuanlüe*, p. 103.

18. Ibid., pp. 103–104.

19. Ibid., pp. 100–102; Chen Shihui, "Guanyu fandui Gao Gang," pp. 99–100; *Liushinian Dashi Jianjie*, p. 406; Xiao Xiaoqin and Li Liangzhi, *Gemingshi*, pp. 28–29; and oral source.

Ironically, according to Deng Xiaoping in 1955, "Guanyu Gao, Rao," p. 520, Gao Gang had demonstrated organizational laxness by lowering the standards of Party members. Assertedly Gao attacked the 1951 First National Organization Conference because it required *raising* standards. This is doubly ironic since that conference was dominated by Liu Shaoqi and subsequently attacked in the Cultural Revolution on the grounds that the standards it set were ideologically suspect. See chapter 1, n. 110.

20. Chen Shihui, "Guanyu fandui Gao Gang," p. 100; *Liushinian Dashi Jianjie*, p. 406; and oral sources.

21. For a discussion of this campaign, which lasted from 1951 to early 1954, see Teiwes, *Elite Discipline*, chap. 4.

22. *Mao Xuanji*, 5:146; *Hangzhou Ribao* [Hangzhou Daily], August 17, 1977; Deng Xiaoping, "Guanyu Gao, Rao," p. 515; oral sources; and above, p. 80. One well-placed oral source stated that the essence of the Organization Conference was "Gao and Rao making an alliance," thus implying a further development from the Financial and Economic Conference.

23. *Liushinian Dashi Jianjie*, p. 406.
24. See above, p. 67; and below, pp. 86–87.
25. The issues of the 1951 criteria for Party membership and the question of rich peasant Party members. While Gao Gang raised the latter issue during the Financial and Economic Conference, there is no direct evidence of Mao expressing a view on it in 1953. See above, chapter 2, n. 26, and pp. 72–73.
26. See above, p. 80.
27. Chen Yeping and Han Jingcao, *An Ziwen Zhuanlüe*, pp. 103–104; and Chen Shihui, "Guanyu fandui Gao Gang," p. 100.
28. Rao Sushi, "Wei Shixian Dang de Zhengzhi Renwu he Zuzhi Renwu er Douzheng" [Struggle to Realize the Party's Political and Organizational Tasks] (October 27, 1953), in *ZDJCZ*, 20:119, 128–29; and oral sources. Rao's speech did, however, praise various organizational practices developed in Gao Gang's Northeast (pp. 119, 122–23). According to Deng Xiaoping, "Guanyu Gao, Rao," p. 516, Zhang Xiushan declared after the conference that it had not solved problems and it was necessary to wait for an opportune time.
29. See Shanghai Jiaotong Daxue Maliezhuyi Jiaoyanshi [Marxist-Leninist Teaching and Research Office of the Shanghai Communications University], ed., *Zhongguo Gemingshi 250 ti Jieda* [Answers on 250 Topics in Chinese Revolutionary History] (Beijing: Zhanshi chubanshe, 1983), p. 197; and Jiangxi Dangxiao, *Dangshi Baiti Jieda*, p. 303.
30. See *WM*, pp. 421–22. The stated purpose of distributing the extract was so participants could better understand the various leaders' speeches.
31. See *Short Course*, pp. 323–33.
32. This was one of several times nominated by oral sources as possible occasions for Gao's first effort to seek Mao's protection for Rao. Cf. above, n. 11. This seems the most likely alternative given the claim that Rao was in "big trouble," which was more clearly the case after his rebuff at the Organization Conference than at any other time before the end of 1953.
33. *Mao Xuanji*, 5:147. On the alliance issue, it is quite conceivable that Gao attempted to intervene on behalf of a *tacit* backer.
34. See Chen Yeping and Han Jingcao, *An Ziwen Zhuanlüe*, pp. 107–108. Since An ceded control of daily work to Zhang Dingcheng after the February 1954 plenum that endorsed the defeat of Gao and Rao, the circumstances remain unclear. However, they most likely were to do with An's Politburo list (see below, pp. 96ff.) and thus reflected one of the main issues used against An by Gao and Rao. In any case, this career setback at minimum suggests that An's position had not been fully restored by the praise he received at the Organization Conference. Several oral sources do not believe that An suffered a political setback and nominated ill health as a reason for any lessening of activities, but the biography by Chen and Han suggests a very active An in the 1954–55 period.
35. *SW*, 5:131n.
36. For the text of the directive, see NCNA, Beijing, January 8, 1954, in *CB*, no. 278, pp. 1–13.
37. "From October to the end of the year" Deng was reportedly away; Jiang Boying, *Deng Zihui Zhuan*, p. 385.
38. Chronologies of the activities of Zhou and Zhu place neither at the conference, and Zhou reportedly was in Shanghai on holidays in early November. Huai En, *Zhou Dashiji*, pp. 365–66; and *Zhu De Nianpu*, pp. 370–71.
39. See chapter 1, n. 63. Unfortunately, I did not raise the question of attendance at this conference with oral sources.
40. *SW*, 5:139.
41. Party histories refer to Mao's comments "at the time of" the conference; e.g., He Xin et al., *Dangshi Jiangyi*, p. 311.

42. See above, p. 43.
43. *SW*, 5:100.
44. Ibid., pp. 93–94, 100.
45. *RMRB*, July 2[2], 1953, in *CB*, no. 255, pp. 5–8; see also Jiang Boying, *Deng Zihui Zhuan*, p. 303. Cf. chapter 2, n. 66.
46. *Zhongguo Qingnian*, April 1, 1954, in *CB*, no. 305, p. 5.
47. See Deng Zihui's September 10, 1954, discussion of this point for 1953 in the Cominform journal, *For a Lasting Peace, For a People's Democracy*, in *CB*, no. 320, p. 2.
48. In spring 1953 over 2,100 of 5,800 cooperatives in Hebei province were disbanded. See "Agricultural Cooperativization in Communist China," in *CB*, no. 373, January 20, 1956, p. 5. An authoritative oral source believes that Mao had expressed his discontent on this score to Gao, although given the timing of his open raising of the issue (see below) this is somewhat problematic.
49. See Teiwes, "Mao and His Lieutenants," pp. 13–15, for a discussion of Deng's willingness to stand up to Mao.
50. *Mao Xuanji*, 82, 117, 120, 123.
51. See Jiang Boying, *Deng Zihui Zhuan*, p. 310; *DSYJ*, no. 3 (1981): 23; *Xinhua Wenzhai*, no. 7 (1981): 187; and *SW*, 5:224–25. Liu Shaoqi's responsibility for the "four big freedoms" was widely claimed during the Cultural Revolution; see Teiwes, *Politics and Purges*, pp. 111n, 113–14.
52. *SW*, 5:135. Cf. Jiang Boying, *Deng Zihui Zhuan*, p. 385.
53. *SW*, 5:137.
54. Jiang Boying, *Deng Zihui Zhuan*, pp. 305, 307–308. Cf. above, n. 48.
55. Ibid., p. 304.
56. *SW*, 5:137.
57. Jiang Boying, *Deng Zihui Zhuan*, pp. 304–305.
58. Ibid., p. 306; *SW*, 5:132, 135–36; and NCNA, Beijing, January 8 and 9, 1954, in *CB*, no. 278, pp. 2, 4, 11, 14, 18.
59. *SW*, 5:131, 137, 138; and NCNA, Beijing, January 8, 1954, in *CB*, no. 278, pp. 4, 10, 13.
60. *SW*, 5:114.

Chapter 4

1. E.g., Xiao Xiaoqin and Li Liangzhi, *Gemingshi*, p. 28.
2. Although the standard formula in post-1978 Party histories merely says that Gao left after the Financial and Economic Conference, one well-informed oral source claims a clear memory of reading a document stating that Gao left Beijing during September. According to the Hong Kong U.S. Consulate General's biographical files, Gao made a series of appearances in Beijing from September 12 to 18 and then appeared in the capital on October 1 and 2 but not again until November. This suggests that Gao may have interrupted his trip to return briefly at the time of National Day celebrations.
3. E.g., *Liushinian Dashi Jianjie*, p. 406.
4. According to oral sources, when Gao was in Hangzhou for talks with Lin he also approached a considerably lower-ranking official, Anhui Party Secretary Niu Shucai, who was later dismissed.
5. *Deng Xiaoping Wenxuan*, p. 257. Cf., e.g., He Xin, Wang Jiaxun, and Chen Mingxian, *Gongchangang Shigang*, p. 375.
6. In "Mao and His Lieutenants," p. 27, I stated there was a gap of "about two months." While this is perhaps the best estimate, it is by no means a certainty.
7. Ibid., p. 405; Chen Shihui, "Guanyu fandui Gao Gang," p. 99; and Shanghai shi Gaoxiao, *Gongchandang Lishi*, p. 262.

8. *Pi Tao Zhanbao* [Criticize Tao Combat Bulletin] (Beijing), April 10, 1967, in *SCMP*, no. 3962, p. 9. I have found no post-Mao sources confirming this incident, while some oral sources are skeptical it took place. There is no doubt, however, that Tao was involved in the Gao Gang affair to some degree; see above, p. 75.

9. "Resolution on Kao-Jao," p. 4.

10. Xiao Xiaoqin and Li Liangzhi, *Gemingshi*, p. 28; and Chen Shihui, "Guanyu fandui Gao Gang," p. 99. Chen Shihui's description applies to arguments made at the Financial and Economic Conference, but they were undoubtedly repeated on Gao's southern trip and thereafter.

11. *Politics and Purges*, pp. 198–205.

12. Hao Mengbi and Duan Haoran, *Liushinian*, p. 425; [Luo] Diandian, *Feifan de Niandai* [Extraordinary Times] (Shanghai: Shanghai wenyi chubanshe, 1987), p. 149; oral sources; and above, pp. 73–74.

13. *Selected Works of Mao Tse-tung* (Peking: Foreign Languages Press, 1965), 3:198.

14. While the predominance on the pre-1953 Politburo by base area and army leaders taken as a bloc is clear (see Teiwes, *Politics and Purges*, p. 199n), if one focuses solely on the great military commanders of the revolutionary period only Zhu De and Peng Dehuai were represented.

15. See *SW*, 5:161–62.

16. Chen Shihui, "Guanyu fandui Gao Gang," pp. 99, 101; and oral sources. There were some differences in the understanding of oral sources. I have reported the view of the source apparently best informed on the question below. Several oral sources supported this account while others, who admittedly had only sketchy knowledge of the matter, differed in that some believed the preparing of the list was a routine task of the organization department, and one source was of the opinion that Lin's name actually was omitted by An rather than being an invention on Gao's part.

According to Zhou Enlai in February 1954, Gao's "fabrications" further included accusations of Liu Shaoqi's favoritism in staffing both central departments and provincial work posts. "Zhou Fayan Tigang," p. 268.

17. Chen Shihui, "Guanyu fandui Gao Gang," p. 101, also states that Liu had no knowledge of the list.

18. Ibid., p. 99, also claims that Lin Biao's name actually was on the list. According to "Deng, Chen, Tan guanyu Rao," p. 273, however, An's proposal was his "personal opinion."

19. *SW*, 5:161; and Chen Yeping and Han Jingcao, *An Ziwen Zhuanlüe*, p. 99.

20. *Mao Xuanji*, 5:146.

21. There is no direct evidence that An accepted fault in this instance, but the assertion of An's sympathetic biographers that he had committed a mistake at this point suggests that he would have admitted error. Chen Yeping and Han Jingcao, *An Ziwen Zhuanlüe*, p. 99. On An's failure to defend himself, it is quite possible that he did not even know that his list was supposed to have excluded Lin Biao since this allegedly was only a rumor spread by Gao.

22. Other prominent members of this group included Liu Lantao, Yang Xianzhen, and Hu Xikui. *Gemingshi Ziliao*, no. 1 (1980): 5, 6ff.; and oral source.

23. At a less exalted level, at the time of Communist takeover many old cadres from the revolutionary base areas reportedly looked down on veteran underground workers as people they had "liberated." See *Xinhua Yuebao* (November 1950): 27.

24. If Party leaders believed the new Politburo members on An's list consisted of Bo Yibo, Rao Shushi, and Deng Xiaoping, only Deng would have been highly regarded for his military accomplishments; see above, p. 21. In this case, it would have appeared that of the ten PLA marshals to be appointed in 1955, eight were excluded from the proposed Politburo. The ten marshals were the nine included in table 3, below, plus Nie Rongzhen.

306   NOTES TO CHAPTER 4

25. According to an authoritative oral source, Deng's outstanding contributions as a leader of the Second Field Army, particulary in the Huai-Hai campaign in 1948–49, gave him great prestige and widespread acceptance of his increasing prominence.

26. Information on this list and its significance was provided by an authoritative source who carefully checked the names from documentary materials. The most notable omissions from the list were 1945 Politburo members Zhang Wentian, a former member of the discredited Returned Student group, and Kang Sheng, who had been out of favor since the mid-1940s and had gone on sick leave in 1949, and Nie Rongzhen, the only one of the ten marshals chosen in 1955 not included. On Kang Sheng, see Zhong Kan, *Kang Sheng Pingzhuan* [Critical Biography of Kang Sheng] (Beijing: Hongqi chubanshe, 1982), pp. 96, 106–109. The absence of Nie Rongzhen is puzzling since he held the very responsible position of acting PLA chief of staff in the early 1950s.

27. In 1956 Bo was elected to the last alternate position in the Politburo, thus ranking twenty-third in the hierarchy overall.

28. Chen Shihui, "Guanyu fandui Gao Gang," p. 99, claims that Gao thought he could win the support of four of the six regions, but this is an obvious ploy to avoid acknowledgment of Peng Dehuai's involvement.

29. While there are no known cases of this happening in the early 1950s, an analogous situation developed between the regional and provincial levels in the Central-South region. There resistance to land reform by local Guangdong leaders caused the regional authorities to send in a new local leadership. See Ezra Vogel, *Canton under Communism: Programs and Policies in a Provincial Capital 1949–1968* (Cambridge: Harvard University Press, 1969), chap. 3.

30. See above, pp. 65–66, 74, 75, 84; and below, pp. 130–32.

31. *Selected Works of Deng*, p. 278.

32. Chen Shihui, "Guanyu fandui Gao Gang," p. 99; Tan Zhongji et al., *Shinianhou*, p. 61; and oral source.

33. This letter is noted in Tan Zhongji et al., *Shinianhou*, p. 61. This account implies but does not specify sinister content. Ye Qun, Liu's wife, assertedly tried to whitewash the letter by saying it was meant to criticize Gao, a claim which is not inconceivable if Lin had by that time been informed of Mao's new attitude toward Gao (see below).

34. Chen Shihui, "Guanyu fandui Gao Gang," p. 99; *Liushinian Dashi Jianjie*, p. 406; oral sources; and above, p. 39.

35. See chapter 1, n. 27. With regard to the immediate period, Lin was not identified at any public function in 1953 by the biographical files of the U.S. Consulate General, Hong Kong, and had ceded his Central-South posts to Ye Jianying on a temporary basis in May. He was not listed among the top leaders who met Peng Dehuai at the Beijing Railway station upon his return from Korea on August 11, the day before the closing of the Financial and Economic Conference. According to oral sources, Lin did not attend the conference.

36. Cf. the comment by Deng Liqun, "Answers to Questions Concerning the 'Resolution on Certain Questions in the History of the Party since the Founding of the PRC' " (July 30 and August 11, 1981), in *CLG* (Fall 1986): 45, in which he asserts that he himself, someone who had worked closely with Liu Shaoqi, thought Lin Biao acceptable when Mao replaced Liu with Lin as the successor in 1966. On leadership reservations concerning Lin as successor, see Teiwes, "Mao and His Lieutenants," p. 50n.

37. See Teiwes, "Mao and His Lieutenants," pp. 63–64 et seq. The degree of Mao's trust in Lin is indicated by the report of a very well-informed oral source that at the 1956 Eighth Party Congress Mao received all the votes for Party Chairman save one—his own, which went to Lin Biao.

38. Deng Liqun, "Answers to Questions," p. 44.

39. While there is little doubt that Lin had health problems both in this period and later, there is some question as to just how serious these were in the early 1950s. According to a very well-informed oral source, Lin's health was not as serious as it was treated. Lin, by this account, turned down Mao's offer of command of Chinese forces in Korea on health grounds when in fact he disagreed with involvement in Korea as "firing on oneself"; this reportedly was told to Deng Zihui by Lin at the time and revealed by Deng after Lin's disgrace in 1971. My source, however, claims that Mao was convinced of the poor state of Lin's health and very solicitous of it to the extent of dispatching his personal physician to attend to Lin. Coincidentally, according to Deng Xiaoping, "Guanyu Gao, Rao," p. 520, Gao Gang also was initially opposed to China entering the Korean war.

40. This speculation is shared by an authoritative oral source, who, upon hearing this story for the first time, offered his interpretation that Gao was using it as a ploy to attract Lin rather than making a serious proposal.

41. *Lishi Yanjiu*, no. 9 (1978): 8; [Luo] Diandian, *Feifan de Niandai*, p. 150; and oral source. Oral sources could offer little specific information and no insights as to what might have been involved in Gao Gang proposing Lin for this role.

42. For Soviet constitutional arrangements as they applied in 1953, see Aryeh L. Unger, *Constitutional Development in the USSR: A Guide to the Soviet Constitutions* (London: Methuen, 1981), pp. 144ff. The Supreme Soviet system was not adopted in the 1954 PRC Constitution, which instead opted for a state chairman.

43. See the resolution of the Lushan plenum on Peng Dehuai in *The Case of Peng Teh-huai*, p. 41. According to a Cultural Revolution account, in 1962 Mao claimed Peng was the leader of the Gao Gang group ("Selected Edition on Liu Shao-ch'i's Counter-revolutionary Crimes," April 1967, in *SCMM*, no. 652, p. 31), while an oral source reports that at Lushan, Peng rejected accusations of close private relations with Gao. Concerning Zhang Wentian, oral sources state that there is no evidence to link Zhang to the Gao Gang affair.

44. Cf. the failure to mention Peng's role in attacking Luo Ronghuan and Liu Bocheng at the 1958 Military Affairs Committee meetings; Teiwes, "Peng and Mao," pp. 88–89.

45. See, e.g., *Dapipan Tongxun* [Big Criticism Bulletin] (Guangzhou), October 5, 1967, in *SCMP*, no. 4124, p. 2.

46. This may reflect a misunderstanding since it is unclear which position, commander of Chinese forces in Korea or chief of staff in Beijing (then held on an acting basis by Nie Rongzhen), would be higher. The remark is recorded here for the weight it lends to a recurrent theme of this study—the great attention accorded to status within the CCP leadership.

47. For a discussion of both the issues involved in the criticism of the Hundred Regiments campaign and Peng's resultant bitterness toward Mao, see Teiwes, "Peng and Mao," pp. 85–86. My oral source believes that while the criticism concerning the 1942 Japanese attack on the Taihang regime was well-founded, that concerning the Hundred Regiments was unfair.

48. According to an oral source; cf. below, p. 108. Peng, like most Party leaders, was not identified in public for the remainder of August after his return from Korea; see above, n. 35. As with Gao and other leaders, Peng is again identified on September 12 in Beijing at a central government meeting. Presumably Peng might have been contacted in Beijing before, or perhaps after, Gao's southern trip.

49. The above understanding of Gao's approach and Peng's response comes from an authoritative oral source. Another source believes that Peng actually rejected Gao's criticism of Liu, but on balance this appears a far less reliable account.

50. Oral sources. One source claims this view was also put by Gao to Peng Dehuai, but this is doubtful given Peng's role as a leading Long Marcher. On the "North Shaanxi saved the Center" notion, see the generalized Cultural Revolution attack on the idea in *RMRB*, April 18, 1968, in *SCMP*, no. 4176, p. 5. Cf. Kuo, *Analytical History*, pp. 159–61.

51. An apparently well-informed article in the Hong Kong journal *Zhen Xiang* [Truth] (August 1984): 34, claims that Liu Shaoqi sensed Gao's activities and proposed promoting Xi to GAC secretary-general, an appointment that came to pass in September 1953, in an effort to isolate Gao. This same source reports that in this period Zhou Enlai engaged in an effort to drag Deng Xiaoping away from Gao, and as part of this Liu and Zhou had Deng transferred to the position of Party secretary-general. On the latter point, see below, p. 117.

52. Xi took over from Lu Dingyi as head of propaganda as a result of the propaganda authorities taking a more radical approach toward the national bourgeoisie than that approved by Mao. Cohen, *Communism of Mao*, pp. 17–18; and oral source.

53. *Lishi Yanjiu*, no. 9 (1978): 8. My oral sources did not know of this incident. Moreover, they were puzzled by the approach to Luo since Luo had served under Lin Biao in the Fourth Field Army and therefore, they reasoned, there was no need to approach him with Lin Biao on side. Cf. above, pp. 99–100.

54. Based on a similar conversation between Gao and Luo Ruiqing in December; see below, p. 119.

55. See Klein and Clark, *Biographic Dictionary*, 2:646–47.

56. Cf. Mao's claim, *SW*, 5:165, that it was not until the autumn and winter of 1953 that the "conspiracy" was discovered. The possible December dating is based on references strongly implying that the approach to Chen Yun came at that time, as well as one implying the same specifically for Deng. See *Liushinian Dashi Jianjie*, p. 406; and below, n. 66.

57. *Deng Xiaoping Wenxuan*, p. 257. Here Deng simply lumps together too many things, including some that clearly happened before November.

58. See He Xin, Wang Jiaxun and Chen Mingxian, *Dangshigang*, p. 375.

59. The text in the English edition of *Selected Works of Deng*, p. 278, translates *zhengshi tanpan* as "serious talks," but "formal negotiations" more accurately reflects the Chinese meaning.

60. *Deng Xiaoping Wenxuan*, p. 257.

61. Ibid.

62. Bachman, *Chen Yun*, p. 45, hypothesizes that Gao's approach was based on a perception of Chen's weakness. While such an interpretation might be plausible if unconvincing for the first part of 1953 (see above, pp. 29–30), it is highly unlikely from the summer on given Chen's several telling interventions at the Financial and Economic Conference.

63. Given Deng's emerging responsibilities within the GAC in the economic sphere and his close cooperation with Chen in fall 1953 on the question of the planned supply and marketing of grain and edible oils, it is plausible that he supported Chen's cautious approach; see above, p. 30. On the other hand, a seemingly well-informed Hong Kong source, *Zhen Xiang* (July 1984): 21, pictures Deng together with Mao as impatient to transform all private industry into joint state-private industry in contrast to Chen's fear of adventurism in this regard.

64. See Bachman, *Chen Yun*, pp. 31, 51. Chen's critical attitude seemingly grew as the FFYP unfolded after Gao's defeat.

65. *Deng Xiaoping Wenxuan*, p. 257.

66. See *Liushinian Dashi Jianjie*, p. 406; and Chen Shihui, "Guanyu fandui Gao Gang," p. 100. These sources discuss the approach Gao made to Chen after noting the early December meetings, but I have seen no written source explicitly claiming the approach was in December. Chen Shihui's version, in fact, further clouds the issue by referring to the approach that Gao had *already* (*ceng*) made to Chen.

67. The intriguing, seemingly well-informed Hong Kong source cited above, nn. 51 and 63, depicts a Mao-Deng conversation on the conflict between Liu and Gao during which Mao sought Deng's opinion, and Deng replied with a quotation from Confucius

critical of those driven by ambition to overreach themselves. As the author commented, by this subtle conversation Mao and Deng understood each other. *If* this is an accurate account, and *if* it refers to Deng's "report" to Mao, it suggests a far more guarded encounter than Deng's version of immediately going to Mao to expose Gao's approach. *Zhen Xiang* (August 1984): 34.

68. *Deng Xiaoping Wenxuan*, p. 257.

69. Chen Shihui, "Guanyu fandui Gao Gang," p. 100, claims that "many comrades" who had heard the anti-Party propaganda of Gao and Rao exposed the matter to the Center, but this appears to be in the context of the December showdown, which exposed Gao and Rao and may have been in response to the talks (see below) initiated by Deng, Chen, and others. Concerning Huang Kecheng, an oral source recalls that Huang's report came before Gao's exposure, sometime after the Organization Conference, although details are lacking.

70. *Selected Works of Deng*, p. 329.

71. The Hong Kong journal *Zhengming* (November 1980): 18, in an account based on oral sources, claims that Mao's disgust was indeed a pretense. In this view, as the situation unfolded Mao weighed his options and decided to sacrifice Gao. Interpretations of motives aside, this account is broadly compatible with my oral sources but differs in some particulars. See below, n. 76.

72. The primary source for this conversation, [Luo] Diandian, *Feifan de Niandai*, p. 149, places it at "one day in 1954," but this is clearly wrong. Oral sources have variously dated it in November or December 1953, while Chen Shihui, "Guanyu fandui Gao Gang," p. 100, implies it took place in December.

73. Mao's meaning here is perhaps that Gao did not nominate Lin Biao as a vice-chairman.

74. [Luo] Diandian, *Feifan de Niandai*, p. 149. In the original text "XX" appears where Chen Yun's name has been inserted.

75. Chen Shihui, "Guanyu fandui Gao Gang," p. 104.

76. Tan Zongji et al., *Shinianhou*, p. 61; and oral source. See the somewhat different Hong Kong account in *Zhengming* (November 1980): 18, which asserts that Deng held talks with Rao, Peng, and Lin but makes no mention of efforts by Chen or by Mao and Zhou.

77. Peng's awareness and intention are asserted in Peng Cheng and Wang Fang, *Lushan 1959* [Lushan 1959] (Beijing: Jiefangjun chubanshe, 1988), p. 160. By this account, Peng realized Gao Gang was behaving "abnormally" after a "1953 Politburo meeting" which in the context of the Gao-Rao affair almost certainly was one of the sessions held in December before the 24th; see below, pp. 115–16. Of course, what may have caught Peng's attention was less Gao's "abnormal" activities than possible signs of Mao's diffidence toward Gao. The account further claims that after talking with Deng he promptly opposed Gao's "splitting activities."

78. Huang Yao, Li Zhijing, and Yang Guoqing, *Luoshuai Zuihou Shiwunian* [Marshal Luo's Last Fifteen Years] (Beijing: Renmin chubanshe, 1987), pp. 24, 55, reports that "at the end of 1953" during a conference of high-ranking military cadres which began on December 7 under the auspices of Peng Dehuai, Deng Xiaoping paid a visit to Luo's home. The only outcome of the visit noted in this account is that Deng, after noting that Luo's house was too small for the size of his family, arranged for him to move into a new residence.

79. Cf. *DSYJ*, no. 4 (1982): 22; and *Xinshiqi*, no. 8 (1981): 17. The references are somewhat different from the meaning here in that Peng Dehuai is not mentioned, and the four regions referred to include Gao's hopes to win over Deng and the Southwest rather than his more successful efforts concerning Peng and the Northwest.

80. Both oral sources and Chen Yeping and Han Jingcao, *An Ziwen Zhuanlüe*, p. 104, point to the reports of Chen and Deng as the turning point.

Chapter 5

1. Most sources refer to this meeting either simply as a central meeting (*zhongyang huiyi*) or as a Politburo meeting (*zhengzhiju huiyi*). The only reference to an *enlarged* Politburo meeting I have seen is in the English edition of Mao's *Selected Works*, 5:162, where *zhongyang huiyi* is rendered in this manner. My assumption is that this usage is not sloppy translation but rather reflects the knowledge of the editors as to the precise nature of the meeting. This assumption also fits the apparent wide participation in the meeting (see below).
2. See Xiao Xiaoqin and Li Liangzhi, *Gemingshi*, p. 29.
3. [Luo] Diandian, *Feifan de Niandai*, p. 151.
4. See *Geming he Jianshe Wenda*, p. 84; and Hao Mengbi and Duan Haoran, *Liushinian*, p. 425.
5. This is solely my conclusion, but it fits with Luo Diandian's notion of Mao devising strategies and the statements of oral sources about the Chairman making preparations for dealing with Gao Gang.
6. Thus, statements that Mao raised the "two fronts" question "at the end of 1953" (e.g., *Selected Works of Deng*, p. 278) seem to mean that he raised it *again* at this time.
7. Chen Shihui, "Guanyu fandui Gao Gang," p. 100. Official accounts found it necessary to picture Gao's aims as directed ultimately at Mao although this patently was not the case. Thus, in his 1955 report on the affair, Deng Xiaoping, "Guanyu Gao, Rao," p. 517, claimed that Gao calculated that it would not be to his advantage to oppose Mao first, but if he eliminated Liu and Zhou he could then openly oppose the Chairman.
8. On the letter, see chapter 2, n. 124.
9. Oral sources. According to these sources, Mao suffered from a nervous disorder in 1946 following the Chongqing negotiations and had a particularly severe case of exhaustion in 1948. During the PRC's initial period he was overworked as a result of the Korean war, various mass campaigns, and the general line, but it was only with the formulation of the general line that he decided on a rest.
10. Oral sources. It is unclear to what extent Liu's handling of routine matters was a regular feature of his role as Mao's top assistant within the CCP and to what extent it was due to Mao's health, but I draw the inference that Mao's usual attention to detail eased somewhat in 1953 given his physical condition.
11. Oral source. This was not an overly onerous task, but at the time Mao aired his complaints in 1953 he was carrying the full load of receiving credentials. Once the new constitutional arrangements were made in 1954, Mao did receive some relief with PRC Vice-Chairman Zhu De, not NPC head Liu Shaoqi, receiving the credentials of two of the six new ambassadors to China in 1955. See U.S. Consulate General, Hong Kong, *Index to the Publications of the Press Monitoring Unit 1953–1954*, pp. 340–43; and ibid., *1955*, pp. 310–12.
12. See the discussion of Mao's subsequent succession arrangements and the "two fronts," including his statement that he deliberately let power "slip away," in Roderick MacFarquhar, *The Origins of the Cultural Revolution*, vol. 1: *Contradictions among the People 1956–1957* (New York: Columbia University Press, 1974), pp. 152–56.
13. Oral sources. Deng was officially named secretary-general in April 1954; *Dangshi Nianbiao*, p. 261.
14. Cf. chapter 4, n. 51, for a Hong Hong account attributing Deng's appointment to the efforts of Liu and Zhou to win him away from Gao Gang.
15. A less credible reason for the holiday suggested by an oral source is Mao's depression upon the death of his eldest son in Korea. Doubts arise concerning timing since by late 1953 Mao's son had been dead for three years; see MacFarquhar, *Origins*, 2:397.

16. One oral source, in discussing the closely related issue of the "two fronts," stated that Mao *asked* who could take over the "first front" and Gao proposed rotation.
17. Chen Shihui, "Guanyu fandui Gao Gang," p. 100; *Liushinian Dashi Jianjie*, p. 406; and *DSYJ*, no. 4 (1982): 23.
18. Red Guard sources also claim that Zhu lent support to Gao on the issue of leadership by rotation; *Dongfanghong* [The East Is Red] (Beijing), February 11, 1967, in *SCMP (Supplement)*, no. 172, p. 21. Similar Red Guard claims that Peng Dehuai also supported rotation (see *Gongnongbing* [Workers-Peasants-Soldiers], September 1967, in *SCMM [Supplement]*, no. 27, p. 24) are not confirmed by oral sources. The view that Peng did not back rotation fits with the information that he had been informed of Mao's anger with Gao Gang by Deng Xiaoping.
19. This source claims that a similar development occurred at the Lushan meetings in 1959 when he spoke out for Peng Dehuai because he did not know what was going on. Zhu, in his view, was "always the innocent."
20. Xiao Xiaoqin and Li Liangzhi, *Gemingshi*, p. 29; and *Liushinian Dashi Jianjie*, p. 406.
21. [Luo] Diandian, *Feifan de Niandai*, pp. 149–50. This account appears to conflate two separate Politburo meetings, an earlier one where Mao raised the issue of acting chairman and the December 24 session exposing Gao Gang. It records both Gao's approach to Luo after the meeting, which probably happened after the first meeting, and Gao's acceptance of Mao's harsh criticism, which definitely took place on December 24. It should be noted that Luo Ruiqing had been dead for nine years when the book appeared and could not be consulted, and that Luo Diandian had seriously misdated these events (see chapter 4, n. 72). If this was a single meeting, however, then Gao's activities were not stopped by Mao's actions on December 24; see below, n. 26.

If we assume the general as opposed to detailed validity of Luo Diandian's account, Mao's Cultural Revolution claim in 1967 that Luo Ruiqing was involved in the Gao-Rao affair seems particularly perverse. See *Xuexi Wenxuan* [Selected Study Works] (n.p., 1967), 4:147.
22. NCNA, Beijing, December 10, 1953, in *SCMP*, no. 707, p. 24.
23. *SW*, 5:162.
24. *Liushinian Dashi Jianjie*, p. 406; Xiao Xiaoqin and Li Liangzhi, *Gemingshi*, p. 29; and *Geming he Jianshe Wenda*, p. 84.
25. *Mao Xuanji*, 5:147.
26. Xiao Xiaoqin and Li Liangzhi, *Gemingshi*, p. 29; Chen Shihui, "Guanyu fandui Gao Gang," p. 102; [Luo] Diandian, *Feifan de Niandai*, pp. 149–50; *DSYJ*, no. 4 (1982): 24; and oral source. "Serious warning" is a formal Party disciplinary sanction just below a demerit in severity.

A few sources suggest that even after December 24 Gao was undeterred: see, e.g., above, n. 21; and Xiao Xiaoqin and Li Liangzhi, *Gemingshi*, p. 29, which claims that even after December 24 Gao and Rao turned a deaf ear to Mao's warning and continued their activities. The weight of evidence, however, strongly suggests that Mao's intervention ended the threat.
27. Cf. above, pp. 74–75.
28. Chen Yeping and Han Jingcao, *An Ziwen Zhuanlüe*, p. 105. Mao's destination of Hangzhou is given in [Luo] Diandian, *Feifan de Niandai*, p. 149.
29. Arguably, Mao's scheme concerning the "two fronts" might have produced a new emphasis on Liu's position as the successor without the Gao Gang affair, but there is no way of knowing how this issue would have developed in different circumstances.
30. *ZDJCZ*, 20:256; *Lishi Yanjiu*, no. 2 (1980): 58; *Dangshi Yanjiu Ziliao*, 6:718; and Gong Yuzhi, *Zai Lishi Zhuanzhe zhong*, p. 367.
31. *WS 1949–1957*, p. 43, presents a single paragraph dated February 1954 under the

title "Guanyu Zengjiang Dang de Tuanjie de Jueding (Zhailu)" [Excerpt from Resolution Concerning Strengthening Party Unity], and this paragraph was included in the resolution passed by the Fourth Plenum on February 10, 1954 (see *ZDJCZ*, 20:262–63). It differs, however, from the corresponding section of the resolution as paraphrased in the communique released one week after the plenum, in that the latter document reversed the order of the tasks. See below, n. 61; and appendix VII-1. The assumption here is that this was Mao's draft either as originally put forward on December 24 or as amended before the plenum, while the final version given in the communiqué was adjusted during the discussion sessions convened shortly after the plenum.

32. NCNA, Anshan, December 25, 1953, in *SCMP*, no. 715, p. 2.

33. NCNA, Beijing, January 20, 1954, in *SCMP*, no. 733, p. 1. Rao Shushi only made one recorded public appearance after December 24, on January 1.

34. See the photo in this volume from *Deng Xiaoping*, p. 72, where Gao is identified seated in the front row of conference participants while Rao apparently stands in the second row.

35. *Chen Yun Wenxuan (1949–1956)*, pp. 230–31.

36. On the challenge to Khrushchev in mid-1957 by the Soviet "anti-Party group," see Roy Medvedev, *Khrushchev* (Oxford: Basil Blackwell, 1982), chap. 11.

37. Xiao Xiaoqin and Li Langzhi, *Gemingshi*, p. 31. Even at the end of the February discussion meetings Rao, but not Gao, was identified as "comrade." See *ZDJCZ*, 20:267–69, 272–76.

38. See above, p. 39.

39. Oral sources report that Gao approached "many people" (*henduo ren*), but I was unsuccessful in getting them to elaborate on exactly who was involved apart from those already mentioned, and on who actually undertook self-criticism on this score at the Fourth Plenum. While this clearly reflected a lack of knowledge, I had the feeling that for one of the few times in my interviews the respondents were holding back. I have no explanation for this; while it is tempting to argue that since this issue was pursued during the difficult days of May 1989 these larger circumstances were at play, I did not encounter difficulties in raising sensitive issues on other topics during this period.

40. Oral sources; and above, p. 108.

41. *Case of Peng*, p. 41. Peng Cheng and Wang Fang, *Lushan 1959*, p. 160, report that Peng took the initiative to make a self-criticism at the Fourth Plenum; the context suggests the Gao Gang affair was a central aspect of this self-criticism.

42. Chen Shihui, "Guanyu fandui Gao Gang," p. 103.

43. *Liu Xuanji*, 2:129–30; and *ZDJCZ*, 20:262–63.

44. *Zhou Xuanji*, 2:120–28. Zhou, p. 125, welcomed the first steps to self-examination by those who had seriously damaged unity and hoped they would go further. Cf. Zhou's letter to Liu about Liu's report, which suggested a softening of the text; *Zhou Shuxin Xuanji*, p. 499.

45. *ZDJCZ*, 20:257, 261.

46. *Chen Yun Wenxuan (1949–1956)*, pp. 229–32.

47. *RMRB*, February 18, 1954, in *SCMP*, no. 751, p. 7. Cf. above, p. 86.

48. Hu Hua, *Shehuizhuyi Jiangyi*, p. 89; Chen Shihui, "Guanyu fandui Gao Gang," p. 103; "Deng, Chen, Tan guanyu Rao," p. 272; *Geming he Jianshe Wenda*, pp. 84–85; He Xin, Wang Jiaxun, and Chen Mingxian, *Gongchandang Shigang*, p. 376; and oral sources. Hu Hua gives the date of Zhou's speech as February 25, while *Geming he Jianshe Wenda* states it was on the 24th, and the outline of Zhou's speech in *ZDJCZ*, 20:267, is simply dated February 1954. Oral sources describe the records of the discussion meetings as "semi-open" to Chinese scholars.

49. On Chen Yi, see above, p. 45. On Tan Zhenlin, see chapter 2, n. 124.

50. See Tan's biography in Klein and Clark, *Biographic Dictionary*, 2:797–99, which traces the career ties of Tan and Chen Yi from the late 1920s. According to an authoritative oral source, Tan was very close to Deng Xiaoping and not particularly close to Rao Shushi. During one of the epic battles of the Chinese revolution, the 1948–49 Huai Hai campaign, the front committee consisted of Deng Xiaoping (secretary), Liu Bocheng, Chen Yi, Su Yu, and Tan Zhenlin; *RMRB*, February 26, 1988, in FBIS, March 7, 1988, p. 34.

51. "Deng, Chen, Tan guanyu Rao," pp. 272–76. Cf. Chen Shihui, "Guanyu fandui Gao Gang," p. 103; *Geming he Jianshe Wenda*, p. 85; and He Xin, Wang Jiaxun, and Chen Mingxian, *Gongchandang Shigang*, p. 377.

52. "Zhou Fayan Tigang," pp. 267–68; and Hu Hua, *Shehuizhuyi Jiangyi*, p. 89. Liu Shaoqi was not openly named as the target of Gao's activities at any point during the mid-1950s, although the general point of sectarian activities against leading comrades of the Center was made in 1955.

53. See above, pp. 25–26.

54. *SW*, 5:108–109; and above, p. 69. It is difficult given the question of distortions in volume 5 to determine who was Mao's target in each instance, but his criticism of Bo Yibo for not reporting to the Central Committee (p. 107) clearly was the type of "decentralism" that upset Mao. On the other hand, Mao concludes his long discussion of the problem of decentralism with the observation concerning the shameful nature of undermining Party unity (p. 109), a remark ostensibly directed at Gao Gang.

55. See the discussion of the criticism of such deviations in Teiwes, *Politics and Purges*, pp. 175–78. See ibid., pp. 121–24, for an analysis of the efforts to deal with similar problems before the Gao-Rao affair came to a head.

56. *Dangshi Dashi Nianbiao*, p. 261; and Hao Mengbi and Duan Haoran, *Liushinian*, pp. 428, 431.

57. According to Mao in April 1956, "[The large regions] had shortcomings which were later exploited to a certain extent by . . . Gao Gang and Rao Shushi. It was subsequently decided to abolish [them] and put the various provinces directly under the central authorities." *SW*, 5:293–94.

58. An authoritative oral source states that Mao's 1956 reference to Gao's "illicit relations with foreign countries" (*SW*, 5:340) was merely the Chairman's way of talking, not a formal verdict.

59. "Zhou Fayan Tigang," p. 268.

60. Ibid., p. 269; and Chen Shihui, "Guanyu fandui Gao Gang," p. 103, report Gao trying to excuse his suicide attempt during his February 24 self-criticism. According to an oral source, Gao tried to shoot himself using one of the guns all high- and middle-ranking cadres carried at the time.

61. This is a speculative suggestion based on the new order of first merciless struggle against the unrepentant and then rectification of those willing to reform in the paraphrase of the resolution on strengthening Party unity included in the communique of the Fourth Plenum published in *RMRB*, on February 18, 1954, four days into the discussion meetings. See *SCMP*, no. 751, p. 5; and above, n. 31.

62. See above, p. 124. On possible personality factors and the sense of betrayal, see also above, pp. 36–37, and chapter 1, n. 100.

63. "Resolution on Kao-Jao," p. 4; and oral source.

64. *Zhou Dashiji*, p. 369; and oral sources.

65. For an earlier discussion of these meetings and the process of defining the scope of disciplinary action, see Teiwes, *Politics and Purges*, pp. 178–82.

66. *Selected Works of Deng*, p. 279.

67. Chen Shihui, "Guanyu fandui Gao Gang," p. 105; "Resolution on Kao-Jao," p. 5; and oral sources.

68. *Pi Tao Zhanbao* (Beijing), April 10, 1967, in *SCMP*, no. 3962, p. 9; and oral source.

69. See Teiwes, *Politics and Purges*, pp. 179–80. These meetings add a further puzzle to the role of Tan Zhenlin in that Tan, along with East China propaganda chief Shu Tong, "carried out criticism and self-criticism of the work of the East China Bureau and their own work" at one of these meetings, and Cultural Revolution sources claim Tan and Chen Peixian conspired to make "false self-examinations" concerning the Gao-Rao affair. However, as noted earlier, recently available documents suggest that the self-criticisms of Tan and Shu had nothing to do with Gao or Rao. See chapter 2, n. 124.

70. Only individuals definitely identified as suffering career setbacks as a result of the Gao-Rao affair by contemporary or post-Mao sources are included in table 4. For others who possibly suffered, see Teiwes, *Politics and Purges*, pp. 180, 188, 654.

71. While this of course can be taken as indicating Gao's lust for dominance, it can also be seen, in the words of one well-placed oral source, as reflecting Gao's good point of "daring to use able people," presumably without regard for status considerations.

72. Cf. Deng Xiaoping, "Guanyu Gao, Rao," p. 518.

73. E.g., Zhang Xiushan stood with Gao in a tense meeting in 1935 when the North Shaanxi leadership was under attack as right opportunists; *Geming Huiyilu* [Revolutionary Reminiscences], 10 (July 1983): 40.

74. See above, p. 84.

75. Chen Shihui, "Guanyu fandui Gao Gang," p. 106.

76. *Xinhua Wenzhai*, no. 1 (1987): 169–70; *ZDRZ* (Xi'an: Shaanxi renmin chubanshe, 1985), 25:47; *Wenshi Ziliao Xuanji* [Collected Materials on Literary History] (Shanghai: Shanghai renmin chubanshe, October 1982), pp. 30, 35–36; and oral source.

77. *ZDRZ*, 25:41–43.

78. *Mao Zedong Zhuzuo Xuandu* [Selected Readings from Mao Zedong's Writings] (Beijing: Renmin chubanshe, 1986), 2:880.

79. *Wenshi Ziliao Xuanji*, October 1982, pp. 35–36; and oral source.

80. Ke's ties to Jiang Qing and his consistently leftist orientation were noted by an authoritative oral source. It is not clear, however, how strongly developed Ke's ties to Jiang were as of 1954–55. It is my conclusion that Ke used the situation to strengthen his own grip on Shanghai.

81. Li Tao, ed., *Chen Yi Yuanshuai Fengbei Yongcun* [Marshal Chen Yi's Everlasting Monument] (Shanghai: Shanghai renmin chubanshe, 1986), pp. 518–19.

82. *Mao Xuandu*, 2:880.

83. *Liushinian Dashi Jianjie*, p. 409.

84. Among the possibilities are that military leaders still believed An's list had excluded Lin regardless of the facts of the matter, that even if they accepted the story of Gao's misrepresentation of the list they had become sensitized to the issue of PLA Politburo representation, and that current claims notwithstanding, the list did actually exclude Lin, perhaps for health reasons. Also, as noted earlier, actual Politburo membership up to that point did shortchange the major military commanders of the Chinese revolution; see chapter 4, n. 14.

85. According to an authoritative oral source, Lin went on sick leave in 1954. This undoubtedly reflected his poor health, but this source suggests he may have felt vulnerable due to his involvement in the Gao-Rao affair. In any case, Lin may simply have continued his already existing sick leave; see above, p. 21.

86. Bachman, *Chen Yun*, p. 46. On May 1, only Liu, Zhou, and Zhu were listed as "close comrades-in-arms"; NCNA, Beijing, May 1, 1954, in *SCMP*, no. 799, p. 2.

87. Liu was strengthened by virtue of delivering the political report to the Congress, moves toward implementing the "two fronts," and the creation of the position of Honorary Party Chairman for Mao. See MacFarquhar, *Origins*, 1:100, 105–107. The case of Peng

Zhen is more confusing as he actually dropped slightly in formal rank. Peng ranked tenth as compared to seventh before the Congress. Deng Xiaoping, Lin Biao, and Party elders Lin Boqu and Dong Biwu now ranked above Peng, while Kang Sheng was dropped below him. See ibid., pp. 145–46, 165. I would judge Peng's appointment as the second ranking secretary after Deng on the new Secretariat as more indicative of his continued high status and power.

88. Kang Sheng and Zhang Wentian of the 1945 Politburo, neither of whom were included in *The Great Soviet Encyclopedia*, were dropped to alternate status in 1956; all others except for Gao Gang retained their places. The new 1956 Politburo of seventeen full members included all of those selected for the *Soviet Encyclopedia* (see table 3) except Gao, Rao, Deng Zihui (who clashed sharply with Mao on agricultural cooperativization in 1955), and marshals Ye Jianying and Xu Xiangqian. The only figure selected for the full Politburo not on the encyclopedia list was Minister of Finance Li Xiannian; an authoritative oral source believes Li's promotion represented recognition of the Fourth Front Army.

89. *WS*, 1969, p. 35. Cf. Zhou Enlai's comments to the Fourth Plenum in *Zhou Xuanji*, 2:121.

90. At the 7,000 cadres conference in early 1962, Liu rejected Peng's rehabilitation on the erroneous grounds that he had formed an anti-Party clique or "military club" and had conspired with foreign countries, and also attacked his participation in the anti-Party activities of Gao and Rao. "Selected Edition on Liu Shao-ch'i's Counter-revolutionary Revisionist Crimes" (April 1967), in *SCMM*, no. 652, p. 30; Jin Chunming, *Jianguohou Sanshisannian* [The Thirty-three Years after the Founding of the Country] (Shanghai: Shanghai renmin chubanshe, 1987), p. 144; and oral source.

91. For a recent analysis of the dynamics of the Peng-Mao clash at Lushan, see Teiwes, "Peng and Mao," pp. 89–91.

92. See above, pp. 104–105.

93. The three men served as leaders of one of the constituent bases of the North Shaanxi area, the Shaanxi-Gansu base. Liu Zhidan was military commander, Gao Gang political commissar, and Xi Zhongxun chairman of the local Soviet. Wang Jianying, *Hongjun Renwu Zhi* [Red Army Personnel Records] (Beijing: Jiefangjun chubanshe, 1988), pp. 111, 317, 535–36; and *ZDRZ* (Xi'an: Shaanxi renmin chubanshe, 1981), 3:212.

94. Fang and Fang, *Zhou Enlai*, pp. 41–43; and oral source. In addition to Xi, others removed from office as a result of this affair were SPC Vice-Chairman Jia Tuofu and Vice-Minister of Internal Affairs Wang Ziyi.

95. According to Fang and Fang, *Zhou Enlai*, p. 43, Zhou and Chen Yi, purportedly speaking for Mao, sought to reassure Xi that all was not lost. The thrust of the story, however, seems to be a somewhat unsure effort on the part of Zhou and Chen to talk Xi out of a possible suicide attempt rather than to offer a well defined path to rectification.

Chapter 6

1. "Down with Liu Shao-ch'i," in *CB*, no. 834, p. 7, claims she served as Liu's secretary in 1941. The same source, p. 5, states that Xiang Ming, a member of the Gao-Rao "clique," was Liu's secretary earlier in 1938.

2. See Fang and Fang, *Zhou Enlai*, pp. 41–43. It is unclear, however, to what extent this closeness had developed by 1953.

3. *Jinggangshan* [Jinggang Mountains] (Beijing), January 1, 1967, in *SCMP (Supplement)*, no. 162, p. 14.

4. It is important to note that the great fluidity of the revolutionary period meant that most leaders had contacts beyond a single "mountaintop" even where there was a strong primary identification. One of the consequences of this is that many of the new assignments

brought together people who had some prior contact. Cf. the relationship of Zhou Enlai and Deng Xiaoping; above, p. 30.

5. For a discussion of specialist bureaucratic involvement in policy formation during a later period, see Nina Halpern, "Economists and Economic Policy-Making in the Early 1960s," in *China's Intellectuals and the State: In Search of a New Relationship*, ed. Merle Goldman with Timothy Cheek and Carol Lee Hamrin (Cambridge: Council on East Asian Studies, Harvard University, 1987).

6. Guo Feng, one of the members of the Gao-Rao "alliance"; see chapter 1, n. 96.

7. Gao and Rao assertedly were "aware it was a gamble"; *Zhongguo Qingnian*, April 16, 1955, in *SCMP*, no. 1036, p. 13. Cf. above, p. 62.

8. An undertaking made all the more improbable by Gao's apparent argument that Lin Biao was Mao's true successor; see above, p. 103.

9. See above, chapter 2, n. 124.

10. See above, pp. 109ff.

11. See Mao's April 1956 remarks in *SW*, 5:301–302.

12. Although the circumstances were very different, Zhou Enlai's reported willingness to approach Mao on the question of protecting cadres during the Cultural Revolution only "when everything else failed" is instructive. See Fang and Fang, *Zhou Enlai*, p. 165.

13. In April 1956 Mao contrasted Gao's destructive activities to the constructive criticism made of erroneous views at the Financial and Economic Conference; *WS*, 1969, 35–36.

14. See Teiwes, *Politics and Purges*, chap. 3.

15. Mao undoubtedly would have approved any sections not in the original but added to his draft and incorporated at the Fourth Plenum. See above, pp. 122, 125, and chapter 5, nn. 31, 61.

16. For an able general discussion of Mao's particular areas of interest, see Michel Oksenberg, "The Political Leader," in *Mao Tse-tung in the Scales of History*, ed. Dick Wilson (Cambridge: Cambridge University Press, 1977), pp. 95–98.

17. Even as late as the onset of the Cultural Revolution, some leaders still expected Mao's forgiveness; see Teiwes, "Mao and His Lieutenants," pp. 20, 74.

18. Note the comment in Liao Kai-lung, "Historical Experiences," in *Issues & Studies* (November 1981): 92, that [in the early 1950s] "final decision-making power rested with one man alone."

INDEX

"agrarian socialist thought," 42–43, 69–70, 73, 76, 150, 290n117
Agricultural Mutual Aid and Cooperativization Conference. *See* Chinese Communist Party, conferences
agricultural policy. *See* rural policy
An Ziwen, 6, 10, 22, 24, 28, 47, 66, 73–74, 79–87, 96–99, 102–6, 113, 121, 127, 131, 134–35, 143–45, 148–51, 157, 164, 166, 168, 213–17, 231, 246–47, 259, 265, 290n110, 295n26, 301n4, 302nn6–10, 303n34, 305nn16, 21, 24, 314n84. *See also* Chinese Communist Party, Politburo list
Anhui Party School, 10, 157

"base area"/"white area" appeal, 5–6, 18, 25, 39, 41, 45, 66, 73–74, 80, 83, 95–100, 110, 113, 124, 127, 135, 143–44, 164–65, 168, 214, 221, 241, 263, 300n114
Beria, L. V., 125, 236–37
"blind rash advance." *See* "rash advance"
Bo Yibo, 6, 9–10, 13, 22–24, 28–30, 33–34, 36–37, 52–53, 56, 62–78, 94–99, 102, 105–6, 112, 127, 129–30, 135, 137, 142, 144–45, 149–52, 157, 163–64, 177–81, 183, 193, 195, 198–207, 279n22, 290nn117, 118, 297nn59, 67, 298nn68, 73, 299nn94, 109, 301n129, 305n24, 306n27. *See also* taxation policy
bourgeoisie, 9, 33–37, 42, 52–55, 58–63, 66–71, 76–77, 91, 110, 118, 142, 145–47, 150–52, 162, 164, 188–92, 196, 203–4, 217, 238, 244, 253, 256,

bourgeoisie (*continued*)
267–68, 296n37, 308n52
Bukharin, N. I., 50, 61, 66, 73, 125, 296n48, 297n66

Central Committee. *See* Chinese Communist Party
Central People's Government, 13, 70–71, 159, 181, 207, 264, 284n32, 285n46, 288n95
centralization, 20–21, 26–27, 33, 35, 51, 128, 205
Chen Bocun, 132, 263, 273
Chen Boda, 137
Chen Duxiu, 125, 204, 236–37, 255, 272
Chen Peixian, 130, 300n124, 314n69
Chen Shihui, 10–12, 38, 45–46, 67–70, 96, 112–13, 157, 201, 280n37, 287n72, 291n130, 301n129, 305n10, 308n66, 309nn69, 72
Chen Shutong, 59, 64, 192
Chen Yi, 16, 22, 24, 45–46, 97, 99–100, 126–27, 130, 133, 136, 148, 160–61, 170, 245, 247–48, 252–53, 261, 265, 284n39, 301n124, 313n50, 315n95
Chen Yun, 7, 10–11, 18, 20, 22–23, 25, 27–32, 60–61, 64–71, 79–82, 88, 93–94, 100–1, 104, 109–14, 118, 122–26, 135–36, 142, 144–50, 152, 172, 180–81, 187, 190–91, 198, 207–12, 222–23, 228, 282n10, 283n32, 286nn56, 63, 65, 287nn67, 70, 71, 293n156, 296n43, 298n81, 308nn56, 62–64, 309nn69, 76;
health of, 29, 65, 81, 180–81, 284n32
role in Gao-Rao case, 30, 32, 109–13, 221–23, 228; self-criticism, 124

318 INDEX

Chen Yun (*continued*)
  Issues and events:
    on bourgeoisie, 60–61, 67, 110, 118, 147, 152; on socialist transformation 67, 190–92; on taxation policy 64–65, 67, 71, 147, 152, 207–10
  Relationships with others:
    Bo Yibo, 30, 65; Deng Xiaoping, 30–31, 145, 286n63, 308n63; Gao Gang, 10, 22, 27–30, 32, 60, 65, 79, 93–94, 109–11, 114, 144, 222, 286n56, 289n96; Li Fuchun, 30, 286n65; Lin Biao, 23, 102–3, 113; Mao Zedong, 30, 32, 39, 65, 68, 110–12, 135, 148, 150, 287n67, 298n80; Peng Zhen, 32; Zhou Enlai, 30, 65, 111
  Speeches, reports:
    to Central People's Government Council, 13, 70–71, 207–12; to Financial and Economic Conference, 13, 53, 60, 67, 298n81; to Fourth Plenum, 10, 122, 125; to National Party Conference, 171
Chinese Communist Party (CCP):
  factionalism, 4–5, 16, 18, 50–51, 65–66, 71–74, 79, 81, 83–84, 95–101, 121, 126, 135–39, 144, 158–60, 245, 277n3, 278nn9, 10; resolutions, 96, 157, 221; unity, 3, 8, 15–20, 38–39, 70, 75–77, 85–87, 112, 120–25, 140–43, 153, 158, 166, 169–75, 217, 235–43, 256–58, 273–76, 300n124, 313nn54, 61
  Central Committee:
    directives, 34, 43; membership, 94, 159–60, 170, 214, 236, 261; plenums (of the Seventh Central Committee) First, 159; Second, 42, 53, 56–57, 64, 67–68, 158, 186, 196–204; Third, 42, 190, 197, 282n15; Fourth, 7, 10, 40, 108, 116, 119, 121–25, 170–71, 174, 235–57, 260, 271–74, 278n13, 296n48, 312nn31, 39, 41, 313n61; Fifth, 134, 172; (of Eighth Central Committee) Tenth, 141; (of the Eleventh Central Committee) Third, 10, 105

Chinese Communist Party (*continued*)
  resolutions, 125, 169, 235–40, 256–58, 272–74, 312n31, 313n61
  Conferences:
    Agricultural Mutual Aid and Cooperativization (1953), 79, 87–92; Financial and Economic (1953), 6, 9–10, 34, 52–87, 162–67, 177–79, 183–212, 215–16, 293n3, 294n7, 300n124; National Party, (1955), 7, 11, 46, 74, 116, 129–31, 171–75, 230, 254–76; Organization Work (1951) 81, 302nn11, 19, 22; Organization Work (1953) 6, 79–87, 92, 163–67, 213–17, 258–60; regional and local conferences (1954), 121, 129–30, 171, 261
  Congresses:
    Seventh (1945), 18, 98, 159, 282n8; Eighth (1956), 32–33, 121, 134–35, 223
  Politburo:
    list (An Ziwen's), 6, 10, 74, 81, 83, 96–103, 106, 113, 121, 127, 134–35, 143–44, 157, 164–68, 231, 241, 303n34, 305n24, 306n26, 314n84; meetings, 7, 53, 59–60, 115–20, 169, 171, 187, 191, 228, 230, 237, 279n31, 310n1, 311n21; membership, 18, 26, 96, 99–101, 134–39, 159; resolutions, 41
collectivization. *See* rural policy
commercial policy, 63, 177–79, 193–95, 210; National Commercial Conference (1953), 63, 178–79, 193–94
Conferences. *See* Chinese Communist Party; commercial policy
Congresses. *See* Chinese Communist Party; National People's Congress
cooperativization. *See* rural policy
Council of Ministers, 103–4, 107, 119, 162, 226–27, 230, 242
Cultural Revolution, 3–11, 19, 54, 65, 73, 98, 131, 143, 147, 151, 169, 221, 226, 288n89, 289n97, 290n110, 291n123, 300n124, 302n19, 304n51, 307n50, 311n21, 314n69, 316n17;

Cultural Revolution (*continued*)
  claims of sources, 13, 41, 44, 47–48, 57–58, 65, 117, 126, 224, 235, 301n124
culture, 4, 18–19, 36–37, 147, 151, 158, 204

"decentralism," 127, 196, 205–6, 313n54
Deng Xiaoping, 7, 10–11, 20–26, 28–32, 54, 61, 67, 70, 77, 83–85, 87, 93–94, 97–102, 106, 108–114, 117, 123–29, 134, 136, 142–45, 148, 150, 166, 170–73, 181, 206, 221–28, 254–76, 278n15, 283nn26, 28, 293n156, 299n94, 301n124, 305n24, 306n25, 307n39, 308nn51, 56, 63, 67, 315n87
  role in Gao-Rao case, 30, 108–9, 111–13, 134, 221–22;
  self-criticism 124, 295n35
  Issues and events:
  on bourgeoisie, 256–57; on Gao-Rao case 129, 157, 222, 256–76, 310n7; on general line, 85, 166, 259; on "independent kingdoms," 25; on socialist transformation, 61, 255–58; on "two-line struggle," 10; on unity of CCP, 85, 109, 166
  Relationships with others:
  Bo Yibo, 22–23, 30; Chen Yi, 22; Chen Yun, 30–31, 145, 286n63, 308n63; Deng Zihui, 23; Gao Gang, 7, 54, 67, 84, 93–94, 102, 108–11, 129, 222, 288n94, 302nn19, 22, 308n51; Li Fuchun, 30; Lin Biao, 23, 309n76; Liu Bocheng, 23; Luo Ronghuan, 113; Mao Zedong, 23, 26, 31–32, 108–9, 112, 117, 134–35, 150, 285n44, 309n67; Nie Rongzhen, 22; Peng Dehuai, 23, 113, 309n76; Rao Shushi, 127, 222, 245–52, 309n76; Tan Zhenlin, 23, 126, 313n50; Zhou Enlai, 23, 30, 111, 316n4
  Speeches, reports:
  at discussion meeting on Rao Shushi, 126–27, 153, 170, 245–53, 260–61, 301n124; to Organization Work Conference, 85, 166, 217; to National Party Conference,

Deng Xiaoping (*continued*)
  10–11, 171–72, 254–76
Deng Zihui, 21, 23, 26, 28–29, 39–40, 79, 88–90, 101, 138, 146, 181, 295n33, 297n66, 304n47, 315n88
Dong Biwu, 100, 101n, 123, 136, 172, 315n87

"economic cabinet," 30, 164, 264. *See also* Gao Gang
"equality between public and private." *See* taxation policies

fan maojin. See "rash advance"
Fang Weizhong, 293n3
FEC. *See* Financial and Economic Committee
FFYP. *See* First Five-Year Plan
Financial and Economic Committee (FEC), 27–30, 34, 60, 62, 110, 285n47. *See also* Chen Yun
Financial and Economic Conference. *See* Chinese Communist Party, conferences
First Five-Year Plan, 20, 27, 29, 53, 55–56, 82, 88, 171–74, 196, 254, 271
"first front." *See* "two fronts"
Five-Anti Campaign, 34, 44, 55, 58, 62, 63, 81, 201, 249, 268. *See also* Three-Anti Campaign
"five deficiencies," 201
"five excesses," 201
"five tiger generals," 25, 284n36
foreign relations, 35, 47–49, 128, 197, 242, 255, 292n148. *See also* Korea; Soviet Union
"four big freedoms," 89, 92, 295n33, 304n51

GAC. *See* Government Administration Council
Gang of Four, 9, 167, 169, 175
Gao Gang: "alliance" with Rao Shushi, 12, 46, 66, 74, 84–86, 115, 130, 140, 165–67, 224–25, 230–32, 254–76; "base area"/"white area" appeal, 95–99, 135, 164, 168, 263; biographical information, 6, 20, 35, 159–61, 283n30, 304n2; "conspiratorial activities," 8, 52, 115, 120, 127, 162–72, 175, 213, 216,

320 INDEX

Gao Gang (*continued*)
223, 230–34, 258–59; discussion meeting on, 11, 116, 126–29, 166, 170–71, 235, 240–45, 260–61; "economic cabinet," 30, 164, 264; expulsion from CCP, 7, 121, 172, 254, 273; factional activities, 5, 126, 130, 159–62, 170, 241; "holiday," 6, 93, 95, 165, 224, 259; "independent kingdom," 5, 7, 25, 101, 127–28, 242, 263–64, 284n39; knowledge of Marxism-Leninism, 37, 66, 103–4, 168, 190, 242, 296n48; lobbying activities, 93–94, 101–11, 221–27, 254–76; personality, 24–25, 36–37, 46, 124, 127, 129, 146–47, 159–60, 264, 289n96; relationship with North Korea, 47, 267, 292n146; relationship with Soviet Union, 5, 47–48, 51, 110, 128, 151, 160, 190, 242, 277n7, 292nn144–49, 313n58; report on, 254–76; "roving talks," 93, 95, 116, 165; self-criticism, 125–26, 170, 243–44, 261, 313n60; suicide, 4–5, 7, 121, 124, 129, 141, 170, 240–41, 244, 261

Issues and events:
on bourgeoisie, 36, 61–62, 71, 110, 147, 190, 267, 297n50; foreign policy, 267; on New Democracy, 61; rural policy, 36, 267, 288n91; on socialist transformation, 61–62, 77, 118, 149, 190, 296n48; taxation policy, 62–66, 71, 147; and trade unions, 40

Relationships with others
An Ziwen, 97, 164; Bo Yibo, 6, 9, 62, 65–68, 130, 148, 163–64; Chen Yun, 10, 22, 27–32, 60, 65, 79, 93–94, 109–14, 144, 222, 286n56, 308n66; Deng Xiaoping, 10, 21, 108–9, 114, 222; Li Fuchun, 22, 30; Lin Biao, 7, 21–23, 74, 79, 93, 102, 105, 108, 113–14, 140, 142, 165, 213, 222–23, 226, 304n4, 307nn40, 41; Lin Feng, 25, 160; Liu Lantao, 22; Liu Shaoqi, 5, 39–40, 47–48, 95, 115, 122, 144, 157, 159, 163–68, 177, 215, 308n67; Luo Ronghuan, 107–8, 114–15, 226–27; Ma Hong,

Gao Gang (*continued*)
130–31, 297n65; Mao Zedong, 6, 12, 24, 25–26, 30, 34–40, 44, 47, 58, 61–62, 74, 104–5, 112–13, 118, 127–28, 142, 147, 149, 157, 160, 281nn47, 49, 288nn85, 95, 292n149, 300n117, 309n71; Peng Dehuai, 6, 21, 79, 93, 104–6, 113–14, 140, 142, 307n43; Peng Zhen, 16, 24, 32, 39, 289n104; Rao Shushi, 12, 44–47, 66, 71, 74, 84–86, 115, 127, 130, 134, 143, 148, 161, 165–67, 213, 230–34, 252–53, 259–60, 295n31, 302nn11, 22; Tao Zhu, 224–25; Xi Zhongxun, 23, 106–7, 145; Zhang Wentian, 307n43; Zhang Xiushan, 314n73; Zhou Enlai, 5, 29–30, 32, 47, 159, 163–64, 167–68, 215

Speeches, reports, statements, 36–37; at Financial and Economic Conference, 65–66, 163–64, 215–16

general line, 4, 33, 42, 49–61, 69–70, 79, 82, 85, 94, 145, 162–63, 166–70, 173, 183–87, 202, 207, 217, 248, 259
generational issue, 4–5, 47–49, 147, 293n156
Government Administration Council (GAC), 24n, 27–30, 53, 59, 64, 104, 145, 164, 167, 180, 185, 285nn45–49, 296n43
Great Leap Forward, 105, 140–41
Gu Mu, 130
Guo Feng, 11, 84, 132, 231–32, 263, 273, 280nn39, 40, 284n36, 289n96, 316n6
Guomindang, 39, 41, 73, 81, 98, 131, 133, 202, 215

Han Jingcao, 215–16
Han Tianshi, 133
"hasty retreat." *See* "rash advance"
He Long, 24, 100, 137, 284n38
Hu Hua, 281n45
Hu Qiaomu, 82, 86, 138, 190, 217–18
Hu Xikui, 305n22
Hua Guofeng, 9
Huang Kecheng, 28, 93, 102, 105, 111, 124–25, 138, 309n69
Huang Yanpei, 59, 64, 191–92
Hundred Regiments campaign, 106, 307n47

INDEX 321

"imperialist encirclement," 125, 151, 162, 237, 255–56
"independent kingdoms," 5, 7, 25, 101, 127–28, 230–31, 242, 250, 263–64, 284n39. *See also* Gao Gang; Rao Shushi

Jia Tuofu, 28, 139, 185, 315n94
Jiang Qing, 131, 133, 140–41, 281n45, 282n9, 314n80
Jiangxi Soviet, 26, 96–97
jizao maojin. See "rash advance"

Kaganovich, L. M., 48, 293n156
Kai Feng, 224
Kamenev, L. B., 296n48
Kang Sheng, 137, 140–41, 306n26, 315nn87, 88
Ke Qingshi, 133, 314n80
Khrushchev, N. S., 47, 124, 292nn147–49, 312n36
Korea, 7, 15, 17, 24n, 47, 105, 197
Kosygin, A. N., 292n146

Lai Bozhu, 247
Lai Keke, 84, 131, 133, 260, 297n67
land reform, 19, 41, 73, 164, 225, 267, 269, 306n29. *See also* rural policy
Lenin, V. I. *See* Marxism-Leninism
Li Fuchun, 22, 24, 28, 30, 32, 53, 61, 66, 68–69, 82, 101, 136, 197, 217, 286n65, 292n153
Li Lisan, 40
Li Weihan, 28, 34, 53–54, 58–62, 66, 76–77, 138, 142, 145, 189–91, 280n44, 295n36, 296nn37, 41, 43, 48, 297n50
Li Xiannian, 137, 315n88
Li Xuefeng, 138
Li Yu, 270
Li Zhuchen, 192
Liao Luyan, 88–89
Lin Biao, 8, 18, 21–24, 28, 39, 74, 79, 93, 96–110, 113–14, 119–20, 124, 134–36, 140, 142, 145, 150, 159, 164, 167, 175, 213, 221–23, 226–30, 270, 281n45, 293n156, 301n124, 305nn16, 21, 306nn35–37, 307nn39–41, 314nn84, 85, 315n87, 316n8
health, 21, 53, 99, 102–3, 119, 124,

Lin Biao (*continued*)
134–35, 145, 150, 223, 230, 283n27, 307n39, 314n85
Relationships with others:
Chen Yi, 22; Chen Yun, 23, 102–3, 113; Deng Xiaoping, 23, 309n76; Deng Zihui, 23; Gao Gang, 7, 22–23, 74, 79, 93, 102–5, 108, 113, 140, 142, 165, 213, 222–23, 226, 301n124, 304n4; Liu Shaoqi, 105, 113, 140; Mao Zedong, 23, 39, 103, 108; Nie Rongzhen, 22; Peng Dehuai, 23, 105–6; Peng Zhen, 39, 102–3, 124; Rao Shushi, 120; Zhou Enlai, 23
Lin Boqu, 100, 101n, 136, 190, 315n87
Lin Feng, 22, 24n, 25, 127, 130, 139, 160, 263, 284n37
Liu Bocheng, 23–24, 100, 136, 307n44, 313n50
Liu Changsheng, 247
Liu Lantao, 22, 28, 138, 290n118, 305n22
Liu Mingfu, 297n65
Liu Ren, 74
Liu Shaoqi, 6–8, 13, 22–23, 39–87, 95–98, 112–22, 147–50, 159, 163–69, 183, 187–90, 206, 213–18, 221–26, 229, 236–41, 262, 283n32, 288n89, 289nn97, 99, 101, 103, 105, 290nn108, 110, 111, 116, 118, 121, 291nn123, 130, 131, 292nn144, 149, 306nn33, 36, 307n49, 308nn51, 67; Cultural Revolution criticisms of, 288n89, 289n97, 290n110, 291n123, 295n33; "fatal materials," 73; self-criticism, 122, 206; as successor, 6, 18, 41, 45, 49–51, 93, 103–4, 113, 121, 135, 142, 147, 149, 161, 306n36, 311n29
Issues and events:
on bourgeoisie, 42, 60, 72, 188, 238; on general line, 166, 217; on Marxism-Leninism, 238–40; on New Democracy 57–58, 149–50, 183, 295nn25, 32; rural policy, 19, 41–43, 90, 149–50, 163–64, 225; on socialist transformation, 57–58, 60–61, 125, 187–90, 238–40, 295nn28, 32; taxation policy, 64–65, 144, 279n22; Tianjin talks, 41–42, 72–73, 122

Liu Shaoqi (*continued*)
  150, 163–64; and trade unions, 39–40, 122; on unity within CCP, 125, 166, 237–40
  Relationships with others:
    An Ziwen, 47, 79–84, 98, 105, 144; Bo Yibo, 22, 52, 65–66, 98, 144; Chen Yi, 22; Deng Zihui, 23; Gao Gang, 5, 36, 39–40, 47–48, 95, 115, 122, 144, 159, 308n51; Lin Biao, 105, 113, 140; Lin Feng, 22; Liu Lantao, 22; Mao Zedong, 6, 8, 13, 32, 37–38, 40–44, 47–48, 52, 58–60, 65, 72–74, 87–90, 97, 117, 128–29, 135, 140, 146, 149–50, 153, 157, 181, 279n24, 282n15, 290nn111, 121, 314n87; Peng Dehuai, 105–6, 113, 140, 289n105, 315n90; Rao Shushi, 22, 45–47, 81, 97, 161, 217, 291n131; J. Stalin, 49; Tan Zhenlin, 23; Wang Ming, 41; Zhou Enlai, 42, 60; Zhu De, 119
  Selected Works of, 40, 280n33
  Speeches and reports:
    to Fourth Plenum 10, 122, 125, 169, 236–40; on land reform, 19; on mutual aid and cooperativization, 42; to Organization Work Conference, 302n19
Liu Xiao, 247
Liu Yalou, 222
Liu Zhidan, 35, 140–41, 315n93
Long March, 35, 96, 106, 255
Lu Dingyi, 137, 308n52
Luo Diandian, 229n4, 309n72, 310n5, 311n21
Luo Ronghuan, 93, 101, 107–8, 113, 115, 119, 124, 136, 221, 226–27, 307n44, 308n53, 309n78
Luo Ruiqing, 112–16, 119, 138, 150, 167, 228, 308n54, 311n21
Lushan meetings (1959), 104–5, 124–25, 140, 289n98, 307n43, 309n77, 311n19, 315n91

Ma Hong, 11, 28, 37, 66, 74, 102, 130, 132, 145, 232, 263, 273, 280nn39, 40, 284n36, 297n65
Ma Yinchu, 28
Malenkov, G. M., 48, 51, 242, 292n154,

Malenkov (*continued*)
  293n156
Mao Zedong: health, 5–6, 33, 48, 117–19, 152, 230, 287n75, 289n103, 299n111, 310nn9, 10, 15; holiday, 7, 115–18, 121, 129, 147, 149, 166, 169, 236, 310n15; leadership style, 3, 17–20, 44, 142–53, 277n1, 280n43, 282nn9, 10, 12, 16, 288n87; role in Gao-Rao case, 4–5, 8–9, 11, 93, 97, 142–43, 149, 230
  Issues and events:
    on bourgeoisie, 9–10, 37, 42, 54–55, 59–61, 77, 91, 118, 142, 146, 150–52, 202–4, 218, 296n37, 308n63; on "decentralism," 127, 205–6, 313n54; on "four big freedoms," 89, 295n33; on general line, 33, 42, 49, 53–60, 89, 91, 183–90, 202, 207, 295n32, 298n72; on generational issue, 4, 48–49; on Great Leap Forward, 140; on "imperialist encirclement," 151; on "independent kingdoms," 127, 230–31; on land reform 19, 73; on Marxism-Leninism, 151, 175, 202, 218, 271; on "mountaintops," 16, 74–75, 97, 144, 165; on New Democracy, 57–58, 61, 149–50, 184, 295n26; on "rash advance," 37, 43, 61, 77, 89–91, 146, 205; rural policy, 26, 37, 42–43, 87–91, 146, 149, 152, 184–86, 203–4, 304n48; on socialist transformation, 37, 60, 79, 87, 118, 146, 150, 184–92, 281n6, 289n99, 294n17; on Soviet Union, 48–49, 124–25, 151, 292n152; taxation policy, 13, 37, 62–65, 69–71, 76–77, 84, 91, 129, 144–46, 148, 151, 165, 177, 202–3; on Tianjin talks, 42, 72–73; on trade unions, 40; on "two fronts," 32, 112, 115–18, 162, 222, 229, 310nn6, 12, 311nn16, 29; on unity within CCP, 3, 17, 20, 38, 70, 75–77, 86, 94, 98, 112, 114, 120–25, 141, 143, 149, 151–53, 165, 169, 201, 206, 217, 237–39, 313n54

INDEX   323

Mao Zedong (*continued*)
Relationships with others:
An Ziwen, 98; Bo Yibo, 9, 67, 70, 84, 98, 112, 129, 133, 142, 144, 148, 151, 157, 179–80, 201–7, 290n117, 313n54; Chen Yi, 22, 161n; Chen Yun, 30, 32, 39, 65, 68, 110, 112, 150, 287n71; Deng Xiaoping, 23, 26, 31–32, 108–9, 112, 117, 134–35, 150, 206, 283n28, 285n44, 308n67; Deng Zihui, 23, 26, 89–90, 146, 280n43, 285n42, 315n88; Gao Gang, 6, 12, 24n, 25–26, 30, 34–40, 44, 47, 58, 61–62, 66–68, 74, 104–5, 112–13, 118, 127–28, 142, 147, 149, 157, 160, 165, 228–34, 281n49, 284n37, 288n95, 289nn98, 100, 103, 292nn148, 149, 298n70, 300n117, 306n33, 309n77, 311n18, 313nn54, 58, 316n13; Huang Yanpei, 191; Li Weihan, 58–59, 295n36, 296nn37, 43; Lin Biao, 23, 39, 103, 108, 306n37, 307n39; Liu Bocheng, 23; Liu Shaoqi, 6, 8, 13, 32, 37–38, 41–45, 47–48, 52, 58–60, 65, 72–74, 87–90, 97, 117, 129, 135, 140, 146, 149–50, 153, 157, 177, 181–82, 206, 279n24, 282n15, 289nn99, 100, 290nn110, 111, 121, 299n111, 314n87; Luo Ruiqing, 113, 167, 228–30, 311n21; Nie Rongzhen, 22; Peng Dehuai, 23, 106, 140, 282n15, 307n47, 315n91; Rao Shushi, 19, 44, 66, 82, 85, 94, 112, 119–20, 133, 161, 165, 215; Stalin, 4–5, 125, 146, 151, 279n24, 292n152; Tan Zhenlin, 23, 148; Wang Ming, 18, 282n15; Yang Shangkun, 97, 181–82; Ye Jianying, 23; Yudin, 49; Zhou Enlai, 6, 37–38, 41, 47, 52, 58, 72, 90, 92, 106, 129, 135, 146–47, 153, 157, 282nn12, 13, 289nn99, 101, 297n63, 314n86; Zhu De, 135, 161n1, 314n86
Speeches, statements, letters, circulars, 39, 42, 58; to Central Committee (1956), 279n24; to Chen Shutong,

Mao Zedong (*continued*)
59, 64; to Financial and Economic Conference, 9, 54–55, 69–70, 75, 77, 145, 165, 201–7, 298n72, 301n129; to Huang Yanpei, 59, 64; to Liu Shaoqi, 41, 282n14, 290n110; to National Party Conference, 171, 175, 230–34; to Organization Work Conference, 86; at Politburo meeting (Dec. 1953), 119–20; to Second Plenum (1949), 57; to Yang Shangkun, 217–18
Selected Works of, 9, 49, 69–70, 181, 192, 201, 207, 230, 279n24; *Wansui* collection, 8–9, 58, 70, 235, 278n20, 279n24
Marxism-Leninism, 16, 49–50, 61, 66, 69, 151, 158, 162, 174–75, 199–202, 218–220, 237–42, 245, 258, 275, 293n157
Mikoyan, A. I., 129
military, Gao Gang's appeal to. *See* "base area"/"white area" appeal; Chinese Communist Party, Politburo list; Gao Gang, relationships with Lin Biao, Peng Dehuai
Molotov, V. M., 48, 293n156
mutual aid. *See* rural policy

national bourgeoisie. *See* bourgeoisie
National Organization Work Conference. *See* Chinese Communist Party, conferences
National Party Conference. *See* Chinese Communist Party, conferences
National Party Congress. *See* Chinese Communist Party, congresses
National People's Congress (NPC) (1954), 32, 121, 134–35
New Democracy, 57–58, 61, 149–50, 183–84
New Three-Anti Campaign, 80–81, 85, 214, 288n87, 301n3
Nie Rongzhen, 22, 24, 139, 288n87, 306n24, 307n46
Niu Shucai, 93, 102, 132, 304n4
NPC. *See* National People's Congress

"oppose rash advance." *See* "rash advance"

Organization Work Conferences. *See* Chinese Communist Party, conferences

Pan Hannian, 130–34, 148
Panyushkin, A. S., 292n147
Peng Dehuai, 6, 8, 21–24, 28, 53, 79, 93, 99–100, 104–8, 110, 113, 120, 123–25, 130, 134–36, 140–42, 150, 222n1, 226, 278n12, 282nn12, 15, 293n156, 301n124, 305n14, 306nn28, 35, 307nn43, 44, 47–50, 309nn76–79, 311nn18, 19, 315nn87, 90, 91; critique of Great Leap Forward, 140–41; at Lushan meeting (1959), 104, 125, 289n98, 307n43, 315n91; rehabilitation, 105; role in Gao-Rao case, 104–5, 125, 134, 140; self-criticism, 125, 312n41
  Relationships with others:
    Deng Xiaoping, 23, 113, 309nn77, 78; Gao Gang, 6, 21, 79, 93, 104–6, 113, 140, 142, 301n124, 307nn49, 50; He Long, 24; Lin Biao, 23, 105–6; Liu Bocheng, 23, 307n44; Liu Shaoqi, 105–6, 113, 140, 315n90; Luo Ronghuan, 307n44; Mao Zedong, 23, 106, 140–41, 289n98, 307n47, 315n91; Nie Rongzhen, 22; Rao Shushi, 120; Xi Zhongxun, 23, 105; Ye Jianying, 23; Zhou Enlai, 23
Peng Zhen, 16, 18, 22, 24, 28, 32, 39, 74, 80, 98–100, 102, 110, 123–24, 135–36, 288n87, 289n104, 314n87, 315n90
Plenums. *See* Chinese Communist Party, Central Committee
Politburo. *See* Chinese Communist Party
political culture. *See* culture

Qian Ying, 82, 217

Rao Shushi: "alliance" with Gao Gang, 12, 46, 66, 74, 84–86, 115, 130, 140, 165–67, 224–25, 230–32, 254–76; biographical information, 6, 20, 44, 131, 160–62, 176, 181, 214, 246, 249, 283n29, 293n156; "conspiratorial activities," 8, 120, 162–75, 213, 216, 230–34, 258–59;

Rao Shushi (*continued*)
  during Cultural Revolution, 131; discussion meeting on, 11, 116, 126–29, 170–71, 235, 245–52, 260–61; expulsion from CCP, 7, 121, 172, 176, 254, 273; factional activities, 5, 7, 71–76, 112, 160–62, 246; health, 44, 249, 265; "independent kingdom," 250, 284n39; personality, 44, 46, 127, 148, 158–59, 170, 250–51, 264–65, 284n39; report on, 254–76; security issue, 131–34; self-criticism, 125–26, 170–71, 245, 251, 261
Issues and events:
  on bourgeoisie, 268; on "branches against areas," 80–81; on New Democracy, 58; rural policy, 269; on socialist transformation, 58; on unity within CCP, 85
Relationships with others:
  An Ziwen, 79–83, 145, 148, 166, 213–17, 246–47; Chen Yi, 16, 24n, 45–46, 97, 126–27, 133, 148, 160–61, 247–50, 253, 265, 284n39; Deng Xiaoping, 222, 309n76; Deng Zihui, 23; Gao Gang, 12, 44–47, 66, 71, 74, 84–86, 115, 127, 130, 134, 143, 148, 161, 165–67, 213, 230–34, 245–53, 259–60, 295n31, 302n22; Lin Biao, 120; Liu Shaoqi, 22, 45–47, 81, 97, 161, 163–64, 166–68, 213, 215, 259–60, 291n131; Mao Zedong, 19, 44, 66, 82, 94, 112, 119–20, 133, 148, 249, 282n12; Pan Hannian, 131–34, 148; Peng Dehuai, 120; Tan Zhenlin, 23, 126, 148, 313n50; Yang Fan, 133–34; Zhang Xiushan, 231; Zhou Enlai, 163–64, 167–68, 215
Speeches, reports, statements:
  to Financial and Economic Conference, 83, 85, 163–64, 215–16; to Organization Work Conference, 85, 259–60, 280n38, 303n32
"rash advance," 34, 37, 43, 61, 77, 89–91, 146, 205, 287n78
rectification, 35, 70, 80, 84, 122, 124–25, 129, 158, 166, 180, 205, 214

"red areas." *See* "base area"/"white area" appeal
"red capitalists," 42
Red Guard, 8, 94, 143
regionalism, 4–5, 22–26, 99–101
Ren Bishi, 80, 81, 282n8
Resolution on Strengthening Party Unity (1954), 120, 122, 125, 169, 235–40, 312n31, 313n61
Rong Zihe, 297n59
rural policy, 21, 26, 33–34, 36–37, 41–43, 53, 56, 87–92, 146, 149–50, 152, 163–64, 184–86, 203–4, 269, 290nn116, 117, 297n66, 304n48

"second front." *See* "two fronts"
seven "fatal materials," 73
Sha Qianli, 190
Shanxi cooperatives issue (1951), 42, 73, 122, 150, 152
shougou. See socialist transformation
Shu Tong, 253, 314n69
shumai. See socialist transformation
Sino-Soviet relations. *See* Soviet Union
"sixty-one traitors," 98
socialist transformation, 33, 37, 53–61, 67, 71, 76–79, 87–91, 118, 125, 142, 145–46, 149–52, 157, 162, 174, 183–91, 196, 199, 237–38, 255–56, 275–76, 281n6
Soviet Union: as a model, 16, 20, 35–36, 42–43, 49–51, 61, 104, 110, 125, 143, 147, 151; assistance to China, 35, 48, 122, 270; Communist Party of, 16, 51, 124, 128, 175, 218–20, 236, 297n66; differences with China, 16, 43, 50–51, 278n7; factionalism, 50–51; *Great Soviet Encyclopedia*, 99–101, 135, 315n88; role in Gao-Rao case, 5, 47–49, 160, 240, 277n7; Sino-Soviet relations, 47–49, 128, 160, 242, 278n8, 292nn148, 153
SPC. *See* State Planning Commission
Stalin, J. V., 4–5, 47–50, 66, 86, 92, 104, 125, 146–47, 151, 277n7, 279n24, 292nn148, 152, 296n48, 297n66
State Planning Commission (SPC), 27–30, 34, 36, 59, 77, 110, 114, 118, 181, 258, 285nn45–50, 286n54, 288n82. *See also* Gao Gang
State Statistical Bureau, 27

Su Yu 44, 249, 313n50
succession issue, 6, 18, 41, 45, 49–51, 93, 102–4, 113, 121, 135, 142, 145, 147, 149, 161, 292n154, 293n156, 306n36, 310n12, 311n29
sufan campaign, 131
Sun Qimeng, 190

Tan Zheng, 138
Tan Zhenlin, 22, 23, 24n, 126–27, 130, 138, 148, 170, 190, 245, 252–53, 261, 278n18, 300n124, 313n50, 314n69
Tao Zhu, 75, 93–94, 99, 102, 104, 130, 221, 224–26, 278n16, 305n8
taxation policy, 4, 6, 13, 33, 37, 52–56, 62–71, 76–77, 84, 91, 144–47, 151–52, 163, 177–83, 192–203, 207–12, 279n22, 298n68, 299n101
Three-Anti Campaign, 44, 81, 158, 201–2, 249, 288n87
Tianjin talks, 41–42, 44, 72–73, 76, 122, 150, 163
trade unions, 39–40, 122, 290n108
transformation. *See* socialist transformation
Trotsky, Leon, 125, 296n48
"two fronts," 32, 50, 115–18, 162, 222, 229, 310nn6, 12, 311nn16, 29, 314n87
"two-line struggle," 8–10, 221–22, 233

Ulanfu, 137

Wang Fu, 80, 214
Wang Guangmei, 42
Wang Jianying, 24n, 29n, 101n
Wang Jiaxiang, 137
Wang Ming, 18, 41, 205, 224, 281n45, 287n67
Wang Shoudao, 139
Wang Ziyi, 315n94
"white areas." *See* "base area"/"white area" appeal
worker-management relations. *See* trade unions
Wu Yuzhang, 123

Xi Zhongxun, 21, 23, 28, 84, 106–7, 138, 140–41, 145, 217, 278n12, 308nn51, 52, 315nn93–95
Xiang Ming, 74, 80, 84, 102, 131–32,

Xiang Ming (*continued*)
 260–61, 266, 269, 273, 297n67, 315n1
Xu Dixin, 59–60, 187, 190
Xu Teli, 123
Xu Xiangqian, 101, 139, 315n88
Xue Muqiao, 28

Yan'an, 19, 35, 39, 41, 45, 68, 96, 105–6, 130, 205
Yang Fan, 131–34
Yang Shangkun, 82, 86, 105, 138, 181, 217–18, 224, 289n103
Yang Xianzhen, 305n22
Yao Wenyuan, 9
Ye Jianying, 23, 101, 139, 174, 283n27, 306n35, 315n88
Ye Jizhuang, 28
Ye Qun, 223, 306n33
Yudin, P. F., 49

Zeng Shan, 28, 247
Zhang Chunqiao, 9
Zhang Dingcheng, 303n34
Zhang Guotao, 18–19, 125, 204, 236–37, 255, 272
Zhang Mingyuan, 132, 232, 263, 273, 284n36
Zhang Wentian, 98, 105, 123, 137, 224, 306n26, 307n43, 315n88
Zhang Xi, 28
Zhang Xiushan, 84, 132, 224, 231–32, 259, 263, 273, 284n36, 303n28, 314n73
Zhang Yunyi, 247
Zhang Zishan, 202
Zhang Zuolin, 292n144
Zhao Dezun, 132, 232, 263, 273, 284n36
Zhao Han, 80, 214
Zheng Xinru, 190
Zhou Enlai, 5–6, 10–11, 18–19, 22–25, 29–30, 32, 47–77, 80, 85–86, 90, 92, 96, 111–14, 116, 118, 122–23, 126–29, 135–36, 144–50, 159, 163–67, 172–73, 180, 183, 185–200, 214–15, 221, 235–36, 240–59, 262, 266, 279n22, 283n32, 293n156, 294n18, 298nn72, 83, 300n124,

Zhou Enlai (*continued*)
 301nn126, 127, 3, 305n16, 308n51, 312n48, 315nn89, 95
Issues and events:
on bourgeoisie, 60–61, 188, 196; on general line, 49, 53, 56, 60, 82, 145, 183, 189; on industrialization, 185, 196; on New Democracy, 58, 185; on "rash advance," 77, 90; on rural policy, 56, 90, 185–86; on socialist transformation, 56, 58–61, 185–92, 196; on taxation policy, 56, 64, 67–68, 71, 193–98; on unity of CCP, 75–76, 165
Letters:
to Liu Shaoqi, 312n44; to Mao Zedong, 56, 183–86
Relationships with others:
An Ziwen, 81; Bo Yibo, 30, 64, 199–200; Chen Yun, 30, 65, 111; Deng Xiaoping, 23, 30, 111, 315n4; Gao Gang, 5, 29–30, 32, 47, 165, 183, 185, 240–45, 305n16; He Long, 24; Li Fuchun, 30; Lin Biao, 23; Liu Shaoqi, 42; Mao Zedong, 6, 19, 37–38, 41, 47, 52, 58–72, 90, 106, 129, 135, 146, 153, 157, 282nn12, 13, 297n63, 314n86; Nie Rongzhen, 22; Peng Dehuai, 23; Rao Shushi, 165, 282n12; Stalin, 49; Xi Zhongxun, 145; Ye Jianying, 23
Speeches, reports:
at discussion meeting on Gao Gang, 126–29, 170, 240–45, 261, 298n71, 312n48; to Financial and Economic Conference, 10, 55, 68–70, 192–201, 298n72; to Fourth Plenum, 10, 122, 125, 171, 315n95; to Organization Work Conference, 82
Zhu De, 18, 24, 61, 82, 85, 88, 105, 118, 123, 135–36, 149, 161, 166, 217, 236, 282n8, 283n32, 305n14, 310n11, 311nn18, 19, 314n86
Zinoviev, G. E., 296n48
zuotanhui. See discussion meetings on Gao Gang and Rao Shushi

FREDERICK C. TEIWES is a Reader in Government at the University of Sydney. He has written widely on various aspects of Chinese affairs and is the author of the authoritative *Politics and Purges in China* (1979), of *Leadership, Legitimacy, and Conflict in China: From a Charismatic Mao to the Politics of Succession* (1985), and a contributor to *The Cambridge History of China*.